C0-AYO-294

The Decline of Rome

The Decline of Rome

JOSEPH VOGT

Translated from the German by
JANET SONDHEIMER

THE NEW AMERICAN LIBRARY

First printing

Published by The New American Library, Inc.
1301 Avenue of the Americas, New York
New York 10019

Library of Congress Catalog Card Number: 67-23462

Printed in Great Britain

CONTENTS

ILLUSTRATIONS

(between pages 148 and 149)

ACKNOWLEDGEMENTS

The publishers are grateful to the following for providing illustrations for this volume:

Izrada, Jugotourist, Belgrade, plate 17; Vienna, Kunsthistorisches Museum, plate 34; Victoria and Albert Museum, plate 83; Elisabeth Schulz, Basel, plate 87; Fototeca Unione, Rome, plates 1, 53, 90; Adolfo Tomeucci, plate 6; Alinari, plates 8, 12, 19, 32, 55; Anderson, plates 22, 33, 79, 80, 82; Alinari (Amilcare Pizzi) 84; Victor von Hagen (photos by Tošo Dabac), 9, 46, 60; Josephine Powell, plates 11, 42, 81; Landes Museum Trier, plates 13, 36, 37, 38; Max Hirmer, plates 4, 5, 14, 15, 23, 24, 26, 28, 30, 43, 47, 48, 50, 51, 52, 57, 61, 62, 65, 66, 67, 68, 69, 71, 86, 88; The Mansell Collection, plates 20, 56, 58; National Tourist Organisation of Greece, plates 21, 54 (N. Hadjistylianos); André Held, plates 29, 44, 45, 49, 72; Museo Capitolino, Rome, plate 31; Ministry of Works, plate 35; German Archaeological Institute, Rome, plates 27, 40, 63, 64; Gabinetto Fotographico Nationale, plates 39, 41, 73; Bill Pepper, plate 70; Bildarchiv der Österreichisches Nationalbibliothek, plates 74, 75, 76, 77, 78; British Museum, plate 85; Oscar Savio, Rome, plate 89.

PREFACE

In the title of this book the formula 'the decline and fall of Rome' which Gibbon launched with such success on the world of modern historical scholarship has been left to stand undisturbed. In justification, he could point to the collapse of the Roman empire, which in the west gave way to the new states founded by the Germans, and to the conviction of the many generations of Romans, from the days of Cato the Censor onward, who bewailed the moral decay of the governing class. But here the subtitle 'the metamorphosis of ancient civilisation' has been appended as an indication of the real subject of this exposition. The intention is to show how something new emerged from the ruins, how the ancient world transformed itself, how in state and society, in thought and belief, in architecture and literature the elements of a new cultural unity became visible during these centuries.

With such a wealth of historical phenomena passing before our eyes, it has been necessary to direct attention first and foremost to the social classes and intellectual and spiritual forces which forge the link between the ancient world and what are known as the Western Middle Ages; Byzantium will have a volume to itself in the *History of Civilisation.* In selecting and interpreting the data I have had to make those personal decisions which fall to the lot of the professional historian. I have given my reasons, and have been grateful to draw on the results of modern research in all the relevant fields. The problems of antiquity in decline have in recent decades been investigated with ever-increasing energy by historians and archaeologists, students of ancient literature and philosophy, specialists in religious and ecclesiastical history. In the bibliography it proved possible to mention only a fraction of the numerous learned works to which I feel myself indebted. In recent years I have also had the welcome experience of putting certain of the problems raised in this book to interested colleagues in Trier, Rome, Paris and London. Further valuable stimulus was given by the conference held at Salzburg in 1961 under the auspices of the International Society for the Comparative Study of Civilizations, which was devoted to problems connected with the higher civilizations.

Above all I want to thank the many students who gave me their close attention in lecture and seminar rooms and assisted me with their contributions. The list is a long one, starting from the dissertation on complaints about German treachery in ancient literature and leading by way of the study of the burial of Constantine the Great down to the book on Augustine and ancient Rome.

INTRODUCTION

The subject of this volume is the history of Mediterranean civilization during the last centuries of the ancient world, from about AD 200 to 500. The chronological boundaries have been left deliberately vague, as a truer reflection of the historical process than the conventional dates, the accession of Diocletian in 284 and the end of the Roman empire in the west in 476. By the year 200, the age of the Severi, changes in the structure of the Roman empire and its culture had already made themselves felt. Serious attacks on the frontiers were forcing the emperors into bitter defensive wars; the principate was becoming a military monarchy. An absolutist régime, whose tendency was to make all members of the empire equal, meant an end to the superiority of Roman citizens and the privileged position of Italy. On the intellectual and spiritual plane there was an unprecedented mingling of various philosophical systems and religious sects. Certain reforms introduced by the house of Severus marked the beginning of a process which would continue for centuries. In the succeeding period, the state, now fighting for its life, imposed strict controls on the social and economic life of its citizens. Religious syncretism and the conflict between the various cults ended in the triumph of Christianity, with the Christian church in a position of considerable political power. All Roman efforts at defence failed to prevent foreign invaders from penetrating to the heart of the empire, and German states were set up in its western territories. The latest of these foundations, the kingdom of the Franks, was so close in structure and religious complexion to the *Imperium Romanum* and yet so clearly orientated towards the future, that we may legitimately regard it as the basis of a new unity, the basis of western Europe.

I shall here be concerned with this process as a whole, with the conflict between forces of conservatism and innovation in state and society, culture and religion. It is not the intention to concentrate on one particular facet, as Kahrstedt does, for example, in his *Kulturgeschichte der römischen Kaiserzeit*, a distinguished piece of work which deals only with the early empire. I have also rejected the plan, followed by Mattingly in his

Roman Imperial Civilization, of concentrating the main political events in a single introductory chapter, since my aim has been to seek new historical insights from the interaction of politics and culture. The everyday life of Rome, although rich in interest as Carcopino has shown, will also be relegated to the background. The main themes will be the changes in the political and social structure, the rise of new spiritual and intellectual forces, above all Christianity, and the incursion of new peoples into the zone occupied by classical culture. It will be clear from what has already been said that except in the early period the main arena will be the western part of the empire, leaving Byzantium to stand on the periphery. Even this restricted field leaves us with a wealth of historical phenomena, so that it becomes necessary to highlight only the most significant of these events. In making his selection the historian is naturally influenced by his subjective view-point; having made his choice, he must justify it to the reader and be prepared for criticism.

The nature of the task will become clearer if we consider briefly the way these centuries have been discussed and presented by historians of modern times. The questions posed by eighteenth-century scholars when faced by the decline of the ancient world were framed in the spirit of the Enlightenment; their answers were for the most part drawn from the ancient writers, and had already been put forward by the humanists of the fifteenth and sixteenth centuries. Eighteenth-century scholars saw the history of the later Roman empire as the decay of the state and the dissipation of its cultural heritage. Following Sallust, Tacitus and other writers, they found the causes of this decline in the crumbling of political and moral fibre rather than the catastrophes produced by invasions of the so-called 'barbarians'. When Gibbon published the first volume of his grand-scale *History of the decline and fall of the Roman Empire* in 1776, he sounded a note whose echoes have still not completely died away. In the general observations on the fall of the Roman empire in the west which Gibbon appends to Chapter XXXVIII, he compares Imperial Rome with its Republican predecessor, and suggests that the decline set in at an early date: Roman conquests, particularly under Trajan, had so extended the boundaries of the empire that the whole framework was strained. The mainspring of Roman resilience had suffered lasting damage as the result of soft living; the independent spirit of the citizen had given way to the submissive mentality of the subject. This widespread loss of morale became increasingly marked as Romans started rubbing shoulders with provincials and even with 'barbarians' from outside the empire. Gibbon leaves us in no doubt that he regards the Christian religion as one of the enervating factors. In his fifteenth and sixteenth chapters he gives a detailed account of the progress of the new religion and its relations with the Roman government. Despite the circumspection with which the author treats his theological opponents, it becomes quite clear that in his view Christianity made capital out of a process of moral and intellectual decline which was already well under way, and that the Christian church had usurped political power from the state. The history of the Roman empire from the second century to the final *coup de grâce* administered by the Turkish conquest of Constantinople in 1453 was thus one of unbroken decline. The decadence of Rome and Byzantium which Gibbon postulates has been measured by the yard-stick of the Enlightenment and calls for critical examination. Just how thoroughly Gibbon was permeated by the self-confidence of his age is shown by a remark he could make only a few years before the outbreak of the French Revolution and the catastrophes of the Napoleonic period: 'The reflections which illustrate the fall of that mighty Empire will explain the probable causes of our actual security.'

In the nineteenth century, great advances in historical method made it possible to study Greek and Roman history in the light of an ever-increasing body of source material. At first interest was concentrated on the earlier centuries, in which it was generally considered that Hellas and Rome had reached their zenith. One result of these researches was a veneration for the history and culture of the Greeks and Romans treated as a single unit, classical antiquity, held to be sharply distinct from the ancient east and medieval Europe which lay on either side. The clearer men's conception of the unity of classical culture, the more pressing became the question of how and why it met its end. Was this an example of cultural dissolution brought about by the Christian religion? Or did the end come about as a catastrophic annihilation at the hands of the barbarians? Should we perhaps see an upheaval in the social and economic life of the empire as the root of the phenomenon, the transition from urban civilization to feudalism? Many solutions to the problem were suggested, of which only a few of the most typical can be mentioned here.

Exponents of historical materialism, which sees the organization of the means of production as one of the determining forces of history, classified ancient civilization as a slave-owning society, in sharp contrast with the feudal organization of the Middle Ages. The Communist Manifesto claims that the transition from one form of society to another is a result of the class struggle. Nevertheless, it seems from their writings that Marx and Engels could find no evidence for a heightening of the class struggle under the empire. Rather it is their contention that since slavery was becoming extinct, and free men despised manual labour, the Roman world had reached an impasse; it was the Germans who found a way out, with their system of using serfs for the cultivation of the fields, which became a substitute for slavery. It is true that Marxist historians, particularly in the Soviet Union, have recently tried to fit slave rebellions within the Roman empire into the picture. This question has for some time been a controversial issue among Russian historians, whose debates have not always been free of political influences. Some scholars in the Russian camp, who recognize that there were no really large-scale slave revolts under the empire, explain the collapse of slavery by suggesting that the slaves and the *coloni* (peasants attached to the soil) made common cause with the foreign invaders. This is an appropriate place to mention the theories of an English historian, F. W. Walbank, who regards slavery as the root cause of the general loss of vitality. He maintains that since all the heavy work was done by slaves, who had no rights, there was no incentive to devise labour-saving techniques which might have made agriculture and the craft trades more efficient. This explains why technical invention came to a halt under the empire, why no-one had the initiative to invent a mechanical loom, a steamship or firearms. The death of ancient civilization was brought about by technological paralysis. Although it would be too much to say that these theories are a solution to our problem, there is no doubt that they open up fresh fields for investigation.

The problem has also been tackled by an opposing camp, which offers an anthropological interpretation of the great break in historical continuity. Its protagonists point to the fall in population, its racial dilution and the shrinking ruling class as the primary causes of the great debacle. This is the position adopted by a German historian, O. Seeck, whose great *Geschichte des Untergangs der antiken Welt* (which started to appear in 1895) covers the period from the time of Constantine the Great to the end of the Roman empire in the west. For Seeck, who deals with politics and culture with especial emphasis on religious developments, the political life of Rome – and indeed of ancient states in general – was governed by a fatal plan of self-destruction. Invoking the Darwinian theory of selection, Seeck sets out to discover whether the forces of struggle and natural selection were given free play in bringing those most fitted to govern to the head of affairs, and concludes that the opposite was the case, above all at Rome. During the civil wars of the Republic and again under tyrannical emperors, the ablest men were immediately liquidated, again and again the best blood was spilled. After prolonged internal struggles the field was left to men of inferior character, with an inherited slave mentality, and from this poor material the rot spread to affect the whole body of citizens. Seeck is not thinking primarily of the admixture of foreign racial elements, whether Germanic or oriental; for him outstanding ability was a personal quality, not the hall-mark of a particular race. The *damnosa hereditas* of the ancient world in its political aspect was this systematic 'extermination of the best'; the old ruling families had contrived their own destruction, leaving a vacuum to be filled by men of inferior worth, whether from the lower strata of Roman society or from outside; the collapse of the ancient world was the result of unnatural selection. It should be sufficiently obvious that this is a decidedly one-sided interpretation. But it must be acknowledged that the demographical problems, as set out by Seeck in his first volume, have yet to receive a full-scale treatment.

While the scholars so far mentioned were insisting on the gulf which seems to separate the ancient from the medieval world, others were taking note of the political, social and cultural threads which connect these two periods and stages of civilization. To counter-balance the ancient historians, with their emphasis on the moral degeneration of the Roman people, and the humanists, for whom the European Middle Age was a dark millenium interposed between ancient and modern civilization, there were now scholars of various nationalities who laid stress on the survival of ancient institutions and culture. The region first investigated for evidences of historical continuity was Gaul, where contacts between Romans and Germans were closest and most significant. Starting in 1874, Fustel de Coulanges published a series of works dealing with the connections between the institutions of the later Roman empire and the organization of the Frankish state. He succeeded in demonstrating that certain essential elements in institutions and government survived, above all in the forms taken by the monarchy and in feudalism. More recent research has, in many ways, reinforced the view that ancient civilization in Gaul was not totally destroyed by the Germanic invasions. In his *Wirtschaftliche und soziale Grundlagen der europäischen Kulturentwicklung von Caesar bis auf Karl der Grossen* (1918), A. Dopsch surveys all the territories affected by the German invasions for traces of continuity, drawing on the results of archaeological excavations as well as literary sources. Some of the theories advanced in this book have since had to be modified; it is now recognized that there were significant differences in the settlement and economy of the various regions, and that the germanic peoples had something worthwhile of their own to contribute. But scholars have continued to come forward in defence of continuity in the western parts of the empire – no-one has ever seriously maintained that there was any marked break in the east between ancient and Byzantine civilization. Above all, Christopher Dawson has shown in an outstanding book, *The Making of Europe* (1935), how closely western civilization is indebted to the ancient world for its culture and Christian mode of life. Mention must also be made of H. Pirenne, whose *Mahomet et Charlemagne,* published in 1939 and since become famous, was a bold bid at redrawing the line dividing ancient from western civilization. The break in continuity was not brought about by the German invasions, nor even by the end of the Roman empire in the west; Merovingian Gaul was still in genuine communication with the late Roman world and kept up its trade with the whole Mediterranean region. It was the Arabs who cut the Frankish kingdom off from the Mediterranean, leaving it landlocked within the continent; and it was only at this point that the thread of continuity was finally broken.

This and many other theories about the end of the ancient world and the continuity of cultural development will be kept steadily in view in this survey of the period AD 200–500. There will also be occasion to refer to some of the scholarly expositions of the many problems presented by the history of the late Roman empire, regardless of whether they make any fresh contribution to the question of continuity: for example the work of J. B. Bury, E. Stein, A. Piganiol, S. Mazzarino and now, above all, A. H. M. Jones. Our historical horizon has been greatly enlarged thanks to the researches of F. Altheim, who looks to the Persian and Arab worlds for light on declining Rome; he has also added to our knowledge of the Huns and even brought China into the picture. F. Lot made the interpenetration of the Roman and German worlds his life's work. One could recite at length the names of scholars who have helped to trace the history of the German peoples from their origins through their wanderings to the foundation of their kingdoms, not to mention those who have done so much to elucidate the history of the early Church and its relations with the Roman state in its pre-Christian form. Historical studies continue to branch out in new directions. Specialists in Roman and Byzantine antiquities and in the development of their languages both have much to tell us, especially if we want to understand how the ancient world came to be divided into a western and an eastern sphere. Classical archaeologists and art historians have taught us to recognize the distinctive character of the art of these later centuries. The changing language of art forms can be traced in the sculpture of the later Roman empire and in the buildings and mosaics of Rome and Constantinople, Trier and Ravenna. We now realize how fallacious it is to think only in terms of the debasement of classical art. The men of these centuries – whether pagan or Christian – experienced a new vision of the human and the divine, which made them capable of new forms of expression. In Germany the period we are concerned with here is known as the age of *Spätantike*, in recognition of its individual quality. Although I do not propose to adopt this label, I shall give great prominence to the contribution made by art history to the understanding of cultural change.

This brings us back to a point already made, the need to fasten on a few essential phases in the historical process by which the culture of antiquity was transmuted into a new, western European, form. The historian will do well not to treat a phenomenon of this kind in isolation. Similar cultural changes can be observed at other periods and in other parts of the world. The science of history, working alongside allied disciplines such as ethnology and sociology, has long been engaged in defining criteria for distinguishing between a primitive and a developed culture and for plotting the birth, maturity and decay of a culture group. It is impossible to refer here to the works on universal history and sociology which from the eighteenth century onward have prepared the way for a morphology or classification of cultures. But mention must be made of two twentieth-century pioneers in the study of civilizations, whose genius has illumined our present subject, along with many others: Oswald Spengler and Arnold Toynbee. There can be no doubt that several of the historians mentioned earlier have been influenced by this new approach, although they might hesitate to say so or even be unaware of it.

However greatly Spengler and Toynbee may differ in outlook and use of evidence, they have one view in common: the drama of human history covers the whole surface of the earth and the study of developed civilizations everywhere is essential to true historical understanding. For Spengler, who was influenced by the vitalist philosophy, a civilization is an organism. The high civilizations of history correspond to the plant and animal organisms of nature: they are self-contained living creatures, entities filled with the breath of life. Whatever was produced by these organisms possessed such inner harmony that men's historical actions became a formal expression – indeed a symbol – of their culture. The rise and fall of civilizations follow natural laws, like the life cycle of plants. In the area covered by the Mediterranean and the near east, the civilizations of Egypt and Babylon were followed by what is known as classical civilization (also described by Spengler as Apollonic), whose essential imprint was that of Greece. It was a hall-mark of this civilization that men saw existence as corporeal, that the sense of reality always took a bodily form. After the death of Graeco-Roman civilization the Arab or 'magical' made its appearance, to hold the stage for roughly the whole of the first millenium after Christ. The men who lived in this mental climate experienced the historical drama as the struggle between body and soul, between good and evil; this attitude was common to Christianity, itself oriental, Byzantium and Islam, and brought them close together. Signs of the impending birth of western or Faustian civilization only start to appear round the year 1000. This summary enumeration of only a few of the civilizations discussed in a book as universal in scope as Spengler's *Untergang des Abendlandes* does scant justice to the wealth of historical interpretations from which the reader may profit, even if he discards the morphology as unfounded. Spengler's interpretation of the phenomenon of the end of classical civilization still remains stimulating, although professional scholars have rejected, on convincing grounds, his interpolation of an intermediate stage between the ancient world and the west.

Toynbee, while acknowledging his great debt to his predecessor, argues against Spengler over the existence of the 'magical' civilization and questions his basic assumptions. Toynbee is not attracted by the idea of civilization as a natural organism, which leaves the possibility of human action upon history in doubt and denies the existence of any living continuity between different civilizations. As a professional historian he brings precise knowledge and a comprehensive empiricism to support his case. For Toynbee, the civilized societies known to historical science are the social atoms of which history is composed. In all essentials the growth and development of these societies are determined not by natural law but by human decision. Man is constantly presented with challenges from his natural environment and the historical circumstances of his day; the response he makes affects the structural growth of his society – where it is positive his civilization flourishes, where it is negative, it will collapse. Classical – or as Toynbee calls it hellenic – civilization sprang from the civilization of ancient Crete and was built up by the creative endeavours of the Greeks over the centuries. At a decisive moment the Greeks failed to meet the great test of creating an international commonwealth of city states, and it was this initial refusal, in the time of the Peloponnesian War, that marked the beginning of the end for classical civilization. It is true that the Romans did in fact create a universal state as a vehicle for classical civilization – every civilization produces a universal state at some stage in its history – but it was a state founded on force. Thus at the time when the *Imperium Romanum* had reached its fullest extent this society was being undermined on two sides. The ruling and tyrannical minority within the empire was resisted by whole sectors of the population who turned away from the state in search of higher values, to worship new gods; the devotees of the oriental mystery religions may serve as an example. Toynbee describes these elements as the internal proletariat. At the same time, the empire was under attack from without. The surrounding peoples, Thracians, Scythians, Arabs and Germans, who had hitherto shown themselves appreciative of what a higher civilization had to offer, now took the initiative against the empire; this was the attack from the external proletariat. The combined effects of these onslaughts from within and without led to the collapse of the whole society. It was at this point that Christianity, the universal religion, emerged from the womb of ancient civilization, and it was the church, a kind of chrysalis civilization, that produced men whose creative response to the call to action led to new societies: on one side western Christian civilization, that is to say our own, on the other the Orthodox Christianity of Byzantium, which sent out a shoot into Russia.

There is no need here to take up a position with regard to Toynbee's *Study of History* as a whole. But so far as our present undertaking is concerned, it must be said that Toynbee has provided some very rich food for thought on the subject of civilizations in general and the metamorphosis of classical civilization in particular. If it is granted that writing the history of a civilization concerns something dynamic rather than static, then we shall have to take account of how by their actions and decisions the men of the age between Septimius Severus and Clovis determined and reacted to the events which shaped their culture. We shall have to examine how internal and external resistance – that is to say creative understanding of the world and the vigour of new nations – shattered the structure of the old society and laid the foundations of a new order. Here is the nub of the question : was the seed of our western culture sown in the ancient world ?

CHAPTER 1

THE CRISIS OF THE ANCIENT WORLD IN THE THIRD CENTURY

1. *Political, social and economic life*

An analysis of the political and social constitution of the ancient world in the third century and of its intellectual climate will be a fitting overture to the drama of the decline of Rome and the rise of a new culture.

In this drama the emperor always had a leading part. The successes of the Roman people in conquering and subduing foreign lands had led, by an inexorable destiny, to their progressive loss of political control. In the last years of the Republic the People's Assembly had already become a tool in the hands of the great political bosses. When Augustus brought peace to Rome and the empire he ruled in collaboration not with the citizen body but with the senate, an aristocratic advisory council. The senate was composed of important magistrates, members of the Italian landowning nobility who had made politics their profession. Augustus as victor received authority for his monarchical rule from the senate, and – in form at least – collaborated with the senate in the conduct of affairs. Men of senatorial rank were entrusted with the highest administrative offices in the provinces and with commands in the army. The People's Assembly was restricted to a very subordinate role and soon ceased to play any part in politics. The only men to be taken directly into the imperial service were the 'knights', members of the gentry class which occupied second place in Roman society; at first used sparingly, soon they were required to fill a whole series of civil and military positions whose place in the hierarchy was very precisely defined. The Augustan constitution was a compromise. In form the monarchy was a limited one and some vestiges of Republican freedom remained: it seemed as though personal rule had been reconciled with civil liberty, *principatus et libertas*.

It is astonishing that the principate based on this contrived solution should have endured for more than two hundred years. Even so, modifications started to appear from quite an early date. Each change of ruler raised the question whether the senate still possessed sufficient power and prestige to choose the new incumbent or at least confirm his accession. Some emperors declared open war on a rebellious senate and preferred to work through knights, whom they placed in positions of authority in the civil administration and the army. The Senatorial Order had undergone a far-reaching transformation. Many noble families, both Roman and Italian, had died out, others had been liquidated because of their opposition to the emperor. Their places had been taken by families from provincial aristocracies, whose members had reached high office and secured a seat in the senate. Most of them were notables from Roman cities in Gaul and Spain, but the elite of the bourgeoisie in the Greek cities of the east was also represented. This variegated senate of the second century was easy to manipulate: Antoninus Pius and Marcus Aurelius still found it expedient to indulge its pretensions, but Commodus flouted it with open contempt. In the meantime the political power of the army was steadily increasing. At first it was the Praetorian cohorts, the emperor's guard stationed at Rome, who took the initiative on the death of a ruler; later the powerful armies on the empire's threatened frontiers took a hand, elevating their own commanders to the throne. It was particularly after a state of war had become permanent that the voice of the legions carried more weight than the wishes of the 'fathers' at Rome.

The emperors of the house of Severus profited from this new situation. Septimius Severus (193–211), the founder of the dynasty, came from a romanized family of the town of Lepcis in Tripolitania, his wife Julia Domna was a member of an important priestly family from Emesa in Syria. The emperors Caracalla and Geta, who were children of this marriage, were succeeded by descendants of the Syrian branch of the family. Modern scholars are divided as to how far the policies of the dynasty were influenced by the national stock from which it sprang. But the emperors' descent from families of Punic and Syrian origin must certainly have widened the breach with ancient Roman tradition still further, leaving the way clear for an absolute monarchy. Nevertheless, the chief object of this daring break with the past was to secure the safety of the whole empire, from the Roman wall in northern England to Mesopotamia, the new province east of the upper Euphrates. If this was to be achieved it was inevitable that the emperor should rely chiefly not on the senate but on the army, although the custom of allowing the senate to ratify the soldiers' choice long continued to be observed. Members of the Order of Knights now gained access to the highest offices of state and to legionary commands. Within the legions it became possible for ordinary men to reach the rank of centurion and finally gain admission to the Order of Knights. An increase in the number of legions, higher pay for the troops and the various privileges now attaching to garrison duty all combined to produce in the frontier provinces a new type of soldiery, living side by side with the civilians and rooted in the soil. Tradition has it that as Septimius Severus lay dying at York he exhorted his sons : 'Stick together, pay the soldiers, and never mind all the rest.'[1]

The military monarchy was provided with the legal and religious foundations necessary to make it an institution. The emperor made laws without reference to the senate. For advice he relied on the lawyers sitting in his council of state (*consilium principis*), the body which issued imperial laws or *constitutiones*. Eminent legal scholars, usually holding the office of a *praefectus praetorio*, became influential councillors and might even deputize for the ruler : Plautian and Papinian under Septimius Severus, Ulpian and Paul in later reigns. These men, who had the privilege of delivering binding decisions on disputed points of law (the *ius publice respondendi*), were also the authors of voluminous legal treatises. It is clear from the Digest, the learned commentary which the emperor Justinian appended to his Corpus Iuris, that these third-century jurists based their exposition not on abstract legal principles but on carefully selected cases, and by this method produced a jurisprudence which reflected changes in institutions and outlook. Roman classical law was in fact their creation. Within its framework the absolute power of the monarch was set on a legal basis, and it was recognized that service to the state was the first duty of a citizen : an unmistakable departure from the Augustan principate. Henceforth the ruler was sole commander of a huge army, sole law-giver, sole proprietor of a good part of the best farming land within the empire ; he stood on an eminence far above the ordinary citizen, far indeed above the world of men in general, since he now received the formal honours paid to a divine being. In the past the state religion had countenanced only the worship of dead emperors alongside the gods ; but now sacrifices were also offered to the living ruler. Subjects addressed the emperor as 'our Lord', 'our God', the imperial house was the *domus divina* and anything connected with the emperor was described as sacred (*sacer*). The cult of the ruler and his house assimilated many of the features already displayed in oriental, Greek and Roman veneration of men endowed with superior power and wisdom : the idea of the god-king, the apotheosis of the hero-benefactor, devotion to the father of the fatherland. There can be no doubt that in the crisis-ridden third century, when men could not fail to be perpetually aware of their dependence on powers mightier than themselves, an element of sincere belief must have entered into the worship of the emperor.

The influence of the new monarchy was felt in all parts of the empire ; its militarization was both beneficial and dangerous. A soldiers' emperor naturally made the defence of the empire and the defeat of its alien invaders his life's work. But what was to prevent some body of troops from choosing a new man if the fancy took them? It was in fact quite common for an army stationed on the frontier to set up their own commander in opposition to the reigning emperor. The annals of the third century are filled with the reigns of short-lived rulers who fought one another; from the middle of the century military anarchy gained the upper hand, and the stability of the régime was only restored by the most strenuous exertions. For the subject, the effects of the reorganization initiated by the Severi were more permanent still. Absolutism was a great leveller of differences between regions and social classes. The Senate's loss of political power was not the only casualty; Rome, the imperial residence, and Italy, the home of Roman citizens, lost their former precedence over provinces inhabited by non-citizens, foreigners (*peregrini*). The emperor had now begun to use his title of proconsul, the mark of his supreme military power, in Rome itself, the city dedicated to civil liberty. Septimius Severus had no scruples about stationing a legion not merely in Italy but in the immediate neighbourhood of Rome; the regiments of guards, once the preserve of Italians, were now thrown open at all levels to Illyrians and Orientals.

It must be said that in placing Italy and the provinces on an equal footing the Severi were carrying a long-term policy to its logical conclusion; the protection of the provinces had been a major concern of the government since the days of Caesar and Augustus. From the outset it was a maxim with the emperors that the provinces were not to be plundered of their wealth as they had been by their Republican governors, but that their economic resources should be developed by long-term planning and their inhabitants prepared for admission to the full status of citizens. Many methods were devised for lessening the differences which divided citizens from subjects (*cives-peregrini*). The most thoroughgoing was the foundation of cities. In the eastern provinces imperial Rome continued the urbanizing policy of the hellenistic kings. In the west numerous citizen-colonies had already been established in the days of Caesar and Augustus. These communities, often settled by retired legionaries, became centres for the diffusion of the Latin tongue and Roman way of life in the provinces. In what is now Spain there were the colonies of Hispalis (Seville), Corduba (Cordova), Augusta Emerita Merida and Caesarea Augusta (Saragossa); in Gaul, Lugdunum (Lyons), Augusta Raurica (Augst), Aventicum (Avenches) and later, towering above the rest, Augusta Treverorum (Trier). Ara Ubiorum on the Rhine was originally a legionary camp, but when the troops departed the settlement was raised to a colony (Colonia Claudia Agrippinensium – Cologne). Augusta Vindelicum (Augsburg) should probably also be included in this early group. There were four colonies of this type in Britain, Camulodunum (Colchester) Lindum (Lincoln),

Glevum (Gloucester) and Eburacum (York); at Londinium (London) a civilian settlement of mixed population grew up round the fort. In Africa there were the colonies of Thamugadi (Timgad) and Cuicul (Djemila). The colonies mentioned in this list were only the most important of the military foundations, places where legionaries were stationed. The auxiliary regiments (*auxilia*) also made their contribution to the progress of urbanization. These were composed of soldiers drawn from the subject populations who were rewarded with Roman citizenship on discharge after long service. They swelled the numbers of new citizens in the provinces and wherever they settled helped to promote the levelling policies of the emperors. Moreover, many towns inhabited by provincials gradually advanced in standing, often by way of the grant of Latin status (*ius Latii*) which was the formal preliminary to the full status of *civitas Romana*. Romanization of the governing class in a provincial society was often accomplished by granting hereditary Roman citizenship to notables whose families had served for a generation or two on the local council and had deserved well of the Roman state. A steadily expanding circle of provincials was thus admitted to full citizenship.

This systematic extension of the franchise was accompanied by a silent process of romanization brought about by the introduction of Roman legal principles and practices into the provinces, a process which has recently attracted the attention of modern specialists in the history of Roman law. Whereas in modern law single citizenship is the normal rule, Roman civil law permitted common citizenship with non-Roman states and cities. Citizens of provincial cities could hold Roman citizenship without losing their former status. Since a provincial city might number among its inhabitants several notables who had been honoured with Roman citizenship, it is not surprising that the local code of law (left untouched by the governor) was gradually infiltrated by Roman laws and practices. This was all the more possible because from the end of the Republican period Roman jurisdiction and jurisprudence had been developing institutions of private law and procedure which were valid for both citizens and subjects, that is to say, they covered the whole field known as the *ius gentium* (the law of all nations). Emperors who extended to the provinces edicts originally intended only for Rome and Italy (for example the laws concerning tutelage and the treatment of slaves) were following the same trend. It was the merging of citizens and subjects that made the wide dissemination of Roman law possible, and brought life in the provinces into line with Roman law and practice.

The long process of romanization reached a resounding conclusion with the edict issued in 212 by the emperor Marcus Aurelius Antoninus (commonly known by his nickname, Caracalla), the *Constitutio Antoniniana*, under which all free-born provincial subjects (apart from a few small categories) became Roman citizens. The effect of this imperial edict is startlingly clear from official papyri which have survived from Egypt, preserved by the desert sand : native inhabitants are found with the surname Aurelius, named after the emperor who had granted them the franchise. But the reverse of the medal is equally plain : the provinces now had to pay tribute. It is possible that the edict of Caracalla was in fact inspired by fiscal considerations, as one authority explicitly states. There is no denying that the new citizens in the provinces were burdened not only with the usual tribute but also with the tax liabilities of older citizens, in particular the taxes on inheritance and manumission. But this does not alter the fact that the general grant of Roman citizenship finally concluded the protracted process of making Italy and the other regions of the empire equal before the law. Roman law was now accepted everywhere. Admittedly, the numerous codes of local law (already somewhat adapted to accommodate Roman usage) still remained in force; their compatibility with Roman law now received formal recognition.

It would be a mistake however to suppose that there was now complete uniformity among the provinces as a result of the assimilation of subjects with citizens. In the lands imprinted by hellenism the legal tradition formed over the centuries was maintained. Greek was still spoken in cities throughout the east, not only in Greece and Macedonia but also in Asi Minor, Syria, Egypt and Cyrenaica, wherever Greeks had settled in the past. The urban bourgeoisie of these regions clung to their Greek culture and learning through all the trials of war, epidemics and confiscations. In literature Greek maintains a clear lead over Latin throughout the third century; the histories of this period are written by Greeks, Herodian and Cassius Dio. We shall see later how Greek philosophy reasserted its sway throughout the Roman empire in the course of the third century. It is true that the Greek language and urban civilization were confined to the fringes of the eastern provinces. In central Anatolia and Galatia urbanization progressed slowly and the Celtic tongue was retained at least into the fourth century. In Syria native dialects continued side by side with the official Greek, while Arabic and Aramaic made further inroads in frontier districts. The peasant population of Egypt still spoke their ancient ancestral tongue. Whatever the headway made by the Greek language and Roman law, the importance of the oriental cults, extending far beyond their homeland, makes it clear that the cultural life of the eastern provinces had a distinctive quality of its own.

The real successes of romanization were concentrated in the western provinces; here Latin gained the upper hand, the socially ambitious took to urban life, and provincials turned citizens cast their artistic and religious aspirations in a Roman mould. Gaul and Spain were the chief beneficiaries of romanization, followed closely by large parts of north Africa, in particular what is now Tunisia and parts of Algeria; the impact on Britain and the German provinces was less pronounced. Naturally, even where Latinization was at its strongest, remnants of the native speech and way of life survived. Celtic personal names continued to be used in Gaul, to a certain extent. It was not uncommon for the inhabitants of Gaul and Spain to be bi-lingual, which explains why the Latin of the western territories is so markedly provincial in flavour. Celtic continued to be a living tongue in the outlying regions of Gaul and Britain, in Africa the Punic and Libyan languages were still alive – as were the ideas and practices of the older religions. But whatever reserves one makes, the fact remains that the romanization of Gaul and Spain was sufficiently thorough to be a historical reality, enabling those provinces to withstand the influence of their Germanic invaders.

Roman successes were equally spectacular in some parts of the Danube provinces. Here the chief agent of romanization was the army, stationed in strongly fortified encampments and numerous smaller forts to guard the river frontier. Certain Illyrian and Pannonian tribes were completely won over to Rome, attracted by service in the army. In the third century, and even as late as the beginning of the fourth, Illyrian and Pannonian troops formed the core of the imperial army. At a time when emperor-making had become a matter for soldiers, it is not surprising to find these legions constantly putting their own commanders on the throne. As the researches of Alföldi have shown, these emperors of Illyrian and Pannonian descent became completely Roman in outlook; from the mid-third century they had indeed become the chief protagonists of the Roman idea of empire and its essential bulwark in the face of political anarchy and economic crisis.

As late as the fifth century, the poet Rutilius Namatianus is still loud in his praises of Rome. Rome, he says, has given the diverse nations of the world a single fatherland; Rome has turned government into a blessing for her subjects, and by receiving conquered peoples into communion with her laws has made the whole earth a single city-state.[2] We can agree with this eulogistic estimate to the point of admitting that equality among the peoples was indeed achieved and that ultimately there was one law common to the whole empire. But at what a cost! The tribes had forfeited their freedom, the cities their self-government. Rome might be the fatherland, but Roman citizens had lost their political independence. The populations of Gaul and Syria might live under Roman law, but absolutism excluded the citizens from any share in making important political decisions. This negative result is all the more deplorable in view of the substantial efforts made in the early days of the principate to take the subjects of the provinces into partnership, a gesture which deserves close attention. Augustus and his successors had set up provincial assemblies in most of the western provinces, regional councils like those established by the leagues of hellenistic city-states. Cities and tribes chose representatives to attend meetings of the council (*concilium*), which were usually held annually. The first assembly of this type known to us is the *Commune Asiae*. In Gaul, which had been conquered by Caesar, assemblies of the three provinces came together at Lyons to form the *Concilium Galliarum*; similar institutions were to be found in other provinces. One of their principal tasks was to conduct the ceremonies of emperor-worship, which expressed the common bond uniting all parts and peoples of the empire; the assemblies also discussed political and administrative questions so far as they affected the provinces. Representatives from the provinces had access to the emperor outside the usual magisterial channels. The activities of the councils are known to us in some detail, mainly from inscriptions and monuments. Much of their attention was given to the formalities of emperor-worship – building temples, arranging for sacrifices, holding games. But there is also evidence of direct political action. The councils could send ambassadors to present their petitions to the emperor, thus by-passing the governor altogether; and they could also express their opinion of the governor by voting a special resolution, whether to decree him honours or, just as likely, to complain of grievances, in which case proceedings might follow. It is plain that the provincial assemblies provided a measure of control over the governors and at times were instrumental in bringing abuses to light. But this was the historic limit of their usefulness; the weapon of initiation placed in their hands was never pressed home. The internal cohesion of the provinces may indeed have owed much to these *Concilia*, but the councils themselves never developed to become organs of independent opinion. The basic reason for this surprising lack of initiative on the part of the delegates is probably connected with the role these provincial notables hoped to play as servants of the emperor, which meant that their sympathies were wholly with Rome. Their orientation was towards the universal empire, to the neglect of the territory or city from which they sprang; their energies were devoted more to securing a foothold on the imposing bureaucratic ladder of Roman magistracies than to augmenting the rights of their own communities. The fate of these provincial institutions thus provides yet another demonstration of Roman imperialism successfully at work. By the third century the councils were unmistakably in decline; local initiative, whether civic or regional, was all but spent. At this point it is important to notice that the activities of the councils had to be paid for by the office-holders. It hardly needs saying that in this period of economic crisis such huge expenditure was an intolerable burden, and the councils fell victim to the general impoverishment. When they were revived, in the much diminished provinces of the period following Diocletian, they were no longer representative of opinions and peoples but acted as official organs of the administration.

The important part played by the provincial aristocracy in the *Concilia* leads us on to a closer examination of the social and economic structure. One consequence of the urbanizing policy of the emperors during the first two centuries of the empire had been the formation of a prosperous bourgeois class in both eastern and western cities. We might say that this urban bourgeoisie occupied the place of a middle class in the social structure, standing below the Senatorial Order, which had lost its political power but not its wealth, and the Order of Knights, which absorbed a steady stream of the most successful social climbers. Well-to-do families were entitled to fill the offices and seats on the city council (*curia*), which changed annually; the names of the eligible families were kept on a special register, the *album decurionum.* These wealthy townsmen had long been proud to shoulder the considerable financial burdens attaching to their office, both in provincial communities and in cities of full Roman status. Where civic revenues were insufficient to meet the costs, the ancient rule that personal wealth carried public obligations continued to be honoured.

The heaviest expenditure was on buildings; this was the face the city presented to the world, impressing on every visitor with what success the provinces could emulate Rome their great exemplar, city of cities. Urban settlements always tended to follow the same pattern, irrespective of the region. There was a central square (the *agora* or *forum*), flanked by the main public buildings, the town hall (*curia*), the roofed hall or basilica which served as the commercial centre or law-court, colonnaded streets, and temples, which often included a Capitol, dedicated to the three supreme deities of the Roman religion. No important city was without its theatre, amphitheatre and circus, schools and libraries, sports gymnasia and baths. Wealthy citizens were not infrequently responsible for building and maintaining the town walls. This passion for building among the well-to-do, and the vitality of their civic life, have their memorial in the ruins still to be found in all parts of the empire. The Odeon at Athens, an enormous hall at the foot of the Acropolis used for dramatic and musical presentations, was only one of the many buildings put up by a wealthy Athenian named Herodes Atticus, patron of the arts and artists, archon of his native city in 127 and Roman consul in 143. There are beautiful tombs from Trier and its environs dating from as late as the third century whose reliefs, executed like paintings, depict the life of the prosperous citizen, above all the merchant: Moselle boats with wine-casks, *coloni* paying their rents, scenes from school life.

Expenditure on the sacrifices, feasts and games which punctuated the calendar had to be just as lavish. Each temple had its priesthood and sacrifices, each gymnasium its contests. Most costly of all were the innumerable public spectacles which were maintained through all the vicissitudes of war and want in celebration of the joys of urban life. These displays also had the virtue of obliterating, at least for a short space, class distinctions based on property; they also concealed the grave blemishes on the face of urban civilization. Just as in the imperial city itself the lowest classes of the population were bribed with bread and circuses, so was it the custom in every large city to keep the proletariat in poverty and idleness by lavish doles. Nor was there any pretension to higher things in what was presented in the theatre or arena. Plays were rarely performed; the bill was usually filled with pantomimes depicting the love-life of the ancient gods and other titillating subjects, to the accompaniment of flute and lyre music, with perhaps a little solo or ballet dancing thrown in. There was an avid public demand for chariot races in the circus: the crowd went into frenzies over the champions who steered their two-wheeled, four-horse chariots to victory along the long narrow tracks. The displays in the amphitheatre were a purely Roman invention which, although frowned upon, were imitated throughout the Greek parts of the empire. Every important city built its own amphitheatre, modelled on the Coliseum at Rome: Carnuntum, the garrison town on the Danube, had two; the city of Thysdrus (El Djem), which lay near the coast just south of Carthage, put up a gigantic building 148 m. long, 122 m. wide and 36 m. high, capable of holding 60,000 people. The shows in the amphitheatres gratified the crude appetites of high and low alike. The gladiators, skilled swordsmen who were often recruited from slaves or criminals, fought one another to death with swords and a variety of other weapons. The games were advertised by wall posters stuck up all over the town and drew vast crowds, keen connoisseurs with a taste for blood; when a contestant was finally brought down and begged for mercy it was for the donor of the games, or even the audience, to decide whether or not he should be finished off. Animals were also hunted in the amphitheatres, wild beasts imported from both Africa and northern Europe: lions, tigers, panthers, leopards, elephants, bears and auroches. Experienced hunters were set to fight the famished beasts, which they had either to vanquish or become their next meal. Felons – even men who had been tried and found innocent – were sometimes despatched by this road, when men had a whim for turning an execution into a popular show. These coarse entertainments were enormously expensive; procuring, transporting and maintaining the animals swallowed up huge sums, and the most popular animals were always the rarest. Even as late as about 400 we find a leading Roman senator, Symmachus, writing countless letters to his friends and disbursing 2,000 pounds in gold to secure exotic beasts and expert fighters for the games he was preparing for his son.

The wealth which made such expenditure by senatorial families and upper class provincials possible came chiefly from the land, as Rostovtzeff has convincingly shown in his brilliant work on the economy of the Roman empire. From time immemorial, money spent on the purchase of land had been the most convincing proof of membership of the old or new aristocracy. Emperors and senators possessed properties all over the empire, while the civic nobility was buying up all the land round their cities. Agriculture long remained profitable, although to what extent varied greatly with the quality of the soil and the type of farming. In Italy corn was now the chief crop; the needs of the great city of Rome were met by cereal grown in Africa and Egypt. Vines and olives were cultivated in parts of Italy and in the Greek provinces, but chiefly in Spain and southern Gaul. There was nowhere in the Mediterranean region where stock-farming was very advanced, which meant a dearth of natural manure; artificial fertilizer was a poor substitute. In corn-growing areas the deficiency had to be made up by frequent ploughing. In lands with a Mediterranean climate there was always a danger that the ground would become too dry in summer; again, frequent deep ploughing was the answer. Constant working of the ground was also necessary where olives and vines were cultivated, in order to conserve moisture.

All branches of agriculture thus required considerable expenditure of effort. Even in the days when proprietors gave their estates every attention and could count on the annual harvest to increase their wealth, the total yield was insufficient to prevent famine, at least in bad years and in times of war. The absence of any improvement to farm tools – ploughs and other implements – was a further drawback. As may easily be imagined, large estates often lacked the man-power such intensive cultivation demanded. Slaves had long been hard to come by; fewer prisoners were taken in war than in the palmy days of Republic. It is true that slaves could be bred from slaves, but the results fell far short of satisfying the demand.

Faced with this critical situation, some landowners of the first and second centuries had already discovered a new way of providing themselves with labour. Reserving the best land on their extensive estates for their own farms, they leased out the inferior and more remote portions in parcels to tenants who were called *coloni*, a word originally applied to all settlers on the soil; this agrarian system is known to modern historians as the colonate. It seems certain that this institution was introduced into the western Mediterranean from the hellenistic kingdoms, in particular Egypt. In the provinces of the Roman empire the relationship between tenant-farmer and proprietor was initially governed by a contract which stipulated only that the tenant was obliged to surrender part of his harvest and to perform labour services on the master's farm at seed-time and harvest. But as time went on the coloni became more and more dependent on the proprietors of latifundia and also on the principal lease-holders of imperial estates. Inscriptions from imperial estates in Africa show that for a time the emperors made efforts to protect this class of small tenant; but the stupendous burden imposed on the state by the incessant warfare of the third century lured the emperors, in the hope of a guaranteed revenue from taxation, into a fateful alliance with the great proprietors, to the detriment of the labour force. There was now no-one to intervene as the landowners hauled their tenants step by step into a subjection which later received legal sanction. In the northern European provinces the process was more protracted, since there was always a source of potential tenants just beyond the frontier, the so-called barbarians. But in lands with an older agrarian civilization, in Egypt, Africa and Italy, it was easier for the great landowners to devise methods for depriving their coloni of their liberty and chaining them to the soil. Soon, too, we find these *possessores* trying to withdraw their estates from the fiscal administration of the cities to which they belonged, and so create independent territorial units. The estate worked by a peasantry bound to the soil was already well over the horizon. Mosaics from African villas give us the clearest picture of what such an estate looked like: the master's residence, a great country house fitted out with all the luxuries of urban civilization, stood in the middle of his demesne, surrounded by farm buildings which included stabling for race-horses; at a slightly further remove stood the dwellings (*casae*, *vici*) of the coloni belonging to the estate. The great house, which was sometimes protected by walls and ditches, formed an economic unit on its own, a new type of community planted in the middle of the countryside. The sources leave us in no doubt that the suppression of a free peasantry made agriculture less productive. As will appear later, pockets of unrest started to form in various parts of the empire. The properties owned by provincial *curiales*, on average much smaller than imperial and senatorial estates, experienced the change as a more gradual process; but they too became less profitable. As farming incomes fell, so did the standard of living in towns. Expenditure on buildings and entertainments dwindled and civic office lost its attraction.

The stagnation in agriculture was all the more noticeable because other sources of wealth were drying up. The upper class of the urban bourgeoisie took little part in craft trades and industry, since manual work was considered degrading and craft work did not rank high as a profession. This was the province of the lower classes, including freedmen; slaves found that work in essential trades such as baking and carpentry offered a road to freedom and social betterment. Practitioners of the various crafts banded together in gilds (*collegia*), which chose their own leaders, established a communal fund and held regular meetings. The trade gilds long enjoyed the same freedom as was extended to religious sects and burial clubs. Some enterprising spirits went in for large-scale manufacture, but in general work-rooms were small; an undertaking which employed a hundred workers, whether slave or free, counted as a large factory. There is both literary and epigraphical evidence of steady industrial activity throughout the whole Mediterranean region under the early empire, and it is clear that some places produced a surplus for export. The ancient cities of Asia and Syria specialised in linens, ornaments, bronzes and vases, using well-tried traditional techniques; in Egypt the papyrus plant was made into the writing material most commonly in use and glass was also a leading industry; in Italy Campanian metal-ware and Etruscan pottery (Arretium ceramics) were world-famous. While urbanization was still the order of the day, the building trades also prospered; quarries and mines (most of them imperial possessions) supplied the necessary materials. Imperial peace guaranteed the safety of trade and commerce. Men of the middle class who were unable to live off their land and spurned craft-work turned in large numbers to commerce and banking. The imperial and civic governments did much to improve and maintain roads, bridges and harbours. Admittedly, the great road system was designed primarily for the army and to facilitate official communication; it had become quite normal for troops moving from Gaul to Syria to travel by land rather than sea. The imperial postal service (*cursus publicus*), with its numerous stations en route for changing horses and for overnight or longer halts, was established so that officials and public intelligence might journey about the empire with the greatest possible despatch. But there was no reason why this marvellous network of communications – one of Rome's proudest titles to fame – should not also carry traffic in men and goods, and enterprising merchants (*negotiatores*) and ship-owners (*navicularii*), who traded in both commodities, took advantage of it. Gilds of merchants from all over the empire had their depots in the great entrepôts, Puteoli and Ostia, Aquileia and Narbo, Ephesus and Berytus, Alexandria and Carthage. The trade routes extended far beyond the boundaries of the empire. Amber was brought back from the shores of the Baltic and the North Sea. Trade with India, the home of precious stones and spices and the intermediary for the silk trade with China, could be carried on either by the land route, which followed in the tracks of

Alexander the Great, or else by the sea passage linking Alexandria in Egypt directly with India. The interior of Africa yielded ivory, ostrich feathers and negro slaves. But there was one irksome restriction on the free movement of trade over this vast field, namely the customs duty (*portorium*) which was levied not only at the frontiers but also within the empire. In part, remarkably enough, these internal customs dated from the period before the various provinces had become absorbed into the Imperium Romanum; but there was in addition a new customs organization, divided into circumscriptions often larger than a province and covering the whole empire, Italy alone excepted. Wherever there was a customs office all goods entering or leaving or merely in transit were subject to an official duty, on average two-and-a-half per cent of their value, rising to as much as twenty-five per cent on luxuries imported from outside the empire. The whole purpose of the system, which from the second century was an established part of the imperial government, was fiscal; it was never an instrument of economic policy. The revenues were indeed so high that their contribution to the public purse was second only to the tribute from the provinces.

Eulogists of Rome down the centuries have praised the emperors for bringing peace to the empire and the blessings of a common law and free trade to its peoples. But by the third century trade and industry also show signs of regression. Internal wars and plundering raids by alien tribes had banished security from both land and sea. Yet the fundamental causes of the decline lay in the economy itself. Industry had itself become an export, and was now brought up against an insuperable obstacle. The techniques for producing the wares traditionally associated with Greece, Italy and the ancient lands of the East had travelled north and west, leading to the establishment of rival workshops on the periphery. The provinces of Gaul and Germany were soon manufacturing all the glass and pottery they needed. The central regions of the empire were badly hit by these developments in the outlying provinces. In the light of our modern experience we might be tempted to point to the markets for industrial products still awaiting exploitation outside the empire. But here we run up against the firmly held Roman conviction that the frontiers of the empire were coterminous with the frontiers of civilization, both actual and potential. At this particular period the idea must have taken an even firmer hold, since the peoples beyond the frontiers had now awoken to their opportunities and were starting to acquire the goods of the civilized world by plunder rather than purchase. Nor was any effort made to expand industries for internal consumption and little money was invested in new undertakings. Yet there was still plenty of money about, and thanks to a highly developed banking system loans were available at a rate of interest which rarely exceeded six per cent.

Even so, men still preferred less adventurous forms of investment, in landed property and house purchase. Industrially speaking, the spark of private initiative was soon quenched. Moreover, little was done to improve techniques in the established branches of industry. After the brilliant advances of the hellenistic period, science and technology had fallen into a decline and few fresh discoveries were made. It is insufficient to point to slavery as the reason for this stagnation. We may grant that a manufacturer employing slave labour had less incentive to look for improved and faster methods of work than a modern capitalist who buys his labour in a free market and must use it to the best possible advantage. But slaves were disappearing from the industrial as well as the rural scene, and manufacturers would certainly have reaped some advantage from new mechanical processes with which to eke out their labour force. On closer examination we find that some advances were made even in this later period, but that they were confined either to trades such as building or weapon-making which were vital to the state or else to the manufacture of luxury articles for the rich, sumptuous glass-ware and gold and ivory ornaments. This was the plutocratic streak in society; it was felt that the everyday utensils of the masses should be as cheap and nasty as possible. Practically nothing was done to raise the general standard of living or indeed to stimulate demand among the poorer population.

Until the time of the Severi the imperial administration had practically abstained from interfering with the economy. But the burdens of the state had now greatly increased and revenues were falling with the general regression. There was war on several fronts, against the Germans on the Rhine and the Danube, against the neighbouring eastern kingdom in the south-east, not to mention the civil wars between contenders for the imperial title nominated by the armies. The population was subjected to the strain of heavy taxation, the requisitioning of supplies and billets for the troops and compulsory labour on road-works and on building walls round threatened cities. Epidemics took their toll; our authorities give a horrifying picture of the loss of life in both town and country from the plague which made its appearance in the reign of Marcus Aurelius and again under Decius. There can be no doubt that from the third century the population was falling, although the extent of the decline varied considerably with the region. In view of the nature of the sources, it is impossible to give any exact indication of the numbers involved. Scholars have been trying to calculate the size of the population of the empire ever since the sixteenth century, and have arrived at very different answers. Modern research has chiefly concerned itself with the city of Rome; figures for citizens liable to be called up on defence duties and for recipients of the public corn doles have been examined and checked against what can be ascertained about the divisions of the city from the topographical layout. But even these improved techniques have failed to produce wholly convincing results. We may perhaps assume that in the time of Augustus the population of the empire was about seventy million, that of Rome about half a million. There is admittedly still considerable doubt about this starting figure, but the fact still remains that under the empire the curve followed a downward trend. The written authorities testify to a falling-off in the ruling classes of Greece and Rome even during the last years of the Republic, and it is plain from edicts issued by Augustus, Trajan and Nerva in an attempt to arrest the decline that the process continued into the first and second centuries. Then came pestilence, hunger and war, which affected all classes of the population. Inscriptions tell their own story, for example this petition from the people of the village of Skaptopara in Thrace, complaining of oppressive treatment by soldiers and officials (238) : 'we have made it plain that we are at the end of our tether and intend to leave our ancestral homes because of the brutality of these visitors. Once we householders were many, now we are only few'.[3] When cities in Italy and Gaul came to repair their war-ravaged walls they found they could make the circumference much smaller. The inhabited surface of a new walled city often occupies only a third or even a quarter of the original area.

Faced with this serious crisis, the state embarked on a drastic intervention in social and economic affairs. The measures of which we hear may seem as shortsighted as they were brutal. But in evaluating the economic policies of the third and fourth centuries it must be remembered that there was no expert staff of planners at hand, armed with a wealth of experience and clear-cut aims, to set the economy on an even keel and take a long-term view. The government of the day saw the defence of the empire as its prime task and set itself to devise whatever methods would most speedily procure the money and manpower needed to carry on the struggle. The actions of the state were often measures taken in blind self-defence.

As in our own day, the minting of coins offered the state an effective means of influencing currency and prices. But it was in this very field that the policy of the imperial government misfired, as the detailed investigations of numismatists have shown. It appears that a partial exhaustion of the gold and silver mines had provided excuse for a depreciation in the fine metal percentage of silver, which first occurred in the time of Marcus Aurelius. The direct consequence was a fall in the value of money and a rise in prices. When in the third century it became necessary to depreciate the gold coinage as well, a prolonged crisis of monetary confidence developed. Men spurned the debased coins and started to pay high prices for coins of the full standard, including those of earlier periods, and, in Egypt, even the silver coins of the Ptolemaic kings. A harsh decree against black market trading in currency has come down from the town of Mylasa in Caria (210): free citizens guilty of this offence are threatened with heavy fines, slaves with flogging and imprisonment. Further evidence of the general mistrust felt for the debased noble metal coinage is provided by the hoards which were buried here and there in times of need, to be unearthed by later generations. The hoarded coins dating from this period (they have also been recovered from places outside the empire) are mostly of copper. The monetary system was in such disarray that in some instances men were already resorting to barter. The well-attested rise in prices and wages are symptoms of persistent inflation. Using the mass of documentary material which has survived from Egypt – accounts, receipts, taxation orders – Heichelheim and others have shown that this inflation meant a perceptible fall in the standard of living for the ordinary population.

The general impoverishment is equally noticeable from the tax returns. Here, too, the government had resorted to harsh methods to further its military ends. Throughout the empire the basic unit for taxation was the area administered by municipal governments. If the imperial officials charged with collecting taxes from the provinces failed to amass the amount due, the short-fall had to be made up by the *curiales*, the municipal councillors and office holders, who also had to pay any arrears owed by their city from their own pockets. While there is no evidence of open rebellion against this system, it is clear that well-to-do townsmen took refuge in a form of passive resistance, by refusing to fill the offices and council seats they had once so eagerly coveted. Again, from the third century onwards the state used coercion to ensure the continuance of the public services (*munera*) previously performed by various sections of the population or put out to tender in a free market. At this period the most pressing tasks were the building of town walls – after 271 even Rome had its massive circular fortification erected by the emperor Aurelian – keeping the armies in weapons, food and clothing, and by no means least, maintaining food supplies to the capital, which for centuries had been forced to rely on imported cereals to maintain its large and unproductive proletariat. In the course of the third century these responsibilities were loaded onto the corporations of craftsmen and merchants, as a matter of compulsion. It was not long before membership of these gilds, once voluntary, became obligatory. Lowly tasks (*munera sordida*), such as road-building and transport connected with troop movements within the empire were performed by the common people, without compensation. Admittedly, a few state factories were set up for the manufacture of textiles and weapons, but this marked the limit of the government's efforts at self-help. In general it is still true to say that all the responsibilities officials could no longer discharge by using the resources of a free economy were now imposed as a compulsory duty on municipal governments and on various groups within the population.

Such were the drastic methods by which the military monarchy obtained the money and man-power it needed, and so initiated a process of social upheaval unparalleled in the history of the ancient world. Individual voices now often express the despair induced by the totalitarian tendencies of the régime and its attendant terrors. 'The provinces lay trembling in their bondage' – the words are those of an orator describing this past bondage in a panegyric addressed to a new emperor – 'spies went hither and thither in the cities listening to men's talk, no man could speak or think freely. All that was just and reasonable in liberty was suppressed and each man shuddered at his own shadow.'[4] But the mass of the population kept silent and even the upper classes of the bourgeoisie bowed themselves to the yoke, for there were still individuals who managed to infiltrate into the imperial service and thence into the new aristocracy, to amass more wealth and power than ever before. We cannot fail to see that with the decline of the bourgeoisie the urban way of life revealed its ancient, hidden blemishes. The cities whose benefits were available to only a small proportion of the population had enjoyed an existence which can only be described as parasitic. Oppressed peasants on the land and rightless slaves in households and workshops had made for prosperity – but only so long as the empire remained at peace and the social order stood firm. The wealthy had tried to ingratiate themselves with their poorer fellow-townsmen by gifts of bread and circuses. This substitute for culture had not staved off the crisis. Where now, we may ask, were the intellectuals who down the centuries had proclaimed the state the guardian of justice and its citizens free men?

2. *Intellectual and religious life*

The crisis of the ancient world is nowhere more evident than in its intellectual life. Education, literature, philosophy and religion all show a profound disturbance of existing values. Yet it is here, if anywhere, that signs of the approach of an entirely new order first make their appearance. Ancient man would emerge transformed from the crisis of the third century.

At first glance the educational opportunities which existed in the Greek cities of the east, and had become available in Roman communities from the beginning of the empire, seem impressive. Around the turn of the third century grammar and rhetoric were being taught to the youth of townspeople in civic schools throughout the empire. In some intellectual centres the emperors had used public funds to set up professorships of language and literature, and later of medicine and law. Cities which attracted an exceptionally large number of gifted teachers may be described as university towns, thus Alexandria, Antioch and Berytus in the east, Rome, Carthage and later Milan and Bordeaux in the west. Teachers at this level enjoyed many privileges, of which the most important was their total exemption from civic responsibilities. If we ask what was the aim of this education, it becomes immediately apparent that there was no attempt at providing an introduction to a philosophical understanding of the world; the schools of philosophers continued their work outside the public institutions, whether state or municipal. The specialized disciplines and their methods were equally neglected. Mathematics, mechanics and the natural sciences formed no part of the ordinary curriculum; the solitary exponents of the exact sciences had long resigned themselves to the preservation of some small corner of their great hellenistic heritage through the compilation of unambitious handbooks. The aim of the state and municipal schools was strictly vocational: an education in rhetoric opened the door to the legal profession, the imperial civil service and perhaps even a position at court. Eloquence was still an overwhelming asset in public life. In the age of absolutism panegyrics of the emperor stimulated the art of rhetoric to its finest flights, as may be seen from the masterpieces preserved in the *Panegyrici Latini*, especially those composed at the end of the third and the beginning of the fourth century. There is no reason to suppose that eulogists of despotism were lacking even when the crisis of the third century had reached its climax.

Literary activity, still intense in the second century, especially in the Greek provinces, was seriously affected by the decay of the civic bourgeoisie. Yet there were still some writers who enjoyed a certain prestige, particularly in the early third century when some of the Severi and their ladies were known to move in literary circles. The authors of these decades were neither Italians nor Greeks but natives of remoter provinces. The historian Cassius Dio, whose work is proof both of the survival of the Thucydidean method of historical writing and of the intellectual influence Rome exerted as a world power, came from a family who had held office in the Bithynian city of Nicaea: he himself passed through all the grades of a career in the Roman public service and was consul for the second time in 229. Although a Greek, he was so completely at home in the Roman world that he felt competent to write the history of Rome from the arrival of Aeneas in Italy down to his own day, ending with his consulate of 229. Having assiduously collected his material, he wrote a work composed of eighty books; about a sixth part of the whole has come down to us and parts of the lost portions are known to a certain degree from excerpts made by later writers. This historian was strongly influenced by rhetoric, as is evident from the numerous speeches inserted into his narrative and still more from his florid set pieces. Yet one can say that as a piece of political history his *History of Rome* is still in the mainstream of the best classical tradition. No other Greek work written under the empire comes so close to an understanding of the Roman state and its problems. In any case, Dio appears all the greater because he was unique in his generation. His contemporary Herodian, who wrote a small book on Roman history from the death of Marcus Aurelius, confines himself to empty descriptions of palace revolutions without attempting to uncover the political motives behind them. The only name in Latin historical writing is that of Marius Maximus whose work is now lost; we can, however, form some idea of its plan and character from its use by later writers. Marius Maximus attempted to emulate Suetonius by writing the biographies of the Roman emperors from Nerva to Elagabalus; he stuck to the stereotyped pattern for biographical writing, his reporting was uncritical, his narrative longwinded – manifestly he must be classed among those literati who had lost the sense of political values which informed the greatest historical writing.

When we turn to the specialized disciplines we find that by far the most eminent writing came from the jurists we have already encountered as councillors of the emperor in the time of Septimius Severus and later, the men who provided absolute monarchy with its theoretical foundation. Papinian, Ulpian and Paulus were the authors of copious treatises whose purpose was partly to assist in the administration of justice and partly to further the education of law students; surviving fragments and excerpts reveal these works as the classics of Roman law. As comments on the *jus civile*, but at the same time concerned with the law for all men, they are a dazzling reflection of the spirit of the age in which the inhabitants of the provinces had become citizens of Rome. All other branches of learning remained stagnant; there was no new writing of any consequence in the fields covered by geography, mathematics, philology and medicine. Nevertheless there was still some interest in knowledge of every kind, although writers were content to fasten on isolated eye-catching snippets from the inherited body of learning. They produced miscellaneous compilations of anecdotes from natural and human history, anthologies of a type which had long been popular: for example, the all-embracing *Learned Banquet* compiled by Athenaeus of Naucratis. This author's gleanings cover a wide range of subjects: habits and customs from all periods, food and drink, games and dancing, flatterers, slaves, hetairai, in fact everything the taste of the period found interesting or amusing. The book, which is not alone of its kind, is a clear enough indication that learning was treated rather as a game than as the basis for new advances in knowledge.

How are we to account for this intellectual inanition? Is it really enough to point to the ravages of war, the blight which settled on the towns and the impoverishment of the bourgeois middle class? Such an explanation would be unsatisfactory. For the fact is that this century saw poetry as well as science brought close to extinction. It has not a single dramatic or epic poem to its name, and no lyric poet worth mentioning. The only branch of imaginative writing to show any merit is the romance. The classical romance has its roots in the hellenic era, at a time when Greece was still untouched by Rome. Under the empire travellers' tales and love stories were the most popular forms of romance. In a society increasingly cut off from political reality there was a constant demand for tales of free invention in which elements of myth and history were combined. Longus, in his famous pastoral romance *Daphnis and Chloe* transformed a titillating erotic episode into a literary work of art. Heliodorus in his *Aethiopica* succeeded in capturing the variety of the world and the interaction of events, while at the same time showing divine guidance in operation behind the scenes of the love affair. Recently scholars have drawn attention to the religious complexion of these late classical romances. With this in mind it seems appropriate to mention here a book which, although ostensibly the biography of a real person, is in fact a romanticized and much embroidered portrait of a holy man with quite exceptional gifts, the life of Apollonius of Tyana written by Philostratus at the request of the empress Julia Domna. Apollonius, who lived under the Flavian emperors, belonged to a sect named after Pythagoras which imposed a strict régime of life on its adherents. The Godhead was to be worshipped not through sacrifices but by self-purification, and this sage set himself the high goal of becoming godlike through virtue. He was active in Rome and his extensive journeys led him to Spain as well as Ethiopia and India. Everywhere legends sprouted concerning this miracle man, who was credited with the gift of prophecy and the possession of psychical powers so compelling that he could drive out demons and bring the dead to life. In choosing to set out the life of this Pythagorean saint as a traveller's tale Philostratus intends the reader to admire the teacher of wisdom rather than the wizard. His hero attains to supernatural powers not through magic but through his knowledge of God; Apollonius of Tyana is thus made to appear the prophet of a new faith.

And so we come to religion, the territory in which the third century produced something really new; philosophy must also be included under this heading, since knowledge of God was for the moment its sole aim. An immense and multifarious field spreads out before us: the religious rituals of town and country-dwellers, together with the official worship of the state deities; the oriental cults and their mysteries, not forgetting the magical and occult arts; the high endeavours of philosophers; the sublimest forms of mystical piety. Literary sources, inscriptions, papyri, figurative and monumental art all bear witness to the fact that the men of this generation had been inundated by a new faith in religion. The creative energy of this century shows itself in the worship of divinity and the longing for union with the Godhead. This is just as true of those who clung to the names of the old gods as it is for the many who were now turning to the Christian message. All the same, this was no bolt from the blue; the spiritual metamorphosis which overtook the men of the later Roman empire is best regarded as the final product of the thought and religious experience of antiquity as a whole, which is the view of scholars such as M. P. Nilsson, L. Bréhier, E. R. Dodds and A. J. Festugière who are well qualified to judge. It is true that the intellectual culture of these later centuries exhibits features directly opposed to the mentality of the classical epoch. The Greek spirit of rational enquiry, which had also captivated educated people in the Roman world, started to droop under the empire. Philosophers no longer strove after a new interpretation of the world which should surpass the systems of Plato and Aristotle and the hellenistic schools; the perpetuation of received theories was the limit of their ambition, and for the most part they contented themselves with commentaries on individual works. As we have already seen, exponents of the exact sciences, mathematics, astronomy, mechanics and medicine, were no longer throwing up important new problems. This paralysis may partially be accounted for by a defective understanding and aptitude for experiment, which in antiquity did not occupy the place in natural science that it holds today. There was little increase in experimental data, which meant that speculation was to some extent carried on in a void. 'Greek rationalism spent itself like a fire which dies for want of fuel' (M. P. Nilsson). Henceforward the world picture of Greek and Roman scholars assumed a form which was regarded as final: the earth is the central point of the universe but also the scene of change and therefore of decay, above it lies the region of the air, inhabited by all manner of daemons, high above that there is heaven, which knows no dissolution, and over all the highest, transcendental God. The antithesis between the terrestrial world and deity was deeply felt. The burning question was, how could man escape from this separated state? How could he attain truth? How could he find God and so achieve the only happiness? By the time we reach these latter-day generations of the ancient world the problems men set themselves have become theological and moral.

It has been said that this shift in thought and attitudes was brought about by the invasion of the Graeco-Roman world by oriental thinkers and their ideas; some have even gone so far as to speak of an 'orientalization of classical man'. It is true that for centuries there had been an appreciable influx of people from the eastern Mediterranean, especially Asia Minor and Syria, into Greece, Italy and the western provinces, and that the newcomers had made themselves at home in Latin or Greek (or even both), often becoming Roman citizens after years of outstanding service in their professions. Throughout the whole course of Greek and Roman history there was more movement of population from east to west than in the contrary direction. In the third and fourth centuries individuals of eastern origin played a particularly conspicuous role in the political and intellectual life of the Roman empire. Ulpian, the jurist, came from Tyre, the philosopher Plotinus from Egypt (as did the poet Claudian, somewhat later), the historian Ammianus from Antioch in Syria. These names may well stand as representatives of a larger group of men who on the surface appear to be Greeks and Romans, but who in their youth had imbibed their native oriental traditions, much of which may well have stayed with them. It is thus not surprising that many elements in the religion and philosophy of this period seem to have affinities with the teachings and conceptions of Asia and Egypt. But however important this oriental influence, its main office in the western Mediterranean was to release subconscious impulses already present. If we look closely at ancient culture in all its diversity, we realize that at this period the Greeks and Romans were again cultivating dispositions and energies they had always possessed but which had been overlaid by others. There is no denying that the use of reason was a characteristic feature of the classical centuries; but in their early days the Greeks and still more the Romans, had allowed the irrational to dominate essential parts of life. Divinely inspired seers foretold the future; teachers of wisdom saw the body as the prison of the soul and sought release through abstinence and spiritual discipline (asceticism); priests of the official religion consulted their secret books for prophylactics against the wrath of the gods. It was these primitive attitudes that were once again laid bare, changing the mental climate completely. Many men found by experience that knowledge of truth could be attained not only through human enquiry but also through visions and revelations of God. Piety was no longer merely a matter of offering sacrifices; now men gave themselves up to prayer, silence and contemplation and sought union with God through severance from the material world, through self-abnegation, through ecstasies. The religious life of this late period was mystical in tone. But to make the picture complete we must mention that superstitious and magical practices of a quite primitive character were also present.

Certain features of this new feeling for religion are to be found in all provinces and in all municipal cults. Numerous inscriptions and votive offerings from Greece and neighbouring territories testify to the continuing worship of the old municipal deities. If evidence of these traditional cults becomes scarce from the mid-third century, this may partly be explained by a falling-off in public contributions attributable to the general economic crisis. What is striking is that the cult centres which flourished longest were those which met men's longing for supernatural aid : the temple of Aesculapius, god of healing, at Epidaurus, the oracles at Didyme and Clarus, the temple at Eleusis. The secret initiations which had long been practised at Eleusis were a guarantee of men's happiness in the after life. Many people who were scornful of the means to salvation offered by the oriental religions may still have turned their steps towards Eleusis, which continued to be a centre of hellenic worship. The emperor Gallienus (260–8) who made the revival of Greek culture part of his political reforms, encouraged the Greek cults, himself becoming an archon of Athens and an initiate of Eleusis. Contemporaries hailed this return to the ancient holy places as a tribute to 'hellenism', but it is clear that the road trodden by the emperor and others like him did not lead to the gods of Olympus.

A similar harking back to archaic traditions is noticeable in the Roman state religions ; here too a new feeling for religion is at work. The emperor Augustus had made the worship of the state gods a cornerstone of Roman policy ; he revived ancient temples and priesthoods, ceremonies and rituals, and introduced the cult of the emperor into his modified principate as the religious expression of belief in monarchy. Observance of this political religion (the worship of the state gods, the *di publici populi Romani*) was encouraged by all his successors, both in Rome and in the provinces ; indeed the ruler himself always held the office of chief priest (Pontifex Maximus). The Capitoline gods were worshipped wherever Roman magistrates ruled ; shrines were dedicated to Mercury and Hermes wherever Roman citizens settled ; Mars and Victoria were invoked wherever Roman soldiers had their camps ; the cult of the emperor was observed without question by citizens and non-citizens alike. Although observance of these official cults frequently became a mere formality, in times of danger Romans everywhere united in the conviction that the gods could intervene and that Roman rule was invincible so long as men venerated the gods. Horace's dictum 'as long as you obey the gods you will rule'[5] was accepted as an article of political faith. The third century emperors, even when they were uncouth soldiers from Pannonia and Illyria, clung to the idea that the gods could be wooed through sacrifices. As the number of gods who won acceptance increased, so did exhortations to defend the ancestral religion, even at the price of prohibiting what was new. Even the historian Cassius Dio ranges himself among the champions of this politico-religious orthodoxy when he ascribes the following advice to Maecenas, the councillor of Augustus. 'Everywhere worship divinity according to the customs of the fathers and compel all others to do the same. Those who import anything alien into the worship of the gods must be condemned and punished, not only to do the will of the gods, whose contemners indeed have no respect for anyone, but also because men who wilfully introduce new gods seduce many others into an alien habit. So are conspiracies, factions and secret societies born, all things injurious to monarchy. Therefore tolerate no godless men and no magicians.'[6] It was not long before this advice was translated into reality. An edict issued by the emperor Decius in 250 ordered all members of the empire to be present when sacrifices were offered at the altars of the Roman gods. As will be seen, this edict was aimed principally at the Christians, but what is important to notice here is that the crisis of the empire had goaded the emperor into an act of primitive superstition which would have been impossible in the days of Pericles and Caesar. The gods are to be coerced by forcing all men to unite in their worship – a desperate recourse to state-magic.

If it is granted that the essential characteristics of the new religious feeling were men's longing for personal union with God and the assurance of happiness in an after-life, we shall find these features displayed most clearly in the oriental religions which had long been spreading into the empire from their homelands in the east. The cult of the Great Mother of Gods had been brought to Rome from Phrygia in the desperate days of the war against Hannibal; protected by Rome, the cult had continued to attract believers. The Egyptian gods Sarapis and Isis had their worshippers in the western as well as the Greek provinces, and a temple in the heart of Rome, built by the emperor Caracalla. Soldiers of the Roman army had an especial devotion to the Persian Mithras; the underground crypts used by Mithraic congregations have been found on many camp sites. The Syrian deities had a strong appeal because of their connection with the celestial bodies. Elagabalus, whose cult was brought to Rome by the Roman emperor who took his name, was a sun god whose worship was imposed by his name-sake on the empire as a whole. In general, however, the victory of this or that alien god was not primarily due to the intervention of individual emperors on their behalf; as F. Cumont has shown, the form these deities assumed and the ritual they demanded satisfied the religious yearnings of many men, without requiring them to abandon the worship of their native gods. The new gods belonged to no one people or city; they appealed to all mankind, their sphere was as universal as the imperium. Men of oriental origin, merchants and slaves, may indeed have been the most active in these cults and the most eminent in their priesthoods, but converts of every race and nation were received into their fellowship as brothers. The rites and ceremonies must have had a tremendous drawing power, consisting as they did of processions to the sound of sonorous music and sacred dramas showing forth the passion, death and resurrection of Attis or Osiris, in which the worshippers were called on to consummate the divine act, all within the setting of secret sanctuaries. Many of the sects claimed that their religious teaching could solve the riddles of the universe and of human existence which had defeated the philosophers. Above all, the obligations laid on the believer were far more personal in character than those demanded by the observance of the state and municipal cults. Ritual actions were prescribed which brought purification and healing; asceticism was enjoined through prayer and fasting; priests, who could be identified as such from a special form of dress or tonsure, exercised what amounted to a cure of souls. When the neophyte had passed through all the successive stages which marked him out as belonging to the god and his flock he was at last initiated into the ultimate secrets and through participation in the most arcane rites (mysteries) achieved union with the god and thus assurance of immortality: he was in fact totally transformed, born again, god-like. The forms of initiations were many and various, ranging from acts of crude sensuality to rites of high spirituality. In the *taurobolium* of the Great Mother the neophyte sprinkled his eyes, ears, nose and mouth with the blood of the slaughtered bull and thus baptized, received the adoration of the worshippers. Apuleius has left us a description of initiation into the cult of Isis with which he concludes his romance *The Transformation of Lucius*, otherwise known as *The Golden Ass*. 'I approached the very gates of death and set one foot on Proserpine's threshold, and yet was permitted to return, rapt through all the elements. At midnight I saw the sun shining as if it were noon; I entered the presence of the gods of the underworld and the gods of the upper world and stood near and worshipped them.'[7] (Transl. R. Graves.) What actually happened remains cloaked in mystery; all the initiate was allowed to say openly was that after this solemn rite he was shown to the people dressed in royal raiment, crowned with a radiant chaplet, a lighted torch in his hand – decked out like the sun. Yet even with all this strange variety of rite and doctrine, and despite the proselytizing activities of their priests, there was no serious enmity between the cults. There was nothing to prevent the zealous from belonging to several sects. At bottom the conceptions and practices of the mystery religions were so closely akin that a formal mingling of deities and cults, by a process of syncretism, was genuinely possible. All the same, the priests of Mithras or Sarapis or whatever god one likes to mention remained convinced that theirs was the highest god. They each had their watchword: 'there is but one

God, Mithras', 'there is but one God, Sarapis', but what this meant was that the god in question had assimilated all others to himself; the existence of other deities was not denied (henotheism). As astonishing proof that the oriental religions carried all before them we need only point to the action of the emperor Aurelian (270–5) in importing the Syrian sun-god to Rome, to be worshipped there with full Roman honours: Sol Invictus was now to be the highest deity in the state religion, lord protector of the emperor and the empire.

The spread of the oriental religions appears to some extent to have been promoted by systematic missionary activity. The success of such evangelism was most marked in the lower classes of the population, both in town and country. Educated people were often repelled by the fanatical modes of worship associated with the cults. But the tide of new religious feeling by no means passed them by. A large collection of religious texts in Greek assembled under the name of Hermes Trismegistus and apparently composed in the period AD 50–250 has come down to us. These writings, which treat of the origin of the world and the descent and salvation of man, purport to be the revelations of the Egyptian god Thoth, the lord of knowledge and wisdom, known to the Egyptians as 'the great great', to the Greeks as 'Hermes three times greatest'. We are endebted to the learned activity of A. D. Nock and A. J. Festugière for the publication and elucidation of these texts. The regions where the hermetic teaching originated can now be identified, and it has been established that Egypt was of less importance than the name of the god suggests; the Near East, Greece and late Judaism all made some contribution. Hermetic teaching centred in the fundamental doctrine of a single and supreme God, creator of the world, and the parlous state of man, abandoned to the material world, the world of evil, poised between the influence of the heavenly bodies and of daemons, living in fear of punishment for his actions after death. In this predicament the revelation of Hermes offered liberation to the elect, gave wisdom through illumination and led to the knowledge of God. The one who knows may rest in God, saying: 'Whither shall I look to praise thee, upwards, downwards, inwards, outwards? All is in thee, all from thee, thou givest all and takest nothing, since thou hast all and there is nothing thou hast not.'[8] Mention of an elect shows that hermetic teaching did not produce large communities of worshippers but rather small sects of a prophetic character. Although the texts are full of contradictions, the revelation of Hermes attracted men from the educated classes and led many to a mystical piety through its teaching of the heavenward journey of the soul, the ascent of man to God.

In a few of the Hermetic writings the true knowledge reached through the contemplation of God is described as gnosis. The use of this expression to denote sublime knowledge, and the deification of man achieved by this means, was not exclusive to Hermetic circles; it was also current in the Greek philosophy of this period and agitated Christians of the second and third centuries. One might say that gnosis is a key word of the new religiosity. Modern scholarship has seen gnosis, or gnosticism as it is more generally called, in a number of different lights. Attention was initially concentrated on gnosis in its relation to Christianity, in particular the fierce battles between the Church and the gnostic heresies which were held to represent an acute phase in the great movement towards the hellenisation of Christianity (A. von Harnack). Later it was shown that gnosis had a connection with earlier Greek religion and with the oriental cults; gnosis was explained partly as the revival of long-forgotten religious concepts which had once been believed, and partly as an attempt at intellectualizing the oriental salvation religions. More recently still there has been an important addition to gnostic literature through the discovery of a library belonging to a gnostic community settled in Upper Egypt. The collection comprises more than forty texts in the Coptic tongue translated from the Greek and going back to originals which probably belong to the second century; they include apocalyptical writings and apocryphal gospels. In the light of our present knowledge we can say with certainty that gnosis was no mere reaction to the catastrophes which overtook the ancient world and the loss of political power by the educated classes. Its roots lie far deeper and reach out into a variety of cultures. The dualist conception which sets Light and Dark, Good and Evil in direct opposition, is to be found in the Ancient East, in Judaism and in Persia. From the beginning of the empire there were men in Graeco-Roman society who saw the world as evil, the creation of an evil spirit, and who thus held one of the fundamental tenets of gnosis. The further development of this teaching ran as follows: man must recognize his plight on this earth and discover how to deliver himself, he must conquer carnal enjoyment so that through the contemplation of God his soul may gain access to the kingdom of light. It was this basic conception of God and the world, of the fallen nature of man and the posibility of his return to the kingdom of God, that was disseminated within the great gnostic systems, which proliferated in mythical and symbolic figures and subtle concepts. Gnosis drew a wide circle of educated men into the tangled web of its speculations.

The religious life of the third century was thus many-sided. We find emperors and their magistrates, cities and their temples all opening the gates to a new tide of belief, worshippers of new gods appearing in the great centres of commerce and in army encampments, hermetic and gnostic sects emerging into view. Yet there were also many men in all ranks of society who found no comfort for the pains of existence in revelations and mysteries but longed for concrete information about the immediate future and practical recipes for subduing matter. Even these demands could be met, since at this period practitioners of astrology and magic were extending the principles and methods of their trade, borrowing piecemeal from the religious systems and even encroaching upon science. The notion that the heavenly bodies exert an influence for good or ill can be traced far back in the history of the Ancient East. It received its fullest theoretical and practical treatment in Babylon; the Chaldeans in particular were renowned for their mastery of the art of predicting men's future by calculating the position of the stars. Since this could only be done by the application of mathematical skills, astrologers came to be known simply as *mathematici*. Some schools of ancient philosophy raised objections to the teaching and practice of astrology and the Roman government had repeatedly expelled the Chaldeans and Mathematicians from Rome, admittedly without permanent success. Under the empire astrologers were employed by people of the highest social eminence and some emperors and generals had their horoscopes cast. Interrogating the stars for information about the death of the ruling emperor was strictly forbidden but widely practised; rich men consulted Chaldeans before undertaking a journey, rich and poor made astrological enquiries about the future of a new-born child. In combination with the oriental cults, especially the Syrian religion, reading the stars developed into a formal astrological belief, and it cannot be denied that in the century of catastrophes astrological fatalism had what was in many ways a crippling effect.

The theories and practices of magic were more widespread still. At all periods and among all peoples one meets the superstition that if prescribed words are uttered and specific actions performed a certain effect will ensue, whether it be the death of an enemy or the kindling of love in the person desired. In more advanced civilizations science comes to the aid of magic: recognition of regular patterns in natural processes is just as helpful to magic as to mechanics and technology. Finally, as religions degenerate, they too add their contribution to the enrichment of magic. In the ancient world the Babylonians and Egyptians, and indeed the Persians, evolved numerous methods for controlling the wicked daemons of the world; by its very name magic reminds us of its connection with the wise men of Persia, the Magi. There is plenty of evidence that the black art of the magicians played a malefic role in the declining centuries of antiquity. The emperors might declare open war on the magicians, arraigning them in their laws with murderers and poisoners, but magic still maintained and indeed enlarged its influence. There are reports of magicians engaging in practices contrary to the criminal law, using corpses of executed criminals for magical purposes, or sacrificing a child in attempts to conjure up the dead. Innocuous forms of magic were very widespread: the wearing of amulets, the magical manipulation of letters and figures, belief in the miraculous powers of metals and precious stones. A large number of lead tablets inscribed with formulae of imprecation have survived, together with innumerable papyri containing magical texts to cover every conceivable eventuality. The power of magic had indeed become so ominous that one might well be tempted to say that a magical culture was in process of developing.

The temptation will be resisted; I would suggest rather that the creative energy of the men who lived in this late phase of ancient civilization is more clearly reflected in the religious ferment and in leanings towards mysticism. In support of this view I suggest that the cults, mysteries and sects were of less importance than the two phenomena which display the religious temper of the century at its purest and strongest, the Neoplatonist philosophy and the theology of the Christian church. The former represents ancient thought at its most spiritualized, the latter introduces a metaphysic in which the divine, the eternally fixed point, descends into the world of men and transforms historical existence at its innermost core.

In the course of the second century philosophers of the Graeco-Roman world had already ceased to concentrate on the differences between the various schools of philosophy; instead they now emphasized the features which all schools held in common. This swing to eclecticism again brought to the fore an earlier conception of Greek philosophy, that of a deity remote from the world and withdrawn from men, accessible only to the pure in spirit; the material world, far below the divine, was a zone of evil from which man must free himself through asceticism. When the philosophers of the imperial period came to elaborate these ideas they evoked Pythagoras and 'divine' Plato in their support. By the turn of the second century this Platonic current – a Platonism with a markedly religious imprint – was already flowing strongly. The teachers who adopted this position belonged for the most part to the prosperous and educated middle class; they addressed themselves to a select circle of listeners and demanded from their disciples a life of sustained philosophical endeavour, in graduated stages. These teachers held that the unity of the All was manifest in a hierarchy of many forms of being, which descended from perfect to less perfect appearances; they taught a way of knowledge which although it began in the material world saw this only as the reflection of higher spiritual reality, and attained final perfection by ascent from one region to another. One of the earliest names in the neo-platonic school is that of Ammonius Saccas who lived out his philosophy in a small community at Alexandria during the time of the Severan emperors. Among his pupils were Origen, whom we shall meet as an important Christian theologian, and Plotinus, with whom neo-platonism reached its apogee.

Plotinus was born in 205, perhaps at Lycopolis in Upper Egypt; after a lengthy period of study at Alexandria, he accompanied the emperor Gordian on his campaigns against the Persians (243) and ended by settling in Rome, where he was active among a circle of enthusiastic disciples until shortly before his death in 270. After he died his treatises containing the essence of his teaching were published by Porphyry (one of the inner band of disciples) in six groups of nine 'Enneads'. Our understanding of this important work has recently been substantially advanced by philologists and philosophers such as L. Bréhier, A. Armstrong, W. Theiler and R. Harder.

The philosophy of Plotinus starts from the fixed image of a cosmos which has no temporal beginning or end, which is bounded and exhibits an unchanging order. In all Being the quality of Being depends on the degree of unity possessed by the parts: something living has a higher degree of reality than a heap of stones whose components are simply placed side by side. Every reality in which the unity of the parts is not perfect presupposes a higher and more perfect unity beyond it, and each reality will only be understood as it relates to a more perfect unity: the One is nothing but the principle of Being, the primal hypostasis, in which there is no more division. But this prime essential Being cannot subsist alone and for itself, since everything that is perfect produces something from its superfluity; this is an eternal process, not just a creation at a point in time. This creation is a radiation or emanation, an effusion from which the creator suffers no loss. But what is produced stays close to its source, turns back towards it, and this centripetal movement forms the second hypostasis; the intelligible world, the Intellect, is at once Being and Understanding. One side of this second hypostasis is the multiplicity of the world, an immutable chain of Being from the highest to the lowest, the other is Intellect which discovers the richness of the intelligible world. In thinking of itself the Intellect-hypostasis apprehends its own existence and at the same time certainty of its content. From Intellect comes the third hypostasis, the Soul. The Soul is the link between the world of Intellect, from which it comes, and the material world, which it keeps in check. Below these three hypostases comes Matter, which is a further hypostasis: Matter is indeterminate, insensible and by itself incapable of receiving form and meaning. Everything evil comes from the alliance the Soul has entered into with Matter. The Soul may indeed be able to guide the body, in so far as she pays attention to the world of Intellect and is thus her own Intellect. But where the momentum of the Soul is insufficient to direct her own reflexes, then she becomes subject to the material world of change; this is the descent of the Soul, her sin, for which she must do penance in the after-life. The task of a philosophical education is to lead back the Soul to her original state of contemplation. This is achieved through thought, at a higher level through intuition and finally, through contact with the highest, in ecstasy. At this point there is no difference between the knowing and the known: the contemplator is absorbed into the One, in that he himself becomes It.

Such, in outline, was the way taught by Plotinus for achieving understanding and liberation from the material world. It is hellenic in so far as the harmony of the cosmos is preserved and man is considered capable of delivering himself; creation is not accomplished by a single divine act, redemption is not accomplished by the revelation of God in history. Yet a deep gulf separates Plotinus from classical Greek philosophy. In Plotinus man no longer concerns himself with the material world in order to know and master it, but only because it is an image of the Intellect and thus makes possible the ascent into Being, which is far above existence. Thought withdraws itself from this world, from the beauty of corporeal appearances and the hazards of political life. This being so, it is not clear what Plotinus intended when he urged the emperor Gallienus, one of his admirers, to establish his philosopher's city of Platonopolis in the Campania. Did he envisage a centre for common contemplation? As Bréhier has said, Plotinus turned philosophy into 'a way of describing metaphysical landscapes, which the soul may reach through intellectual discipline.' Thus a door was opened for the metaphysical contemplation of the divine, and in the centuries to come many thinkers and poets would cross its threshold.

The attitude of Plotinus' successors to the state religion and its traditional forms of worship shows the continuing influence of his system under another aspect. Plotinus himself did not use the word 'God' of his Primal Principle; he spoke of the heavenly bodies as gods, and so far as they were concerned was content to accept polytheism. He also mentioned observation of the stars as a means of prediction and had no objection to ritual practices. He explains that the efficacy of a prayer or of honours paid to the statue of a god arises not from the intervention of a deity in the world but from the sympathy subsisting between the individual parts of the world. But Porphyry, Iamblichus and other later followers of Plotinus went much further to accommodate the forms of popular piety as we have learned to know them, defending astrology and belief in the wisdom of oracles. Porphyry provided a philosophical foundation for the ritual practice known as theurgy – a procedure for procuring divine influence at will – and Iamblichus was happy to defend the gods, heroes and daemons of late paganism. In the generations after Plotinus many who called themselves Platonists were thus in retreat from the spiritualization of philosophy. Neoplatonists of this type became allies of the last pagan emperors, defending the forceful measures they took in compelling Christians to outward observance of the state religion.

When we come to set neo-platonism beside the theology of the Christian thinkers of the third century, the contrast and the kinship between the two will become equally apparent. First, however, we must cast a backward glance at Christian belief and the Christian mission in its earlier phase. The beginnings of Christianity in the Roman empire have been closely scrutinized by many generations of scholars; here it will suffice to mention only those of the present century, A. von Harnack and H. Lietzmann, L. Duchesne and J. Daniélou. Even so there is still much that is mysterious about the rise of this religion.

At its centre is the belief in a God who is personal and who created the world from the void. This was the idea accepted by Israel and sustained throughout the thousands of years of its history. Belief in a personal God entailed the rejection of polytheism and pantheism, as also of any philosophy which recognized a plurality of gods. The Christian gospel declares – and here it parts company with Judaism – that in the fulness of time God through Jesus, who is Christ, redeemed fallen mankind, cancelled out sin and restored the world to divine grace. Christ is thus set in the middle of history; man as an individual is called to responsible action and world history becomes the history of salvation. There is no place here for redemption myths which revolve in a cycle of perpetual rebirth, no place for the gnostic systems which speak of a mystery that has never come to pass but is perpetually immanent. On the contrary, what Christians have to do is to seize the grace of redemption: with the annulment of the Old Covenant they are the 'new people' – succeeding Israel, they are the 'third race' – succeeding the Greeks and the Jews they are appointed through purity of life and sacrificial love towards all mankind to prepare the way for the coming kingdom of God. The code of Christian behaviour does not merely consist of injunctions to refrain from certain actions, as in the Decalogue; nor is it concerned with the good citizen morality and recipes for happiness propounded by Greek and Roman philosophers. The gospel, by its call to positive action, cuts across the mood of resignation and doubt which had settled on so large a part of humanity in the ancient world; it is a new beginning struck in the soil of a torpid world. The proclamation of the gospel went out to all mankind, Jews, Greeks, men of alien races; its universality overlaid the national religions and extended beyond the frontiers of the Roman empire.

It is impossible to describe here in detail how the Christian religion was carried by the apostles and their successors from Jerusalem to Syria and then eastwards into the Aramaic-speaking region, to Mesopotamia, westwards into Asia Minor, Greece and Rome. In the Mediterranean world the proclamation of Jesus who is Christ was initially made in the Greek tongue, from the outset in combination with concepts originating in hellenistic thoughts and beliefs. But the Hebrew origins of the gospel meant that the mission had many links with Jewish communities of the Diaspora, hellenized groups of Jews within the Roman empire. This early contact, however, was soon followed by a rupture with the Synagogue. In turning towards pagans, especially Greeks, the Christians cut themselves off from the ritual law of Judaism and soon ceased to look for a Messiah who should gather in the dispersed people and bring them to rule over the heathen. It was not long before many cities of the ancient world had small communities of the new faith called Ekklesiai (congregations) on the model of the mother church at Jerusalem. Meeting at first in private houses, the Christians joined together in divine service at which the gospel was preached and the Lord's supper celebrated. Their common life was based on the sacraments and on acts of charity to the suffering world. By the second century we find the episkopos (bishop) taking precedence over the presbyters (who were modelled on the elders of the synagogue) in leadership of the congregations; his position is monarchical, he represents Christ to the community, his is the highest authority in preaching and discipline, he is responsible for safeguarding the unity of the congregation against individual opinion (heresy) and faction (schism). Bishop, priest and deacon make up the hierarchy of officials within the community; initiated through a religious ceremony, they form the clergy as opposed to the laity, the body of the faithful.

The numerous congregations which sprang up one after another were linked by personal visits, correspondence, and writings of various kinds, in which Greek literary forms make their appearance. For a long time the Roman government made no serious attempt to curb the spread of the new religion. Emperors and magistrates were in general tolerant of new gods, and the Christians were careful to conduct themselves as loyal subjects of the empire. Admittedly, under their creed the state as such had no divine authority, but they adhered strictly to the Pauline precept that the powers that be are ordained of God, so that new establishments took care not to be drawn with Jews into opposition to Rome. Such, at least, was the view of the communities in general, the position adopted by the Church as a whole. But the possibility of a dangerous conflict was present from the beginning. Christians, like pagans, prayed for the safety of the emperor and the state, but they held aloof from the ceremonies offered to the gods and refrained from emperor-worship. It was over this question that conflict shortly arose. Even so, throughout the second century and even in the early part of the third, the Roman government relied on a formula which aimed at avoiding a general conflict between the state and the new religion and the formal persecution of Christians. The emperor Trajan had decreed that only Christians who refused to sacrifice to the gods when explicitly ordered to do so should be punished by death. It is true that the sect was at the same time declared illegal, but it was expressly stated that there should be no attempt to track down its members. The initiative for taking proceedings against Christians thus lay with the pagan and Jewish populations of the cities in which the small communities were established, and with provincial governors, who were left with a wide discretion over acting on information received. The evil insinuations which were spread abroad about members of the new faith, who in many ways formed tightly-closed communities, often led to delation and not infrequently to prosecution, which could end in the death sentence executed in a hideous form. The valiance of Christians who remained true to their faith aroused the wonder and admiration of many pagan observers. To the communities themselves the victims were martyrs (blood-witnesses), and their deeds were often written down as *acta,* on the hellenistic model; they were held up as an example, as witnesses filled with the Spirit who gained immediate entry into eternal bliss, so full of grace that they could also restore back-sliders to the faith. Veneration of the martyrs forged a powerful bond between the separate communities and led many to the new faith : as Tertullian was to say not long after, the blood of Christians was the seed of new Christians (*semen sanguis*).[9] In fact, up to the beginning of the third century Christianity was spreading in all directions. In the east it had won fresh ground in Mesopotamia, where Edessa Callirhoë was an active centre ; there were now numerous Christians in Egypt, where an important community was well-entrenched at Alexandria. The success of the gospel was especially marked in the provinces of Asia Minor. In the west there was a strong community at Rome, the imperial city, which added to its power of attraction ; Carthage held a commanding central position in North Africa, in Gaul communities stretched from the mouth of the Rhône up to Lyons ; Irenaeus, bishop of this city, mentions the existence of communities in the Germanic and Spanish provinces towards the end of the second century. Moreover the faith had long since ceased to be confined to the lower classes of society ; Christians were now to be found among officials, in the army and at the imperial court, especially in the time of the Severi, when a few of the emperors of this house showed themselves open to the new religious influences.

The increased spread of Christian communities and the rise of some Christians in the social scale was accompanied by developments in doctrine. A few Christian groups were strongly affected by external influences; gnosticism and a new form of apocalyptical eschatology entered from the border zones of Judaism, from Hellenism came the concept of the Logos and elements of ethics as taught by the Stoic and Platonic philosophers. In the meantime there was also something of a revival of primitive Christian enthusiasm, whose prophetic modes of preaching clashed with the institutions of bishops and clergy. The dust of these battles has been preserved in numerous Christian writings, initially written mostly in Greek but later also in Latin, since the protagonists of many deviant doctrines had settled in Rome. In the course of this struggle with heterodox teachings, which here and there resulted in the formation of separatist churches, the doctrine of God and the concept of the Church received a more precise formulation. In combatting gnosticism of whatever shade it was especially important to arrive at a definition of the divinity of Christ, and in particular his relation with God the father. The authority of a few outstanding bishops who stood for the apostolic tradition and the defence of church unity carried particular weight in these internal theological controversies. Other Christian writers took up the dialogue with the pagans and used the same literary forms in defence of their faith as the Jews had earlier in justifying their religion to the hellenistic world. The second half of the second century is rich in apologetics aimed at establishing Christianity on an intellectual footing, providing it with a generally agreed philosophy, and at reconciling it with the Roman state. It is claimed that there is no fundamental distinction between the Christian faith and philosophical thought, but on the contrary, that Christian doctrine has entered into the heritage of Greek culture. Polytheism is vigorously attacked, with much the same arguments as the pagan philosophers had used; toleration is demanded for the new religion, on the principle that each man must be left free to choose his own religion. There is also the surprising assertion that the Christians are loyal subjects of the state, that they obey authority and pray for the emperor, and furthermore that Christians want nothing better than to be the emperor's first allies and associates in upholding the existing order. The state could not fail to benefit – so one apologist maintains – if all men shared the moral outlook of the Christians. In conclusion we should take particular notice of a suggestion which had far-reaching effects, namely that the Empire and Christianity are locked together into history, since both began in the days of Augustus; Roman power has advanced continuously since the rise of this religion, and so long as Christianity has its protection will continue to advance. The letter in which this idea first makes its appearance was addressed to the emperor Marcus Aurelius; many such apologies carry imperial addresses as a matter of literary form. But despite so much effort, the goal of all this apologetic, to secure formal toleration for

Christians, was not achieved. Where they did succeed was in presenting Christianity to a growing circle of educated people as a type of philosophy.

The reply from the opposition was not long delayed. Celsus, a philosopher of the Platonic school, published his fierce polemic against the Christians as early as the reign of Marcus Aurelius. He stigmatizes the Christian mission, with its appeal to the lower classes, as destructive of social order, denouncing the Christians for deserting the empire in its hour of need by their disengagement from public life. But the main burden of his accusation is directed against the intellectual claims of the new religion. Celsus rebukes the Christians for their open preference for the uneducated and the criminal; he tries to show that essential parts of their doctrine contradict the reflections of an understanding mind, for example the doctrines of the creation of the world, original sin and redemption, and above all the dogma of the resurrection of the body. Pagan religious practices are supported with philosophical arguments. The gods are presented as the intermediaries between the supreme divinity and the world, their plurality justified by reference to the plurality of nations. It is claimed that the forms of worship paid to the gods and the rules of ritual are hallowed by tradition; the nomos is beyond all modification. The Christians are thus branded as deserters, seditious agitators and criminals. To us the political reasons which prompted this stinging polemic may seem clearer than the author's philosophical position, since the basis of Celsus' thinking is obviously the Platonism he shared with many Christian writers of the period. It has been shown, in fact, that he probably extracted his philosophy of history from the Apology of Justin, who died a martyr in 165.

In later literary battles and periods of intensive persecution pagan philosophy and Christian theology drew closer still; the Christian faith had begun to take its place in the history of Greek culture. The first real progress along this line was made in Alexandria, for centuries a seat of Greek learning and a place where Egyptian beliefs and Jewish wisdom still flourished. Here more than anywhere the Christians were compelled to justify their faith through debate and analysis. The Christian philosopher Clement, who was born into a pagan, perhaps Athenian, family and became a Christian by his own choice, taught there for several years at the turn of the second century. The titles of his works epitomize the stages through which he thought pagans and Christians should pass on their initiation to the faith. The first essential, as indicated by his *Hortatory Discourse to the Greeks*, a work in the traditional style, is that men should discipline themselves to philosophical thinking. Polytheism is rejected as an office of slavery, imposed on man by daemons. On the other hand, it is stressed that pagan philosophy has helped to prepare the way for recognition of the true God; full recognition was brought about through the Logos, Jesus Christ. Clement's second book, *Paidagogos*, is also directed to the educated section within the Christian community, and presupposes a knowledge of contemporary thought. Here he explicitly alludes to Greek wisdom as *propaideia*, that is to say, the essential preliminary to Christian humanism; this hellenic contribution to understanding, which was the work of a human Logos, has been completed by the divine Logos: Christ as the divine teacher exceeds all former wisdom. The Logos Paidagogos, by his life and teachings which are recorded in Holy Writ, set up the standard of the perfect life. These theses set out the substance of Clement's teaching. The numerous questions which must have occurred to his religious-minded contemporaries are thoroughly dealt with in another book entitled *Stromateis*, literally 'carpet bags' which as its name suggests is a work of general and variegated content. The hellenic stamp of his theology once again makes its appearance in what is said of the knowledge of God and in the ethical teaching. The world was made and God revealed to man through the Logos, who is united with the Father and Spirit in the Trinity; the true law is inscribed in the heart of every man, Moses and Plato were both philosophers, true friends of wisdom. But in the fulness of time God himself becomes man, redeems mankind, and provides the means of grace; above all, as the exemplar of perfection, the Logos guides man to right conduct. For man the source of righteousness is no longer the law of the state but the love of God; the Christian belongs to the heavenly city (Uranopolis), where Christ reigns as he does in the terrestrial Church, which is formed after the model of the heavenly. In his striving after virtue, in his aspiration to true wisdom, valour, righteousness and moderation, the new man is no longer driven by fear and hope; virtue has become its own reward. But the final goal of all striving is God himself. The Christian who is schooled in philosophy will so immerse himself in the gospel that he becomes assimilated with Christ, even the image of God. The Christian religion is the true gnosis which leads to bliss. If, says Clement, a Christian gnostic were offered a choice between knowledge of God and eternal blessedness (always supposing that these two inseparables could be parted), he would unhesitatingly choose knowledge of God, nothing else[10] – which sums up for us the philosophical creed of this Christian in whom experience of the gospel and of Greek culture had united.

Greek influences were also fruitfully at work in Origen, who followed Clement in establishing a comprehensive system of theology. The son of Christian parents, he was born in 185 and studied literature and philosophy at Alexandria, where he was also a pupil of Ammonius Saccas. At the request of the bishop of Alexandria he undertook the instruction of the catechumens and eventually, in connection with this school, gave public lectures which were a general introduction to philosophy and theology. Shortly after 230 he came into conflict with his bishop and moved to Caesarea in Palestine. Here he founded a theological academy, but his advice was also sought by other Christian communities and occasionally by members of the imperial court, so that he visited Athens and Antioch and had considerable influence in the Roman province of Arabia, which was an Alexandrian mission field. His prodigious literary output, which embraces a host of commentaries, sermons and tracts of every description, has come down to us only in fragmentary fashion, as his theology was soon attacked and in the sixth century he was declared a heretic. From his work we receive an overwhelming impression of a scholar who has introduced the forms and style of Greek learning into theology and called the interpretation of scripture a mode of philosophizing. Interpretation of the Bible occupies the greater part of his work. In order to arrive at a scientifically established text Origen placed the primitive Hebrew version of the Old Testament alongside the Greek translations accessible to him, and thus produced a recension in six columns (*Hexapla*). Many of his commentaries and sermons are devoted to exegesis of the scriptures, in which he attempts – as the Platonists had with Homer – to extract the higher meaning from the literal text and thus make the Old and New Testaments rewarding reading even for philosophers. Origen used this biblical foundation as the basis of a theological system which appears to have been set out in his *De principiis*. Modern scholars who have tried to reconstruct the whole edifice of his thought differ widely in their interpretations, but it is generally agreed that Origen regarded Holy Writ and the apostolic tradition as the sources of the faith and that his intention was to elevate the wisdom of faith into a system of philosophy. In this attempt he leaned more towards the Platonists than the Stoics and was also stimulated by influences emanating from Judaeo-gnostic circles, which makes his contribution clearly distinct from that of Clement.

Origen sets out a doctrine of the Trinity and the redemption of fallen man which seems to contain the kernel of the bitter controversies of later generations. In Origen's theology only the Father is himself God; the Son, begotten of God from eternity, is of the same essence with the Father, he is Logos and Redeemer, second God; the Spirit is called into being by the Father through the Son. The creation and redemption of the world took place as follows: God first made the world of spirits, to which the souls of men also belong. The exercise of free choice by the spirits led to the Fall and the condemnation of spirits and souls to seek their purification in the material world. Redemption is accomplished through the Logos who unites himself with a spirit-essence and can thus take human form, becoming God-man. Just as this redemption entails a necessary manifestation of the God-world relationship, so is the purification also understood as an eternal process, which continually adapts itself to new cycles of world history. In the end all souls, including evil spirits, will submit as purified beings to the guidance of the Logos and enter the kingdom of God; this is known as the apocatastasis, the renewal of all things. Origen's doctrine of the Trinity, creation and redemption can be seen as the theological counterpart of the graduated structure presented by neo-platonism. One might say that his theology is Hellenic in that the origin of the world and the course of history are seen as phases of an eternal necessity – a hypothesis which leads to the implicit denial of the unique historical character of Christianity. But for all his involvement with Greek philosophy and Jewish gnosticism, Origen confesses to the Christian faith and as a theologian stands rooted in the Christian community. Since Christ is the great teacher of all mankind, the only road to perfection is the imitation of Christ, which leads from faith through asceticism to mystical union with Christ. Theological thinking thus parts company with philosophy and the community of believers turns its back on everything achieved by the *polis* of antiquity – the Church, indeed, emerges as the *politeia* of the Gospel, in opposition to the Roman state; Origen thus becomes the founder of a Christian spirituality, and the contemplative monasticism of later years had good reason to invoke his name.

This union of Christian doctrine with the Christian life – at once an imitation and a deviation from hellenic philosophy – is perhaps justification enough for the attention paid here to the Alexandrian theology of Clement and Origen at the expense of other works from the great wealth of Christian literature. The aim of these theologians was not merely to counter pagan objections on the intellectual plane but also to show how the life of Christians, inhabiting the city of God, was superior in deeds and achievements to the ideal laid down by the philosophers. Origen, who was imprisoned and tortured under the Decian persecution, declares in the foreword to his polemic against Celsus that the true defence of the faith proceeds from the Holy Spirit of Christ: 'Jesus defends himself through the conduct of his true disciples'. As we shall see, the defence of the Christian fellowship against the state, now in league with the pagan philosophers, constitutes the great psychomachia of these late centuries of antiquity.

3. *Enemies of the ancient world – external and internal*

When Roman historians reflect on the historical role of the empire, when poets glorify Rome's eternal mission, they always point to the benefits Roman rule conferred on the subject peoples and the peace it brought to the whole world. Their view of what constituted the world was restricted to the lands ringing the Mediterranean, the sea they called 'our sea', the land complex they called 'our world'. Making a prudent assessment of Roman resources, Augustus had checked further expansion in the east and the north and set limits to the empire, on one side the three great rivers, Rhine, Danube and Euphrates, on the other the desert belt of Africa and Arabia. Here and there some of his successors moved forward beyond these limits, but only in order to afford more secure protection to their frontiers by means of an advanced defensive zone. Such was the motive behind the conquest of Britain, of the Neckar region between the upper reaches of Rhine and Danube, and of Dacia north of the lower Danube; Septimius Severus eventually succeeded in creating a similar outpost across the upper Euphrates, the province of Mesopotamia. Where the natural frontiers of ocean, river or desert were lacking, the borders of the empire were protected by fortifications – palisades, forts, ditches and walls, depending on the terrain – so that the entire field of ancient civilization formed one vast enclosure.

In the third century a serious threat developed to several sectors of the imperial frontier as numerous tribes settled outside the empire went over to the attack. The Picts in Scotland were pressing on Hadrian's wall in the north of England, and from the middle of the third century the desert tribes of the Blemmyes were making raids on Egypt, thus threatening the empire at its southern extremity, the first cataract of the Nile. Desert peoples were now using dromedaries, whose value had long been proved in peaceful traffic, for military purposes. This innovation meant that long-distance forays were possible, so that Arabs could now direct their raids against Syria and Mesopotamia and it was not very long before the nomads south of the fortified frontier in Algeria also started to attack. The empire had two major enemies of long standing, both of whom profoundly influenced the fate of ancient civilization, the Persians and the Germans. Writing in the reign of Nero, the poet Lucan extolled the lands beyond the Tigris and the Rhine as retreats of freedom, regions unblemished by tyranny. It was from these very regions that the empire was now to be continuously attacked.

In the first centuries of the empire Rome had had as its neighbour in the extreme south-east the kingdom of Parthia; although there was frequent warfare, no life and death struggle had developed. The Parthians had indeed shown themselves susceptible to the influences of Mediterranean civilization, Greek was still understood in the cities between the Euphrates and the Tigris and western cults had gained a foothold there. Intensive archaeological excavation of the city of Dura-Europus, which up to AD 165 had belonged to Parthia, has shown that temples of Greek and oriental deities stood side by side and that Christianity was also present. Now, however, Persians who had long been settled in the south of the Iranian highlands rebelled against Parthian rule and against all alien, non-Iranian elements in the country. This nationalist movement was led by a member of the Sasanian princely house, Ardashir (Artaxerxes). His Persian forces defeated the last king of the Parthians and went on to undertake extensive campaigns which secured his rule as far as India; in 226 he was crowned Iranian king of kings in the old capital of Ctesiphon. The house of Sasan was thus established on the throne and a kingdom founded which we call the Sasanian empire.

Ardashir linked the revolt of his house and people with a revival of the ancient Persian religion; politically he claimed the heritage of the ancient Persian empire of the Achaemenids, which under Darius and Xerxes had united the lands from India to the Hellespont and the Bosphoros. The fighting forces of the Persian people and of the principalities absorbed into the empire were deployed as armoured cavalry; as a weapon, the horse and rider covered in mail had long been a feature of warfare in these parts, and its further development made the Persian army the most up-to-date attacking force of the age. The Roman border provinces on the Euphrates were attacked, and from the time of Alexander Severus the Imperium Romanum was saddled with the war against the Persians as a new and heavy responsibility. Although the Roman army was quick to imitate the armoured weapon of its opponents, the Persians achieved some important successes. The extent to which the situation in the east had been transformed was revealed when Shapur I was crowned in 242, proclaiming his pretension to universal rule by assuming the title 'king of Iran and non-Iran'. Rejecting the many other religions which had penetrated east of the Euphrates, Shapur made the ancient Persian faith the sole religion of the state. This consisted of the sacred pronouncements of Zoroaster concerning the eternal conflict between the spirit of good and the spirit of evil, Ahura Mazda and Ahriman, and the duty laid on men, especially Persians, to fight for the victory of the good. The Magi, the priests of the Persian people, freed the religious tradition of its alien accretions and produced a purified text of the Avesta. Deviant cults and sects were suppressed. The priest, Karter, who can be regarded as the architect of the Persian state-church, tells in a ceremonious inscription how he rose from being a simple priest to chief Magus and judge of the whole empire, acting in this capacity as the guardian of orthodoxy; Jews, Buddhists, Brahmans, Nazarenes and Christians were all expelled, fire-altars set up and Magi appointed wheresoever the horses and warriors of the king of kings made their appearance. Shapur himself set out the achievements of his reign in a rock inscription near Persepolis. Amongst his other triumphs he exults above all in the defeat of the emperor Valerian and the capture of his 70,000 strong army. The capture of Valerian (260) became a victory motif in Persian art, and one finds the momentous scene on rock reliefs and carved stones which show the Roman kneeling before expectant Shapur, who towers above him on his horse. The event was not only a temporary military defeat for the Romans but also a severe set-back for romano-hellenistic civilization in the east. The Roman frontier provinces were henceforth drawn into the Iranian orbit. Mesopotamia supplied new adherents to the Persian religion; and the Persians were able to recruit traitors and spies even among the Roman ruling class throughout the whole intermediate zone in which men's sympathies hovered between east and west. The far-reaching cultural effect of the Sasanian empire is all the more evident when we discover Persian influence starting to appear a little later in the insignia and ceremonial of the Roman emperors. It is also possible that the advantages of linking the state with a single form of religious belief, as seen in the Persian state church, encouraged Roman emperors to secure a new form of religious sanction for the Imperium Romanum, whether in the exclusive worship of the old gods or by turning to the God of the Christians.

But despite its support by the state, the official Persian religion did not succeed in capturing all the inhabitants of the Persian empire. The years which saw the establishment of Zoroastrianism in Persia saw also the proclamation of the doctrines of Mani and the first Manichaean mission. In Mani, who was born in Babylonia in 217 of a noble Parthian family, a personality of world-wide importance appears on the scene. Brought up in a Christian baptist community, he claimed that his call to prophesy came through an angel of God, and that what he preached, as the last in the line of great teachers following Buddha, Zoroaster and Jesus, was the revelation of heaven. Mani devoted the earlier part of his mission to his kinsmen, but afterwards spent many years preaching in India and was also active in the central regions of the Persian empire. King Shapur admitted him to his immediate retinue and for a long time encouraged him equally with Kantir, the priest who was eventually to gain the upper hand. In the course of extensive missionary journeys about the Persian empire and in Egypt Mani attracted numerous disciples and founded many communities. He was venerated as a miracle-worker like any other founder of an oriental religion, but his success was in large part due to his talent for organization and his high artistic gifts. He devised magnificent ceremonies for divine worship, wrote and preached in a Syrian tongue and was a master of all forms of poetic expression. Since his mission was to the whole world, Mani's works were translated into many languages. His long and successful career ended when the Magi accused him to the king (Shapur's next successor but one) of corrupting their religion; after a stormy trial he was condemned to imprisonment, and it was in prison that he died (276). But the religion which Mani founded continued to spread, to Egypt and the African provinces of the Roman empire, to Arabia, and as far east as China, travelling by way of Sogdiana. It has been possible to reconstruct the Manichaean religion with the aid of texts in Arabic, Syrian, Iranian and Chinese tongues supplemented most recently by the important letters and homilies in a Coptic dialect which have been discovered in Upper Egypt (H. C. Puech, G. Widengren). It is clear that in Mani's teaching basic Iranian conceptions receive a gnostic imprint. As in Persian dualism, two supreme Principles are postulated, the Father of Light and the Lord of Darkness. Together with their attendant princes and spirits both are active in the great world process which works through hard-fought contests towards the separation of light from darkness, until at the last the kingdom of light is victorious and peace reigns. A myth tells how the Father of Light comes to the aid of men with self-knowledge by sending them a messenger. Buddha, Zoroaster and Jesus were just such messengers, but their message has been falsified. Mani is the last of the line and will conquer both east and west; he comes to proclaim the great duty of men, which is to increase the light in themselves by abstaining from flesh and wine and sexual pleasures. Only the elect will be able to live as saints, the mass of followers must follow a roundabout path to salvation.

It was to practise this creed and these disciplines that the Mani communities assembled together. The church had a single head and under him apostles, bishops, priests and teachers; some monastic communities were established, rules of fasting laid down and confession introduced. The Manichaeans accepted parts of the New Testament writings and often referred to Jesus as the leader of the soul, while Mani is seen as the Spirit and paraclete whom he sent. This gnostic aspect of their doctrine made it easier for Manichees to penetrate individual Christian communities within the Roman empire; we know from the life and writings of St Augustine how sorely the Christian church was tried in its struggles with Manichaeism. But the Roman state, too, was distrustful of this sect which abhorred the world and often veiled itself in secrecy; the Persian origin of the religion and the danger that its adherents might be in collaboration with the enemy of the empire made it suspect from the start. In 297 the emperor Diocletian issued a savage edict against the Manichees addressed to the proconsul of Africa.[11] In this he declares that the Manichees, members of an enemy nation, have spread over the world like monsters, committing numerous crimes, stirring up cities and infecting the peace-loving Roman people, indeed the whole world with their poison. It is therefore decreed that the leaders of the movement be burned, together with their writings, and their camp-followers beheaded; high-placed Roman citizens who belong to the sect are to be condemned to compulsory labour in the mines. It is possible that the Manichaeans had been involved in the rebellion which broke out in Egypt about this time; what is certain is that the Romans were continuing to outlaw alien religions. Yet despite all the counter-measures taken by the state, Manichaean groups survived within the empire to become a fruitful soil for the formation of new sects in medieval Europe.

We have seen that in the east Rome was confronted by a powerful and unitary enemy, the neo-Persian empire. By a fateful conjunction this was the very period when the Germanic peoples were starting to attack, so that the Roman army was forced on to the defensive on a second and widely extended front, which ran the entire length of the Danube from its mouth to its origin and then followed the Rhine to the channel. On this front, however, there was no unified leadership or systematic plan of campaign to contend with. It is true that the modern observer can see these scattered groups as part of a complex whole; but this is because he knows that almost all the peoples pressing on the Rhine and Danube were Germanic by origin, governed by similar political and social customs, and that their attacks formed part of a general movement of populations which had affected the whole of eastern Europe.

By the beginning of the third century the germanic world was no longer divided into the numerous small tribes described by Tacitus in his famous book. In the century which had passed since Tacitus' treatment of the subject the picture had altered, because of changes in habitat among the germanic peoples and because of their partial coalescence into larger groups – a move which had important consequences, since the resulting tribal federations were capable of a more sustained attack on the Imperium Romanum. It will be useful to single out the most important of these groupings, as they are known to have existed at the beginning of the third century. The first to catch the eye are the east Germans, tribes who had migrated from Scandinavia to settle initially in eastern Europe. The Gothic tribes, from Sweden, moved first into the land round the Vistula and from there pressed on through southern Poland to reach the Black Sea. The Ostrogoths (Greuthungi) settled extensively in the Ukraine, while the Visigoths (Thervingi) occupied a wide region from there to the lower Danube. This long association with the Greek cities on the Black Sea and their Sarmatian neighbours in southern Russia brought the Goths into contact with both classical and Iranian civilization. Meanwhile, also in the second century, the Vandals had been moving south-east from Silesia to reach the eastern border of the Carpathians. The geographer Ptolemy, writing in the second century, tells us of a third east German group settled between the middle Oder and the middle Vistula, namely the Burgundians; but well before the middle of the third century we find the Burgundians on the upper and middle Main, where they had made contact with west German tribes who had long been settled in central Europe. The territory occupied by these west Germans followed the middle Danube to its source and then straddled both banks of the Rhine. The Marcomanni and the Quadi threatened the Roman frontier from Carnuntum to Regina Castra (Regensburg), the Quadi being for the moment the greater danger. In 213 we hear for the first time of a new group, the Alamanni, who were pressing south against the upper German *limes*; they belonged to the Suevi tribes of central Germany, who had produced a great leader Ariovistus, as early as the time of Julius Caesar. Around the middle of the third century the name of another new amalgamation appears, that of the Franks, which had absorbed a number of small groups from the lower Rhineland: Bructeri, Teucteri, Salians and Ripuarians. Lastly we have the Saxon tribe, which embraced the various germanic peoples living round the mouth of the Elbe and the Weser.

The Roman empire was thus hemmed in by an arc of powerful German tribes, from the Black to the North Sea. We can no longer rely only on Tacitus for our picture of germanic habits and customs at this period, but must supplement his account by references to later writers and above all to archaeological finds. There can be no doubt that all the Germans engaged in agriculture. It is equally certain that they were exploiting metal ores and salt deposits; here and there one finds evidence of incipient industrial activity. Settlement might take the form of isolated homesteads, hamlets or villages, but the east Germans, at least, were not yet rooted in the soil. Although the west Germans were by now sedentary, since most of them had to contend with land which was wooded and often marshy as well, they were very ready to abandon their clearings and go off in search of ground which was better and less cramped. Politically speaking the dominant form of association was the tribe; and membership of the tribe was conferred not by rights of citizenship of the type which could be acquired, as in contemporary civilized states, but by blood. All the free men of the tribe of an age to carry arms came together to form the (*Thing*), the council of war, which handled matters of public concern, notably issues of peace and war, and the discharge of legal functions. It was this assembly which had the deciding voice, no matter whether the tribe had a king or was led to war by several chieftains. The institution known as the following or retinue is to be found among all the germanic peoples and was of great antiquity: a leading warrior bound others to him by ties of friendship and loyalty, maintaining them in his household and leading them to battle and death. The formation of small groups of this type is characteristic of a society whose communal life was governed by spontaneous human relations rather than a legally graduated class system. As an institution the following thrived on war; and warfare was in fact the normal condition of life among the Germans at this period, whether it was whole tribes feuding with each other or separate groups embarking on independent ventures. This bellicose mode of life is also reflected in germanic religious ideas and practices. It is true that deities associated with fertility, growth and death were everywhere worshipped, and from an early date; these were the Vanir, whose cult took forms that we meet among other Indo-germanic peoples. On the other hand, belief in the Aesir, supernatural figures with the power of intervening in human life and even of assuming human shape, was peculiar to the Germans. It is highly significant that the three principal deities, Wodan, Ziu and Donar, whom Tacitus identifies with Mercury, Mars and Hercules, are all connected with war. It is Wodan, as lord of the tempest, who kindles the battle-lust of the warriors, Donar the thunderer who wields the sword and Ziu who decides the outcome. The idea that fallen warriors wake to life again in a higher kingdom is also part and parcel of this religion based on war. There was no separate order of priesthood and no temples; true, we hear of seers and wise women, people with special insight into sacred things, but in general it was the kings and chieftains who were responsible for paying the gods the reverence due and declaring their will.

The preceding account describes germanic life as it was at the beginning of the migration period in places still largely untouched by outside influences. In fact the tribes had already been in touch with the outside world; they had become familiar with alien gods and evolved their runic script from an Italian alphabet. Prolonged contact with Rome produced a general veneer of civilization, of varying depth, and an approximation to Graeco-Roman ways of life; these preliminary encounters were more fruitful in some places than in others, but in general they were sufficiently important to determine in many ways the relations between the tribes and the Imperium Romanum once the frontiers had been crossed. In the Rhine provinces of the empire, where there were also Celts to add their contribution to the melting pot of peoples and customs, a close collaboration developed between Romans and Germans. Here the combination of the Roman and indigenous way of life produced a specifically Roman-provincial culture. The provincials learned horticulture and wine-growing from the Romans; the use of stone for building became the rule and urban settlements appeared, whether as Roman colonies or as civil communities attached to Roman camps. Areas were set aside for temple sanctuaries and bridges and aqueducts constructed to make the practical business of living easier. Industrial production markedly increased and Roman techniques were now being used in the local manufacture of textiles, glass-ware and pottery. House mosaics and funerary reliefs, portraying merchants at work and the various relaxations of urban life, reflect the everyday activities of the indigenous upper class. Nor did Roman influence stop short at the provincial frontiers. The Romans had long operated a system of buffer zones under which the chieftains of tribes living just over the border were given definite responsibilities, while retaining the semblance of independence. Client states of this type had been entrusted (with or without subsidy) with the outer defence of parts of the Rhine and Danube frontier, or were ruled by a king imposed on them by Rome. These areas also offered a convenient outlet for the Roman economy. The Hermunduri, for example, who were settled in northern Bavaria, carried on a steady trade with the province of Rhaetia. But Roman traders also reached even the most remote tribes, as has been demonstrated by archaeological finds. Table-ware, ornaments, and wine—a highly prized commodity – were all being exported to the Baltic and Scandinavia ; in return the merchants brought back raw materials, furs, amber and slaves, often paying for them in Roman money. In these transactions neither party was the loser.

In another field of Romano-German relations, the enlistment of Germans into the Roman fighting services, the advantage on balance lay with the Romans, although it was not without risk. From the beginning, the magnificent physique and fighting spirit of the Germans had convinced Roman observers that here were born mercenaries (*vivi ad arma nati*).[12] In Italy under the empire fair-haired blue-eyed men were not to be met with every day, which made these exotic features all the more prized. It was probably just such a preference for tall handsome youths that had prompted Augustus to create a German bodyguard for his household. This small corps of guards (*Germani corporis custodes*) had loyally served the emperors on the Palatine for almost a century. Some later emperors also liked to have Germans in their retinue ; Caracalla, for instance, was very proud of his 'lions', the troop of German horsemen clad in national dress and armed with native weapons who accompanied him on his travels. The use of Germans in regular units of the army had more weighty consequences. Germans from the provinces of upper and lower Germany are found serving as auxiliary troops (*auxilia*) and in special regiments (*numeri*) from quite an early date ; after a time, however, they ceased to be used on their home ground and were sent to fight elsewhere. Germans were also admitted to the legions ; from the second century it became customary to fill up detachments by local conscription. As the supply of citizen soldiers from Italy dried up, the opportunities for provincials correspondingly increased. In the second century, however, the Germans in the Roman army were outnumbered by Gauls and in the third century by Pannonians, Illyrians and even Orientals; it was Constantine who made the higher commands accessible to the Germans. Meanwhile Roman policy had found another use for German energies. In the years of the Marcomannic war Marcus Aurelius had started the practice of using tribes settled outside the empire for the defence of the frontiers and in fighting enemy tribes. The purchase of this assistance from the allies was to have dire consequences; but at first the method seemed to justify itself. Recruitment within the empire had been seriously affected by the decline in population and the total withdrawal of the urban citizen class from all forms of military activity; this being so, it was natural to look increasingly to the Germans of the border states, who appeared ideally suited by their armament and tactics to repel German invaders – so much so indeed that in the third century the Roman army itself adopted some of their methods and gear. The Romans took to wearing breeches in the Batavian style, and the short Roman sword was replaced as a cutting weapon by a long blade, the germanic spatha. There was an increase in the number of horsemen and lightly-armed troops. With arms and equipment of this type, running conflicts became more usual than the pitched battles ending in hand-to-hand fighting which had formerly been the rule; the legionary infantry were gradually being demoted from their all-important role. The Roman army was thus being subjected to German influences even before the time of Constantine. Germans were also slowly making their way into civilian life. We often hear of slaves of germanic descent, although Syrians and Phrygians are just as numerous. Here too it was Marcus Aurelius who was responsible for an important innovation, designed to alleviate the shortage of labour in the Danube provinces brought about by wars and epidemics; he set free German war prisoners assigning them to Roman proprietors and leaseholders of imperial domains in these provinces to work their estates. These Germans thus acquired a legal status as peasants on Roman soil which linked them just as much with the institution of the Roman colonate as with that of germanic serfdom; their descendants would inject fresh life into the Roman army.

The major incursions by the great germanic confederations which had formed on the far side of the Rhine and the Danube were thus preceded by a long and various history of contacts between Romans and Germans. The crisis within the empire in the third century undoubtedly led to a reduction of strength on the frontiers, which helped the attackers. But it must also be noticed that the Germans in south-eastern Europe were themselves under pressure from the Sarmatians, a powerful Iranian people who had long been gaining ground between the Caucasus and southern Russia, with such success that isolated groups had already penetrated to the plain between the Danube and the Theiss. This explains why east German attacks on the empire were so often accompanied by demands for land. But as motivating forces the spirit of adventure and thirst for booty animating individual warrior-bands were even more important than the tribal quest for land. There was a widespread notion that the Roman empire possessed an abundance of costly treasures. Roman money had made its way into German hands in some quantity, whether as payment for goods supplied or as the annual subsidy for activities in defence of the frontier. Table-ware and ornaments of every description were heaped on chieftains by way of bribes or rewards. Gold treasures of Roman origin have come to light on German soil along the whole front from the Black Sea to the North Sea. Favoured by the crisis of the empire, bands of Germans now started to seize the riches of the civilized world by force. The Roman frontier provinces were plundered and this was followed by marauding raids deep into the heart of the empire. In 251 the Goths contrived the defeat and death of the emperor Decius in the province of lower Moesia, and shortly afterwards – using ships which they must have obtained from the Greek cities on the Black Sea – executed a series of daring raids against the coasts of Asia Minor and Greece, carrying off plunder and prisoners. On one of their forays the Alamanni reached Milan, while the Franks could sweep through Gaul to arrive at Tarraco. It was only by slow degrees that the emperors succeeded in overcoming the crisis, setting up a new frontier organization which entailed political and military reforms. Taking a realistic view of the situation as a whole, the emperors decided to evacuate the provinces lying beyond the river boundaries. This decision made it possible for the Alamanni to occupy the land round the Neckar and the part of Rhaetia north of the Danube (*c.* 260); shortly afterwards (*c.* 270) the Romans withdrew their garrison and administration from the province of Dacia. Then, in order to give the river frontiers cover against simultaneous pressure on the various sectors, the emperor Gallienus created a cavalry troop which was stationed not in the frontier provinces themselves but in the rear, to be thrown into action where the need was greatest; Gallienus also made far-reaching changes in the high military commands. Under his successors a sustained effort was made, lasting over several decades, to secure the river frontiers by erecting a system of fortifications. Defence posts were also set up along internal roads and towns provided with walls, gateways and turrets. The Porta Nigra at Trier epitomizes the grim grandeur of this late phase in the history of an empire determined to defend itself to the uttermost.

The modern historian is in a position to compare the relationship between the Roman empire and the youthful germanic peoples with the circumstances attending the dissolution of other great civilizations.

When Egypt and China were declining they too enlisted foreign mercenaries and called on neighbouring peoples for military help. In Egypt and China foreigners also rose to high positions and ended by seizing power. These observations appear to yield a universal rule for the sequence of events in dissolving empires. But since the educated classes of the Graeco-Roman world knew all too little of the history of alien peoples, they were unable to draw much profit from these lessons. Even granted that their historical frame of reference was limited, one wonders how closely Romans from the time of the Marcomannic wars (in the reign of Marcus Aurelius) were observing the movements of their German neighbours; whether they were aware of the tribal incursions into the north-eastern parts of their empire as part of a general process and whether they prepared their minds for meeting the onslaught. Tacitus, whose monograph on the Germans was written around the year AD 100, reveals an astonishing knowledge of the germanic world and an early presentiment of its vital energies, perhaps even of its future historic role. But in the century of crisis there was no-one of the stature of Tacitus to appraise and clarify the situation in which the empire found itself. The short lives of the emperors made long-term defence planning increasingly harder. The possibility that a pacific approach might reduce the antagonism between the old world and the new was apparently never canvassed. Official opinion remained true to its conviction that all peoples living outside the empire were to be classed as barbarians, a conviction which made it difficult for the ancient world to take a critical look at itself. The word barbarian was still used, as it had been a thousand years earlier when the Greeks first invented it, to designate all who spoke an outlandish tongue, all foreigners, despite the fact that constant experience had shown them as people possible to talk to, with ways of life worth imitating. The barbarians were still regarded as uncivilized children of nature, wild men; though at the same time, there were many Greeks and Romans who sensed that the pristine spontaneity of these peoples was brimful of promise and noble ideals. The Romans who used *barbari* (as also *gentes*) to cover all tribes innocent of urban institutions and the classical polis, were blind to the possibility that the social virtues of freedom, courage and loyalty were more secure among peoples whose communal life was founded on blood ties and personal allegiance than in the curias and corporations of the Roman empire, which were held together by force. Finally, there was a dangerous self-deception in treating the barbarians generally as robbers and aggressors while constantly calling on their support; so many of these alleged thugs were already serving in the Roman army that in ordinary speech the word *barbari* can on occasion simply mean 'soldiers'. Despite so many generations of actual contact with these foreigners, the illusion that a high degree of human civilization was attainable only within the Roman empire still remained unshattered and the expression barbarian retained its derogatory meaning. Pictorial representation of battles between Roman and non-Roman warriors show the latter as uncouth figures deserving to be beaten and crushed under foot, the primordial stuff of conquest (*materia vincendi*), as can be seen with great effect on the huge Ludovisi battle sarcophagus, which dates from the third century. But if we want to understand the folk migrations and the transformation of culture we shall do better to dispense with the word 'barbarian' altogether, especially in view of its equally depreciative effect in our modern usage, relegating what it describes beyond some moral pale. Where the term is met with in the sources, the rendering chosen must fit the situation in question, so that the expression actually used – foreigners, enemies of the empire, aliens, new peoples – will depend on the context.

From the third century warfare on the Persian and German fronts was continuous, with only short interruptions. The army, on which the security of civilian life throughout the whole empire so manifestly depended, grew steadily in importance and staked out still higher claims. Units in the frontier provinces vied with one another in making emperors, and from the middle of the century civil wars and imperial assassinations were the order of the day. In this confused period parts of the empire were thrown back on their own resources, no longer receiving directives from the centre and economically isolated. The unity of the empire was severely tested by this crisis in the imperial régime. Some modern scholars claim to detect a political trend towards particularism, towards provincial autonomy, and even speak of a separatist movement within the ancient world. They point above all to those regions which were still not fully romanized, to peoples and nations (*gentes* and *nationes*) who had kept their own speech and in times of stress were an easy prey to the temptation of setting local patriotism above loyalty to the empire. It is true that there were many regions where local languages and traditional ways of life had been preserved; we have already noticed the Galatians and Phrygians of Asia Minor, the vitality of Syrian and Aramaic dialects and the role of Coptic in Egypt. Remnants of the Punic and Berber languages had survived in North Africa, in Gaul and in Britain there were areas exclusively inhabited by Celtic-speaking tribes. Some native tongues were actively supported by the Christian mission, which helped to promote Syriac and Coptic as literary languages. Altogether there was a notable divergence among the provincial cultures which grew from the soil of the empire, and this is most clearly illustrated from their artistic output. In figurative art, especially portraiture, the single cosmopolitan style splits up into local forms, so that soon we find a Roman,

Greek and oriental style of portraiture. But whatever importance may attach to these distinctively regional forms of life and art, on the political plane they produced no national uprisings and no separatism. When emperors were being made in the provinces, the initiative lay neither with the tribes nor with the mass of the provincial population; the decisive voice was always that of the Roman frontier armies, stationed on the Rhine, the Danube and the south-east front. Admittedly, these army units already contained a substantial admixture of local elements, but the first concern of the legions and of the emperors they created was always the defence of the frontiers; they had no ambition to detach provinces from the empire.

The strength of the bond of unity, even at a period of supreme crisis, is apparent from the two lordships which came into being on the extremities of the empire in consequence of the Persian wars and the catastrophic defeat of Valerian, one in Gaul and the other on the borders of Syria. In 259 the army on the Rhine acclaimed its own commander, Postumus, as emperor. Although the new ruler drew his support from the population of Gaul, he still saw the defence of the Roman provinces against the Germans as his main task. When attempts at combining his rule in Gaul with allegiance to the central Roman government, which on Valerian's capture had passed to his son Gallienus, proved fruitless, Postumus set up a regional administration with its own senate and annually appointed magistrates; this *Imperium Galliarum*, in which the provinces of Britain and Spain also joined, continued for more than a decade. The emperor Gallienus was quite incapable of subduing this rival imperium; his successor Claudius was fully engaged in countering Gothic attacks on the Danube. The defeat of the Gallic emperor (Postumus' successor Tetricus) was finally accomplished in 273 by Aurelian, whose prodigious energy succeeded in restoring the central power of the empire. Although it existed for so long, the *Imperium Galliarum* was far from being a national Gallic state: the Roman administration continued everywhere in being and the government in Gaul knew no higher aim than to preserve the empire and its culture.

In the south-east, however, there was a more positive attempt at the creation of an independent state. This movement had its origin in Palmyra, the oasis-city in the Syrian desert which was the junction of caravan routes linking the Black Sea and the Mediterranean with Mesopotamia, Arabia, Persia and even India and China. Palmyra was ruled by prosperous merchant families who had succeeded in securing a degree of autonomy for their city within the framework of the Roman empire. We find the Palmyrenes using Greek alongside Aramaic in their inscriptions and adorning tombs of both men and women with portrait reliefs whose stylization and hieratical aspect reveal a distinct oriental influence. For Rome the great attraction of this powerful mercantile city lay in its customs and dues and still more in the military help it could provide for the war against the Persians. As a result of striking successes in defence of the Roman frontiers, a Palmyrene nobleman, Septimius Odaenathus, acquired such prestige that after the capture of Valerian he was able to asume the royal diadem, while still continuing his successful prosecution of the war. The emperor Gallienus found himself obliged to recognize this prince on the periphery of his empire; conferring on him the titles *dux* and *corrector totius orientis*, he entrusted Odaenathus with an exalted military command and the civil government of the eastern part of the empire. In practice Odaenathus became the ruler of all the eastern provinces from Asia Minor to Egypt, but although so powerful, he still maintained the link with Rome. It was not until after his death, when power passed to his widow Zenobia, that the Palmyrene principality became hostile to Rome. This remarkable woman planned to unite in her kingdom the intellectual forces of hellenism and the east; the neo-platonist scholar Longinus was an influential member of her court and she maintained relations with Paul, the disputatious bishop of Antioch. It was she who prompted her son Vaballath, when he started to rule in his own right (271), to assume the name Augustus and have coins struck in his own image. Palmyra had thus become a separate kingdom in hellenistic form. Since the danger of permanent separation from the Imperium Romanum was here much greater than in Gaul, Aurelian made the defeat of the Palmyrene anti-emperor his first charge. After twice attacking, he succeeded in breaking the power of Palmyra, razing the walls of the city and leading Zenobia captive to Rome. The entire East was now restored to Roman rule. The failure of the Palmyrene experiment demonstrates once again that nationalist forces were too feeble and too disparate to withstand the central power. In 274, as the saviour of Roman unity and *restitutor orbis*, Aurelian deservedly celebrated a triumph, with the conquered Zenobia and Tetricus in its train.

Political regionalism had thus shown itself short-lived. But there remains the possibility that the lower strata of the provincial populations were becoming disaffected in their allegiance to the emperor and the empire. Do we find signs of an impending social revolution in this century? The distinguished and erudite Rostovtzeff sought to show that now the urban bourgeoisie, so long the mainstay of ancient culture, had been broken by the policy of the soldier-emperors, the soldiers of the army, in alliance with the peasants, were increasing their power. According to this interpretation, the interests of soldiers and peasants coincided and they therefore pursued a common struggle against the existing ruling class. A critical examination of the evidence makes it clear that although soldiers and peasants did work together here and there, the alliance was transitory and can be accounted for quite naturally by the close connection between army units and the countryside surrounding their encampment. There is no evidence of any united revolutionary action by soldiers and peasants. If this is accepted, we are still left with the question whether there were any peasant revolts as such in this century. Soviet scholars maintain that the hard-pressed peasant class was now in revolt, and that over the generations they so managed to distort the whole social structure that the final upshot was the new system of feudalism. There is plenty of evidence that the rural population was oppressed and had much to suffer from being forced to provide billets and supplies for a violent and unlicensed soldiery. It is also true that there are isolated instances of peasant revolts. In Gaul between the years 283–5 there was a rising of peasants who called themselves Bagaudae, (a Celtic word, apparently the equivalent of 'vagabonds'), organized on military lines with two leaders at the head. This unrest, which had some anarchical features, was soon put down; but we hear of Bagaudae again in the fifth century, this time also active in Spain. Even the first appearance of the movement, towards the end of the third century, must certainly be interpreted as a symptom of serious social and economic disorders; similar conditions provoked the Circumcellionist movement in north Africa during the fourth century, which we shall meet in connection with the separatist church there. But however alarming this Gallic rebellion, the Roman empire of the third century was certainly in no danger from a general revolution embracing dependent peasants, coloni and slaves working on great estates. The institution of the colonate was being introduced on more and more latifundia of the western provinces, where great proprietors had long recognized that tenant-farmers settled on the land offered the best solution to their labour difficulties. But there were still slaves employed on agricultural work, and on the villas of the urban bourgeoisie in the eastern provinces unfree workers remained in the majority. Dependent peasants and slaves were certainly oppressed, but the colonate had not as yet led to the legal attachment of peasants to the soil, and slaves often lived no worse than the poorer elements in the free population; life in the lowest stratum was becoming much the same for all, whether free or unfree. Even so, the imperial government did much to protect the peasantry, whose services in supplying the army and making troops up to strength were quite indispensable. To preserve order in the countryside the emperors and municipalities took energetic measures against the looting which was endemic in times of crisis; military units were sent to flush out brigands and local militias formed to guard settlements and roads. Moreover, there is some evidence that it was still possible for small peasants to attain a modest prosperity and to rise in the social scale by hiring themselves out as labourers. For example there is a third-century funerary inscription in which a reaper from Mactar in Tunisia recites proudly, and in verse, the details of his career. Born poor but free, he had a small plot he could call his own. In his youth his custom was to attend first to his own harvest and then work as labourer on neighbouring estates. Later he left home for Numidia, where he worked for twelve years as reaper; for eleven years he was foreman of a gang and worked so well that eventually he acquired a house and estate; he crowned his achievements by entering the ranks of the decurions and becoming a tax official. This inscription is testimony that wage-earning still offered prospects of advancement.

Our survey of national and social movements prompts the conclusion that the characteristic attitude of the oppressed classes was more passive than revolutionary. The power of the government and the pressure of the ruling classes were strong enough to suppress isolated revolts and to maintain an attitude of subservience. The army provided a means of escape for many who were ambitious enough to want to rise from the depths. Even peasants could make a career in the legions where Illyrians, Germans and Moors found a path to power and office.

Toynbee claims that the alien tribes who attacked the empire from without have their counterpart in an internal proletariat. In making this assertion he is thinking not so much of national and social rebellions but of a considerable class of educated people whose philosophical and moral convictions were alienating them from the empire and its culture: men for whom the state in its majesty and power was no longer the highest good, who were abandoning the classical order of values and turning instead to religious groups whose message was of an otherworldly salvation for mankind. This hypothesis leads us on to the whole question of the intellectual and spiritual revolt against Rome and the emperor, against the empire and classical civilization. The first thing to notice is that the old Roman nobility offered only residual opposition to the soldier-emperors and their policy. Frondist elements in the senate were largely eliminated in the drastic purges conducted by the emperors Commodus, Septimius Severus and their successors. If we turn next to Greek writers, we certainly hear voices raised in criticism both of Rome's despotism and of the greed and coarse pleasures of her citizens. But this lofty dissociation from Roman values could only be effective if the challenge was taken up by other groups with a stronger will to action than was shown by the Greek *literati*. This clearly does not apply to the devotees of the oriental mystery religions, who had no compunction in worshipping the state gods and whose congregations were multiplying in town and country, often under the patronage of the emperor. The Jews on the other hand, whether in Galilee where a sizeable remnant remained or in the communities of the diaspora, had never become inwardly reconciled with Rome. Admittedly they enjoyed privileges accorded them in the early days of the principate; one can say that their religion was tolerated as the traditional faith of a national minority (*religio licita*). But they never forgave the Romans for their destruction of the temple and subsequent establishment of a colony on the soil of Jerusalem, all the more odious because Jews were forbidden entry to their holy places. The expectation that the Messiah would come to destroy Rome was kept constantly alive in new apocalyptical writings, and the Jews were further regaled with stimulating prophecies of the fall of the ruling city couched in Sybilline verses on the Greek model. Even the expounders of Jewish law inveigh against the wickedness and sacrilege of the empire. For a considerable time the Jews continued to be the spokesmen of the traditional oriental hatred for the Romans. There was nothing fortuitous about the reiteration in Jewish writings of the old idea that a king would come from the east to vanquish Rome and make Asia triumph. It was only by degrees that hostility to Christianity impelled some Jews to seek accommodation with the pagans and to join with them in a common front against the rise of the Christian Church.

When we come to investigate the part played by Christians of the third century in the spiritual revolt against Rome we must first recognize that there were Christians and Christians. On the one hand stood the organization which embraced all the congregations and was steadily growing in definition and comprehensiveness, that is to say the Church. On the other were various groups who kept themselves apart and were not infrequently disowned as heretical in tendency. We must consider not only those dogmas and writings calling on Christians to do battle with the idolatrous state, but also the institutions in which the fellowship of Christians had become so consolidated that to the outside world they soon appeared as a state within a state. Here and there we shall have to be content to notice only the most historically significant of these phenomena.

In general, the early Christian view that there was nothing inherently divine in the state was not regarded as inconsistent with respect for authority and its concomitant of civil obedience. But there were always some Christians who rejected the Roman state as a power of evil, a guise in which it already appears in the Book of Revelation: sinful Babylon, the monstrous anti-Christ. Later generations made serious efforts at a rapprochement with the Roman empire, but even so there were occasional outbursts of hatred. The collections of Sybilline oracles which has come down to us from the second and third centuries contains pronouncements of Christian origin which revile Rome, threaten her with the penalties of her wickedness and wallow in anticipatory descriptions of her fall. There were heretical communities for whom all existing states were the work of the devil. Still more significant, at the turn of the second century we find important theologians of the Church, for example Irenaeus of Lyons and Hippolytus of Rome, referring images and allegories from the Book of Daniel to the Roman empire. The iron greaves of the colossus in Nebuchadnezzar's dream (a figure which in a widely accepted exegesis represented the successive empires of history) are equated with the brute power of the Roman empire, while the fourth beast to come up from the sea, he with the iron teeth and nails of brass, is the incarnation of Rome itself – a serious indictment of the empire which still represented itself as pacific and eternal.

At about this time, however, the prevailing view among Christians came to be that the state was a necessary authority for keeping the peace, dispensing justice and raising taxes. But idolatry and emperor worship were of course still held to be sinful, which could not fail to lead to a serious clash with an empire claiming authority from the gods. With the zeal of newcomers, the soldier-emperors set about a massive reinforcement of the bond between the state and the worship of the gods, enjoining strict observance of the traditional ceremonies and demanding a more elaborate emperor worship. This hardening of attitude on the side of the state coincided with the consolidation of the Church. Many Christians must have suffered from clashes with hostile governors even in the time of Septimius Severus, clashes which heightened the sense of identity within congregations, made strong through martyrdom. In the Christian literature of this period we meet a concept of the Church which draws an analogy between Christian and political communities, not forgetting that the community of saints is not of this world. Men speak of the *Politeia Christi*, but emphasize the official status of the congregation directed by the bishop and his clergy and insist that the separation of clergy from laity has a basis in law. This concept of the Church emerges above all from western writings. Here we have the first indication that the theology of western Christendom, as it evolves, will dwell almost as much on shaping the life of the Christian community in a pagan world as on the metaphysical content of Revelation. One can detect this tendency even in Greek spokesmen for western Christianity, such as Irenaeus and Hippolytus, but it is far more marked among the Latin authors whose influence was now becoming great. It was about this time that Latin became the language used for preaching and the liturgy at Rome, while in Africa, where Christians had conducted their services in Latin from the beginning, the Christian apologetic was gaining in dignity, lucidity and strength from the Latinity first of Tertullian and then of Cyprian.

In his combination of sharpness of intellect with passionate feeling Tertullian has no peer. It would certainly be wrong to treat him as fully representative of the Carthaginian Christian community, especially since in later life he was drawn to the extremist Montanist sect and founded his own group. But his *Apology*, addressed to the governors of the Roman provinces, breathes the self-confidence which already inspired Latin Christendom around the year 200. Tertullian is ruthless in his castigation of the worship of the old gods; the persecution of Christians he attacks as unjust and absurd. He points with pride to the Christians in official posts, in the army, even in the senate, and asserts that passive resistance or secession by the now powerful and numerous body of Christians would bring the empire to its ruin. 'We could take up the fight against you without arms and without commotion, merely by passive resistance and secession. With our numbers, the loss of so many citizens in the far corners of the earth would be enough to undermine your empire, our mere defection would hit you hard. Imagine the horror you would feel at finding yourselves thus deserted, in the uncanny stillness and torpor of a dying world. You would look in vain for your subjects – the enemy at your gates would be more multitudinous than the population of your empire!'[13] This was a direct threat which could not pass unnoticed by the Roman magistrates. When he became a Montanist, Tertullian went much further, rejecting military service and all callings which entailed any involvement with idolatry. As against this, the Church now encouraged Christians to enter secular professions and gave its blessing to those who rose in the social scale, though without securing any essential relaxation of the tension between Church and state, between the faith and the official religion. Christian leaders now revived, and tirelessly preached, an idea which had gained currency in earlier times of persecution: the idea that to be a Christian meant to be a soldier (*militia Christi*). As Tertullian constantly hammers home, for the Christian soldier baptism is his military oath, Christ his emperor, the clergy his officers, times of persecution his opportunity for offering battle to the imperial foe. Cyprian, who as bishop of Carthage had to lead his community through some bitter struggles, sees the whole Church as the base camp of Christus Imperator, and has visions of the victors returning triumphant after defeating the enemy, decked with trophies. Origen, too, describes martyrdom as a trial of strength before the eyes of the world, citing the great figures of the Maccabean war as exemplars.

In all this we have anticipated the course of events. It was necessary to show the moral strength of the Christian communities in order to make plain the basic position of the Roman state in its dealings with Christianity. The rulers of the second century, together with the Severan emperors, regarded the new religion as in principle criminal and treated it as such, without launching any systematic persecution. But after the fall of the Severan dynasty (235) the emperor Maximinus issued an imperial decree attacking the leaders of individual communities as the people responsible for the Christian mission. The emperor Decius (249–251) went still further. In times of military extremity the people and the army – and even men of senatorial rank – fearfully acknowledged that all misfortune flowed from the wrath of the gods, for which the Christians were to blame since they refused to offer them fitting worship. In the militaristic fashion of the age, Decius sought to remedy the situation by ordering all inhabitants of the empire to an act of compulsory worship. Urban and rural commissions were set up whose task was to see that sacrifices and libations were duly offered and to issue a certificate (*libellus*) in confirmation. Christians throughout the empire were thus faced with the ultimate decision. Many weakened under this organized demonstration of mass-patriotism, but others heroically endured torture, banishment and death. While the communities were still pondering whether the back-sliders (*lapsi*) could be readmitted, Valerian launched an attack on the clergy, the upper crust of the Christian laity and on Christian worship (257). It is clear that the fiscal interests of the state also came into the picture, but as the Christian leadership remained unshaken these shock tactics proved fruitless. Valerian's son and successor Gallienus stopped the persecution and restored confiscated properties to the communities (260). He seems to have decided on a kind of truce, perhaps in order to allow time for the pagan revival to take effect.

In the ensuing period of tranquillity, which lasted for forty years, the organization of the Church became noticeably firmer. The separate congregations, now attracting more upper-class converts than ever before, were strengthened in composition and their entitlement to possess their own resources was acknowledged. Congregations joined together in a loose provincial organization, which gave recognition to the principle that the bishop of a mother-church had the right to ordain ministers for new foundations. It became customary for the bishops of such provinces to meet regularly in synod and discuss and decide matters of common interest. In the eastern parts of the empire the boundaries of the Church provinces were often made to coincide with the provinces of the empire. Alexandria, Antioch, Carthage and Rome became pre-eminent among episcopal cities. There is evidence of a persistent effort at Rome to assert the primacy of its congregation and bishop. While all this was happening, the mission was achieving successes on a wider front. In Egypt, parts of Asia Minor and in Africa, the rural populations were won over to the faith, which meant a new access of strength to the Christian way of life. In Palestine, Caesarea was a centre of Christian education; in the province of Syria Phoenice, Tyre was a leading Christian city. Evangelism was intensified in the province of Arabia, whilst Antioch in Syria continued to be the base for the propagation of the Christian faith in Mesopotamia and even Persia. Edessa was by now a completely Christian city and from here and from Cappadocian Caesarea the faith made its way into Armenia. Progress in the old province of Asia, in Bithynia, Greece and the whole Balkan area was slower. About a hundred episcopal sees are known to have existed in Italy around the middle of the third century, most of them probably in central and southern Italy. Christianity had reached most of the North African cities and achieved successes on the south-east littoral of Spain. There had been a little penetration of inland Gaul from the Rhône valley; in the valleys of the Moselle and the Rhine the cities of Trier, Cologne, and Xanten are known to have had bishops; and the first evidence of Christian activity is discernible in Britain.

In some regions the evangelization of the countryside gave a new impetus to native languages. In Gaul missionaries preached in Celtic, in parts of North Africa away from the coasts in Punic. The Syriac language made its literary debut with Bardesanes, the Christian gnostic. In Armenia Christianity was now being preached as the national religion in place of the Persian faith; and since Christianity was now the official religion the Church inherited property which had belonged to the temples. Preaching to the people in their own tongue remained a constant feature of the Christian mission, and there can be no doubt that Christianity brought smaller nations to a keener sense of their identity. But it would be wrong to see this as the beginning of a revolt by the small nations against the empire. Hippolytus in his treatise *On the Anti-Christ* and his *Commentary on Daniel* declares that the destruction of the Roman empire will be accomplished through tribes, which he even describes as 'democracies'. But in advancing this view the theologian was influenced by his eschatological assumptions, and his thesis remains an oddity. The Church as a whole saw its historical destiny as bound up with the world-empire. Even Origen, who sets the *politeia* of the Gospel in opposition to the state, maintains in his polemic against Celsus that the universality of Imperium and Church should be understood as a providential disposition, reminding his readers that the gathering of the nations into the empire of the Caesars had prepared the way for the Gospel. In this unitary empire Origen sees no further place for national gods, but looks to the day when the Logos shall unite the multiplicity of peoples into a single Nomos, a form of life everywhere one and the same. This belief points to a future in which the Roman empire, wholly permeated by Christianity, would be essentially transformed.

4. *The ancient world in a state of emergency*

It is astonishing to find the ancient world holding its own for so long against powerful enemies without and persistent opposition from within.

Emperors expended themselves in prodigious endeavours to preserve the unity and substance of the empire. It was Diocletian, with his co-rulers, who first placed all departments of life – political, social, economic and cultural – on a defensive footing: with him, indeed, the state of emergency induced by the empire's struggle for existence became a permanent institution. Diocletian, who became emperor in 284, was a native of the romanized part of Dalmatia; at the time of his accession he already possessed a wealth of experience accumulated in military and governmental posts. As a politician he had an exceptional talent for analyzing existing power relationships and making long-term plans based on his findings. Although the immediate object of his measures might be to remove certain specific abuses, they were so skilfully dovetailed that the result was a fully articulated system of government, both of the periphery and of the centre whose hard core was strong enough to weather many storms. Here our main concern is with the basic principles which guided his planning, since the order established by Diocletian provided the casing in which the process of cultural transformation could continue to work.

Diocletian succeeded in consolidating monarchical power after the long period of confusion. The desperate plight of the empire, perpetually threatened along its far-flung frontiers, was now more than one man could cope with; but prudence and the fear of usurpation restricted the choice of partners to the circle of military commanders. In 285 Diocletian gave his general Maximian, already distinguished by battle-honours, the title of Caesar, naming him as his successor; in the following year, Maximian was raised to the rank of Augustus, that is to say co-ruler. A few years later the number of rulers was increased to four, two senior army officers (Galerius and Constantius) being appointed Caesares, to take their share in the government and add to the number of designated successors. This tetrarchical plan made it possible to divide the huge complex of the Imperium Romanum into four regions while still preserving the authority of Diocletian as senior Augustus: Diocletian ruled the eastern provinces from his seat at Nicomedia, Maximian ruled Italy, Africa and Spain from Milan, Galerius the Danube provinces, from either Sirmium or Thessalonica, and Constantius, based on Trier, ruled Gaul and Britain. There is no need to follow the achievements of this imperial partnership in any detail, nor to trace the vicissitudes of the system after Diocletian's abdication. On the long-term view, what is more important is that the principle of unitary rule was maintained despite the fourfold partnership and that Diocletian's clear formulation of absolutism made it possible to complete the transition from the principate to the dominate. The ancient institutions inherited from the Republic, such as the senate and the annual magistracies, were rendered politically innocuous, and all the officers in the imperial administration placed directly under the sovereign.

In keeping with ancient theocratic tradition, the absolute power of the dominate was held to rest ultimately on the semi-divine nature of the ruler (*dominus*). According to contemporary belief, the emperor was the recipient of divine grace (*charisma*) – indeed the abode of the divine spirit. The divine author of this power, however, was not Sol Invictus, although the cult of the sun-god continued to be observed, as was that of the Persian Mithras, to whom numerous new shrines were dedicated. The gods invoked by Diocletian were the ancient Roman deities Jupiter and Hercules, whose worship had for centuries formed the solid core of army religion. He called himself Jovius, that is to say offspring and protégé of Jupiter; Maximian took the name Herculius, and by thus attaching himself to the lesser of the two gods made plain his own subordination to the supreme ruler; the Caesares were also given a place in the divine family. Gods and emperors were thus part of a single hierarchy, an idea we find expressed in a votive inscription addressed 'to our lords Diocletian and Maximian, the unconquered Augusti, born gods and creators of gods'.[14] The monarchy of the later empire was a theocracy cast in the Roman mould. Further evidence that this was so is to be found in the imperial insignia and court ceremonial, in which hellenistic and Persian influences are now even more noticeable than under the Severan emperors. The ruler of the world has his orb and sceptre, in pictorial representations his head is encircled by the nimbus, in token of the unearthly light streaming from his countenance. The ceremonial garment – though strictly speaking we should call it a liturgical vestment – is of purple silk embroidered with gold and far surpasses all ordinary clothing in splendour and extravagance. The god-like ruler remains in strict seclusion in his palace; a subject summoned to the *Sacrum Palatium* must make his act of adoration, falling to his knees and kissing the hem of the imperial robe. The ruler rarely shows himself openly in the capital; when he does so, his appearance is in the nature of an epiphany, a divine manifestation.

This late Roman monarch, at once emperor by divine grace and god-emperor, possessed unlimited power in the government and administration of the empire. Diocletian used his absolute power to reorganize the central and outlying administrations, casting them in a new and enduring form. The chief governmental departments were concentrated in the imperial residences (of which there were four, one for each tetrarch); the imperial council (*sacrum consistorium*), the chief ministers, the Praetorian prefects at their head, the important jurists and the imperial chancery, which was divided into various sections each with its special function (*scrinia*). The imperial council was purely advisory, the chancery heads were executive officials, law-giving was reserved to the emperor. He might issue *edicta*, which gave orders of a general character, *rescripta*, which were written answers to private petitions or to requests from officials for clarification of the law, *decreta*, which were judgements on disputed cases, or *mandata*, instructions to provincial governors. Whatever form the imperial *constitutiones* might take, they formed the sole source of law. It was for this reason that a start was made on assembling the *constitutiones* of the reigning and previous emperors in book-form; little, however, has survived of the collections made in the Diocletianic period, the Codex Gregorianus and the Codex Hermogenianus.

The decisions emanating from the centre went out to the whole empire, and Diocletian also re-organized the civil government of the provinces and the high commands on the frontiers. His aim was to bring all governors and army commanders under central control; by giving each officer a specific task, he sought to ensure that their activities were both effective and undamaging to the interests of the empire. Here too his arrangements were to have a long life. The provinces were made smaller, so that a tight check could be kept on the administration, and the frontiers provided with maximum security. Even Italy was divided into provinces and so lost the last remnants of its privileged position. Altogether about a hundred provinces were set up, administered by governors (*praesides, correctores, consulares*) drawn largely from the equestrian order. Since the governors were now restricted to purely civil functions, the frontier provinces received in addition a military commander (*dux*); the perpetual threat to the frontiers demanded the appointment of men with specialized qualifications, which made the old practice of combining civil and military power no longer feasible. It was clearly impossible for such a host of governors and commanders to deal directly with the emperor; twelve larger units ('dioceses' or administrations) were therefore created, each embracing several provinces. At the head of every new 'diocese' was a *vicarius*, who as his name suggests represented the Praetorian prefect; the prefect's own office remained attached to the imperial entourage. The *vicarii* were also recruited from the equestrian order, which now gained the upper hand in the imperial administration; the senatorial order lost its political power and was content to become a class of privileged land-owners.

Since the defence of the frontiers continued to be the first charge on the government, the role of senior army officers was all-important. Diocletian not only increased the number of legions but also, more revolutionary still, separated the cavalry from the legionary infantry and organized it in separate regiments; this concentration on cavalry was essential in view of the tactics required for fighting the Germans and

Persians. The experience of having to fight simultaneously on several fronts was responsible for another innovation, the creation of a mobile force composed of mixed units of cavalry and infantry, to back up the armies on the frontier. First introduced by the emperor Gallienus, it was only under Diocletian that these regiments took their final form and were mobilized for instant action at the point of greatest danger. They moved only at the orders of the ruler himself and formed his personal escort, the *comitatus Augustorum;* soon after they came to be known as the *comitatenses*, a name which distinguished them from the frontier regiments who were called *limitanei* or *ripenses*. Altogether the army may now have been some 400,000 strong, a gigantic force which must always have been difficult to recruit and enormously expensive to supply and maintain. In addition there was also continuous expenditure on improving the frontier defences, in particular the cordon of forts on the Rhine and the Danube, the outworks of the *limes* which ran from Tripolitania to Morocco in north Africa and the Syrian defence system, with its roads, watering-places and support positions; the strata Diocletiana, which runs from Damascus to Palmyra and thence to Sura on the Euphrates, perpetuates the name of the military master-builder. Yet all these places, impressive though the list may sound, formed only the basic structure of the enormous fortress which the empire itself now was.

The transformation of the Imperium Romanum into a fortress prepared men for the prospect of a long siege, for the successful handling of affairs in time of emergency. The citizens of such a world had to accept that their first duty was to submit to an all-embracing administrative machine and to foster the needs of the huge army. Here indeed was a situation in which bureaucracy was likely to grow and flourish. It is not surprising to find an Egyptian governor issuing instructions that each imperial estate could have only one steward and not more than three assistants. The methods Diocletian devised for requisitioning supplies for the army and the bureaucracy also helped to feed the swarming proletariat of the capitals. By his great tax reform he laid down the pattern of taxation for centuries to come. The taxes paid in kind, the *annona*, were levied on a standard fiscal unit (the *iugum*) which was worked out from a survey of all the land available; the size of the *iugum* depended on the fertility of the soil and the number of people working it (*capita*). This *iugatio-capitatio* assessment was first applied in 296, when the valuation on which the tax was to be paid (*indictio*) was fixed for five years. But from 312 it became customary for fifteen years to elapse between valuations. Records of later date show that a vineyard *iugum* was equivalent to five acres, while an arable *iugum* might range between twenty and sixty acres, depending on the quality of the soil. Since agriculture remained the most important means of livelihood within the Roman empire, it is easy to see why the fifteen-year indiction cycle came to be adopted as a chronological measure. Trade and industry were of course also subject to taxation, and the sales-tax and customs dues continued to be levied as before. In addition to the various payments in cash and kind already mentioned, there was also a self-contained system of municipal taxes and compulsory works (*munera*), which remained the responsibility of the civic governments. Yet despite these arrangements, the distended bulk of the civil and military apparatus was still too vast for government revenues to support. Lactantius, a contemporary observer who as a Christian was not well disposed towards Diocletian, is severely critical of the tetrarchy;[15] 'There were more people in receipt of payment than there were taxpayers. The energies of the coloni were consumed in meeting monstrous tax-demands, with the result that fields were deserted and good farming land allowed to run wild.' Admittedly, in a pamphlet this is a rhetorical overstatement, but we also have authentic testimony of actual government practice, in the order of an Egyptian governor (297) which sets out the new tax system and threatens with death tax-collectors who fail to fulfil the new norms. The governor is clearly justified in asserting that the new arrangement promises a more reasonable and equitable method of taxation : it was indeed reasonable to use the quality of the soil as the basis of assessment, equitable to set Italian citizens on the same footing as other members of the empire. Even so, the policy still seems short-sighted in that it exploits the economy in the interests of the state whilst ignoring the need to stimulate production and, above all, to improve agricultural techniques. Moreover, the imperial government was all too ready to allow proprietors of the great latifundia to withdraw from the fiscal orbit of the civic authorities, allowing them to collect the *annona* from their own tenants – and at the same time increase their hold over them. The initial trend of fiscal policy had been towards equality, but in practice it worked in favour of the ruling class and to the impoverishment of the mass of the urban and rural population.

This fatal tendency can be observed in other economic policies pursued by Diocletian and the majority of his successors. Earlier emperors had often failed to take advantage of the coinage as a means of influencing trade and prices. It was Aurelian who finally took steps to stabilize the gold currency and who tried at least to prohibit the minting of coins for private interests by forming mint-workers into corporations. Soon after 298, when important military successes on all fronts had brought the government a substantial stock of gold and silver, Diocletian decided on a monetary reform. In order to give the full-standard coins he intended to issue a unified value all over the empire, he put an end to separate provincial issues. He produced a gold coin (*aureus*) and a silver coin (*argenteus*), equivalent in value to one-sixtieth and one-ninety-sixth of a pound in gold. Very little of this precious metal currency, which had a very high value, found its way into the hands of the poorer people. A series of copper coins was issued for everyday use, the chief unit being the *follis;* and these small coins were given half the value they had under the Aurelian system. The new coins aroused general mistrust among the mass of the people, with the consequence of a heavy run on goods and a rise in prices even steeper than was usual. An Egyptian papyrus again gives us a glimpse of how men reacted to the situation in practice. Writing privately to a friend who is doing business on his behalf, a public official asks that all his money shall be laid out on goods, regardless of the price.

To combat this inflation, Diocletian resolved on a bold move never before attempted. In 301 he issued an edict for the whole empire which fixed maximum prices for food, raw materials, textiles, transport, wages and salaries (*Edictum de maximis pretiis rerum venalium*). The edict can be reconstructed from inscribed fragments found in the Greek part of the empire and from another fragment which has recently come to light in Italy, at Sulmona in the Abruzzi, which may have come originally from Ostia or Puteoli. The lengthy preamble has also survived, in which the government declares its firm resolve to take decisive action against the dealers and speculators held to be wholly responsible for the general misery. As the fathers of the human race, the emperors feel called on to act for the common good:[16] 'Who is so dumb-witted or so devoid of human feeling that he cannot have known or noticed that all saleable objects offered for sale or traded in towns have increased so much in price that unbridled greed is no longer restrained even by a superfluity in the market or a good harvest? The men who are behind this business are constantly on the alert, scanning the stars, the wind and the weather, vexed beyond endurance when the fortunate earth is moistened by rain from heaven as earnest of future fruitfulness, since they only pity themselves when favourable weather promises a rich harvest. These men, who have nothing better to do than carve up the benefits sent by the gods for their own advantage, damming up the open-handed favour of heaven and in bad years trading in seed-corn and cornering the market, these men, who are themselves swimming in a wealth which would satisfy a whole people, who think only of their gain and their per cent: subjects! – it is to forbid these men the practice of their greed that we are called by our care for humanity.' Later in this high-sounding preamble the soldiers are particularly affected by these abuses, whether in camp or on the march. Since the miscreants must be put in fear of their lives, infringement of the law – whether by exceeding the maximum price or withholding goods – is made punishable by death. The long tariff which follows names maximum prices for about a thousand articles. The enumeration of prices and wages gives us some idea of wage and salary scales and their relation to purchasing power. For example, unskilled workers, day-labourers and herdsmen earn only half as much as bakers and carpenters; teachers in elementary schools, however large their classes, get no more than bakers, but teachers of higher grades have several times as much. A carpenter has to work at least two days to earn the price of a pair of shoes, and eleven days for a ready-made woollen garment. As others have rightly said, this tariff would have provided even the less well-off classes with a tolerable standard of living. It only remains to add that it was never implemented. Even an edict on maximum prices could not arrest the depreciation of money in circulation; the flight from money to goods continued and prices rose still higher.

When we come to evaluate this experiment, unique in the annals of the Roman empire, we cannot fail to be struck by its one-sidedness. An attempt was being made to regulate prices in the interests of the state, without providing for control of the production and consumption of goods. The prospects for a directed economic policy were inevitably dim if attention was to be concentrated on a single phase in the extended nexus of production and consumption. The violence of the edict's attack on the dealers almost leaves one with the impression that the attention of the populace is being diverted from omissions and failings on the part of government agencies. Since the state was the proprietor of much of the most essential land and had a huge labour force at its disposal, one can think of other ways by which prices and wages might have been brought into alignment. But instead of first putting its own domestic economy in order on rational lines, the government proceeded to set up yet another expensive bureaucratic machine, to operate alongside the already extravagant court and the huge army of soldiers and officials whose demands on the public purse were bottomless. The failure of the whole undertaking bore heavily on the poorer sections of the community and intensified social differences among the population. The army and the bureaucracy had their livelihood guaranteed through the tax system of the *annona*, the proprietors of latifundia found loopholes through which to escape the net of state socialism. Even now the governing classes were scarcely aware of how far their system of a state directed economy had removed them from the idea of freely acting citizens which was an integral part of the classical political tradition. Their single aim was to keep the inhabitants of the empire – the whole human race, as the edict puts it – alive, whatever the cost to freedom.

The enormous power concentrated in the absolute monarchy brought even the intellectual and spiritual life of the ancient world within its sphere of influence. Although bred to a life of military command, Diocletian and his co-rulers gradually came to recognize the all-embracing nature of their office, setting defence of the religion and traditions of the empire alongside concern for its material security. The growing success of their defence measures and the pile of wealth accumulating at the expense of their subjects stimulated the autocrats to employ the powerful resources of the state in a monumental display of their theocracy. Architecture and sculpture were the obvious media for bringing the divinity of the emperors and the virtues of their rule to the notice of present and future generations. During the critical decades in the middle of the century Roman art had suffered a setback; but under the stimulus of an absolutist government, which at the turn of the third century made itself felt in every department of Roman life, creative energies were again released, to find expression in some unique achievements. In fact Roman architecture now reached its zenith. Taking over where the great builders of the Severan age left off, this generation of Roman architects achieved full mastery over the technical and constructional problems presented by their art, and by their barrel- and cross-vaulting lifted to impressive heights the great halls the emperors commissioned them to build. Absolutism had stimulated Roman public architecture to its final flowering.

In keeping with their basic plan, the rulers had removed their residences to points nearer the threatened frontiers, which meant that Rome was no longer the main show-place for buildings embodying imperial majesty. The city, now enclosed by Aurelian's great circular fortification, still remained the seat of the Senate. When their meeting place in the Curia was burned down, Diocletian provided them with a new one as a matter of course, a dignified building near the old forum. He also erected new *thermae* to serve the population at large. This extensive structure stood in the north-eastern sector of the city and formed the exact counterpart of the baths of Caracalla in the south; in both, all the various rooms and halls were housed within one great edifice. Finally, Rome was still the abode of the highest deities of the Roman state and in 303, the year marked by festivities in honour of the twentieth anniversary of the Augusti (*Vicennalia*) and the tenth of the Caesares (*Decennalia*), a splendid monument was erected in honour of the tetrarchs on the sacred ground of the old forum. But the city on the Tiber was to receive no new imperial palace. The rulers preferred to commission buildings in the places where they spent much of their time, to provide quarters for their central administration and households and to assert through their design the self-confidence of the new régime. Since archaeological investigation has so far failed to give us any picture of the Augustan palaces at Nicomedia and Milan, the ruins of Trier and Salonica, capitals of the two

Caesares become all the more eloquent. Trier, the seat of Constantius, had also been occupied by the Gallic *imperator* Postumus; from the evidence it seems almost certain that a unified complex of imperial buildings was created at this period in the north-eastern part of the city; the residence stood on the site of the existing cathedral with the basilica as formal audience hall close by, together with the *thermae*, a building of high artistic merit. The Porta Nigra, which formed a citadel on its own built into the city walls, probably also dates from this period. At Salonica, recent excavations have enabled us to reconstruct the ground plan of Galerius' palace: a residence, Galerius' triumphal arch supported by four massive pillars, giving access to the Hippodrome, and the street which was lined with colonnaded halls, leading up to the central building, the mausoleum of Galerius and his family.

The unflagging energy of this official architecture strikes the modern observer most forcibly when he contemplates the palace Diocletian erected for himself at Split on the Dalmatian coast, not far from his native city of Salonae. The entire structure took the form of a rectangular fortress with guard-turrets and a gate-way in the middle of each wall. The enclosure was quartered, to produce four blocks of buildings which included a temple raised on a podium, probably dedicated to Jupiter, and facing it the domed hall representing the mausoleum, the emperor's burial place. On the south side an arched passage 157 metres long gave access to the sea. Entrance to the imperial apartments lay through a peristyle on the main axis of the complex; this entrance hall had the appearance of a sanctuary, and under its gabled portico the emperor appeared to receive the homage of his subjects. Since Jovius was equal to the gods, his dwelling ranked as a temple. Diocletian planned this palace as a residence for his declining years. It seems likely that Maximian made similar provision. A very large villa has recently come to light in Sicily, at Piazza Armerina north of Gela, which has all the appearance of an imperial construction belonging to this period. This is a loose-knit system of splendid buildings scattered over the landscape, at its centre a large peristyle round a garden, to which the living quarters and official apartments were attached; there are also traces of *thermae*, a gymnasium and a concert hall. In many rooms the pavement is inlaid with magnificent mosaics in the best Roman tradition; the chief motifs are taken from hunting and sport, but myths concerning the gods also figure and the emphasis on the deeds of Hercules seems to point to Maximianus Herculius.

The purpose of this official architecture was to assert that wherever the emperor appeared a god made his epiphany. The theocracy was also made visible in sculpture, in particular historical reliefs and imperial portraits. While the period between the end of the reign of Septimius

Severus and the accession of Diocletian apparently inspired no monumental reliefs, under the battle-fame and creative drive of the Jovii and Herculii the art of triumphal sculpture woke once again to life. Two massive pillars survive from Galerius' triumphal arch at Salonica, decorated on all sides with reliefs of the Persian wars. The representation of the emperor echoes a style which has already appeared on the triumphal arch of Septimius Severus at Rome. The ruler stares out at us full face from the throng of surrounding profile figures shown in motion, so that the artist confronts us, as it were, with the supreme source of all authority. This method of portraying the emperor in relation to a great theme lends an almost iconic quality to the official monument. The same trend also accounts for a style of imperial portraiture which gradually established itself. It is true that during the third century a variety of traditions contributed to the formation of the imperial image: Roman verism, which aimed at an exact likeness, long survived side by side with Hellenic classicism. Provincial artists and traditions still flourished, especially when it came to producing the imperial images constantly in demand for cities and camps and wherever the ruler was worshipped as present god (*deus praesens*). But in the light of catastrophe, the creative philosophers and artists of this century were led to look for permanence behind fleeting appearances, for the idea behind the corporeal form. The sculptured portrayals of late Roman emperors thus tend to devalue bodily appearance. An early example is the head of the emperor Gallienus in the Kassel Museum: here the artist shows us a face in which he sees an image of the new spirituality. Ultimately the whole figure may point to what stands behind appearances and come to serve a symbolic purpose. In the porphyry groups of the tetrarchs which stand on a corner of St Mark's cathedral at Venice there is no attempt at individualizing the heads or varying the movement of the bodies; the rulers are shown embracing, a gesture which proclaims their concord. The monument is an assertion of the abstract idea of the new empire.

In architecture and sculpture the stylistic forms of the period thus express the idea of theocracy. Diocletian was also determined to make the theocracy serve as the basis for reviving the ancient faith and customs of the fathers. He himself made dedications to both Roman and Oriental deities, favouring Mithras in the latter category: he honoured Jupiter, Hercules, Mars and Victoria on his coinage, and before making important decisions consulted the oracles, in particular that of Apollo at Didyme, of ancient fame. Diocletian was thoroughly imbued with the old Roman belief that the good fortune of the state rested on pious conduct. His stern edict against consanguineous marriages issued in 295 contains a warning that the blessing of the gods can only be obtained if all citizens lead lives that are pious, god-fearing, chaste and peaceful;

and two years later, in his edict against the Manichaeans, we find him condemning upstart sects which set themselves up in opposition to the old religions. The great monument erected in the heart of Rome in honour of the Vicennalia was decorated with reliefs showing the offering of sacrifices and vows, an expression of this newly-awakened faith. One cannot fail to recognize that the religious revival had some effect on public life; inscriptions from all over the empire testify to renewed observance of the cults. Official orations – many of which have survived – delivered on ceremonial occasions in the presence of the emperors naturally reflect the political religion practised by the tetrarchs. One orator sums it up when he says 'Best of emperors, you have earned your good fortune by your piety'.[17] For educated men it was important that neoplatonism had now entered on a phase which made it possible to defend belief in the gods and participation in the popular and official cults. Several of Plotinus' successors identified the gods and daemons as intermediaries between the supreme deity and the material world and countenanced their worship in the traditional forms. In the end Greek philosophy had failed to prevail over polytheism; nor had it succeeded in making the official cults any more spiritual. Philosophers and statesmen were now united in the view that true piety consisted in the traditional worship of the gods.

There was but one group which held aloof from this ingathering of religions: the community of Christians. The truce concluded by Gallienus was still in operation. During this untroubled period the Christian mission had met with continued success: in the eastern parts of the empire Christianity had reached out even into the countryside, new converts had been made in the army and among professional men in the towns. But while the state still held back, pagan philosophers were now launching new attacks on this religion which agreed no better with prevailing philosophies than with the observance of ancestral customs. Porphyry, whose work in fifteen books entitled *Against the Christians* was composed soon after 268, wrote from a sound knowledge of the Bible; his fierce polemic is directed not only against the gospels and the apostles but also against Christian doctrines and morals in general. He takes up again the political argument advanced by Celsus, describes the Christians as traitors to their country's laws and regards the whole civil order as in jeopardy from this 'barbarian outrage'. A few decades later, when there was again conflict between the state and Christianity, new polemics appear in which Christians are called on to return to the religion of the emperors. In the years when Diocletian's restoration was in progress, the antagonism between the state and Christianity had a strong political flavour. The Christian apologist who alleged that educated pagans recognized the hollowness of the old religion but kept to the faith, since without its façade they would have found themselves stripped of everything, may well have been right.

What is certain is that the political self-assurance of Christians had been substantially reinforced. The long truce gave their communities confidence to match themselves with the still hostile state, in the conviction that they were the new race, the race of a coming world order. Arnobius, an African teacher of rhetoric, wrote his treatise *Adversus Nationes* c. 300 in the heat of his recent conversion. Once again, we find the old charges against the Christians repudiated and the usual objections to paganism advanced. These arguments are combined with a vehement protest against religious compulsion as being contrary to the will of God, and a general disparagement of the Roman state which suppresses the freedom of its peoples. Arnobius lays great stress on the factors in the contemporary situation which speak in favour of the Christians. It is a fact, he says, that the Christian faith has spread throughout the world; it is a matter of observation that love of Christ has completely transformed the lives of peoples; it is known that highly-gifted orators, grammarians, rhetoricians, legal scholars, doctors and philosophers have been converted to the new faith; and finally there is the proof which speaks for itself, namely that Christians can endure torture, indeed that threats and prohibitions only serve to strengthen their resistance. 'Do you really believe that this happens blindly and by chance, do you believe that such courage comes from only casual influences? Is not this conduct more likely to be God-given and holy? Without God, could such conversions of the soul occur (*tantas animorum fieri conversiones*) that when believers are confronted with the torture hooks and countless other torments they accept the truth revealed once and for all as though they were possessed of a sure delight and the love of all virtues, preferring the friendship of Christ to everything of the world?'[18] This style of reasoning may seem to strike a popular note, but there was no lack during these years of serious argument addressed to cultivated pagans. Lactantius, a pupil of Arnobius, was summoned to teach rhetoric at Diocletian's capital city of Nicomedia and there wrote his *Divinae Institutiones*, a defence of the Christian religion. Adopting the language and style of Cicero, Lactantius proved to an elevated class of readers that academic learning and Christian belief were compatible. He presents Christian monotheism as something essentially new and revolutionary in the intellectual life of the age, invoking human reason against the authority of antique paganism and seeking to discredit official religious coercion by reference to the inward uncertainty he detects among the pagans. Inspired by his eschatological belief that after the time of tribulations God will establish his holy city in the midst of the world, Lactantius enlists himself, as it were, in the militia of Christ, acknowledging the duty binding on all Christians to guard the faith with dogged endurance.

By the time Lactantius' book appeared the great persecution was already under way. The two powers which had for so long stood opposed now entered the decisive struggle : on one side the state, in the full vigour of absolute monarchy, seeking its ultimate justification, valid for all its subjects, in renewed faith in the gods, and on the other the Christian Church, waiting in expectation of the kingdom of God, its organization strengthened, its spirit steeled in many battles. There is no doubt that Diocletian, the originator of theocratic rule, was himself the author of the persecution. He had bided his time throughout the long years of his preoccupation with the defence of the empire and with administrative and economic planning, making no move even when Christians gained positions at his court in Nicomedia. But now the moment had come for drastic measures against 'customs of such barbarous monstrosity and sects composed of criminals', as he puts it in his edicts against consanguineous marriages and the Manichees. This was the hour to mobilize the forces of the state against the Christians, as against these others. In his later work *De mortibus persecutorum*, Lactantius blames the persecution on Galerius, whom he describes as an uncouth pagan from the wilderness beyond the Danube. It is certainly true that Galerius, who drew his support from Illyrian legions as yet little affected by the Christian religion, showed great energy in persecuting Christians. But the general onslaught is all of a piece with Diocletian's theocracy, which rested on the deification of the emperor and aimed at uniformity among his subjects in the service of gods and emperors. It certainly appeared so to those Christians of the day in whose chronology the accession of Diocletian marks the beginning of a new era, the age of the martyrs.

Battle was joined on an issue which brought the two enemies into direct confrontation, that is service in the army. When Christians in one or two places refused military service, Diocletian issued an order that all soldiers who abstained from offering sacrifices were to be expelled from the ranks. A few years later this purge was followed by a systematic persecution. The first edict, issued on the feast of the Terminalia, 23 February 303, decreed that Christian churches were to be destroyed, their sacred books surrendered and burned and assemblies for worship prohibited. More clearly than ever before, the target now aimed at was the Christian God himself, and the war a true theomachy, as the ancients understood it. Yet still no blood had been shed. Now, however, the Christians were accused of having provoked a rebellion in the eastern frontier provinces, with the result that two more edicts followed, which ordered that the clergy were to be arrested and made to sacrifice, any refusal being punishable by torture and death. Since these edicts hit at the leading members of Christian society, the Church was now clearly being attacked as a state within a state. A final edict issued early in 304 ordered a general sacrifice and so brought the horrors of persecution home to the entire Christian population. It was now clear that by a logical application of its own religious principles the state intended the total extermination of Christianity. However, from the way the edicts were enforced it seems that the rulers were not acting wholly in concert: the situation in the east was very different from that of the west, especially the north-west, where the Christian mission had only just started to make headway, setting up a few small communities who presented no substantial danger to the state. The persecuting zeal of the rulers was also unequal; Constantius, who inclined towards monotheism, contented himself with ordering the demolition of churches and refrained from attacking men. When Diocletian abdicated in 305 and a second tetrarchy was formed, Galerius, who had already shown himself a strenuous persecutor, became Augustus of the eastern part of the empire, appointing a convinced pagan, Maximinus Daia, as his co-ruler and Caesar. In the eastern part of the empire therefore persecution continued for several more years. But in the west Maxentius and Constantine (the sons of Maximian and Constantius), who had been passed over when the second tetrarchy was formed, showed such wide toleration that in Gaul and Britain, and even in Italy, Africa and Spain, martyrdoms were only sporadic. This made the plight of Christians in many of the eastern provinces all the more terrible. There is plentiful and reliable testimony to the elaborate tortures and humiliations inflicted on the accused and the slow and painful execution of the condemned. The number of martyrs was by no means small and must be held to include the host of confessors who were condemned to suffer in the mines, having been deprived 'through sheer human kindness' of only one eye or the use of only one foot. The practice of such chicanery in the name of obligatory sacrifice struck even pagans as low-down and disgusting, and the day at last dawned when those responsible became sated with the blood they had spilled. In some cities of the east the Christians were so numerous that a complete extermination of the sect was impossible. But the most important feature of the persecution was that it made public for the first time how far and how deeply the Christian faith had penetrated among the rural populations of Egypt and Asia Minor.

It was Galerius, custodian of Diocletian's standards, who found himself obliged to abandon the struggle. At Serdica in April 311, when he was already gravely ill, he issued an edict in the name of all the rulers which gave the empire toleration as the fruit of the long and bloody battle. Lactantius has preserved the text of this edict in the following form.

In the various edicts we constantly issue for the well-being and advantage of the state we have declared that it is our will to order all affairs in accordance with the ancient laws and political tradition of the Romans, and hence to see to it that the Christians, who have deserted the religion of their forefathers, are brought to a better frame of mind. For some reason these Christians were seized by such wilfulness and folly that they no longer kept the customs of the ancients, which perhaps even their own ancestors once observed but following their own judgement made their own laws, each as he pleased, and abode by them, gathering together here and there sundry groups of followers. When therefore we issued an edict that they should return to the old ways, many were brought to trial and many even expropriated. But since most of them have become even more resolute in their intention, and we have had to realize that they were neither offering service and respect to the gods nor worshipping the god of the Christians, in consideration of our benign clemency and constant habit of granting pardon to all men, we have become convinced that in this case too our grace must freely flow : therefore they shall again be Christians and rebuild the houses in which they meet, always on condition that they in no way act against the public order. In a later decree we shall instruct the judges how they shall proceed. Out of respect for this our gracious act, the Christians shall pray to their god for our well-being, for that of the state and for their own, so that the state may remain unharmed in every way and they themselves live carefree in their houses.[19]

This surprisingly outspoken constitution starts by recalling the serious reasons underlying the persecution, and then goes on to admit that this intervention by the state has been a failure, producing the dire result of making it impossible for Christians to worship any god at all. Since this state of affairs is inadmissible, the Christian religion is to be tolerated, on condition that the Christians do not offend against public order; they are even enjoined to pray for the emperor and the state. The God of the Christians is thus recognized as a divine power – an admission carrying great weight from emperors who had just been persecuting this very same God. It is not too much to say that with the recognition of the Christian God and toleration of the Christian religion, an essential element in Diocletian's restoration was sacrificed. No chronicler relates how the Senior Augustus, in his Dalmation retreat, reacted to the news of this capitulation. If we cast our glance back over the past two centuries, the event acquires an even great historical significance. In contravention of all previously accepted rules, the Christian religion has now become a *religio licita*, the Christian liturgy one form of ritual among many. In future, the question of what religion the state would recognize as its basis was bound to arise, since at this period a polity without religious foundation was inconceivable, and a plurality of conflicting cults would be no support for a viable state religion. The problem of the relationship of the Christian church to the state thus posed itself in a new and still more pressing form.

CHAPTER 2

THE MONARCHY, THE CHRISTIAN CHURCH AND RULING SOCIETY IN THE FOURTH CENTURY

1. *The new age of Constantine*

Today the age of Constantine is linked in people's minds with the epoch-making action of the emperor in granting to the Church, after its period of persecution, not merely recognition but also partnership with the state, so that it was placed in a position of wealth and power. It is pointed out that two dangerous courses were now open to the Church: it might entertain political ambitions and seek to subdue states, emperors and princes – a line of ecclesiastical policy followed in western Europe during the Middle Ages; or it might submit to the orders of the ruler and become an instrument of state – the risk run by the Byzantine church. Some of those who take this long-distance view are impatient of the role still played by state-churches in many countries, wishing to see the last of the new era ushered in by Constantine; the Church, it is said, should shed all political power and concentrate on the salvation of men's souls, if need be at the price of returning to the catacombs. Leaving the problems of the contemporary world to one side, if we concentrate on the fate of antiquity it is obvious that Constantine was indeed responsible for historic decisions which deeply influenced the later course of ancient civilization. In his long reign he destroyed the tetrarchy and its pagan theology but at the same time, by refashioning the system of absolute government, did even more than his predecessors to stabilize the framework of the Roman empire. Leading state and Church in double harness, he was the first emperor to take a lead in church affairs and the first to entrust the Church with public responsibilities. There can be no doubt that this was a momentous revolution, and to demonstrate that this was so we shall have to concentrate on the emperor's actions, on the factual record of his reign. Only passing allusion can be made to the much-debated subject of his character, which turns on the question whether his policy towards the Church was determined solely by his thirst for power and by reasons of state or in part also by sincere devotion to the new faith. The various authorities give very different accounts of the matter. While pagan chroniclers leave a great deal to conjecture, Christians interpret the emperor's actions wholly in their favour. Lactantius, in his *De mortibus persecutorum* which covers events down to the year in which it appeared (about 318), waxes quite fanatical in his efforts to prove that all persecutors came to a horrible end, contrasting their fate with the blessings bestowed on Constantine and Licinius, guardians of the faith. Eusebius, bishop of Caesarea in Palestine and from 325 a personal friend of Constantine, in his *Ecclesiastical History* and still more in his *Life of Constantine*, sets out to portray the emperor as the man of Providence who through his deeds enabled the divine Logos to penetrate the world. Fortunately many of Constantine's own letters, edicts and laws have survived, together with inscriptions, coins, buildings and portraits, and it is these self-revelations which must form the basis of our historical interpretation of his epoch.

This much is clear: Constantine, son of Constantius and Helena, deviated from the path marked out by the tetrarchy and from its religious basis right from the start. When Diocletian re-formed the tetrarchy in 305 Constantine and Maxentius (the son of Maximian) were passed over: in the following year both were acclaimed Caesars by their own armies, amongst whom dynastic sentiment was still strong. Constantine and Maxentius now stood in opposition to the legitimate rulers Galerius, Maximinus Daia, Severus and Licinius. This cleavage shows itself in their religious policies. While the rulers of the east kept up an almost uninterrupted persecution of the Christians, Maxentius, the effective ruler of Italy and Africa, was conciliatory, while remaining staunch in his personal allegiance to the old gods. As ruler of Gaul and Britain, Constantine continued the tolerating policy of his father; father and son were apparently alike in dissociating themselves from popular polytheism. Portrait coins issued in 310 show that Constantine had accepted the sun-god as his personal protector. In the same year a panegyrist declares that Constantine is Caesar by right of birth, and through the grace of the sun-god may expect to receive a universal empire. The assertion that Constantine was called to a single rule by the highest god is clear indication that he was setting himself up against the tetrarchical system and its representatives in the east – the language of the coins and the panegyric must have been inspired by Constantine himself. But however bold the hopes he entertained for the future, Constantine was skilful enough to concentrate his immediate efforts towards an objective which the death of Galerius appeared to bring within his reach: the overthrow of Maxentius, which would give him control of the central regions of the empire. In the eyes of the rulers of the east Maxentius had always been and continued to be a usurper; in Italy and Rome his oppressive political measures had lost him support among the population. In 312 therefore

Constantine embarked on a war which he claimed as a war of liberation, to free the people from the yoke of tyranny. A conquering progress over the Alps and the Appennines was crowned on 28 October by the victory at the Milvian Bridge, a league north of Rome, which cost Maxentius both his rule and his life. After a triumphal entry into Rome Constantine was recognized by the senate as Augustus of the first rank.

In Christian tradition the battle at the Milvian Bridge is linked with Constantine's personal decision to turn to the God of the Christians. When all the evidence is weighed it becomes quite clear that from this time onward Constantine recognized in the God of the Christians a giver of victory; and whether or not one describes this recognition as conversion, it certainly prompted Constantine to some far-reaching conclusions. Lactantius relates that in the night before the decisive battle Constantine was advised in a dream to mark the shields of his soldiers with the heavenly sign of God, and that he carried out his instructions by ordering a sign of Christ to be placed on the shields; from Lactantius' description the sign appears to have been the monogrammatic cross ⳨. On the other hand, Eusebius in his *Ecclesiastical History* says merely that Constantine invoked Christ as his ally in the war. In his life of the emperor, however, Eusebius mentions that Constantine experienced a vision at the outset of the campaign in which he saw a cross of light standing over the sun, accompanied by the words 'In this sign conquer'; this manifestation was followed by a nocturnal vision in which Constantine was guided to use the sign to protect himself against the enemy, whereupon he had a standard prepared bearing a sign in which the letters X and P crossed to produce the contracted name of Christ, the Chi-Rho monogram ☧. However much these accounts differ in detail, they show remarkable agreement in insisting that the sign Constantine actually used was not the plain cross of his vision but a cross which he transformed into a monogram identifying Christ as the victory-giving God. In the manifestos he issued in the years which followed, Constantine repeatedly pays tribute to this God who in times of persecution endowed his worshippers with the strength to endure martyrdom and to overcome. It is plain that Constantine was assisted to his appreciation of the Christian religion by his need for a divine ally in combat. If this God was really capable of such victories, then – in keeping with the traditional Roman view – it should also be possible to win his support through the appropriate ritual acts, for example invoking the power of his name. It was also imperative to see that this protective deity continued to bestow his favours on the state. An experience of this kind, and the gloss Constantine put upon it, was certainly no conversion in the New Testament sense; it more closely resembles the assimilation of a new god after the old Roman fashion.

It is essential to bear in mind that Constantine did not suppress all other deities after the victory at the Milvian Bridge. He was even careful to see that the God of the Christians was not mentioned by name in the few official documents referring to the victory. A panegyric of 313 mentions that Constantine received a special revelation from on high, but goes into no details. The old gods long retained their place on the coinage, whereas Christian symbols were only gradually adopted, and it was some years before their meaning became standardized. In 315 the Roman senate dedicated the triumphal arch erected at the Flavian amphitheatre in honour of Constantine's victory. A frieze running right round it chronicles in traditional style the whole course of the war, from the time the emperor moved camp to the concluding acts of state, taking in the conquest of Verona, the battle at the bridge and entry into Rome. In the portions where the emperor is shown addressing the people and distributing his gratuity, he stares out at the beholder from the centre of the picture, present in all his majesty – the same hieratical stance we have observed in historical reliefs of the preceding period. But there is no reference to the new tutelary deity; here the victory-giving figure is the sun-god. It must be remembered that the arch expressed the views of the Roman senate, which was still wholly loyal to paganism. The inscription merely makes a cryptic reference to the victory obtained 'through divine inspiration' (*instinctu divinitatis*).

But we have other witnesses to the piety of the new ruler of Rome and from these we learn that Constantine gave public expression to his gratitude to his divine patron. The magnificent silver medallion, whose obverse and reverse depicts the conquest and liberation of the city, was probably struck at the mint of Ticinum (near Milan) as early as 313; and on the obverse the monogram appears, on the crested plume of Constantine's helmet. In a prestige issue of this type, the incorporation of the Christ-monogram into the portrait of the emperor could only have been done on the highest authority. Perhaps the most conclusive manifestation of Constantine's acceptance of the new faith was the transformation of the most majestic of all Roman buildings, which was carried out between 313 and 315. The enormous three-aisled basilica erected by Maxentius on the eastern edge of the Forum Romanum was now dedicated by the senate to Constantine, his conqueror. The apse of the basilica, where the judges should have held court, was filled with a statue of the world-ruler, seven times life-size. The colossal head now stands in the court of the Conservatori Palace at Rome: a truly imperial portrait in which the features of the individual are almost wholly obliterated beneath the dignity of the supreme world-ruler, in the words of a court poet *sanctus Caesar, omnipotens Augustus*. Eusebius probably has this statue in mind when he relates (in the *Ecclesiastical History*) how Constantine ordered that an enormous statue erected to him at Rome by the Senate should show him with the saving sign of victory – the Christ-monogram – in his hand.

For Constantine the statesman, display of the victory sign was of secondary importance compared with the need to secure the lasting benevolence of the new God towards the state. This accounts for his prompt action in making over the palace of the Laterani to the bishop of Rome (in the winter of 312-3) and in sponsoring a number of monumental churches within the city. This action becomes all the more significant when we remember that although the Christians had had their burial ground (the catacombs) in the old capital, as yet they had no church there. Hitherto their meetings had been held in private houses adapted for liturgical purposes. The church now built at the Lateran was a five-aisled basilica modelled on secular buildings of this type; it was followed a little later by the basilica in honour of Saints Marcellinus and Peter, martyred under Diocletian. Constantine thus acknowledged that at Rome itself the state was under an obligation to support the Christian religion. He also did everything possible to secure recognition for the new status of Christianity throughout the empire. In the east Maximinus Daia had flouted the Galerian edict of toleration and was again persecuting Christians. But in February 313, at a meeting in Milan, Constantine persuaded Licinius, ruler of the Danubian and Balkan provinces, to join with him in making Christianity a protected religion everywhere in the empire. Admittedly, no edict issued from this conference, but the programme decided upon can be gathered from rescripts sent by Licinius to the governors of the eastern provinces, after his defeat of Maximinus Daia had brought the whole East under his control. From these it appears that the emperors had decided 'to give to Christians as to all others free choice to follow the religion they desired, so that whatever exists of Divinity and Celestial Reality may be amicable and propitious towards us and our subjects.'[1] Joined to this general declaration was an explicit statement that the Christian persecution was at an end, that the communities were to have their confiscated properties and meeting-places freely restored to them. The programme initiated at Milan thus goes much further than the toleration edict of Galerius: the new faith is acknowledged as the source of victory, the Christian communities are recognized in due form as corporations capable of possessing legal rights, their existence as organized entities is endorsed.

During the years which followed the parts of the empire ruled by Constantine were left in no doubt that he was determined to accept the full consequences of making Christianity part of the state religion. A schism had arisen in Africa over the question of whether and in what form Christians whose faith had weakened under the Diocletian persecution could be readmitted to fellowship. Caecilian, who had been elected bishop of Carthage in 312, was rejected by many other bishops of the region on the grounds that he had been consecrated by a bishop who had surrendered the scriptures when required to do so by the state inquisitors. The purists declared the consecration invalid and elected an anti-bishop, Maiorinus, who was to be succeeded in 315 by Donatus, the powerful leader from whom the schism takes its name. Other African cities soon had their Donatist communities, founded in opposition to the churches led by Caecilian; and the Donatists even went to the length of rebaptising Christians who came over to them from the old Church. Some scholars have thought that in seceding from the main, the Catholic Church, the Donatists were directly inspired by the concept of the Church held by Cyprian, the martyr-bishop of Carthage, and that they made this theological position the basis of their claim to autonomy. Any such hypothesis is quite implausible; what is possible, however, is that in Donatist radicalism a fundamentally semitic vein in African Christianity was working itself to the surface. It can be shown that the Donatist church attracted strongest support in Numidia, among the section of the population still imprinted by Berber and Punic influences, that is to say among peoples still incompletely romanized. In these regions, moreover, Donatism found most of its adherents among the lower classes, whose rejection of the Church of Carthage can also be interpreted as an act of hostility towards Roman officials and still more towards Roman proprietors. These sentiments account for the attraction the Donatist church held for the revolutionary movement of the Circumcellions, a terrorist rising of peasant fanatics with a very varied following, which was soon to break out.

The threat of agrarian unrest had yet to declare itself when Constantine first intervened in African affairs. If we accept his own oft-repeated explanation of his actions in Africa, it seems that his primary aim was to ensure that African Christians were worshipping God in due form, so as to protect the welfare of the state. This again sheds light on Constantine's personal attitude towards the new religion. Had he still, in the spirit of a Diocletian, regarded observance of the Roman state religion as the prerequisite for securing divine favour, he could only have welcomed the schism among the Christians. As it was, he believed his duty to the common good obliged him to maintain unity within the Christian faith, and he accordingly went into action, without a full appreciation of what he was doing. A letter to the governor of Africa ordering the restoration of confiscated Christian property was followed by a second which exempted priests of the Catholic Church from all municipal obligations – a tacit avowal that the clerical order, as a professional body, performed work essential to the state. On this occasion, as later, we find that the church of Caecilian is described as the Catholic Church, a designation which earlier writers had employed to describe a Church universal, comprehending the whole empire. There can be little doubt that this line in ecclesiastical thinking had the support of bishop Hosius, now coming to the fore as the emperor's adviser on Christian affairs. In a letter to Caecilian, the emperor speaks of 'the lawful and most holy Christian religion', castigating the schismatics as men of insubordinate temper and hinting that the services of state officials could be called on to enforce their return to the fold. But the Donatists also placed their trust in the emperor and petitioned him to appoint unbiased judges from Gaul to settle the dispute. Constantine agreed to appoint judges but directed Miltiades, bishop of Rome, to investigate and decide the affair. The tribunal Miltiades set up, in effect a Roman synod, passed sentence of excommunication on Donatus. The Donatists appealed from this judgement to the emperor, who took the momentous step of summoning a synod composed of bishops from all the lands under his rule, to meet in August 314 at Arles, in Gaul.

This marks the first occasion on which an episcopal synod was used as a tool of imperial policy. The council of Arles confirmed the condemnation of Donatus and in recognition of the emperor's good offices passed resolutions whose effect was to bring Christians into closer partnership with Constantine's state: Christians were expressly given permission to hold offices which entailed frequent attendance at feasts and games, while avoidance of military service by Christians now incurred the threat of ecclesiastical penalties. The emperor was thus assured that loyal Catholic subjects could be won by means of a synod. But the Donatists were still dissatisfied and appealed to the tribunal of the emperor himself. Constantine's first reaction was to try to persuade the two leaders of the warring churches to leave Africa; when this failed, he resorted to threats and declared in writing his intention of coming in person to deliver judgement. For, he said, it was his duty 'to exterminate errors and staunch all follies, and so see to it that all men profess the true religion in open harmony, offering Almighty God due worship.'[2] Here once again we have a clear statement of a concept basic to Roman rule, that the safety of the state rests on the true worship of divinity. Even this threat failed, however, and unrest in Africa mounted. At length officials were forced to intervene and Donatists were prosecuted; now that they were the persecuted element in an empire in process of becoming Christian, the Donatists could claim that their communities were the true martyr-churches. In 321, after many bitter experiences, Constantine granted the Donatist Church a limited measure of toleration. It was after this, with the fully conscious intention of defending what was the business of the Church from intervention by the state, that Donatus greeted an imperial embassy with the question 'What has the emperor to do with the Church?' while his adherents accused the Catholic Church of betraying the Christians' Lord in order to win Caesar's favour.

Such was the upshot of the first encounter between a Christian emperor and the Christian Church. We have seen the emperor trying to make the Christian religion serve the state, just as the Roman religion had done in the past. While the Church of the mainstream was prepared to meet him, the Donatist Church, despite appeals made by its spokesmen direct to the emperor, now turned away from the state and persisted as a protest movement, at once religious and social. Just how far the Catholic Church, in its new situation, was breaking out of its rectricted circle and invading public life is shown by many of the decisions and constitutions belonging to this period. Constantine made bishops privileged dignitaries and entrusted them with official duties. A law of 316 legalized the enfranchisement of slaves in church in the presence of the bishop as a new form of manumission. This was followed two years later by official recognition of the bishop's jurisdiction, which had long been acknowledged in practice within the Christian communities, as authoritative in civil cases. Next, individual churches secured the right of receiving legacies under wills, which not only confirmed their existence as legal personalities but also made it easier to build up their resources. In 321 Sunday was declared a public holiday, which marked the acceptance of the Christian Lord's Day by the state. These singular concessions raised the Catholic Church above all other religions and communities. Yet Constantine still continued as the High Priest of the Roman state (*pontifex maximus*) and as such remained responsible for the worship of the gods, even though he himself no longer took part in pagan ceremonies. As under his predecessors, certain pagan practices might be forbidden for the sake of public order (secret soothsaying, for example); but paganism retained its official position. Pagans were still being appointed to key offices in the administration and the army and the first duty of the emperor, even a Christian emperor, was still to defend the frontiers of the empire and secure the well-being of all its subjects.

Constantine and Licinius (who after his victory over Maximinus Daia in 313 ruled the eastern part of the empire), were frequently at variance; but it seems that the peace they concluded in 317 was a genuine effort at co-existence. Licinius was in any case engaged in strenuous efforts to raise the level of economic life in the eastern provinces. In his policy towards the Christians he adhered to the toleration agreed on at Milan, without incorporating the organization of the Church – much stronger here than in the provinces governed by Constantine – into that of the state. The more firmly Constantine bound his bishops to the state, the more emphatic became Licinius in asserting his independence of the Church; indeed from 320 he started to favour pagans in his administration and army at the expense of Christians and went so far as to forbid episcopal synods, suppressing all overt Christian opposition by force. In view of these and other differences, one might describe the relationship between the two rulers as a cold war. At length both sides began preparations for an open conflict. The issue at stake was whether Constantine could realize what had always been his aim, a universal monarchy; but the struggle also turned into a war of religion, since Constantine went into battle under the victory-standard of Christ, while Licinius took care to solicit the favour of the old gods through elaborate sacrifices. In the autumn of 324, after bitter fighting on land and sea, Licinius was defeated at Chrysopolis, on Asian soil; soon afterwards, because of his attempt at allying with the Danubian peoples, Licinius was executed as an enemy of the state. Constantine, the champion of Christianity, had made himself sole ruler of the empire.

Before we consider how the relations between Church and empire were affected by the fact that both were now universal, we must glance at the political, military, economic and social framework Constantine imposed on the empire as a whole. After long decades of rivalry within the imperial college a single ruler was now firmly established, and peace reigned along the Rhine, the Danube and the Euphrates. Now was the time, if this peace was to be preserved, for making long-term dispositions. Constantine shared his predecessors' conviction that the realm of civilization was coterminous with the Roman world, with its corollary that alien people must either be held forcibly at arm's length or annihilated. The Christian ruler drew additional inspiration from his belief that power had devolved on him through the grace of God and that to the man of charisma his subjects owed him reverence. Certainly, emperor-worship no longer entailed pagan sacrifices. but an image of the divine order had still to be created, by constructing a hierarchy of offices and dignities throughout the government, administration and army. Constantine's Christian theocracy developed along the lines laid down by Diocletian in his organization of the empire and gave the social structure of declining antiquity its final form.

In the central and provincial government the remaining Republican magistracies were kept in being purely as political decoration. Even so, the office of consul, which was used throughout the Roman world to designate the year, was still highly coveted in old aristocratic circles; the moment when the consul by a gesture of the hand opened the official games was still regarded as the culmination of a glittering social career. Political power, however, was now vested in the offices and careers available through the imperial service. It was now that the various powers and administrations within this system, with a plentiful array of authorities to check their exercise, received final definition. The highest government officials were always at the disposal of the emperor and in his immediate entourage. The Imperial Council (*sacrum consistorium*) was composed of legal advisers and the chief dignitaries of the Palatium. The *quaestor sacri palatii* acted as chief secretary to the emperor; he received all petitions and was responsible for all written answers to them. The quaestor was supported by the heads of the various sections of the chancery and served by a college of clerks (*schola notariorum*). The chancellor or *magister officiorum*, who had assumed the functions of the former praetorian prefect, was more powerful still. As the person responsible for the safety of the ruler he controlled the palace body-guard (*scholae palatinae*); in addition he acted as master of ceremonies at court and head of the secret service, which gave him control of the corps of imperial couriers (*agentes in rebus*). The personal link between these high officials and the emperor is emphasized by the use of the expression *comites* ('in the suite' of the emperor) to describe their rank, a rank which was also held by the two finance ministers, one in charge of the state treasury, the other of all imperial property (*comes sacrarum largitionum* and *comes rerum privatarum*).

The officials of the outer ring of the administration, with all its numerous subdivisions, were subordinate to the centre. The essential features of the structure set up by Diocletian were preserved. Although tetrarchy was a thing of the past, the idea of dividing up the empire into four administrative units was carried over into the universal monarchy, even though there was only one ruler to direct the whole. The office of *praefectus praetorio* was detached from the court and transferred to the outlying administrations, so that there was a prefecture for the East, for the Balkan and Danube region, for the provinces of Italy and Africa and for the north-west, from Britain to Spain. These four prefectures exercised the highest jurisdiction over the provincial governments and were also responsible for maintaining and recruiting the armies; although the office was no longer linked with military command, the prefects, like all high officials including provincial governors, wore military uniform (*cingulum militiae*); even civilian office now ranked as military service. The only high official still to appear in the toga was the city-prefect of Rome (*praefectus urbi*), who was responsible for maintaining public order in the city and for the welfare of its population. This high dignity was reserved for members of the senatorial order; all other offices and careers were open to men of equestrian rank.

In the sphere of military organization, Diocletian's plan of dividing the army into field and frontier troops was now brought to completion and both categories were provided with specialized units of infantry and cavalry. The field army, the strategic reserve, was stationed in the interior of the empire, while the frontier troops remained on the *limites*, where they were provided with grants of land. Army generals or *duces* continued to command sectors of the frontier. For the high command of

tuted two new offices, master of infantry
er peditum, magister equitum). As a bold
n a par with field-marshalships – were
ficers of German descent. The great in-
ans serving in the troops was in fact one
e's army reforms. German horsemen pre-
tinae, the palace body-guard. Soon the
etermined by the proportion of German
ned.
eds of the court, the bureaucracy and the
gious increase in public revenues. In addi-
ift liberality of the emperor and his entire
ained of by pagan writers. Subjects continued
of the taxation system based on *iugatio-capitatio*
an, and there was no falling-off of complaints over

economic distress and price rises. Prices were affected by Constantine's issue of a new coin, which had very advantageous effects for the state and the governing class. This was the gold coin known as the *solidus*, which weighed only one seventy-second of a Roman pound (4.55 g.); every effort was made to preserve its weight and purity. As a high denomination the gold solidus could hold its own, but the silver and copper coinage of the period failed to acquire any fixed commercial value. Constantine's solidus therefore came to enjoy exceptional stability, being used in large-scale transactions and for the payment of salaries to high officials. The people to profit from the new monetary policy were those with more goods at their disposal than they needed for themselves, men in the service of the state, above all soldiers. The poorer sections of the population, who never so much as saw a solidus and had to make do with the inflated coinage, the *denarius communis* or the *follis*, were faced with a further increase in prices. Under Constantine and his sons the manual workers of town and countryside became still more impoverished. Moreover, it was an evil day for the peasantry when the indiction (which fixed their tax liability) was changed to a fifteen year cycle, since years when the harvest failed would now scarcely be taken into account. The possibility of commuting payments in kind into money payments (*adaeratio*) brought no relief, since the assessment of goods against money was quite arbitrary.

Social divisions were becoming deeper and deeper. Coloni on the great estates often tried to escape their contractual obligation and assigned place of work by flight, but the year 332 saw the promulgation of the fateful law binding all coloni to the estate to which they belonged. Henceforth they could neither flee nor be released by their masters, and even their children were bound to the soil, *glebae adscripti*. The long endeavours of landed proprietors to secure a permanent and cheap supply of labour had at last reached their goal. It may be that the enforced settlement of the coloni helped to stabilize the productivity of the great estates; what is certain is that a significant part of the rural population was now demoted to an inferior legal status. The urban bourgeoisie also suffered under the lash of increased coercion by the state, made necessary by the empire's continuing financial needs. What privileges the middle class had managed to retain throughout previous crises were now turned into instruments of servitude. In order to ensure the performance of municipal duties and to halt the drift of families eligible for civic office into other callings or onto the land, the office of decurion was made hereditary by law: the curial order had finally been pressed into the service of the state. Similar rules were applied to the trade corporations on which the army and the large urban proletariat depended for their well-being; for example, membership of the guilds of ship-owners, bakers, lime-burners and pig dealers was made hereditary, with no possibility of transfer to another trade. The process of attaching members of the middle and lower orders to their class and calling, to craft trades and the cultivation of the soil, was thus completed. Two privileged groups remained exempt from the organized pressure of economic and social coercion: the proprietors of landed estates, who were masters of their coloni and at liberty to withdraw their property from the control of the provincial administration, and the high officials of the imperial service, who were in process of forming themselves into a new aristocracy. These were the two ruling classes of secular society in the late Roman empire. As for the role of the Christian Church in all this, it cannot be said to have voiced any protest against the subjugation of the middle and lower orders. But it is at least to its credit that through its charitable organizations the Church helped to alleviate much distress and made a serious effort to penetrate with its new ethos the small cells of family and petty industrial life, so sadly neglected under paganism.

It may be that Constantine's organization of the empire as a whole owes less to Diocletian than I have implied; for his religious conversion, whose first effects we have already traced, also had its influence on the elaboration of offices and dignities and the subjugation of all subjects to the state. In a number of manifestos Constantine issued after his entry upon universal rule, following the defeat of Licinius, he proclaims his sense of being singled out for a special mission. The saving sign is once again acknowledged as the source of victory and the emperor prays that all his subjects may feel themselves drawn to the new faith. However, although he is candid in his condemnation of paganism as a false creed, to the end of his life Constantine refused to entertain the idea of coercion in matters of religion. 'No-one should injure another in the name of a faith he himself has accepted from conviction. He who is quicker to see and acknowledge the truth, let him try to persuade his neighbour, as opportunity offers. But if this is not possible, then he must refrain from the attempt. For there is a difference between battling for immortality of one's own free will and forcing others to do so'.[3] Pagans might if they chose interpret such manifestos as a guarantee that the empire of the first Christian emperor was to be built on freedom to choose between truth and error. Yet Constantine did nothing to support the old religions and on the whole his statements leave the impression that he was willing to let paganism die of its own accord. In later years he even proscribed certain oriental cults, for the most part admittedly those which on moral grounds were also offensive to cultivated pagans, for example the ritual prostitution traditionally associated with certain temples.

It was quite another matter whether this principle of religious freedom could be applied without reserve to the Christian faith itself. Constantine's intervention in Africa had already shown the importance he attached to unified worship of God as an essential means of obtaining divine blessing, which meant that the statesman had a duty to establish the lawful religion – and drive out what was unlawful. The Christians of the oriental provinces, with their numerous Christian communities and long-established episcopal sees and learned academies, had already for generations been passionately engaged in the theological development of doctrine and in perfecting their ecclesiastical organization.

At this very moment far-reaching differences in theological doctrine were coming to a head, differences in which the ordinary Christian was already embroiled. Eastern preoccupation with the eternal nature of the Godhead as a problem of the first importance can be ascribed to the influence of Greek philosophy. The greatest difficulties presented by the doctrine of the Trinity lay in defining the relationship between the three divine Persons. If the Godhead is metaphysical and can have no direct contact with what is finite, how can the origin of the world be accounted for except by postulating a second God? The Alexandrian Church, in particular, was much disturbed by this problem and one of its presbyters, Arius by name, propounded the following thesis : the Father created the Son, who in turn created the world, and appeared on earth, which he redeemed by his teaching and example. On this theory the Son was not eternal in the same sense as the Father but was rather an instrument of creation, a dependent God. Arius' thesis was opposed by Alexander, bishop of Alexandria, who followed the prevailing line in Alexandrian theology, holding that Father and Son were of the same essence (*usia*) but distinct in person (*hypostasis*) ; and a synod summoned by this bishop condemned Arius' doctrine as heretical. Arius then removed himself to Asia, where he found support from several bishops of Palestine and Bithynia; even Eusebius, the learned bishop of Caesarea, was not unsympathetic to the new doctrine. There was now a real danger of a doctrinal split in the East, which might have adverse effects on public worship. We have already remarked that a new fervour in religion was a cardinal spiritual characteristic of the age. It should therefore occasion no surprise to find the true nature of the Godhead becoming a controversial issue within the Christian Church, and the whole body of believers aroused over the question of how God the Father and God the Son were to be defined and worshipped.

News of the affair reached Constantine, bishop Hosius, who was still constantly at his side, perceived some of the wider theological implications of the Arian doctrine. If the divinity of the Logos was doubtful, then the work of redemption would need reinterpretation, in a sense at variance with the received apostolic tradition. It may be that men were already aware of some of the conclusions that might be drawn from the new theology, as they affected the idea of the Church : for example, the Arian view implied that the clergy were not Christ's proxies but merely ministers in the divine service. As for Constantine, his initial intervention in the dispute shows that he regarded differences of theological opinion on a par with disputes between schools of philosophers. For him the vital consideration was that men should unite over essentials; once this was achieved, side-issues would resolve themselves. Constantine was bent on unanimity, as he had already shown by the political line he adopted over the African schism. Moved by his deep-felt conviction that the ruler's duty was to anchor the safety of the state in the favour of God, Constantine exerted his authority more positively than ever before in giving a religious lead to his subjects, laying claim to a species of spiritual authority which he was soon to describe as a general or extra-liturgical episcopacy. On this view he had a duty to intervene in the dispute and to take steps to ensure unity of doctrine. Once again he used ecclesiastical machinery as a channel for enforcing his own will. But since this was not a matter which one bishop could determine, since the synod of a single province was incompetent to give a binding decision on a question of faith which was troubling so many, it was necessary to summon a general council of bishops. This decision on the part of the emperor was a recognition of episcopal authority; at the same time, in the new situation created by the alliance of the Church throughout the empire with the State, it gave the ecumenical council new life as the highest organ of the Church.

In 325 Constantine summoned the bishops to a council at Nicaea in Bithynia. The assembly was composed of some 300 prelates, mostly from the East. Constantine himself presided at the ceremonial opening session, delivering an exhortation to unity. Although a bishop thereafter took charge of the proceedings, Constantine was able to make his influence felt throughout the duration of the council. The decision of the doctrinal issue accorded with the Alexandrian view, a view shared by Christians in the western part of the empire: the Logos was declared to be of the same essence as the Father (*homo-usios*). Arius, together with the handful of bishops who remained loyal to his thesis, was excommunicated by the council and exiled by the emperor. The council also reviewed certain important matters of Church government, and here the emperor's wishes may well have played a leading part. The provincial structure was accepted in principle as the framework for ecclesiastical groupings, which meant that synods would be composed of bishops from a single province, with the bishop of the provincial capital, the metropolitan, taking precedence. The sees of Alexandria, Antioch and Rome, which had long enjoyed a special authority, were confirmed in their jurisdiction over provincial synods, and the shades of difference between the three patriarchates (as they later came to be called) precisely laid down. The canons of the council were published to the churches at large; in addition the emperor wrote to the congregations informing them of his concurrence. On the surface, therefore, it seems as though the co-operation between emperor and Church had ended in a triumph for Constantine. A ruler who professed Christianity, but was as yet unbaptised, had won the right to summon a council; his assent to its canons gave them the force of public law. The bishops, after the long and bitter trials of persecution – whose marks some still bore on their bodies – welcomed the emperor as a colleague in their common task, regarding his relationship with the Church in the nature of an alliance. Constantine, cleaving to the party in possession, as was always his inclination in material disputes, loaded the bishops with honours. Thus with astounding rapidity the emperor had insinuated himself in the direction of the Church, which was from henceforth under a debt of obligation to the State.

The real consequences of this alliance between State and Church soon emerged. Theological disagreement was not brought to an end by the Council. The Nicene formula of *homo-usios* was too imprecise to satisfy the acute minds of eastern bishops schooled in Greek philosophy. Moreover, theological controversy was in some cases intensified by personal rivalries and the competing claims of individual sees. For a time it seemed as though Arius, once he had accepted the Nicene formula, would be reinstated in his position at Alexandria. But Athanasius, his life-long antagonist, who had succeeded Alexander as bishop in 328, was not satisfied that Arius really had revised his beliefs and vetoed his rehabilitation as a presbyter. As a theologian, Athanasius' main concern was with interpreting the message of the Bible, scarcely at all with the final clarification of philosophical concepts. To his way of thinking, any doctrine which endangered the essential unity of Father and Son by further philosophical refinements cast doubt on the message of man's redemption and could only damage the faith and worship of the churches. At the same time he was convinced that defence of doctrinal purity was the responsibility of the bishop, whose duty was also to assert the independence of the Christian community; the emperor could not act as a judge in religious questions. His impassioned teaching of theology won Athanasius a large following, his political manoeuvres, some of them frankly dubious, strengthened his position still further. The first bishop of Alexandria to preach in Coptic as well as Greek, Athanasius enjoyed solid support among the rural population of Egypt, but his intransigent disposition aroused considerable opposition. As the dispute dragged on, the emperor, who had not lost sight of what was happening in the Church, must have felt that this contumacious bishop was the real obstacle to unity. In pursuit of his general aim, Constantine continued to use episcopal synods as instruments of policy, causing them to meet as occasion demanded, setting them specific tasks and when necessary controlled their work. As an initial indication that the bishops were becoming restless under this treatment, we find a synod declaring that no bishop should on his own initiative appeal to the emperor in Church matters. As time went on, eastern opposition to the Nicene formula gathered such strength that in 335 Athanasius himself was condemned by a council which opened at Tyre, and was reconvened by Constantine at Jerusalem, where his magnificent church built over the Holy Sepulchre was to be dedicated. At Jerusalem, Arius and his followers were received back into communion on the basis of an orthodox confession of faith; Athanasius, however, was banished by the emperor to Trier. The statesman might delude himself that the unity he had so imperiously demanded was now a fact; but there were many Christian congregations, especially in the West, who saw the exiled bishop Athanasius as the confessor of the true faith.

Modern scholarship, basing itself on Constantine's letters and edicts, has succeeded in tracing the fundamental outlines of Constantine's Christian faith and sense of mission. He never wearied in his praises of the victory-giving power of the Christian sign and held fast to his conviction that the true worship of divinity was the only means of securing protection for the ruler and his empire. In addition he was convinced that the ruler had a right to order the direction of this worship into proper channels. To him this meant that worship offered on behalf of the Roman state should henceforth be entrusted to the Christian Church, as a guarantee of salvation in this world and the next. Church and State were inevitably linked, since the imperial office was itself bestowed by God. It is clear that Constantine's precise definition of the charge laid by God on the emperor was an amalgam of ideas drawn from a wide range of assumptions and traditions: it included his notion of the episcopal office inherent in the emperor, the idea of the philosopher-king as lawgiver, and the magistracy of the High Priest. Some have also detected an element of the gnostic trends apparent in Hermetic writings, and it is certainly true that at times Constantine seems to regard himself as the heaven-sent bringer of salvation, in whom eschatological prophecies find fulfilment. To appreciate the full extent of the gulf separating Constantine's theology from the creed of the churches one needs only to realize that in all his numerous utterances he makes little mention of the redemptive character of Christ's passion; the theology of the Cross is noticeably absent from his thinking. This probably explains why as an individual he entered no Christian congregation and may perhaps account for his postponement of baptism – which was in any case not unusual at this period. What Constantine did claim for himself was priestly consecration as the emissary of heaven. If he recognized God as his constant judge, he also felt himself in direct and continuous contact with God. This conception of the Christian ruler also allowed him to present the monarchy as a theocracy in the profane sphere. It is true that at times he showed open contempt for polytheism, yet as Constantinus Maximus Augustus he still remained the representative of invisible and supernatural majesty, even in the eyes of the Christian world. True, in his own person he claimed no equality with God and therefore eliminated sacrificial offerings from the cult of the emperor; yet as ruler, elevated above mankind and the fit object of reverence, he could still assume the awesome mask of monarchy worn by his pagan predecessors, complete with insignia, vestments and ceremonial. His personal love of display provided court life with many new embellishments. It was Constantine who introduced the pearl-decked diadem, the symbol of hellenistic-oriental kingship, into the Roman world. Imperial theocracy in its Christian form now took its place among the institutions of the later Roman empire. So great was the force of Constantine's personality, that even with this Christian bias he could bend to his will the men of state and church, government and army. His powerful creative energies also overflowed into cultural life. It is of course hardly surprising that panegyricists, whose role under the tetrarchy has already been mentioned, should also have found ample scope for their rhetoric in the reign of the victorious Constantine, who was not displeased to be hailed *victor omnium gentium*. Among the many praiseworthy deeds ascribed to him, his patronage of Gallic schools – in which he followed the example of his father – deserves special notice. Augustodunum continued to be a centre of learning and Trier was a magnet for scholarly and artistic talent. It was Constantine, as the ancient historians rightly insist, who halted the anti-intellectual trend which had set in under so many of the soldier-emperors. His personal predilection for Christianity opened the imperial court to Christian writers and scholars. That Lactantius, whose compendium of Christian philosophy enjoyed a wide circulation, was summoned to Trier in 315 to act as tutor to the emperor's eldest son, is but one of many indications which place beyond doubt the emperor's intention to form his household and retinue in the Christian mould. Bishop Eusebius of Caesarea, after Nicaea one of the emperor's most loyal collaborators, delivered the ceremonial oration first at the celebration of his vicennalia in Nicomedia, then at the dedication of the church of the Holy Sepulchre in Jerusalem and finally at the festivities held in the new capital to mark thirty years of his rule. The portrait of the ruler that emerges from these orations and from Eusebius' many other writings can be taken as typifying the sentiments of a substantial number of his contemporaries and deserves close study. The poet Optatianus Porfyrius, eminent courtier and for a time a centre of political controversy, may also have been a Christian. The poems of this senator – a respectable figure though long the subject of political controversy – are of slender substance, but the elaborate imagery of his verse, which he brought to artistic perfection, stamps him as a courtier-poet.

When he wrote out his verses on parchment, he would distinguish certain letters, distributed evenly throughout the text, by colouring them red or gold so that they stood out from the main body of the work as an integrated but independent entity. The resulting pattern might take the form of a palm branch or a monogram or some motto, for example *filius atque pater et sanctus spiritus unum*. Whilst playful devices of this kind naturally tell us nothing about the personal beliefs of the writer, they at least show that Christian motifs were among those in demand at court. The emperor's patronage also extended to pagans, for example Nicagoras of Athens, whose family provided priests for Eleusis, and Sopater the neo-platonist, for long a highly respected figure in court circles, until he fell a victim to political intrigue.

Constantine's unusually full legislative activity makes it regrettable that we have no more precise information about the jurists in his entourage. It is clear from the numerous documents which have survived that in style his decrees were strongly influence… quite exceptional degree. So far as their cont… ideas of hellenistic-oriental origin appear … portant as Christian teaching, and inde… guish the two streams. Here only a … starting with slavery. Constantine … sought to alleviate its rigours b… setting some limit to the mast… …g the domestic life of slaves. He j… …on the part of the law by reference to … …w can men countenance the separation of … …ts, sisters from brothers, wives from husbands ?'[4] … …onial legislation made unilateral divorce more diffi… …bited married men from keeping concubines – which cert… …ked an advance towards Christian moral teaching. The same can … said of the law prohibiting gladiatorial combats in a civilian setting and in time of peace. The laws providing a measure of state aid for people in a depressed economic and social position may well have been inspired by the philosophical ideal of philanthropy, working in conjunction with the Christian precept of love. Thus parents whose poverty prevents them from rearing their children are assured of some assistance. Farmers in debt are on no account to be deprived of the plough-slaves and animals essential to their livelihood. Officials collecting debts are enjoined, under pain of death, to refrain from dragging mothers of families from their houses. Even prisoners benefitted from the humanitarian bias of imperial legislation. Captives might be chained, but their chains were not to be used as instruments of torture ; prisoners were not to be wholly deprived of light by day, and by night were to be lodged in the prison forecourt, with a period in the fresh air before day-break. Prison governors and jailers who condemned prisoners to death were to suffer the same penalty. The humane tendency of this legislation appears all the more remarkable when it is realized that in general penal provision and forms of execution continued to be harsh and crude, in keeping with the violent character of this age of decay.

The Constantinian ethos appears at its most majestic in the public buildings he erected as a setting for peaceful intercourse. Like Augustus and Hadrian before him, Constantine realized the potentialities of building as a medium of imperial propaganda and determined the style of public architecture for a long time to come. It is in this field that the adoption of Christianity makes its most obvious impact. Constantine took on himself the duty of providing Christian places of worship from the moment of victory at the Milvian Bridge and his subsequent entry into Rome. Speaking of the churches built in the east, Eusebius tells us that the emperor not only made the resources of the State available but in some cases took a personal share in planning their design and decoration. New churches often received gifts from the emperor in the form of books, plate and landed property. During the preceding century there was already a growing tendency in the East to fashion Christian meeting-houses specifically for worship. As we shall see, Constantine's new foundations were built with the same primary purpose, to accommodate the growing number of Christian worshippers; at the same time they also had an official aspect, since they were built on the basilica plan, that is to say as rectangular hall-shaped edifices divided into aisles by rows of columns and terminating in an apse. The sovereignty of Christ was thus made visible in the structure of his churches; and the motif of Christ in victory also predominates in the Christian sculpture and painting of this period. The emperor's personal form of religion, which retained a substantial element of respect for the past, was responsible for the siting of churches on places hallowed by some holy or heroic event, whether from biblical times or the post-apostolic era. Helena, his mother, also played her part through founding churches in Palestine, which she visited as a pilgrim. Places mentioned in the Old and New Testaments commemorated in this way include Hebron, associated in biblical tradition with Abraham, the Mount of Olives, Bethlehem and Golgotha. The five-aisled pillared basilica of the church of the Nativity at Bethlehem has an octagonal choir in the place of the cave alleged to be the birthplace of the Redeemer. The enormous complex of the church of the Holy Sepulchre, which the emperor intended should surpass in splendour all churches on earth, was linked by an atrium with the rotunda erected over Christ's tomb. At Trier, in the north-west of the empire, we find the old imperial residency transformed under Christian influence; here an enormous double church, whose ground-plan has only recently been ascertained, was built on to the remnants of the imperial palace. At Aquileia, the south church, in all probability founded by Constantine in 325, adjoins the imperial residence. It is significant that Rome itself was dignified by several churches over and above those built directly after the victory at the Milvian Bridge; Peter and Paul, the martyr-apostles, and Laurence the Deacon, a victim of Valerian's persecution, all had churches built over their tombs. It was in 325, at the instigation of bishop Sylvester, that a massive basilica in honour of St Peter was raised on the Ager Vaticanus, at the spot which Roman tradition – recently confirmed by inscriptions – venerated as the scene of his martyrdom and burial-place. Recent excavations have shown that existing graves on the site had to be covered over in the course of building. In pagan eyes this was sacrilege, but no such considerations impeded the builders, whose only aim was to give the apostle's memorial pride of place within the church. Enclosed within a shrine-like structure, the Memoria also became the artistic focus of the building. The dedicatory inscription in St Peter's is testimony to the assurance felt both by the emperor-creator and by Christianity itself, now transformed by its overwhelming confidence in victory:

'Quod duce te mundus surrexit in astra triumphans,
Hanc Constantinus Victor tibi condidit aulam'.
('Because you were the leader when the world rose towards heaven,
Constantine the victor founded this hall in your honour.')

While the imperial city of Rome was becoming a privileged episcopal see, the capital city of the future was rising on the shores of the Bosphoros at Byzantium, whose new name of Constantinopolis was to perpetuate its creator's memory. Because of its permanently beleagured state, the empire's centre of gravity had long since shifted to the frontiers. In his campaign against Licinius Constantine had seen for himself the strategic importance of the straits lying between the lower Danube and the Euphrates: work on developing the old Greek town of Byzantium into an imperial residency started soon after this last rival was defeated. Although the move to the East was eventually taken to signify a rapprochement with the hellenistic-Christian world, initially there was no intention of making the new foundation an exclusively Christian city. Its ceremonial inauguration was attended by pagan ritual, old temples were left standing and some of the new monuments erected were in pagan style. Constantinople was to be the new imperial capital, the second Rome; it was endowed with its own Senate and with an array of public buildings grand enough to compete with Rome. The imperial precincts, containing the palace and hippodrome, occupied the site of the ancient polis, while a second important complex of buildings included a spaccious market with a lofty statue of the emperor. Naturally, the city also had its share of Christian sanctuaries – the church of the Divine Peace (St Irene) was enlarged, plans were made for a church dedicated to the Holy Wisdom. On the edge of the new development, close to the walls, Constantine erected a Martyrium in honour of the apostles, in which he incorporated provision for his burial. Augustus, Hadrian, Galerius and Diocletian had also prepared their own mausolea, but in such a form as to make plain that no divine assistance would be needed to secure their entry among the gods. Constantine, on the other hand, furnished his mausoleum with commemorative cenotaphs of the apostles, leaving the space in the centre clear for his sarcophagus. As Eusebius says, Constantine became numbered among the people of God and received into the communion of prayers offered in this holy place. This was the first time an emperor had received Christian burial, a burial in keeping with this particular emperor's claim to be at once sovereign ruler and general bishop. He took his repose as 'the thirteenth herald of the true faith', to quote a later visitor to his tomb, as the 'equal of the apostles', to use the title bestowed on him by the Orthodox Churches.

Constantine's church foundations, indeed the very lay-out of his tomb, are evidence of the hellenistic influences which affected both his own faith and that of the Church he guided. It was above all in the eastern territories of the empire that his historic achievements and legendary attributes were combined to create the image of the ideal Christian ruler. Even in his own lifetime, a new, historically-centred, Christian theology was growing up round his name. It is surely permissible to accept that Eusebius of Caesarea speaks for many of his contemporaries – and to attach all the more weight to his evidence, as the utterance of a politically active and deeply learned man. Eusebius speaks to us above all as a historian. In his *History* he relates the history of the principal nations of the past; but while he resembles earlier Christian chroniclers in the universality of his field of vision, he is the first to buttress the narrative portion of his history by compiling parallel tables showing events as they took place in the various arenas with which he deals. In short, what Eusebius gives us is a synoptic history of the world. His *History of the Church* inaugurated a new mode of Christian historical writing; instead of writing the history of the nations with a Christian slant, Eusebius brings the history of the new nation, the nation of Christians, to the forefront of his narrative and traces the story of their trials and internal conflicts from the beginning down to the triumph of the Church. Eusebius was also a learned theologian and wrote numerous commentaries on books of the Old and New Testaments, together with substantial treatises to prove the falsity of paganism and the truth of Christianity. The book Eusebius wrote after Constantine's death, as a memorial to the ruler who had ushered in the new age, marks the transition from biography to hagiography.

Throughout his comprehensive writings Eusebius consistently puts forward, in a manner characteristic of his age, a historical interpretation of the world in which the divine salvation is wholly involved in human history. The course of mankind runs from Abraham, with whom his chronology begins, to Christ and thence to Constantine. Christianity, he declares, is not rooted in the law of Moses, which served only to guide the Jews after they had erred and is now superfluous. Eusebius insists that in the beginning true religion was represented by the faith of the patriarchs and their pious mode of life, which agreed so closely with the natural order that the fathers had no need of the Law. The promise made to Abraham has now been fulfilled for all mankind in Christ, the Logos acts as mediator between God and Creation, he is above all the redeemer but also the great teacher who delivers man from ignorance. By a providential dispensation Christ appeared on earth at the time when the Roman empire had reached its zenith, so that the many nations within its world-wide bounds could receive at first hand the word preached by the disciples. Turning to his own day, Eusebius declares that Constantine has come like a second Abraham, his victory is the victory of the Church, he has brought the pagans into the flock and thus accomplished the extension of God's kingdom over all the earth. Constantine himself is seen as an image of God, just as God with his company of angels and heavenly bodies is seen as a great earthly potentate, surrounded by his court. By his leadership of men, through his proclamation of God and through his victories, Constantine has established the kingdom of the Logos on earth. With this event, the development of mankind is complete. The union of Church and State is not an expedient dictated by necessity but a preparation for or indeed even an anticipation of the millennium.

This interpretation of history, like Constantine's own sense of mission, was a compound of biblical ideas, hypotheses taken from Greek philosophy and elements of emperor-worship. When we find a Christian bishop identified with a theology so conspicuously political, we are again reminded that from the moment of its alliance with the State the Church stood in great danger of secularization. The Church in the western part of the empire produced at this period no corresponding image of the first Christian emperor. Sylvester, as occupant of the see of Rome, had defended his office against this ruler by absenting himself from the council of Arles and by his conduct during the early stages of the Arian dispute. And it was around the name of Sylvester that the legend started to accumulate (towards the end of the fifth century) that Constantine had undergone his conversion in Rome and received baptism from its bishop. These stories in turn became the basis of the so-called Donation of Constantine, the great early medieval forgery in which Constantine is made to surrender the imperial insignia and his sovereignty over the western provinces of the empire to the Pope of Rome. For centuries this forgery was made the legal foundation of Rome's claim to power. As a matter of historical fact the claim rested on nothing more than Constantine's concern for the Christian congregations, freely exercised, and in a more general way on the Church's invasion of the secular and political sphere in the period which followed the epoch-making age of Constantine.

2. *State and Church, popular religion and monasticism, in the period after Constantine*

Constantine's sons and successors continued his work. It is true that they fought bitterly among themselves and that some rival emperors also appeared to add to the confusion. The empire devolved initially on Constantine's three surviving sons, Constantine II, who was killed in 340, Constans, who was killed in 350 and Constantius II, who finally ruled alone until his death in 361. But through all the vicissitudes of these decades absolutism retained its firm hold on the government and administration. Moreover, for some forty years after Constantine's death the defensive stance of the empire could not be shaken. Franks and Alamanni might make repeated forays over the Rhine, Goths and Sarmations over the Danube, but the Roman lines of fortification held firm, and here and there on the Rhine frontier the Romans even went over to the attack. The emperors might consider that their achievement vindicated the superiority of the empire and its civilization, even though they settled detached groups from alien tribes on Roman soil. The Persian front also held firm. Constantius proved energetic in repulsing attacks, his successor Julian over-bold in taking the initiative; but in general the situation in the near East remained unaltered.

This display of strength on the borders had its counterpart in the sphere of religion: Christianity was now the avowed creed of the empire, the religion of the Romans. While Christian congregations were making numerous converts in the provinces, missionary activity beyond the frontiers took on a new vigour, reaping both advantages and disadvantages from Christianity's new role as propagator of the Roman religion. Christians in Mesopotamia were often accused of siding with the enemy during the war between Rome and Persia, while Christians within the Persian empire were the victims of bloody persecutions during the fourth century. But to the north and south of the imperial frontiers Christian missionaries succeeded in converting important nations and states to the Gospel. The Goths, who now occupied a territory extending from the former province of Dacia (north of the lower Danube) into southern Russia as far as the Don, had for some time past been in contact both with ancient civilization and with the new religion that had sprung from it. These contacts were made primarily in the cities on the Black Sea littoral, but isolated Christians also reached the Goths by way of Moesia, and there were not a few among the captives brought back by Gothic raiding parties from forays deep into Asia Minor. To one such family, captured in Cappadocia, a son named Ulfilas was born in 'Gothland'. He became a Christian church official (*lector*) and in 341 accompanied a Gothic embassy to the emperor Constantius; it was on this occasion that Eusebius of Nicomedia consecrated him bishop of the Christians living in 'Gothland'. His great influence secured the Christian mission many successes among the east Germans. Here is must be mentioned, for the moment only in passing, that Ulfilas professed a Christianity in keeping with Eusebius' own brand of theology, Arianism. At the same time Nicene Christianity was spreading southwards from Egypt into Abyssinia, the result of a perilous journey undertaken by Frumentius of Tyre from the Red Sea to the court of the Ethiopian king at Aksum, where he gained a position of trust and converted his colleagues to the Christian faith. Consecrated bishop by Athanasius, Frumentius laid the foundations of the Christian church in Ethiopia.

As a further consequence of Constantine's epoch-making decision, his sons, nurtured in the Christian faith, progressively eliminated all traces of the pagan religion from public life. Constantius in particular was convinced that the welfare of the state and the maintenance of the Christian religion were complementary; accordingly he issued a series of laws in which pagan sacrifices were first restricted and then finally abolished, and also ordered the closure of many temples. In their vehemence of tone and harsh penal provisions, Constantius' edicts are in marked contrast with the tolerant attitude of his father; but their application does not appear to have been unduly rigorous. Governmental measures against paganism met with full approval from at least a part of the Christian population, as may be gathered from a work entitled *De errore profanarum religionum*, written by Firmicus Maternus and addressed to the emperors Constantius and Constantine (which means that it must have appeared before 350). Whilst still a pagan the author had written a treatise on astrology; with all the zeal of a convert, he now attacked both the Graeco-Roman cults and the mystery religions of the East. The spearhead of his argument is an idea which in early Christian apologetic had hovered only in the background: whereas the pagan religions distort nature, Christianity vouchsafes a true vision of nature and preserves whatever is wholesome in human commonsense. At several points in this radical-tending pamphlet Maternus categorically urges the emperors to root out the pagan cults and to deliver from error, even against their will, those who resist. The struggle against paganism is vaunted as a campaign fought under orders from God, a call to raise the banner of the faith; by way of tangible rewards, the emperors are offered the prospect of good fortune, victory and substantial accretions to their power. This is in fact an essay in popular Christianity, a Christianity adapted to the world; it may be taken as evidence that a substantial body of Christians were failing to comprehend the new responsibilities which devolved on them as emissaries of the gospel as a result of the alliance the Church had entered into with the State.

The further shaping of the relationship between the State and the Christian Church was to be of enormous significance for the fate of ancient civilization. It was conducted in a thoroughly Constantinian spirit: the Church, as the trustee for the true worship of God, is held to be one of the institutions of the empire; the emperor, as supreme head of the Christian people and of the whole state, is responsible for protecting this religion, so vital to the well-being of the State, and for ordering it in unity. But however clear-cut the path, the actual journey was to prove difficult and indeed dangerous. Constantine himself had left many problems unresolved or provided solutions which proved illusory. His sons, who like their father felt themselves called to intervene in Church affairs, found their attempts to promote unity obstructed by the unprecedented difficulties presented by a multiplicity of theological schools and episcopal factions. Within the Church, the longer conflict continued the more it dawned on many Christians that the faith was itself endangered by submission to the imperial régime. The first Christians to perceive that the Gospel must be a perpetual challenge even to an empire of a Christian stamp were minority groups, if they were not suppressed. Thus in Africa we find the Donatist church standing its ground against the state. Under Donatus' commanding leadership the schismatics strengthened their positions in Numidia and Mauretania, building more and more churches in the towns and villages and installing numerous bishops. After Constantine's death the African provinces fell initially within the dominions ruled by Constans, who sent out commissioners to compel the Donatists to return to the Catholic Church. A Donatist bishop, irked at this coercion by the State, invoked the aid of the Circumcellions, rebellious peasants, and the whole region – in which the native population was oppressed by the ruling Roman proprietors – was soon swept by serious religious and social revolt. The Circumcellions became the radical wing of the Donatists, and the shock-troops they formed often proceeded against Catholics with great savagery. The Donatist ranks included both religious fanatics, who rushed into death in order to become martyrs, and social rebels, who placed themselves at the head of undisciplined mobs to drive out Roman proprietors and compel hated slave-owners to perform servile tasks. The intervention of government troops to quell the rising resulted in blood-shed so that the Donatists could claim with more justice than ever that theirs was the martyr-church. The schismatics were not to be won back, whether by the emperors and their provincial governors or by episcopal synods. Despite a strenuous campaign by Catholic theologians, and despite all the suffering they later had to endure when the heresy laws were used against them, the Donatists kept their Church in being for a full century – a first indication that even within the empire there were limits to the power of Christian emperors and the authority of the Church universal.

In a very much wider setting, the Arian controversy also developed into a trial of strength between emperor and Church. The formula of belief devised at Nicaea, which asserted the Son equal in essence with the Father, had left many questions open; responsibility for their resolution now lay with the schools of theology and the synods. All the philosophical ardour of the East was once again kindled into flame. Whilst Athanasius and his following passionately defended the Nicene theology, other eastern bishops, coming to grips with the problem of giving exact theological definition to the Trinitarian mystery of the generation of the Son through the Father, advanced theses of a markedly divergent tenor; indeed in the East, opposition to the Nicene formula was for a couple of decades predominant. This period saw the formation of major parties within the Church, and above all the invasion of theological controversy by the ambitious strivings of bishops bent on acting as princes of the Church. There is no doubt, too, that the ordinary laity were aroused: reports of everyday conversation among craftsmen and moneylenders show that they had the latest officially approved formulas at the end of their tongues. In course of time, moreover, the theological groupings were to some extent shaped by regional and national influences. In the midst of these many and various currents, the emperor Constantius set his course towards unity by means of dubious political manoeuvres. His personal preference lay in the theological direction closest to Arianism and most strongly represented in the East, that is to say in the part of the empire which originally fell to his share. Where the state professed Arianism, of whatever shade, it was apparently easier for it to intervene in the ecclesiastical sphere, since Arianism cast doubts on the divine origin of the Church; one may suspect that Constantius, and Valens after him, favoured the Arians because they were easier for the government to handle. Constantius played one theological group off against another without scruple, he subdued synods by force or flattery, and made bishops conform to his will; yet for all his efforts, there was still no concord.

Since we are here concerned with the fate of ancient civilization, the vicissitudes of this conflict, which occupied the entire fourth century, are of less importance than the general trends, which were quite fundamental in their bearing since they affected the relationship between emperor and Church and the whole shape of ecclesiastical policy in the future. What first springs to notice is the gulf which started to open between the eastern and the western Church. Initially, it is true, this division arose from the rivalry between two brothers who for ten years ruled the empire between them: Constantius, who was emperor of the East and inclined to Arianism, and Constans, ruler of the western provinces, who championed Nicene theology. Yet tension between East and West continued into the period when Constantius was sole ruler. The Nicene confession found its most zealous defenders among bishops of the western provinces, above all the bishops of Rome: even at this date, western theologians were becoming cut off from the philosophical speculations of the Greek world, and as generations of scholars succeeded one another, penetration of the subtleties of problematic theology became harder still, since the West was losing full command of the Greek language. The western churches were fortified in their beliefs through contact with Athanasius, who endured exile no less than five times during his lengthy career as a bishop (328–73) and used his sojourn in the West to seek support from Rome, succeeding, moreover, in embroiling the western bishops as a whole still further in the dispute. For some time the person of Athanasius, or to be exact the question of his guilt, was an object of violent controversy. At an early stage the Alexandrian bishop made it clear that there were limits to imperial authority in the doctrinal field and openly declared that no-one should allow the seats of theological learning to degenerate into market-places for the bartering of wares. The tension between the eastern and western Church reached such a pitch that at the imperial synod of Sardica (343) communion was formally broken and the bishops on either side actually excommunicated one another. But even when Athanasius was temporarily restored to his see (346), the conflict still continued. After Constantius assumed rule over the whole empire (350), he tried to exact a condemnation of Athanasius from the western bishops and to move them towards the eastern theological position. Constantius' presence at the synods of Arles (353) and Milan (355) turned the scales in his favour, but even so several bishops remained steadfast and went into exile. It was shortly after this that bishop Hosius, now full of years, informed the emperor in no uncertain terms of the limits to his ecclesiastical authority: 'Do not meddle with church affairs, give us no orders about these matters but be instructed in them by us. God has placed imperial power in your hand, the Church he has entrusted to us. Just as anyone who seeks to deprive you of your dominion by stealth runs counter to what is ordained by God, so must you be afraid of incurring the guilt of a serious sin if you arrogate church affairs to yourself.'[5] This clear-cut position continued to have sturdy champions in the West, even after bishop Liberius of Rome ended two years of exile by condemning Athanasius, and Hosius after lengthy brainwashing at the court subscribed to a formula which met the East halfway. But although Constantius summoned frequent synods in both East and West, he still failed to achieve harmony among the bishops. In fact towards the end of his reign Arian theology apparently underwent some extraordinary fluctuations. Formulations of dogma appeared which were clearly somewhat removed from Arius' own position, to be followed first by a thesis, further from Nicaea than ever, which defined the Son as being totally different from the Father (*an-homoios*), and then by a doctrine which defined the Son as similar in essence with the Father (*homoios*), representing a partial return to Nicene theology. In the period which followed, this formula, which satisfied the emperor and was ratified by the synod held at Constantinople in 360, became the official Arian creed. It is true that fresh differences emerged during the reign of the emperor Julian and again under Valens, but in the end even the East showed a growing tendency to draw closer to Nicene theology, which now received powerful reinforcement from the philosophical teaching of eminent Cappadocian bishops, above all Basil of Caesarea. Moreover, once Athanasius was finally permitted to return to Alexandria even he pressed for agreement between East and West. The more the emperors withdrew from the scene, the brighter seemed the prospect for doctrinal unity. However, as we shall see, the feat of reaching a unity binding on the whole empire was reserved for the emperor Theodosius, under whom the full bearing of political direction as a determinant in matters of faith once again stood revealed. Throughout this long and passionate battle of the theologians, the danger always inherent in the emperor's intervention in church affairs had thus showed itself in many ways. In all the confusion of these decades, the consistent conduct of Athanasius, whether he was at work among his flock or living in exile (in which he spent 17 years) calls for admiration. The Church's demand for freedom in shaping doctrine is heard more often in the West than in the East. The western fathers present at the council of Sardica made their resistance to imperial government of the Church clear in the letter they addressed to Constantius: 'There is but one way to bring order to what is confused and to bind up what is broken: namely, that everyone, freed from all fear of enslavement, has complete liberty of decision in the conduct of his affairs.'[6] A handful of exiled western bishops carried on the campaign against imperial coercion through polemical writings. Clearly, these champions of freedom owed their deep insight into the situation of the Church to the emperor's suppression of orthodox belief and their personal experience of banishment. Hilary of Pictavium (Poitiers), in his polemic against Constantius (359), pinpoints the new danger: there are persecutions of the faith but no martyrdoms. The bygone battles, in which a Nero or a Decius was the enemy, are contrasted with the present struggle, waged against a dissembling persecutor, a flattering foe who dispenses money and issues invitations to the palace, who builds up churches but dismantles the faith. Constantius is branded as a tyrant – but his tyranny is over things not of earth but of heaven. Lucifer of Calaris (Cagliari), who wrote five polemics against Constantius, is still more explicit, unmasking a ruler who, he says, seeks to justify his policy as pleasing to God by invoking a shortsighted wholly unchristian argument: if I were in error, then God must long since have venged himself on me; the fact that I am in possession of the imperial rule and remain unscathed by illness is already proof enough that I am pleasing to God! This facile conclusion received the reprimand it deserved in Lucifer's treatise entitled *On the Schismatic Kings*. Lucifer's views were so extreme that he and his followers felt obliged to dissociate themselves from bishops whose inclinations were always on the side of compromise.

The arguments advanced by Hilary and Lucifer struck a blow at the roots of ecclesiastical policy as conducted since the time of Constantine. But these were in the nature of lightning revelations descending on individual protagonists, who had suffered much themselves. For the Church as a whole there was no question of returning to the age of martyrs; on the contrary, from now on the Christian empire found its justification in a new type of political theology, while the Christian Church, in an age which could conceive of no separation between Church and State, kept its place as part of the God-given political order. Adoration of the emperor, as though of a divine phenomenon, ceased; homage was now paid to the chosen of the Lord. In imitation of earlier motifs, portrait coins of Constantius show him with his gaze turned towards heaven, or with a disembodied hand emerging from a cloud to place the diadem on his head, an overt assertion that the emperor was the immediate vessel of divine grace, of that charisma which, for Christians as for others, set him apart as holy. It is thus not surprising that veneration was paid to images of the emperor even under the Christian empire, often, indeed, in a form which differed scarcely at all from the worship of a cult-image. Court ceremonial retained its sacral character, which was so pervasive and powerful that it could even influence the Christian liturgy. Just as the emperor was adored in his palace, so should the God who bestowed his grace on the emperor receive highest honour in a house of palatial splendour and in forms borrowed from ceremonial. In structure the Church remained a hierarchical community, mediating salvation to man, adapting for its own needs yet more institutions and methods of procedure taken from the state. As before, the urban episcopal sees which had been grafted onto the ancient city-constitution remained the cells of Christian life; it was only in the East that a few rural bishops or *chorepiscopi* were created in addition. While synods met by provinces, the oecumenical councils were co-extensive with the empire, and in their case the emperor claimed the right to summon them and publish their conclusions, even if he was unable to preside, neither in person nor even through his deputies. During the fourth century the bishop of Rome acquired heightened prestige in the eyes of the Church as a whole. He was frequently referred to as head of the Roman world and the synod of Sardica, in its deliberations over the rift within the Church, recognized his tribunal as decisive. The Roman see was thus accorded a supreme authority not, indeed, as a disciplinary power, but in questions of doctrine. All the same, the emperor was still in his own fashion a rival in this field, and it was not long before the bishop of Constantinople began to claim a place only immediately below, or even equal, to that of Rome.

Dependence on the emperor was all the more tolerable for the Christian world in that both Church and clergy now occupied a superior position in Roman society. Constantine had already granted the bishops a share in judicial powers; by imperial decree they were now personally exempted from the jurisdiction of the secular courts in all suits affecting the Church. They ranked among the senior officials of the empire and often conducted their business after the manner of Roman magistrates. The clergy, who formed a hierarchy of several grades, retained their immunity from municipal burdens and had still further privileges heaped upon them by Constantius. It is not surprising that the clerical order was gaining substantially in prestige and attraction. Whereas in the old days slaves had been admitted to orders without question, now they were accepted only if their masters freed them at the time of ordination. There was a growing number of clerical recruits from the higher classes, men who were often attracted into orders by the concomitant privileges, above all the freedom from curial burdens; in consequence, it was soon necessary to promulgate imperial legislation in an effort to check this type of evasion. It became the norm for clergy in major orders to refrain from earning a living in secular occupations. But while the clergy now held an eminent and secure position, the interesting fact remains that the celibacy of the priesthood was insisted upon with increasing rigour. In the East it was considered sufficient to prohibit clerics from marrying after ordination; but in the West they were required to observe complete sexual abstinence even in marriage. This celibate régime smacks unmistakeably of biblical asceticism. All the same, reports are not wanting that some prosperous clerics in towns, more particularly at Rome, led fully sensual, not to say degenerate, lives. The day was not far off when Jerome would feel constrained to remark that the Church had indeed grown richer and stronger, but weaker in well-doing.

Rich the churches were indeed becoming, as the offerings of the faithful were swelled by imperial benefactions, of land, plate and ornaments. The legalisation of bequests and legacies under Constantine led to so much exploitation that even fourth century emperors found it necessary to legislate against clerical legacy-hunters. Further visible proof of the churches' growing prosperity was provided by the bishop's palace, now frequently to be found side by side with his church. Yet despite these many deviations in practice, the Christian attitude towards material possessions was still governed by the evangelical precepts of charity and contempt for wealth. Lending money with usury was forbidden. Thus it is not surprising that, for all their wealth, the churches gave little impetus to fresh productivity in the economic field; instead, their funds were lavishly deployed in levelling out crass discrepancies in the resources of private citizens. As in the earliest days of Christian communities, the vastly more powerful churches of the post-Constantian era obeyed the command to relieve poverty and distress, to visit the sick, to care for the fatherless and set the captives free. Christian love still took charity to all men as its standard – in marked contrast with the Graeco-Roman world in which the obligation was restricted to a closed circle of friends and relations. The wealth of the churches and the social prestige of the clerical hierarchy meant that Christian *caritas* could now operate in a more permanent framework. Lodgings for strangers were built as annexes to bishops' houses, following a custom prevalent in the eastern churches. Hospitals, a novelty in the ancient world and another eastern innovation, now sprang up all over the Christian world. While the late Roman state was creating enormous wealth for the upper crust and a degrading poverty among the masses, the Church was shouldering the task of relieving misery wherever it was found. Whether the Church could also succeed in changing men's hearts was another matter.

Two trends converged to make the task of bringing the gospel home more difficult: the Church's involvement with political authority and the abrupt rise in church-membership which took place in the fourth century. Once the emperor was converted, his subjects took to the new faith in large numbers, especially in the cities of the east. With so many flocking into the Church, there was inevitably some relaxation in the conditions imposed on candidates for the new religion. Full membership of the community entailed baptism, and although the long-established practice of infant baptism continued, adult baptism retained all its former importance, with the course of doctrinal instruction, the catechumenate, made less rigorous. Penitential discipline, once so stringent, was also becoming less exacting. For example, the council of Elvira, which met even before the victory of Constantine, issued a tariff of penances which on some points was more indulgent towards sinners, even those who occasionally took part in pagan sacrifices, than would earlier have been conceivable. There can be no doubt that many called themselves Christians without having undergone inward conversion. The Church was faced with the immense task of preserving the essential content of the faith and bringing its moral obligations home to the mass of church-members. The task was all the more complex in that, through its alliance with the State, the Church was wholly committed to the existing social structure. The pressure of the pagan past thus made itself felt from two directions: the State to a large extent determined the public image of the Church, and the mass of believers, only partially converted, brought into the Church a wealth of inherited notions and practices. In the fourth century, therefore, the interior life of the churches was flowing in channels which point towards a growing involvement of Christian communities in the world of antiquity.

This whole process has often been stigmatized as a paganization of Christianity, or indeed as a retrogression to a more archaic stage of religion, a formal betrayal of the primitive Church of the New Testament. The Church was certainly set on a perilous course, but it was one which every religion must take to work its passage in the world. No religious community can subsist on purely subjective piety, and no Christian Church could refrain from realizing its creed of God incarnate through accepting the task of transforming the world. If the Christian community was to be a reality, it was necessary to have at least some degree of ritual, to fashion holy places, to create images and symbols and to accept the duty of bringing Christian standards to bear on public life. Primitive Christianity had already drawn on Judaism and paganism; it had, for example, made use of Jewish and pagan terminology, primarily to express the significance of revelation and grace in human existence. This drastic alteration in the application of words led in turn to a transformation in human thinking. From the time of the apostles Christians were disputing with the Synagogue and with paganism nothing less than possession of the world, always with the implied hazard that whatever was annexed would be thoroughly Christianized. At first, as we have seen, this process led to the formation of organized churches, to apologetic and the development of Christian theology. But it had now reached a crucial phase; alliance with the state had brought in its train the great temptation to surrender to the profane, while the influx of a host of new converts entailed the assimilation of pagan cult-forms. This turn of events can only be described as paganization if one ignores its connection with the heart of the Christian message. Ancient polytheism had given ample scope for the expression of much that is eternally human in every religion. The notion that divinity is present through symbols in the here and now, that through objects and actions it may work on the sense and heart of man, is neither pagan nor Christian but human. Every religion has its conception of how the divine can be addressed through prayer and sacrifice; equally natural is for the petitioner to seek a mediator between himself and the Godhead. In shaping its divine worship and in its forms of popular piety, the Christian Church thus drew heavily on the ancient heritage. Christianity's incursion into the world was indeed a ceaseless process, in which the fourth century has a special significance chiefly as a period of spectacular development and greatly expanded influence. If the modern observer feels inclined to invoke the memory of the primitive Church, he must bear in mind that our evidence for the post-Constantine era is much fuller than for those pristine days: and the more men talk, the more they betray their human nature.

As already mentioned, from the beginning of the third century, principally in the East, the simple meeting-house was being supplemented for purposes of worship by specifically sacred edifices. The vast new structures erected for urban congregations by Constantine, and in lesser numbers by Constantius, show a preference for the basilical plan, which has the effect of transforming the liturgical space into the sacred audience-chamber of God – one senses the Church rejoicing in its vitality, triumphant over all persecutors. At the same time it was entirely consistent with Christian doctrine that the altar, at which the sacrifice was offered, should occupy the central position. In the Latin church it became customary for the celebrating priest to face the people, thus uniting the crowd thronging the great hall with the liturgical event taking place at the altar. Sculpture and painting are also a reflection of the human emotions of the age. Although the council of Elvira had ruled that normally there should be no pictures on church walls, it soon became usual to permit mosaic portraits of Christ, the apostles, martyrs and the Virgin. The spirit of the Constantinian era is again manifest in the sculptor's preference for portraying Christ as victor, and in men's interpretation of the cross as the symbol of victory.

Within these richly decorated interiors divine service became an orderly progression of sacred events. The institution of Sunday and of a calendar of feasts laid the basis of a permanent liturgical framework. With Sunday as a holy day, the weekly cycle of public life acquired a Christian stamp. The Christian calendar first took shape round the festal seasons of Easter and Pentecost, although Easter was celebrated at different times in the various provinces of the Church, as it still is in the Latin and Greek churches of today. The fourth century saw the introduction of the Christmas cycle of festivals. In the Greek East a feast in celebration of the Epiphany or manifestation of the Lord was already being observed in the third century; the chosen date, January 6, was a day on which pagan ceremonies had formerly started in Egypt. This festival was now joined by another in honour of Christ's birthday (*Natalis Domini*), which at Rome was celebrated on 25 December as early as the reign of Constantine – clear indication that the Sun-god (*Sol Invictus*), whose birthday had hitherto been honoured on this day, was now to give way to the Sun of Justice (*Sol Iustitiae*), the Sun of Salvation (*Sol Salutis*). These festivals make the fact of redemption a present reality; in addition, days commemorating the saints and festivals in honour of the Lord's mother were established. Athanasius refers to Mary, long venerated as the unsullied Virgin, as *Theotokos*, Mother of God, and it was probably in the fourth century that the pious theory of her bodily incorruption and corporeal ascent into heaven first gained currency. Celebrations in her honour were held to mark the day on which she brought the child Jesus to the temple forty days after his birth, that is to say 2 February (Candlemas). Although the churches might differ from one another in their detailed observance of the calendar, and commemorative days retained a local flavour, the main outline was by now established. Little by little the rites to be observed in conducting the regular services also took definite shape. The eucharist was celebrated everywhere as a sacrifice, linked with the communal love-feast; from the end of the century this central core of Christian worship is given the name *Missa*. In form the liturgy was undeniably influenced by court ceremonial and by the arcane rites of the mystery religions: lights were kindled, incense offered, holy water sprinkled. Some habits which developed opened up the dangerous possibility that worship would degenerate into a ritual action reserved for the clergy, as for example when priests, even when they were not themselves celebrating, were assigned places in the apse, an elevated structure separating them from the people. From sermons of the fourth and fifth century we learn of the great difficulty felt by many pastors in making every service what it should be,a momentary participation in the fellowship of saints.

Veneration of the saints now became an important feature of Christian worship. Early Christians had already made it their practice to invoke intercession of the dead, to visit their tombs and commemorate the anniversaries of their deaths; the cult of martyrs is attested from the second century. Martyrs were now credited with wonder-working powers and raised to the status of tutelary patrons, whether of individuals or entire cities; their veneration contains such a substantial folk element that in many ways they seem to be regarded as successors to the ancient heroes. Attempts have actually been made to identify individual saints with specific gods and heroes of the past; whatever doubts may be felt on this score, there were certainly places where Christian saints drove out pagan deities and heroes. Vivid narrations of missionaries at work among rural populations, destroying images, sacred trees and other holy places, and building altars and churches in their stead, are common enough. Against this background it is understandable that many features of the old, defeated religion, should have been carried over into the new. The great wealth of literature written in honour of the saints – acts, legends, lives – also contains much that was derived from ancient tales of myth and magic. A further link with the ideas and practices of pagan antiquity is to be seen in the veneration paid to relics of saints. From very early times Christians had eschewed cremation and buried their dead in the earth, out of regard for the promised resurrection of the body. It was not long before the idea arose that touching the corpse or parts of the corpse – if performed with deliberate intent – brought the true believer into communion with the mighty dead. This was the motive which prompted the Christians of Carthage to collect the blood spilled at Cyprian's beheading. The fourth century saw a wide dissemination of the belief that the corpses of martyrs could work miracles and that this power could be released by direct contact. Memorials were erected over the graves of martyrs, which were usually on the outskirts of towns whereas churches serving congregations were in the residential quarters. Soon it became customary for churches lacking local associations with a martyrdom to acquire relics for keeping beneath the altar. It is true that the cult was made the occasion for continual reminders to the faithful of their duty to pray and to emulate the saint's edifying example. But among the mass of the population the cult of relics inevitably held overtones of magic, especially when the clergy took to dismembering saints' bodies in order to have more portions to give away or sell. As time goes on, reports of newly discovered relics and of the translation of corpses to regions where there had been no persecutions – and hence no martyrdoms – become increasingly frequent and significant. One practice found in several places, which was clearly related to pagan ceremonies, was that of holding a feast of the dead (which often degenerated into a drunken orgy) by the side of the grave. Bishops like Ambrose and Augustine had difficulty in suppressing such aberrations.

The tree of popular Christian piety was continually putting forth new blooms. According to the precepts of the Old Testament, it was the custom of all pious Jews to make an annual pilgrimage to the house of Jahveh. In the Graeco-Roman world men were in the habit of visiting the tombs of heroes, and, above all, the temples of renowned gods of healing. Many who regained their health in the wonder-working sanctuaries of Asculepius left behind tablets acknowledging their gratitude, or ordered votive reliefs depicting their cure. The same human attachment to holy places is exemplified by the early Christians who venerated places associated with their Lord and constantly revisited martyrs' graves. Now we find the empress Helena (plate 61) praying at the holy places of Palestine and the emperor Constantine furnishing them with magnificent churches. According to a fourth century legend, Helena discovered the true cross of Christ at Golgotha. At this time pilgrimages to Palestine, the Holy Land, became a common undertaking and the sight they afforded of the holy places helped to bring home to the faithful the fact of their redemption. We know from written narratives that pilgrims from both East and West brought great zeal to their journey. The fervent also travelled over land and sea to visit the sanctuaries of wonder-working martyrs. In the Mareotis, west of Alexandria, a cult grew up around the martyr Menas, who according to legend died in Phrygia in the time of Diocletian and was later buried in his Egyptian homeland. A memorial church was erected over his grave, with a roomy *annexe* for activities connected with the cult. Since the waters of the local spring had healing properties, baths were provided for the pilgrims. Nor did visitors neglect to take home samples of the miraculous water in small phials, for the benefit of the many unable to make so long a journey. Souvenirs were manufactured, tales of wonders started to spread and the town of Menas became famous throughout the Christian world. In Christian times, as earlier, Egypt was a land distinguished both by its especial religious fervour and by its superstition, as the many Christian manuals on magic testify. But Christian names and symbols also figure in the magical incantations and amulets culled from many other regions. The transition from the sacramental use of the cross to superstitious magic was often made quite unconsciously. Many of these debased forms were tolerated by the Church, many it fought only half-heartedly.

In whatever direction we look, it becomes clear that the elevation of Christianity into the religion of the State was endangering the purity of the faith, and that the broadening of the Church to accommodate popular religion was demoting the individual conscience from its decisive role. So much that in the times of persecution was earnest and heartfelt was now masked by the human – often all too human – features of superstitious ritual. But as so often in the course of Christian history, the perils of venturing out into the world were now counterbalanced by the emergence of new forms of renunciation and spirituality. One has the impression that the ascetic trend discernible in the fourth century, which was the period when monasticism took lasting shape, was in some way a compensation for the secularizing tendencies of Constantine and his successors. Monastic ascetism sought perfection in total dissociation from the world – at first, indeed, in total dissociation from the episcopally governed Church, whose place in the Christian polity was now assured. Admittedly, in discussing the origins of Christian monasticism we shall do well to remember that abstinence from the ordinary pleasures of life was enjoined and observed in many of the higher religions. The Jewish community of Qumran on the Dead Sea, which survived until AD 68, renounced property and marriage. The philosophy of the Neo-Pythagoreans and the religion of the Manichees enjoined temperance in the use of physical possessions and in social relationships. But for Christian ascetics the supreme exemplar was the Lord himself, the Lord who watched and prayed, who renounced possessions and marriage and called his true disciples to a life of poverty. Accordingly, the first generations of Christians set a high value on sexual continence and on abstinence from flesh and wine. Isolated instances of really fanatical ascetics begin to appear from the second century, which also saw the institution of an order of virgins whose lives were devoted to prayer and service to the community. In Egypt during the Diocletianic persecution, and still more after peace had been concluded, a number of men were seized by the urge to realize their Christian discipleship by a total renunciation of the world and devotion to a life of pure meditation. Some of these may well have taken to the desert to escape persecution; others, once the persecution was over, perhaps resorted to mortification as a substitute for martyrdom. It is also conceivable that the severe impoverishment of the Egyptian population made a resolve to renounce all the good things of the world somewhat easier to carry out; indeed, many may have been driven into the life to escape taxation and military service. Nor must we neglect the possibility that resort to solitude was often a concealed protest against the growing wealth and power of the Church. But when all is said, there is no denying that this formal adoption of an ascetic mode of life and of disciplined monasticism has offered members of the Christian Church, from that day to this, a fresh road to holy living and mystical experience.

The pioneer of the solitary life (anchoritism) was an Egyptian named Antony, whose astonishing history was chronicled by Athanasius. Antony was born about 251 at Kome in Middle Egypt; one day, when he had already reached manhood, he was profoundly struck by the stark injunction to follow Christ contained in Matthew 19 xxi, which he heard read at a church service. This was probably about the year 311, a time when the persecution in Egypt had died down. Antony accordingly gave his small-holding to the poor and spent several years in solitary meditation on the scriptures. He then went off into the desert – in popular esteem the haunt of demons and therefore a place where ascetics were likely to enjoy complete isolation. However, his reputation as a man filled with the spirit soon attracted disciples, who settled near him to be instructed in the spiritual life. Eventually Antony withdrew even from his disciples and settled at a spot in Wadi Araba not far from the Red Sea and at the foot of a high mountain, which was provided with a spring, a few olive trees and a small piece of fertile ground; here he ended his days. Meanwhile, a disciple of his named Ammonius had introduced eremitical monasticism into the Nitrian desert, settling at Lake Moeris to the west of the Nile delta. Anchorites were also to be found in the neighbouring waste of Scate, under the spiritual guidance of the elder Macarius. Settlements of this eremitical type were loose associations which observed no fixed rule. Attracted to a particular spot by the presence of a distinguished senior, the hermits lived in caves or cells and devoted themselves to ascetic practices, prayer and the reading of the scriptures, often repeating lengthy passages learned by heart. Light handwork, such as weaving mats, was also permitted. Their whole way of life was governed by one main preoccupation, the salvation of souls at the constantly expected hour of judgement. The hermit's highest bliss was to wrest sanctity from the suppression of all desires, to exercise the gifts of miracle and prophecy bestowed on those possessed by the spirit, and through the grace of the spirit to influence not only visitors to his cell but through them congregations left in the world. In his *Vita Antonii* written *c.* 360 Athanasius describes how the saint overcame the world step by step, how he fought with demons and performed wonders. Although this biography may have been modelled to some extent on an ancient life of Pythagoras, the idea of perfection it holds up is identical with the interior discipline of a Christian gnostic. Athanasius' book, which had a wide circulation, was soon joined by other literature: collections of wise sayings uttered by the hermits, travellers' reports of conversations with the monks and descriptions of their way of life, all of which fired other ardent spirits to take this new road to Christian wisdom.

Settlements of monks following a communal life (coenobites) appeared in Egypt at much the same time as those of anchorites. The founder of this new form of asceticism was Pachomius; he was born in Upper Egypt, deserted from the army and received baptism. After living for a while as a hermit, at some time after 320 he gathered several monks round him for the purpose of leading a communal life; this was at Tabennisi, north of Thebes, on the east bank of the Nile. At first the community occupied a single house in which each brother had his cell, then more houses became necessary until the settlement grew into a monastic village, surrounded by an enclosure. Pachomius himself laid down the rule of life for the monastery. The régime was one of poverty and asceticism coupled with unconditional obedience to the direction of the spiritual father (abbas), and all monks contributed according to their capacities to the support of the community, as labourers in the fields, cooks, bakers, gardeners, basket-makers, scribes or readers. The day was punctuated by periods of communal prayer, meals were taken in small groups; the Sunday services were held in the church, usually with outside priests as celebrants. This form of monasticism spread extensively in Egypt and from the beginning included foundations for women. Towards the end of the fourth century Shenoute of Atribe in the Thebaid introduced yet another type of monasticism, with more stringent discipline. For some time the Egyptian ascetic communities not only stood right outside the municipal framework but also held aloof from the episcopal churches; indeed, in the doctrinal disputes they not infrequently followed a fiercely independent line. Later, however, there was a general move to bring the monasteries into lasting association with the bishops and theologians. Many Church Fathers exalted coenobitic monasticism as a kind of re-entry into man's primeval state, a community of saints for whom the institutions of civic life were superfluous.

This view of the ascetic community is found particularly in Syria and Asia Minor, at a time when these regions also had their settlements of anchorites and coenobites. The creative drive of Egyptian monasticism had made rapid headway from its base in the lands of the Nile, finding its first emulators in Palestine and Syria. Hilarion, a disciple of Antony, gathered anchorites around him at Gaza; Epiphanius, after directing a monastery in Palestine, introduced the eremitical life into Cyprus. By the end of the fourth century all the holy places of Palestine had both their hermits and their monasteries. At a very early date there were hermits in the neighbourhood of Edessa; the ascetics who inhabited the wilderness of Chalcis in northern Syria practised extreme forms of mortification, as was customary in Syria as a whole. A unique example is provided by the pillar-saints of the succeeding period: they spent years at a time on a broad platform at the top of a tall pillar, poised between heaven and earth, between life and death, given over to prayer and contemplation, the favoured of the Lord dispensing counsel and blessing to the men in quest of help who camped at the base of their column.

The spread of monasticism into Asia Minor was confined to particular regions. Yet in the hands of one outstanding figure the monastic ideal was here so carefully modulated and spiritualized that it attained permanent and lasting significance, as a means whereby Christians could follow a life of philosophy. Basil was born about 329 at Caesarea in Cappadocia; he studied at Constantinople and Athens and was baptized in 357. His work as a Christian philosopher took him to monastic centres in Egypt, Palestine, Syria and Mesopotamia, after which he settled as a hermit on his family property on the banks of the Iris, among the mountains of Pontus; here he persuaded his friend Gregory of Nazianzus to join him. Having been ordained to the priesthood, in 370 Basil became bishop of Caesarea and as such metropolitan of Cappadocia. Thoroughly acquainted with all forms of asceticism and an experienced bishop, he was also, together with Gregory of Nazianzus and his own brother, Gregory of Nyssa, the author of doctrinal writings and homilies; the theology they developed, in line with the tradition of Origen, lent a new authority to the fruitful relationship between hellenic philosophy and Christianity. This great scholar accepted Pachomius' rule as the most suitable for monastic life, but he was careful to keep his own monastery down to manageable size. In several of his writings, in particular his first and second Rules, he sets out the rights and duties of a monastic superior in the form of question and answer. Provision is made for the reception of disciples, the novitiate, and for the profession of vows; the form of life commended is one of smoothness and order, in which asceticism mingles with manual labour and bible-reading with instruction. Children might also be admitted to the monastery, which entailed the institution of a monastic school. In drawing up his plan, Basil was aiming at a higher form of monasticism; the object was not to produce prodigies of asceticism but to discipline the monk intellectually so that he reached the spiritual state Clement of Alexandria had already projected as man's ideal. It was decisive for the transmission of ancient civilization that Basil also laid down, in his *Letter to youth on the use of Hellenic literature*, directions for secular schools which permitted classical culture to survive as an active influence into the Christian era. While holding to his conviction that a child's religious upbringing is the affair of the family, and preparation for baptism a matter for the priest, Basil considers it proper for classical literature to be read and studied in schools, which were still attended by pagans as well as Christians. He believes that the conflict between the pagan culture of the classical authors and the teaching of the gospel may be resolved if hellenic literature is interpreted as a preliminary stage in Christian education. He thinks it essential that a selection should be made of texts with an important bearing on moral education, arguing that a man who plucks a rose must take heed to the thorns. In taking this intellectual stand, Basil thus acknowledges that the pagans can also be witnesses to what is good. This declaration, the 'Magna Carta of all Christian higher education for the centuries which follow' (W. Jaeger) was taken up and given fuller expression by Basil's friend, Gregory of Nazianzus; but it was his brother, Gregory of Nyssa, who did most to refine this ideal of life. Fired with the spirit of Plato, he made it his life's endeavour to bring Christian man to God through philosophy, and to transplant the Greek ideal, which saw education as the moulding of men (*paideia*), to the soil of the monastery.

The invention and development of monasticism is the last spiritual and intellectual achievement of the Greek east to fall within the confines of this book. The theology of the Greek Fathers, a dazzling exercise in Christian hellenism, and the contribution of late pagan philosophy and literature in the East, both belong to the culture of Byzantium. But monasticism must be given its due, if the history of the Roman West, and above all of the disintegration of the ancient order and the emergence of a new western culture, is to be properly understood: for the pollen of the monastic ideal, both eremitical and coenobitical, was carried westwards, to become an essential agent in the metamorphosis of ancient civilization. The West perhaps first learned of the monastic life from Athanasius, when he visited Rome some time after 339, on his way to banishment in Trier. At all events, it was around the year 350 that the first stirrings of the ascetic impulse made an appearance among the noble families of Rome. Shortly after 373, another exile arrived in Rome, Petrus, who was Athanasius' successor. It was perhaps the influence of these Alexandrians which prompted the elder Melania, a lady of high birth, to adopt the ascetic life and found a monastery in Palestine. Next, we find two learned theologians, Jerome and Rufinus, seeking out the hermits of the East and undertaking the spiritual direction of monasteries at Bethlehem and Jerusalem. The *Vita Antonii*, translated into Latin about 380, made a profound impact on the West. Soon after this date there were hermits at Trier and a monastery at Milan, under the direction of Bishop Ambrose. Even before this, however, Martin had already embarked on his remarkable career in Gaul. Brought up to be a soldier, he turned to Christianity and was baptized, abandoning his calling. Around the year 360 he was living as a hermit in a cell near Poitiers, where he attracted a number of disciples; this spot later became the site of the monastery of Ligugé. Elected bishop of Tours, he spent the rest of his life (he died in 397) travelling up and down the region preaching and performing miracles, converting the peasantry and appointing priests to serve the countryside. During this period he also made prolonged visits to disciples settled in a hermitage on the Loire, the nucleus of the monastery of Marmoutier. All in all, his life was an egregious example of an asceticism which could also embrace the cure of souls.

The monastic movement in the West had its radical wing, which soon came into serious conflict with the Church and the government. Priscillian, who attracted a following in Spain by his asceticism, carried the demand for abstinence to extremes. Starting from a position of gnostic dualism, he made the sharpest possible antithesis between body and spirit; he condemned marriage, took up the cudgels against the institutionalized Church and by his aggressive demeanour secured a large body of adherents in Spain, becoming bishop of Avila. But he was soon confronted by some powerful opposition, both pagan and Christian. He was excommunicated by a synod held at Burdigala and found guilty of magical practices by a secular tribunal. In 385 he was executed, along with some of his followers – the first men to suffer capital punishment on a charge of heresy. This was an extreme case, but monasticism and asceticism were not without their fierce opponents in other parts of the West. Nevertheless, the example of the great figures of Latin monasticism was powerful enough to over-ride all such objections and derogations: men could point to Martin himself, whose life written by Sulpicius Severus was a source of great edification to his contemporaries; Jerome, whose learning bore rich fruit in the western Church and its theology; Paulinus, the Gallic nobleman who left his individual stamp on the monastic ideal. It was not long before new communities of ascetics began to flourish along the coasts of Provence, to become hot-houses for training up priests and bishops. The lonely off-shore islands provided monastic life with a setting comparable with the desert. About 400 Honoratus founded a monastery on the island of Lérins, opposite Cannes, and neighbouring islands were populated soon after. About this time, Cassian, who was familiar with the monasteries of the East, established a community for men at the tomb of St Victor at Marseilles, and another in the same town for women. Cassian was the author of two books which were much read in western monasteries, in which he set out the wisdom he had culled from the eastern fathers and his personal prescription for the achievement of perfection. The monastic ideal he advocates is one of orderliness, as against the disorganized existence of wandering ascetics and fanatics.

The link between monasticism and learning had yet to be forged in the west; the first intimation that the connection would be made dates from the year 395, in which Augustine was elected bishop of Hippo and gathered his clergy together to live a species of communal life. But we must not anticipate. What matters here is that we should pay tribute to the importance, as a historical phenomenon, of the great upsurge of asceticism in both East and West: here was an achievement which owed nothing to the compromised State–Church and was remote indeed from the debased forms of popular religion: a lamp which illumined the gospel ideal of perfection.

3. *The pagan reaction – education, science and technology*

In his edicts and letters Constantine avers that the effect of the religious revolution of his age was to replace a plurality of deities by the one true God. Over-categorical though it may appear, this statement nevertheless touches something fundamental. For centuries the men of antiquity had lived in the belief that the world was full of gods; poets and philosophers interpreted the shapes attributed to the gods as a spiritualization of the reality perceived by the senses. Now monotheism had won the day; worship was due to one God alone, the God who created the world, redeemed man after his fall and kept a continuous control of history. Constantine, who himself experienced the benefit of this divine guidance, had led all his family and circle into the Christian faith; more important still, he had allied the Roman State with the Christian Church. But during his lifetime and after, there were still many pagans who remained true to the old gods; some, indeed, were most vehement in their opposition to the new faith. The derogatory interpretation placed on the emperor's conversion by the historian Zosimus indicates the contempt in which it was held in some quarters. Zosimus' explanation is that Constantine was smitten with guilt for having in 326 contrived the deaths of Crispus, his son by a concubine named Minervina, and Fausta his own wife, on the grounds of their suspected adultery. He yearned to expiate his guilt, but found no religion prepared to purge him of such a sin, save the God of the Christians. This version reflects to the full the disgust felt by many educated pagans for the new religion and its alleged predilection for sinners. There were others, and these were more numerous, who took up no personal position over the conversion of the emperor but quietly continued in their old observance and habit of life. In many remote rural areas of the west, where paganism was still closely bound up with primitive ideas and customs, the old religion remained totally undisturbed. And even in towns, devotees of many mystery religions continued to meet for worship, despite the decrees issued by Constantius.

As a historical phenomenon, the pagan reaction is most clearly evident in areas where belief in the gods was closely associated with the Roman State and Greek culture. As one might expect, the link between faith in the eternity of Rome and worship of the gods was at its closest in the city of Rome itself: were not honours still paid to the Capitoline deities on behalf of the State, did not emperors still assume the ancient office of Pontifex Maximus? Rome still had its buildings and monuments as witness to the piety which had once made Rome's forefathers masters of the world. The senators of the city regarded themselves as custodians of a holy heritage; their attachment to paganism became all the stronger as the emperors found themselves new seats of residence and the city of Constantinople advanced its claim to be a second Rome. Furthermore, belief in the gods was fostered not only among Roman senators but also in the major cities by the current preoccupation with classical literature and art. Higher education and literary culture, as they had been formed over many generations, grew as grafts on the creations of Homer and Virgil, worlds in which gods still abounded. Constantine himself, by assuming once again the patronage of arts and learning as an imperial duty, in contrast with the philistinism of his predecessors over the past century, gave an additional powerful stimulus to pagan culture. Even pagan chroniclers concede that the personal qualities of this ruler helped to reinstate intellectual and cultural discernment among the virtues expected of any ruler, in accordance with the old standards. In fact Constantine and also his sons surrounded themselves with philosophers and men of letters and were unsparing in grants of privilege to physicians and university professors. In Constantine's time – indeed throughout the fourth century – there was a significant upsurge of culture, signalized by a renewed appreciation of classical literature and a revived respect for eloquence as a mark of distinction in speech and writing. A man who had passed through the schools of grammar and rhetoric, where the courses were orientated towards the pagan classics, was eligible for positions of authority in public life. The study of literature was thus the preliminary to a career as advocate or in the civil service, and might lead eventually to a provincial governorship and a high position at the imperial court. Schools specializing in the training of lawyers existed only in the East, at Berytus and Constantinople; and it was only in the East that advocates were required to obtain a certificate of study from an official teacher of law before being allowed to practice. In the West, on the other hand, the bureaucracy was still open at all levels to graduates from schools of rhetoric. Even Christians, however much they might jib at the polytheism of classical literature, followed this scholastic path. We know from one or two papyri that as late as the sixth century Christian schoolboys learned their letters by copying out long lists of mythological names.

Evidence that there was still plenty of opportunity for pagans in the field of education during the period immediately after Constantine is provided by the careers of Libanius and Themistius, two renowned teachers to whom we shall return. Libanius, who came from a family long established in Syrian Antioch, first studied at Athens and then occupied chairs of rhetoric at Nicomedia and Constantinople. From 354 he was teaching with great success in his native city of Antioch, and although a pagan also enjoyed a high reputation among officials of the imperial court. Themistius, who owed his early philosophical training to his father, was in 345 appointed to a chair of philosophy at Constantinople, where his concern to give positive direction to the lives of the young men who sat at his feet brought him into competition with the rhetors. He too was a pagan; yet in 353 he was appointed to the Senate, enjoying high prestige at court and occupying an authoritative position in society; it was largely thanks to him that the intellectual camp managed to gain a foothold in the new capital.

But there were also schools of philosophy whose teaching was in declared opposition to the Christian religion, conspicuous among them the type of neo-platonism which had now come to dominate the scene and which after the death of Plotinus was quite open in its defence of polytheism. Even under Constantine, the Syrian philosopher Iamblichus was busy with numerous works in which he lauded the life of Pythagoras, expounded the Chaldean theology and discoursed on divine effigies and other features of pagan worship. Clearly his aim was to combine pagan gnosis and the wisdom of the mystery religions into a single edifice, ample enough to accommodate the whole of pagan theology from Orpheus and Pythagoras down to Plotinus and the religious experience of all peoples, Greeks, Jews, Chaldeans. Iamblichus came out in favour of ritual ceremonies and sacrifices and defended soothsaying and wonderworking. In his teaching he set out a theosophy which he envisaged as the basis of a mystery-church, a church whose initiations and rituals came close to magic. In the fourth century this sectarian form of neoplatonism became a potent influence, and in the event largely determined the fate of later paganism. For this was the school favoured by Julian, the emperor who reverted from Christianity to paganism, known to history as the Great Apostate (plate 68). Documentary evidence for his reign is supplied by his edicts, letters and numerous other writings; in addition we have the testimony of his contemporaries, for example the historian Ammianus. Julian's tragic life deserves to be studied in its entirety, as a noteworthy monument to the reactionary endeavours of an important pagan sect.

This nephew of Constantine was five years old when his uncle died and the soldiers declared for his three sons, liquidating all other male members of the line, with the exception of Julian and his step-brother Gallus. Although educated as a Christian, Julian also studied the pagan classics, finding that his heart went out to the poetry of Homer. The emperor Constantius was sufficiently distrustful of his cousins to send them away to a remote estate in Cappadocia; here Julian was made a lector in the local church and became familiar with the Old and New Testament writings. After six years spent thus in seclusion, Julian was allowed to return to civilization; he sought out teachers of grammar and rhetoric and was introduced to the philosophy of Iamblichus. Whilst Gallus fell into disgrace and was executed, Julian was allowed greater freedom of movement and was initiated into the Eleusinian mysteries. At a later stage in his career he paid copious tribute to the religious forces which had drawn him in his youth. He identifies his supreme deity as the Sun-god, whom he calls king Helios: that is to say the deity venerated by the first Constantius, founder of the dynasty, and the tutelary power acknowledged by Constantine in the early days of his reign. In Julian's creed the Sun-god, son of Zeus, assumes many shapes, for example he is Apollo and also Mithras; in addition he is the mediator between the idea of the Good and the created world – a definition which appears to be the antithesis of the Christian concept of the Logos. Julian also had a great veneration for Cybele, the great Mother of Gods, whom he describes as virgin and motherless, honouring her as the Mistress of Life who presides over the whole course of the world. Nor did he neglect all the other gods, but assigned each a place and rank, so that the old myths lived again in all their richness.

Towards the end of 355, when he was twenty-three and still immersed in his studies, Julian was raised to the rank of Caesar and sent to Gaul, where the situation was once again threatening. The Franks had just made a surprise attack on Cologne and were entrenched on the left bank of the Rhine. Julian showed surprising energy in defending the empire; in 357 he won a decisive victory over the Alamanni at Strasbourg and then applied himself with great diligence to the administration of his provinces. Later in his career he was to make frequent reference to the experiences of those years – he spent two winters in Lutetia Parisiorum – stressing how refreshing he had found the simplicity and independent bearing of the Celts and Germans, complete strangers to flattery, and what a deep impression their spontaneity had made on him. But soon he was at loggerheads with the emperor. In 359, when Constantius demanded Gallic troops for the campaign he was preparing against the Persians, a revolt broke out in the army; for it was already an almost settled rule that soldiers should remain stationed on a single front. It appears that Julian's well-wishers helped to foment the mutiny. In February 360, to avoid being sent to the East, the soldiers acclaimed their Caesar Julian as Augustus. The form of the proceedings indicates that this elevation, which took place at Paris, was an independent gesture on the part of the soldiers: since no diadem was at hand, they crowned their nominee with a golden neck-chain (a torque) and raised him on a shield in the germanic fashion – a piece of ceremonial which would henceforth have its place in emperor-making. Julian immediately entered into negotiations with Constantius, but when there seemed no prospect of success decided on war and set out with a large part of his army to march against the emperor, who was advancing from the extreme south-east of the empire. Since Julian now made public his transfer of allegiance to the old religion, the war became a campaign on behalf of paganism. It is pathetic to find him sending letters to the Roman Senate and the venerable cities of Athens, Corinth and Sparta proclaiming his kinship with the Hellenes. Educated people of this period understood hellenism as implying championship of the classics, assent to the philosophy of Iamblichus and, above all, belief in the old gods: belief in the gods had now become an integral and essential qualification for membership of the Greek world.

By a momentous dispensation of providence Constantius died on the march, having, it was said, designated his cousin his successor from his death-bed. In 361 Julian thus became sole ruler of the empire. He entered Constantinople and purged the court and administration; yet the proclamations he issued declaring his intention to rule as a philosopher, on the model of Marcus Aurelius, appeared to envisage a régime of religious neutrality. Intensive legislative activity soon followed; careful consideration also had to be given to the defence of the empire's threatened frontiers. Julian resolved to attack the Persian enemy; in the summer of 362, in preparation for his campaign, he took up residence at

Antioch, where he entered into close friendship with Libanius. Nevertheless, he still regarded the revival of paganism as his first charge. In 361 he had already issued an edict proclaiming freedom of worship for all religions, which thus marked a return to the programme projected at Milan in 313. The practice of the Christian religion was not forbidden; but just as Constantine had favoured Christianity, so did Julian now favour pagans. Neo-platonist philosophers and pagan priests gained predominance at court, pagans were preferred for all appointments to high office, temple-building was actively encouraged and Christian congregations were made to surrender confiscated pagan property. The friction created by such actions was greatly intensified when the bishops exiled by Constantius were recalled, to add fuel to the flames of internal dissension among the Christians. It soon became clear that what was in progress was not merely the legislation of pagan worship but also a thorough-going resuscitation of pagan belief. The imperial litterateur became a religious zealot; Julian had no hesitation in performing animal sacrifices in person as pontifex and was vigilant in the defence of pagan orthodoxy, entering into lengthy controversies with philosophers who expressed deviant opinions about the gods. In tune with the spirit of the age, paganism could no longer exist without dogma. For support of this claim one need only look to a text-book of theology written about this time by a certain Sallust, under the title *On the gods and the world*, which is quite simply a primer of religious instruction, a pagan catechism. The Christian Church was to have its counterpart in a pagan hierarchy, in which priests appointed to towns and high priests presiding over provinces all looked up to Julian as Pontifex Maximus; the Pontifex Maximus sent his clergy what can only be described as pastoral letters, giving instruction on matters of doctrine and morals. Prayers were prescribed for daily use and rules drawn up for fasting and sacrifices; priests were to refrain from visiting theatres and avoid reading dangerous books. This strict rule of life was to be combined with kindness and well-doing, true philanthropy. Julian enjoined charity and care for the poor, and had thoughts of establishing pagan communities for men and women on the lines of monasteries. A pagan church was on the verge of creation.

For a time the legal status of Christianity was unaffected. Admittedly, the government had ample opportunity for snubbing Christians, by singling out zealous pagans for distinction and by rewarding towns which abjured the Christian faith. These, however, were pin-pricks, and even the loss of privileges enjoyed by the Christian clergy since the time of Constantine did nothing to alter the situation as a whole. However, influenced by fanatics, Julian went further and made suppression of the Christians, whom he called Galileans, his declared goal. In a fierce polemic, whose argument can be reconstructed from the surviving counter-polemic of Cyril of Alexandria, he again brought forward the objections to Christianity formulated several generations earlier by the neo-platonist Porphyry. In this tirade, showing the customary hostility of the renegade, Julian attacks monotheism on philosophical grounds, combs the gospels for contradictions and hurls at Christians the old charges of disloyalty to tradition. He proceeded to draw his own conclusions from his sinister discoveries: men forbidden by the gospel to draw the sword must be expelled from the army, teachers with no belief in gods and myths could not be allowed to instruct the young. An edict concerning rhetors, issued in the middle of 362, decreed that Christians should no longer be allowed to teach at universities, which meant their permanent exclusion from the educated world. So harsh a measure was condemned even by Ammianus, normally well-disposed to Julian; among Christians who were already finding their own road to the classics, resentment reached unprecedented heights.

Yet Julian was still not content. He was reluctant to follow the example of the soldier-emperors who ordered Christians to sacrifice so as to condemn them; he preferred to attack the Church where it was most vulnerable, and allow it to break under its own stresses. This is also the interpretation to be placed on his plan for the rehabilitation of Israel. In his polemic Julian accused the Christians, with some justification, of having broken away from the Old Testament: from apostolic times onward, Christians had themselves been claiming to be the true Israel, and this dissociation from the Synagogue resulted in theological warfare against the Jews, as a long series of writings *adversus Iudaeos* makes plain. The pagan attitude towards the Jewish people and their religion was very different. So long as there was any danger that the Jews' belief in their destiny as the chosen people of God might lead to the establishment of a national Jewish state in Palestine, Roman policy had been one of ruthless suppression. But once the hot-bed of unrest in Palestine had been damped down, the Jews of the Diaspora enjoyed the benefit of a far-reaching toleration and in fact became privileged. Late pagan writers admittedly deny the Jews any merit in the field of high cultural achievement, but have much praise for their steadfast adherence to the laws and customs of their forefathers. As for Julian himself, although the neo-platonist frame of his theological doctrine did not allow him to recognize the Jewish god as the supreme being, he was ready to regard him as a regent for the world-god, one of those tribal deities whom prevailing philosophical teaching identified as responsible for determining the nature and origin of the different peoples. The religion of the Law, under which divine worship was secure and human life directed towards purity, he regards as exemplary, and praises the Jews for fostering a religious zeal strong enough to arm believers in the face of martyrdom. Given this emperor's high regard for Jewish acts of worship, the destruction of the temple at Jerusalem was bound to strike him as an evil act; and he accepted the restoration of this holy place to the Jews as a duty, in order that worship under the Law might be resumed. We know from remarks made by Julian and his contemporaries that the gesture was also intended as a blow to Christian apologetic, since the destruction of the temple was held to be a sign of God's vengeance against Israel. His animosity led Julian to carry his sophistical calculations one stage further, arguing that since the destruction of the temple was prophesied in the Gospel, its restoration would expose the prophesy as a lie and bring about the triumph of the Old Testament over the New. With such thoughts uppermost in his mind, any thought of winning support from Jews living in the Persian empire, especially those of Babylonia, for the war he was currently contemplating, was of only secondary importance. Early in 363 orders went out from Antioch that the temple at Jerusalem was to be rebuilt at state expense, under the supervision of a loyal servant of the emperor. Julian himself addressed a letter to the Jews, of which only one passage, quoted by a later writer, has survived; the lengthier document still extant, entitled *To the community of the Jews*, can be regarded as a forgery of the late fourth of early fifth century. While it is certain that many Jews approved the emperor's scheme, its reception among strictly orthodox Jews must remain doubtful, since in rabbinical teaching the overthrow of Rome as a world-power was to precede the restoration of Israel as a kingdom. Work started at Jerusalem, but was interrupted by an earthquake; an age prone to see the hand of the gods in such events could only interpret the calamity as a punishment from heaven. The undertaking was at an end; even the emperor abandoned his plan.

This negative outcome disillusioned the Jews, heightened the hostility of Christians and was even a cause of some disaffection among pagans. It was by now evident that Julian was not loved by the people. In the metropolitan city of Antioch, like Alexandria long famed for its anti-imperial wit, ridicule was heaped on this grim-faced unkempt priest, this straggle-beard philosopher who roamed the streets. As a literary man, Julian could retaliate in kind; in his skit *The Enemy of the Beard*, a grosser self-caricature than anything even the Antiochenes had dared, he took the opportunity to draw attention to the real benefits he had conferred on the city. Discouraged as he was, it must have been a relief for the Hellene to turn to the Persian campaign which was to lead him in the steps of Alexander towards the rising sun. This war had long been in preparation and was planned down to the last detail. The emperor marched down the Euphrates as far as the heavily defended city of

Ctesiphon, which he failed to capture. After this it was vital to make contact with the second Roman army operating on the upper Tigris, but as they marched the emperor's troops came under heavy attack from the Persian cavalry; Julian was wounded by an enemy spear and died the following night, surrounded by his friends and in a spirit of philosophical calmness.

With his death the plan for reconverting the Roman empire to paganism fell to the ground. The Christians, who had suffered much from the Apostate and his policy, were bitterly hostile to his memory. The literary campaign they conducted against him engendered the legend that Julian died confessing the religion he had opposed: it is alleged that having allowed the blood from his mortal wound to trickle into his hand, he poured it out like a libation, uttering the words 'Thou hast conquered, O Galilean'. In later centuries the portrait of this enemy of Christians underwent still further distortion. On the other hand, admirers were ardent in his defence: to Libanius, Julian was the darling of the gods, the benefactor of mankind. When Renaissance humanists and philosophers of the Enlightenment came to contemplate the character and achievement of the last of the Hellenes, they credited him with progressive ideals, even to the extent of seeing in this cantankerous individual a forerunner of toleration. To us, today, passing judgement in the course of a critical appraisal of the metamorphosis of ancient civilization, Julian appears a tragic figure. The picture which emerges from his own writings and those of contemporaries is of a man tormented by a restless temperament, by no means innocent of literary vanity, but who nevertheless followed his bent in pursuit of a high ideal. The undertaking itself, however, has all the marks of a convulsive effort at pure restoration Julian fancied he was reviving the brave old world of the classical writers and their gods; in fact what he purveyed was an imbroglio, the confection of a neo-platonist sect which had dissipated itself in notions of magic. Whatever was viable in his schemes came from the Christianity he sought to destroy. The saying 'he who persecutes imitates', often applicable to those who resist a spiritual force, seems an apt summary of Julian: the hunter bent on destruction follows in the tracks of his prey. But Julian was not representative of paganism as a whole. In the generations after him, the paganism which still lived on in the schools and had become rooted in Roman patriotism had its last opportunity for acting as a historical force.

On Julian's death the council of highest-ranking officers chose Jovian as his successor. During his brief reign, Jovian rescinded Julian's decrees against the Christians but continued to tolerate all other religions although he was a Christian. The brothers Valentinian I and Valens, who reigned from 364, also professed Christianity. Under their system of joint rule, although both rulers possessed full legislative powers, the empire was divided into an eastern and a western sphere, to ensure that all frontiers were effectively guarded and to leave no scope for usurpers. To obtain the men and money needed for the continual warfare on the Rhine, Danube and Euphrates, these two soldier-emperors, Pannonians by descent, issued laws which placed civilian life virtually on a siege-footing and outdid their predecessors in harnessing professional corporations to the State, displaying a distinct disregard for property and culture. On the religious question, at the beginning of their reign they proclaimed toleration for the various religions, and by their individual adherence to particular brands of opinion and ecclesiastical faction profoundly influenced the course of the doctrinal battle within the Church. Valens ruled initially from Constantinople, where the massive aqueduct still bears his name, but later moved his residence to Antioch, to become an overt supporter of Arianism and the stern, not to say savage, antagonist of upholders of the Nicene doctrine – and this at the very time when Nicene theology was being illumined by the triple constellation of the Cappadocian fathers. Valentinian, who ruled from Milan and Trier, remained true to the Catholic position, though without any great display of zeal. Ammianus in fact says of him that he remained neutral in the conflict between paganism and Christianity. It is certainly true that his quarrel with the Roman Senate, dominated by the pagan élite, turned not on religious differences but on privileges claimed by the ancient senatorial order. Thus after Julian's death pagans throughout the empire, and especially in the West, still enjoyed considerable freedom of action, which continued even after Gratian succeeded his father in the West in 375.

In the realm of education and culture, followers of the old religion still held a dominant position. In the East, Libanius and Themistius, the two outstanding figures who had received their appointments under Constantius, now acquired the commanding influence they were to retain for so long; their voluminous writings provide a vivid picture of paganism in its last phase. With numerous speeches and over 1,500 of his letters still extant, Libanius must be among the best-documented figures of antiquity; from this material it has been possible to reconstruct not only the circle of his friends and students but also the life of his native city, Antioch. We find the pagan Libanius diligent in wooing the gods, delivering an occasional attack on Christian beliefs yet tolerant of Christians as individuals. There were many Christians among his students, though it is doubtful whether they actually included Basil of Caesarea and John Chrysostom. Libanius continued at Antioch for three decades after Julian's death, teaching rhetoric to the young (he describes himself as a sophist in contra-distinction to the philosophers) and emerging victorious from contests with many personal rivals. He also found himself competing with educational courses of a new type, for example the law school at Berytus, the Latin school at Rome and above all the training in stenography available at Constantinople, which offered the students an easy road to a career in the profession of notarii, whether as assistants in the imperial administration or as public notaries. Oratory as taught by Libanius followed the pattern set by the great classical practitioners, above all Demosthenes: the complete orator should be at once an exemplary citizen of his city and a civilized man, the embodiment of moderation and dignity. Students flocked to Libanius in large numbers, chiefly from Syria but also from more remote provinces of the East, Thrace, Armenia, Arabia. The majority were from prosperous families and embarked on their studies about the age of fifteen, when they were often still in the care of their pedagogues. The course, which included correct speech as well as learning by heart and conversation, lasted at least three years and often extended over five. We have a graphic picture of the way Libanius conducted his classes, seated in the professorial chair, giving all his attention to the students ranged before him on benches. He also supervised their activities outside the lecture-room, steering them away from the dissipations of the big city, chariot-races, theatres and *pantomimi* and, as was proper, restraining them from places of rowdyism, drunkenness and loose women; he also took a close interest in their later progress. Many students from the school of Libanius went on to distinguish themselves in public life; if it produced no poets or scholars, it at least preserved the elements of traditional education and transmitted the ideal character of the orator with such perfection that even Christian Byzantium continued to honour Libanius as a master of Attic speech.

The school of Antioch had its rival in Themistius, professor of philosophy at Constantinople. He too remained a pagan, but was tolerant of Christians, and so tactful in his dealings with emperors that he remained in favour at court for half a century. Under Constantius, Themistius was already a favoured choice as orator on great occasions; Julian was his friend; in 348 he became city prefect of Constantinople, with the title and rank of a praefectus praetorio *honoris causa*; finally he was appointed tutor to the emperor's son Arcadius, admittedly in conjunction with a second teacher who was a Christian. From his writings and lectures Themistius emerges as a philosopher of the eclectical type, since while he paraphrases Aristotle his political theory harks back to Plato. His teaching and writing centred on the problems of politics and ethics. Themistius became a figure of historical importance on account of the long series of panegyrics, running through the reigns of Constantius, Jovian, Valentian, Valens down to Theodosius, in which he provided the monarchy with a philosophical foundation, thereby influencing emperors and forming public opinion. As official orator he was doubtless compelled to project his image of the ideal ruler by showing emperors their duties as the reflection of their alleged virtues, yet no matter who was emperor he could always trace the majestic lineaments of a monarch called to rule by divinity, whose own endeavour would make him godlike: *philanthropia*, love of men, should induce benevolence, mercy should be accounted higher than justice, philanthropy should always prove itself in well-doing, in concern for all men, should leave men free to choose their path to piety – it was in short the cardinal virtue which should inform all the activity of a ruler. This guiding image of the humane emperor, which originated in Greek philosophy, was an example Christian rulers could aspire to follow; the political ethics of antiquity could be reconciled with Christian moral teaching.

The western part of the empire also had its state-universities, Rome, Carthage and Milan. The imperial government was constantly making regulations for the conduct of student life. From a law of Valentinian I we learn that students coming to Rome must have authorization from the governor of their province, that students must notify the authorities of their address in the city, that students must not join societies in the town and that a record had to be kept of their qualifications. A particularly vivid picture of student life as it was at Burdigala (Bordeaux) in the second half of the fourth century can be built up from the literary works of Ausonius, who was appointed to teach grammar there in 334, shortly afterwards becoming professor of rhetoric. Ausonius put into writing all there was to say about himself, his family, his professional activity and personal experience, and won for his poetry the admiration of the age. A native of Burdigala and the son of a doctor, Ausonius resembled most other eminent Gallic families of the day in professing Christianity, but in him Christian belief was combined with a pagan literary culture. Apollo and the Muses were closer to him than the martyrs, the classics more familiar than the Bible. He thus had no qualms about basing his rhetorical teaching on the traditional pagan texts and exemplified for his pupils the same virtues as his pagan predecessors: scholarly refinement, a graceful style and an elegance which refused to be upset by the confusion of the times. Professors of rhetoric in the West also acted as spokesmen for both government and people, on the occasions when they delivered panegyrical orations whose object was make to court and public feel at one; and here, too, Ausonius had conspicuous success. Valentinian I made him tutor to his young son Gratian, in 367 raised to Augustus, and Ausonius spent eight years at the court in Trier. Shortly after Gratian succeeded his father in 375, Ausonius became praetorian prefect of the Gauls and subsequently of Italy as well; his father, son, son-in-law and nephew were also given high offices about this time, so that the entire family was enrolled in the senatorial nobility of Gaul. Ausonius spent several years occupied in his administrative duties and in assisting the emperor with legislation; as he tells us himself, the ceremonious trappings of his high rank – the purple mantle reaching to the knees, the four-horse chariot – were by no means wasted. Eventually he went back to teaching at Burdigala in his beloved Aquitaine, taking up residence on his own estate, where he continued to enjoy the convivial life of a country gentleman until his death (about 394).

Ausonius' life thus embraced all that good fortune could hold for a cultivated man of letters, and the style of his letters and writings is just what one would expect, urbane, scholarly, untroubled by any grave problems. His speeches and letters follow the traditional pattern, his verses extol the love of literature and the intimacies of family life and friendship. Ausonius drew poetic likenesses of his forebears both male and female, and commemorated his deceased professional colleagues at Burdigala in a series of literary portraits. He could also turn his hand to elegiac inscriptions for the heroes of Troy, write verses eulogizing the great cities of the empire, and make the events of his own daily life, filled with the affairs and pleasures of a man of consequence, the theme of an epic cycle. He is exquisite in his praises of Bissula, an Alamannic girl captured in some foray and sent to him as a gift; above all he waxes lyrical over the Moselle, the beautiful river of fish and fishermen, whose banks were adorned with vines and buildings. As poet and teacher, Ausonius stands for a culture of minimal commitment. The cares of empire, the movements of alien peoples, the religious struggles of the age – none of these find a place in his poetry. In old age he was deeply distressed when his correspondence with a younger friend brought home to him the serious and uncompromising character of Christian asceticism; we shall find the same experience occurred in the Christianisation of the educated classes.

It is now time to turn our attention to Rome, at this period the centre of pagan cultural life. Rome, with its temples and victory memorials, must surely have been a potent reminder of the illustrious past, an awesome witness to the eternal mission of Rome and the Roman people. Ammianus tells us that the sight of its marvels impressed even the emperor Constantius, when he visited the city in 356. Rome provided the setting for the most aristocratic senatorial families, whose off-spring were indoctrinated with ancient Roman beliefs and patriotic ideals from their earliest years, first at home and later in their schools. Admittedly, a few noble houses had already adopted Christianity. The initiative was usually taken by women of the family; there is some evidence, from church building at Rome in the fourth century, that individual noble houses played a part in the growth of Christian congregations. But the most distinguished lines continued in the fashion of their ancestors to venerate the gods who had made Rome great and to fill the offices of the Roman priesthood. Their whole ambition was concentrated on the Republican magistracies which would take them from the quaestorship, by way of the praetorship, to the summit of the consulship, to which was now added the city prefecture, the office which controlled the whole government of the city now that the emperors had their residence elsewhere. The outlay entailed by service in the older magistracies was enormous, since praetors and consuls were expected to provide lavish public games at their own expense. But anyone who became consul went down in history, for he gave his name to the year, during which he 'enjoyed the undisturbed contemplation of his own dignity' (Gibbon). These senatorial houses had accumulated great wealth; they possessed palaces within Rome itself and also landed properties in Italy and in many provinces of the empire. The imperial régime, which had deprived the Roman Senate of its political power, allowed the senators many privileges and demanded little of them in return by way of active participation in the cares of government. The Roman nobleman was still left free to shape his life as he wished. Numerous honorific inscriptions and documents relating to eminent personalities have come down to us from this period: their offices are enumerated and their civic virtues praised – virtues such as wisdom, rectitude, and above all a command of oratory. Not a few senators were initiated into the mysteries of the oriental religions and afterwards placed votive inscriptions in the shrine of the Mother of Gods, close to the Vatican. From these texts we learn that they had submitted to the taurobolium, the ritual sprinkling with the blood of a sacrificial bull which led to their rebirth in the congregation of Attis. It is often mentioned that the initiate came to hold several priesthoods in the cult, probably an indication that there were more places vacant than aspirants to fill them. But inscriptions testifying to this religious zeal are also to be found in the sanctuary of the Magna Mater at Ostia, where prominent Romans were still building noble mansions for themselves.

In these inscriptions, as in numerous literary works, we encounter many individuals who belonged to the Roman aristocratic society of the day and can thus discover their family connections and circles of acquaintance. Only a few can be mentioned here. Vettius Agorius Praetextatus, city prefect 367–8, was a man held in high esteem who also enjoyed a reputation as a philosopher. On his tomb-inscription he mentions his priesthoods before his official positions; he and his wife Paulina had sought initiation into several Greek mysteries. This funerary monument is one testimony among many to the important place occupied by women in aristocratic families of the late Roman empire. In inscriptions on the sides and back of the memorial Praetextatus addresses his wife in metres and Paulina answers, in a poem which is deeply personal in its feeling for her husband. Alongside this philosopher we have another ardent supporter of the old religion, Virius Nicomachus Flavianus. He was respected in court circles as a man of high culture; shortly before 383 he was appointed to the ministerial position of *quaestor sacri palatii* and in 389 became prefect of Italy. Nicomachus' family was connected by marriage with that of Quintus Aurelius Symmachus, the celebrated orator. A beautiful ivory diptych, in which both dynasties are named and where the treatment of the figures – priestesses sacrificing – is wholly classical in style, may perhaps commemorate the wedding of the daughter of Symmachus and the son of Nicomachus. (plate 83). As city prefect for the year 384–5, Symmachus came out strongly against the emperor in defence of the old faith and in 391 finally reached the consulship, an office which fell to many generations of his family. His grandfather had been consul, and although his son reached only the praetorship, his grandson and great-grandson were both consuls; the great-grandson became father-in-law to Boethius, the eminent dignitary of the court of Theoderic, whose sons became joint consuls in the year 522. The saying of Symmachus 'blood will always tell' thus seems to be true.

These Roman grandees flaunted their birth and breeding even before the emperors: Symmachus could remind them that the Senate stood next to the ruler, that the emperor was but the first man in the state, as though the constitution of the Principate were still in force. In reality, when compared with their self-assertion, the political power of the senators was minimal and even their field of public action severely limited. We possess about 900 letters written by Symmachus, whose correspondents included not only friends, kinsmen and high officials but also German-born generals and Christian bishops; the tenth volume of his collected letters contains the reports he sent as prefect to the imperial court. The letters were written with a view to future publication; the son who edited the correspondence selected only those whose publication would not spark off political repercussions. But even bearing in mind these precautions on the part of writer and editor, we can still regard these letters as a faithful reflection of the cultured refinement and tranquillity in which eminent senators passed their days. How formal they are, with a daughter addressed as *domina filia,* a son as *amabilitas tua!* How precious is the style, even when describing humdrum events, for example the matutinal reception at the senator's town house, or a visit to the country estate to supervise the manufacture of oil and wine. There was little excitement to disturb the even tenor of this existence. If the Roman mob once again broke out in hunger riots, their lordships withdrew to their country estates. We hear practically nothing of the alien peoples who were invading the frontiers and very little of the government's financial necessities and tax pressures. On the other hand the son's praetorship is a matter of the utmost importance, so much so that his father writes countless letters to procure performers for the games: lions and crocodiles from Africa, horses from the best studs in Spain, gladiators from the land of the Saxons. Great political issues, it is plain, passed the Senate by; the lords of the city of Rome were no longer making history.

The emperors were astute enough to leave the cult of the past as the monopoly of the Roman aristocracy. Alföldi, who attaches great significance to its historical role, has brought to notice interesting evidence on the social and cultural life of the Roman nobility, that is to say the contorniates. These were medallions composed of copper and alloy, which are named from the deep furrow (Italian *contorno*) running round the rim. It was a Roman custom at the new year festival to exchange presents of old coins as tokens of good luck. In Constantine's day the emperor had actually authorized the public mint to stamp and issue commemorative coins with incused edges. These coins were the forerunners of the contorniates, which survive in various series from the middle of the fourth century almost down to the end of the Roman empire in the West. These issues draw on a repertory of types connected with the public life of Rome and distinctively pagan in character: gods, heroes, Roman symbols, circus scenes. On the obverse one may find Alexander the Great and his mother Olympias (proof of the great king's enduring fame in tradition and legend), poets and sages of Greek and Roman antiquity, including Demosthenes, Sallust and Horace, and portraits of celebrated emperors of the first and second centuries. The subjects on the reverse are taken from pagan religion and mythology, not omitting the Mother of the gods, Attis and Isis; symbols standing for the genius of Rome persist to the end. The message is unequivocal: under the guidance of the Senate the face of the city remained unaltered, antiquity lived on. However, one should not conclude that these artistic motifs point to an indestructible core of religious conviction, still less that they were a demonstration against the Christian emperor. As in so much of the literature of the age, this is the language not of sincere belief but of cultivated frippery.

Even so, the more cultivated section of the senatorial aristocracy has one service, voluntarily assumed, indisputably to its credit: the preservation of ancient literature. As is the common experience of devotees of past literatures, the first necessity was to establish and preserve the surviving texts. The improved text of Livy's *History* was the joint work of members of the houses of Praetextatus and Nicomachus. Later copies of various classical authors contain subscriptions indicating that Roman senators of this period worked on their transcription. It was not only a matter of preserving the texts but also of interpreting what was written: and above all of striving to understand a great literature. The Latin grammarians and rhetors set to work with renewed vigour. The linguistic side, the science of grammar, was tackled by a number of authors who aimed at making a compendium of all previous grammatical learning so that it might be available to men of their own day. At the beginning of the century Nonius Marcellus compiled a lexicon of words and objects, a few decades later Aelius Donatus brought out two text-books on grammar which were highly-prized by his contemporaries and in following centuries became the standard works of grammatical instruction in the West. Servius, who taught at Rome in the time of Symmachus, was the author of an extensive commentary on Virgil. Admittedly, his commentary was largely taken up with observations on points of grammar and rhetoric and he had little to say on the deeper questions of poetic conception and form. The philologists, like the lords of the Senate, devoted themselves exclusively to the literature of the past; nowhere in Servius' monumental tome is there the slightest indication of the advent of Christianity as a religious force. There is but one exception to this general conspiracy of silence over subjects whose existence writers preferred to ignore: Gaius Marius Victorinus. He was not merely a rhetor but also a philosopher, a translator of Greek neo-platonist texts into Latin; in 357, to the astonishment of his circle, he went over to the Christian faith. The general submersion in antiquity lasted until the end of the century. The writings of Macrobius, a high dignitary of the empire and member of the uppermost class of senators, were as it turned out the valedictory memorial to this academic classicism; his work was probably complete by the year 386. He even combined philology with philosophy, making his famous commentary on Cicero's *Dream of Scipio* an excellent exposition of Plotinus' teaching on the deity, the cosmos and the soul. His philological treatise *Saturnalia* follows classical models, recording the learned conversation alleged to have passed between Symmachus and his friends on the three days of the December festival held in honour of the god Saturn. All three famous names are there, Praetextatus, Nicomachus, Symmachus, together with others of their circle and a few outsiders, whose questions provide continual material for contradiction and refutation. The talk follows the fashion of cultivated society, concerning itself with language and literature, learning and custom, religion and morality. The book, which is based on an extensive knowledge of the old authors, aims to instruct an educated nobleman in what he should know and how he should behave. Little is said of politics; in the writer's estimation what matters is a good education, which consists of a melange of antiquarian knowledge and a smattering of neo-platonic philosophy. The men of this circle found it absorbing to discourse on the Roman calendar or to recount the witticisms and sayings of the ancients; other topics of conversation included the digestibility of food, the causes of baldness and grey hair, and the reasons why inebriation should be rare in women but frequent in old men. One is left with the impression that the main object was to trot out second-hand knowledge as club-room philosophy. All the same, a few serious themes emerge, and here contemporaries may have detected an unavowed hostility to Christianity: as, for example, in the discussion of the theology of the sun-god which insists that he can assume the guise of many gods, and above all in the well-nigh mystical interpretation of Virgil, whose *Aeneid* is exalted as the epitome of all wisdom, becoming as it were the saving gospel of paganism. But here once again, one cannot fail to see that these intellectuals were living outside their own time. They firmly believed that the good old days (*vetustas*) ended with Virgil and Augustus, and took comfort in contemplating their vanished ideal: 'if we have any discernment, antiquity must always make us bow the knee.'[7]

Since the educated elite was so preoccupied with the past, one may well ask whether at this period the past attracted attention in its own right as a subject for critical and literary exposition, whether in fact there was any historical writing. As we have already seen, Christian authors from the time of Constantine onwards were creating new categories of history. Eusebius taught men to see ecclesiastical history as the story of the historical origin and development of the new people of God; the idea of a Christian world chronicle was taken up and developed, as for example in the compilation made by the 'Chronographer' in 354; hagiography flourished as a medium for writing the lives of divinely-inspired individuals. But can it be said that paganism, so very conscious of itself, was also taking a fresh look at the past and present, reinterpreting them in the light of history? The question is made especially cogent by the fact that Roman senators had a traditional predilection for historical writing. One fact stands out immediately: Symmachus' contemporaries were interested primarily in histories which were themselves already ancient, the narratives of the celebrated classical historians. Livy's *History*, a reverent account of the rise of Rome, were both copied and studied. However, the work as a whole was too voluminous for the now numerous individuals from the lower classes who were rising in the army and administration and needed a rudimentary knowledge of the past to carry out their duties. There was a demand for summaries of the traditional material, for abridged versions of Roman history geared to the capacities of this wider circle of interested persons. This particular task was admirably discharged by Sextus Aurelius Victor in his short book on the Caesars, which covers the main landmarks in the history of the empire down to 360. The author made his career in the public service, becoming in 388 city prefect of Rome; as an historian, he has the capacity for seeing the empire as a whole. An unknown editor subsequently expanded this account of Rome under the emperors into a trilogy; his additional material consists of a brief survey of the legendary royal period of Roman history and a collection of short biographies, starting with Romulus and ending with Augustus. The whole work is entitled *Origo gentis Romanae*, and was clearly intended to present a pagan account of the history of Rome from its origins down to the time of Julian. Still more summaries followed. The emperor Valens instructed Eutropius, the head of his chancery, to write a short history of Rome starting with the foundation of the city. This text-book, distinguished by reason of its clear arrangement, was much read and long remained in use. But even these seventy-five octavo pages were apparently considered too taxing, and Valens commissioned a still shorter work, this time from a writer named Festus. By the time we reach the end of the century we find the unnamed author of an *Epitome de Caesaribus* content to reproduce excerpts from older authorities without making any personal contribution to their arrangement.

All the same, more ambitious works were not lacking. Nicomachus, whom we have encountered as a representative of native Roman culture, wrote *Annals* covering the history of Rome down to his own day and dedicated his book to the emperor Theodosius. Unfortunately nothing has survived of this work, which followed classical models. It is possible, however, that it was used as a source by Ammianus Marcellinus, Rome's last great historian and an exceptional phenomenon in his own right. A Greek from Antioch, Ammianus served in an elite corps of the imperial army; from 353 he was a staff officer with the army command in both East and West; in 359 he was present at the siege of Amida in Armenia and subsequently accompanied Julian on his Persian expedition. On retiring from the army Ammianus lived first at Antioch, but afterwards went to Rome, hopeful of gaining entry into the circle of aristocratic and cultured senators. In this it appears he was not wholly successful, but it is nevertheless remarkable how romanized he became. Although a Greek, he steeped himself in Roman literature; and however mannered his language and style, he certainly achieved a striking competence as a Latin writer. Ammianus 'formerly a soldier and a Greek' as he says of himself, thus bears witness that even after the reforms of Diocletian Latin could still make its conquests in the East. More significant still, Ammianus was so thoroughly imbued with Roman historical and political thinking that he was bold enough to write a continuation of Tacitus.

He composed thirty-one books, covering the history of the empire from the year 96, when Tacitus' *Histories* leave off, down to 378, the disastrous year of the battle of Adrianople. For the earlier part Ammianis relied on written sources; but since books 1–13 are missing, we have no means of knowing which of his predecessors he used. The surviving portion of this work, books 14–31, provides us with a detailed survey of the period covered by his own lifetime. His courage in tackling the recent past lifts him far above the Roman antiquarians. Equally praiseworthy is his method of constructing the history of these decades around his notes and memories and the reports of reliable authorities known to him personally. He expressly asserts his intention of writing impartially, with an eye only to the truth; the modern critic can see for himself that Ammianus often surpasses his master Tacitus in factual accuracy and unprejudiced observation.

Ammianus' magisterial gaze takes in the whole Roman empire in its decline. He had personal experience of the threat to its borders in Persia and Germany, recognized the labile character of the absolute monarchy, was familiar with the intrigues of the court and perceived that the tortuous methods of the secret police and trial by terror were no bar to usurpation and conspiracies. As an historian, he knew how to organize his narrative in a procession of powerful tableaux and exciting episodes, threading its way through the various theatres of war, the struggles for power at the imperial court and the treason-trials in the cities. He, if anyone, possessed the insight born of fellow-feeling and the command of rhetoric required to do full justice to this century, characterized by brutal warfare, spectacular triumphs, mass slaughter, torture and denunciation. But he had a further specific gift which kept him from surrendering completely to the temptations of rhetoric: he combined a huntsman's eye for detail with a high skill in literary reportage. While constantly professing that his intention is to concentrate on the most important events, again and again it is the small things, the marginal happenings, that catch his eye: hence he gives us lightning impressions of campaigns and state occasions, finds space for anecdotes with human appeal and adventurous escapades and deploys his talent for telling detail in vivid sketches of important personages. The story-teller in him is indulged on occasion with narratives which read like something from romance. His account of his own breath-taking escape from the stronghold of Amida, just after it had been taken by the Persians, is unparalleled in ancient literature.[8] But he also belongs to the generation which bowed the knee to its own transfigured idea of antiquity. He is at pains to place the particular events, whose import it is in his power to grasp, in the appropriate category of historical examples familiar from the literature. Ammianus is thoroughly conversant with the collections of

Defence of the Empire

1 The walls of Constantinople near the Edirne Gate. Early fifth century

2 *above.* The walls which Aurelian built to defend Rome; the Porta Tiburtina

3 *below.* The multangular tower and Roman wall at York, built by Constantius Chlorus, father of Constantine the Great

4 Stilicho, a 'barbarian' who became one of Rome's greatest military leaders

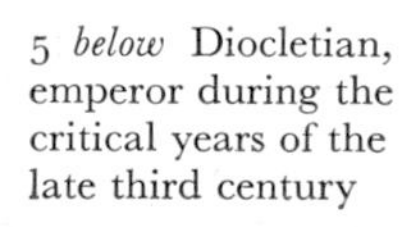

5 *below* Diocletian, emperor during the critical years of the late third century

Christianity in the Roman Empire

6 A view of the Milvian bridge in Rome, where Constantine defeated Maxentius and was converted to Christianity

7 The Christian chi-rho symbol, a fourth-century bronze

8 Lamp with figures of the Apostles Peter and Paul

9 Roman graveyard at Salona, Yugoslavia, one of the largest centres of early Christianity

Church leaders. 10 *above*. Symmachus, Pope from AD 498 to 514. 11 *right*. St Ambrose of Milan, an early fifth century mosaic

Baths and Domes

12 The ruins of Diocletian's baths in Rome

13 Trier, the imperial baths

14 S. Vitale, Ravenna. The great thermal halls were the precursors of this type of domed building

15 *above*. The exterior of Santa Sophia, Constantinople

16 *opposite*. The interior of Santa Sophia

The Basilica

17 The peristyle of Diocletian's palace at Split

18 Mosaic of a basilica from Tabarka, showing the central nave with its rows of columns

19 The church of S. Sabina, a long-nave basilica

20 *above*. The basilica of S. Damaso, an early Christian church on the Via Appia

21 *left*. Foliate capital from the basilica at Philippi, Greece

22 *opposite*. The long-naved church of S Apollinare Nuovo, Ravenna, one of the finest Christian basilicas

PALA TIVM

23 Interior of the baptistery of the Orthodox, Ravenna

24 Interior of S. Costanza, Rome

26 *above*. The mausoleum of Galla Placidia, Ravenna.

27 *right*. Ravenna, the mausoleum of Theoderic.

25 *opposite*. The baptistery of the Orthodox, Ravenna.

Portrait Sculpture

28 Portrait of the emperor Decius

29 Stone head of Amalasuntha, late fifth or early sixth century

30 Head of high official, from the baths of Aphrodisias early fifth century

31 Bronze head of Constantius II

32 *left*. The emperor Caracalla

33 *below left*. Philip the Arab, a contemporary portrait

34 *below right*. Portrait head from Ephesus, second half of the fifth century

Art in the Provinces

35 Mosaic floor of the Roman villa at Lullingstone, Kent

36 Gravestone from Trier, showing a domestic scene

37 Trier, grave-relief of a school lesson

38 Payment of taxes, from a grave-stone at Trier

39 The myth of Prometheus, from a sarcophagus of the late third century

40 Fragment of sarcophagus showing a philosopher reading

41 Fourth-century mosaic ceiling in the north ambulatorium of S. Costanza, Rome, with Bacchic scenes

42 Detail from mosaic in the south ambulatorium of S. Costanza

43 *below*. The sarcophagus of the prefect Junius Bassus (died AD 359). Christian tradition in a classical setting

44 Christianisation of the secular: 'the triumph of the Christian empire', a panel from the doors of S. Sabina

Old Testament Themes in Christian Art

45 *opposite*. 'Adam and Eve', a wall painting from the catacombs of SS Pietro and Marcellino, Rome

46 *below*. The Israelites crossing the Red Sea, a relief from Salona, Yugoslavia

New Testament Themes in Christian Art

47 *opposite.* Detail from the sarcophagus of Junius Bassus. *Above.* Christ as the judge of the world, between Peter and Paul. *Below.* Christ's entry into Jerusalem

48 *right.* Ivory casket from Brescia, showing scenes of miracles. AD 360–70

49 Relief showing the good shepherd, from a sarcophagus of the third century.

Images of Christ

50 Christ giving the laws to Peter and Paul, apse mosaic in S. Costanza

51 Christ enthroned on the globe of the world, apse mosaic in S. Costanza

52 *left.* The heritage of classicism, Christ as a youthful philosopher

53 *right.* Christ-Helios, sun-god and Christian Lord, from the mausoleum of the Julii under St. Peter's, Rome

54 *left*. Christ-Pantocrator, the Byzantine image of an all-powerful Christ, mosaic from the church at Daphni, Greece

55 *below*. Crucifixion scene from the doors of S. Sabina, fifth century

56 *opposite*. Christ with the Virgin Mary, apse mosaic in the church of S. Maria Maggiore

MARIA · VIRGO ASSVPTA E · AD ETHEREV THALAMV IN QVO REX REGV · STELLATO · SEDET SOLIO
EXALTATA EST · SANCTA · DEI GENITRIX · SVPER CHOROS ANGELORVM AD CELESTIA REGNA

Imperial Buildings

57 The north front of the Porta Nigra at Trier, one of the imperial capitals in the late empir

58 Part of a mosaic floor of the imperial villa at Piazza Armerina in Sicily

59 An eighteenth-century etching of Diocletian's imperial city of Spalatum (modern Split) in Yugoslavia

60 *opposite*. A view of the Porta Aurea, on the northern side of the palace at Split

Imperial Monuments

61 Imperial coins of the age of Constantine:
1 and 2: Gold solidi of Constantine the Great
3 and 4: Reverse and obverse of a gold medallion of Constantine
5: Aureus of Constantius I
6: Double solidus of Helena, mother of Constantine

62 The arch of Constantine in Rome, viewed from the north

63 and 64 *opposite*. Details from the arch of Constantine: People listening to the emperor, *and* Soldiers of Constantine in battle

65 and 66 The obelisk of Theodosius in the Hippodrome at Constantinople. *Above*. The relief on the south-east side, showing the emperor Theodosius and his sons watching a chariot race. *Below*. North-west side of the obelisk, Theodosius with Arcadius, Honorius and Valentinian III, with Persians and Dacians bearing tribute

67 *above left*. Roman consul with a 'mappa', marble statue of about AD 400

68 *above right*. Marble statue of the emperor Julian the Apostate, AD 359–363

69 *left*. Late Roman bronze statue of an emperor, from Barletta

70 Giant head of the emperor Constantine, part of a statue from the basilica of Constantine in Rome

Decorative Arts in the Late Empire

71 The art of the miniaturist: Sardonyx cameo of Honorius and Maria

72 Portrait on gilded glass, third century

73 Consular diptych representing the emperor Honorius, commissioned by the consul Sextus Anicius Probus

74 God's bond with Noah

75 Abraham and Melchisedech

76 The drunkenness of Noah

77 The saving of Lot and the destruction of Sodom

74 to 78 The Vienna Genesis Bible, an early example of the miniaturist's art used in the decoration of the holy scriptures. 78 *above*. Noah's disembarkation from the Ark

79 *opposite.* The ivory throne of Archbishop Maximian at Ravenna, about AD 550

80 *below.* Craftsmanship in marble, the high altar of S. Vitale

81 *above*. St Lawrence with his grill and book-case containing the four Gospels, one of Ravenna's many magnificent mosaics

82 Ravenna, church of SS. Giovanni and Paolo, marble pulpit

83 The diptych of the Symmachi, right wing, showing the priestess of Bacchus before the altar of Jupiter

84 *overleaf*. The mosaic in the dome of the baptistery of the Arians

85 The silver platter from the Mildenhall treasure, fourth-century work

86 The magnificent carved wooden doors of S. Sabina

87 The 'Achilles' platter from the fortress of Kaiseraugst, Switzerland, about AD 355

88 The missorium of the emperor Theodosius I, dating from the year AD 388, from Almendralejo (Badajoz), Spain

89 Marble intarsio floor, showing a tiger attacking a calf, from the basilica of Annius Bassus (consul AD 331) on the Esquiline, Rome

90 The decline of Rome: a column from the early empire re-erected as a monument to Phocas, emperor of the East, by Smaragdus, exarch of Italy

Exempla current in the schools and makes use of them freely, persuading himself by learned disquisitions that the deeds of his own time are less significant than those of former days. Exact precedents are adduced to match every case, the present is always seen reflected in the mirror of the past. This way of writing history is a barrier to deeper historical understanding. Ammianus recognizes the crisis of the empire, but preoccupied with the greatness of the preceding age attributes its decline primarily to moral degeneration. Court society no longer honours the values upheld by the ancients, officers are unfitted for their posts, soldiers have become soft, officials are corrupt, and all fall short of the standards set by their historical prototypes, his cherished ideal. In two famous excursuses he gives a melodramatic description of the corruption rampant in the city of Rome, whose taint infected high and low alike; but he remains blind to the political and social causes of this dissolution. Even Ammianus failed to see that the position of the Imperium in the world had radically altered; the crude energy which drove the alien peoples as they pressed against the empire gave him no food for reflection – his knowledge of the Germans was in any case only superficial. It remained a mystery to him why society should have become so rigid, with a privileged upper crust still reaping personal advantage from political upheavals while the urban bourgeoisie remained sunk in torpor and the masses were exploited. The historian has indeed noted the existence of Christianity, describing it with some respect as 'a simple, self-contained religion' (*religio simplex et absoluta*). This degree of attention is already remarkable, given the general tendency of educated pagans to pass over the new religion in complete silence, but even Ammianus remained oblivious to the full extent of the religious transformation. He was true to the old gods, attaching the greatest value to the performance of sacrifices and observation of omens; he believed that faith in 'the eternal deity' would guarantee the empire's permanence. The defeat of Adrianople, with which his work concludes, appears to him a catastrophe unparalleled since Cannae; but were not the Cimbri, Teutones and Marcomanni eventually driven from the empire? Ammianus is confident that Rome will emerge from this desperate plight, as from so many previous reverses. But then he lapses into exhortation, preaching moral regeneration at the Roman people, exhorting them to return to the simplicity and self-sacrifice of earlier generations; he has no concrete plan of action. This everlasting ball-game, in which the events of past and present are kept simultaneously in play or even juggled in mid-air, is typical of the ancient world's approach to historical experience and the task of historical exposition. The historicism of this latest phase of antiquity robbed historical experience of its uniqueness and in so doing, we might add, hindered men's freedom of action.

Another historical work, whose disengaged erudition rivals that of Ammianus although in other respects it falls far below him in attainment, is the collection of imperial biographies, running from Hadrian to the period just before Diocletian, known to modern scholarship as the *Historia Augusta*. In the received text authorship is attributed to six named writers; they worked, it is said, in the time of Diocletian and Constantine, to them a few of the biographies are actually dedicated. In rhetorical embellishment the authors of these lives surpass even Suetonius, or indeed Marius Maximus. They parade their learning with far-fetched quotations, etymological interpretations and antiquarian lore; furthermore, they gratify their fashionable public's curiosity – or thirst for sensation – by recounting anecdotes and scandal of every description. Buried in the clutter, however, is a mass of factual information, all the more vital to us since we have no Tacitus or Ammianus to report the one hundred and sixty-seven years covered by these reigns. As a general rule, however, we ought to trust the biographers only when their evidence is confirmed or made probable by information from another quarter; for if their historical understanding was defective, so too was their critical discrimination in using their materials. They were even quite prepared to invent letters and records and ascribe them to specific emperors. Most of the documents quoted in the text have been shown to be false; and the falsifications were used chiefly to pad out the lives of emperors of whom little definite was known. The problems presented by this composite work have attracted much scholarly attention over the past seventy years: its credibility has been tested at many points and attempts made to clarify both the origins of the Corpus and the question of its authorship, that is to say, whether the authors were really those named, writing at the time alleged. Philological studies have produced some useful results, certain anachronisms in statements of fact have been detected; another line of enquiry has been to see whether there exists a distinctive viewpoint imputable to post-Constantinian authors; and the religious and political assumptions of the biographies have been tested against the contemporary background. So far, however, these researches have had divergent results. The date claimed for the work in the texts themselves, the reigns of Diocletian and Constantine, is still a valid possibility. Some knowledgeable authorities think the biographies were written in the reign of Julian and suggest the book was written to give literary support to his pagan religious policy. Others, basing themselves on utterances which appear to favour fundamental toleration between pagans and Christians, suggest a date as late as the beginning of the fifth century; and they think that a recognized technique was established for the defence of paganism against the Christian interpretation of history which made such great headway at the turn of the century, a technique which refrained from open criticism while making its point through more or less open insinuation. Weighty arguments in favour of the late date have recently been advanced by J. Straub and others, but the question remains undecided. But whatever date may be assigned to its origin, this composite work is still an illumination of late paganism; it is an outstanding achievement in the art of regaling the reader with a medley of true and false stories, enfolding him within the mantle of an honourable aristocratic tradition and at the same time deceiving him as to the author's personality.

When we come to consider the other specialized disciplines, we must constantly bear in mind that in the natural sciences and medicine, as in philology and history, the creative force of antiquity was long since spent. By 100 BC hellenistic science had already exhausted itself and was not revived even when the Romans took over from the Greeks as leaders of the Mediterranean world. Furthermore, Christianity when it appeared directed men's probings and enquiries into paths which led away from the rational interpretation of the world. It is therefore not surprising that the fourth century produced no new systematic works of exposition dealing with the exact sciences. In this field, too, the demand was solely for compendia which summarized the gist of all received knowledge, mainly for use in schools. In mathematics, mention can be made of commentaries composed by two Alexandrian Greeks whose activities as teachers led them to elucidate and amplify the writings of earlier mathematicians, Pappos at the beginning of the century, Theon at its end. Agriculture was far from being the exact science it had once been. However, Palladius, a landed proprietor who perhaps lived in Gaul, showed some initiative in casting his *Opus agriculturae* in the form of a calendar of agrarian and household tasks, suitable for domestic use. Medicine and veterinary medicine are again represented by compilations, for example the revealing collection made by Oribasius, Julian's personal physician, from earlier writers on medical science. In law there is a headlong descent from the heights scaled by the classical authorities, who even in the time of the Severi were still making pioneering advances. Absolutism, under which imperial legislation was the sole source of new law, helped to fetter creative legal thinking. Accordingly, from the middle of the third century jurists resigned themselves to adapting classical texts to the needs of their own day and making abstracts from them. It was also about this time that men started to compose collections consisting of excerpts from imperial legislation and the writings of the jurists, a procedure which would find its grand culmination in the codifications of Theodosius and Justinian. It is characteristic of a period of decadence that men no longer felt equal to mastering the whole range of legal opinions as represented in the classical authors and accepted only five authorities: Gaius, Papinian, Ulpian, Paulus and Modestinus. A formal 'law of citations' promulgated in 426 laid down exact rules to be followed in evaluating opinions expressed by the great five. However, thanks to the activity of law schools and the initiative of individual emperors, there was a resurgence of legal science in the East during the latter part of the the fifth century, which in turn led to a revival of classical jurisprudence – at a time when in the West law and jurisprudence were sinking into vulgarism.

It is particularly striking to find a complete absence of scholarly writing in the fields of engineering, architecture and all technical subjects. In this whole area the Romans continued to live on their ancient Etrusco-Italian inheritance and on the discoveries of hellenistic thinkers and inventors. This received knowledge made possible some most impressive technical achievements, which continued even into the later period. Romans such as Frontinus, the author of a treatise on aqueducts, could claim with some pride that whereas the ancient Egyptians had built useless pyramids and the Greeks non-functional works of art, their own buildings and constructions were of service to mankind. Intensive and ceaseless building activity went on in towns and on extensions to the frontier fortifications; the roads, bridges, and aqueducts built by Roman engineering art continued to be of a high standard. These works were not undertaken merely from practical necessity; they were also intended to proclaim to the world the imperial might of Rome. It even appears that in building aqueducts the principle of communicating pipes, which was already understood and would have made possible a pressurized water-supply, was deliberately ignored, just because the landscape-dominating arches required to carry water by gravity were such obvious manifestations of the Roman presence in different parts of the world. Roman mastery of techniques of high-building is demonstrated by a long series of basilicas and thermal installations; harbour buildings, ships and war-machines were still being produced with routine efficiency. But there were no great new discoveries in any of these fields. Industry, in which the State itself was more actively engaged than formerly, stuck closely to the traditional processes, in mining, metal-working, ceramics, textiles and even in milling. The manufacture of lamps, in which no advance was made on a small and technically far from perfect type of vessel, is perhaps the most telling indication that lassitude had set in. In the whole field of technology, the stagnation already observed at an earlier date became a settled fact, so much so that the few isolated discoveries still being made were not put to general use. For example, the screw press with direct pressure transmission mentioned by the elder Pliny failed to establish itself; even watermills, already known to Vitruvius, were used only sporadically, mostly on large estates; hand-mills operated by women-workers and the capstan-mill of the baker still predominated. Yet it had been realized from the outset that the new invention could greatly reduce the amount of human labour required. The thought is expressed in a noteworthy epigram composed by the poet Antipater of Thessalonica, in the time of Augustus:

> Cease from grinding, ye women who toil at the mill; sleep late, even if the crowing cocks announce the dawn. For Demeter has ordered the nymphs to perform the work of your hands, and they, leaping down on the top of the wheel, turn its axle which with its revolving spokes turns the heavy concave Nisyrian millstones. We taste again the joys of the primitive life, learning to feast on the products of Demeter without labour.[9]
>
> [*Transl. W. R. Paton, Loeb Library*]

This period, however, evinced no desire to return to the Golden Age, when work was unknown. One may cite here a very instructive tale told by the biographer of Vespasian. When the great reconstruction of the city was in progress, an engineer discovered a way of transporting massive columns to the Capitol at very small cost. Vespasian rewarded the man for his inventiveness, but dismissed his project, remarking that the poor must be allowed their chance to earn at least a pittance. This principle of allowing the poor – who existed and must exist – their heavy labour and meagre earnings worked to ever greater effect as the gulf between the classes widened during the third and fourth centuries.

Passivity in methods of production was thus just as characteristic of this late period as the lack of originality in writings about science. There is one lonely exception, a miraculous bloom in a barren field, the small work entitled *De rebus bellicis* (A Tract on Warfare), whose merits have recently been stressed by E. A. Thompson. The author, nowhere mentioned by name, probably belonged to the urban middle class and was apparently writing about 370, under the joint-rule of Valentinian I and Valens. He lays before the emperors a whole series of reforms and suggestions for mechanical contrivances. The title of the work is justified by the author's conviction that his proposed administrative reforms must be put into operation if warfare is to continue and the frontiers to be defended. In his preface he shows himself at once deferential towards the emperors and confident of his own abilities, affirming that the inventive mind owes nothing to high birth and the study of rhetoric but is a natural endowment, met with even among barbarians: 'where the exigencies of the case have forced me to speak somewhat freely on any point, I think I should be protected by your indulgence, for if I am to carry out my promise I must be assisted for the sake of the freedom of science' (Transl. E. A. Thompson). He starts straight away with his cardinal proposition, that emperors should cease to be so lavish with their donatives to soldiers and officials; this prodigality, he seems to suggest, means that booty gained in war is squandered, so that new wars are necessary to replenish the treasury. Our anonymous author believes that he has hit on a possible remedy, namely the reform of the currency. He claims that the gold issues introduced by Constantine made great houses wealthier but had very damaging effects on the poor, which was why they had taken to crime and brigandage. Since the time of Constantine, he continues, these coins have been adulterated by the fraudulent practices of certain persons, with the result that they have either been rejected as currency or used for black market transactions. To inhibit adulteration, all workers employed in minting coins should be relegated to an island and carry out their duties in strict isolation from the outside world. New types must be brought out for bronze and gold coins, following designs appended by the author. He then turns to the provincial administrations, castigating the extortionate methods of governors, especially in levying recruits and in requisitions of every description. He calls for a rationalization of the military establishment, although the nature of this proposed reform is not altogether clear : the lower ranks of the army should contain more men than are needed for the higher grades, and this surplus could then either be discharged or used for other duties, perhaps on the land. Next he lists his inventions ; recognizing that the empire is threatened, 'by the frenzy of the baying hordes which surround it' he is convinced that only new engines of war will overcome the advantages barbarians derive from their natural cover. His sketches and descriptions include plans for new ballistae, new lead-weighted javelins, an improved armoured combat vehicle, a portable bridge made of skins and a war-ship propelled by paddle-wheels, without necessity for sails or oars. He suggests an arrangement by which frontier forts could be financed by contributions from land-owners, in proportion to the amount of land they possessed in the sector concerned. His final demand, for a condensation of imperial legislation to put an end to the existing legal confusion, places him in line with the movement among the urban bourgeois class which led later to the great codifications.

Here speaks a far-sighted reformer, who combines new guiding principles for internal policy with bold proposals for the conduct of war, and of offensive warfare at that. Although his technical inventions aroused the interest of the early humanists, many have been rejected by experts as impracticable. Nevertheless, it would be a mistake to dismiss this man, as some have done, as 'a crack-pot inventor'. He must be given his due as the one man who did not attempt to grapple with the crisis merely by moralizing. Most striking of all is his idea for a thorough-going mechanization of the Roman army ; he becomes all the more remarkable when one compares him with Vegetius, the fifth century author of a small manual on military organization who continues to advocate the old, long outdated military system and thinks solely in terms of defensive warfare. Our anonymous author found no-one to echo his belief that improvement can make the world a better place; his very uniqueness confirms that in science and technology his was indeed a barren century.

4. *Christianity as the state religion – the end of pagan Rome*

Recent research has taken note of signs indicating that the fourth century was to some extent a time of economic recovery and social consolidation. It can be agreed that in the period between Constantine and Theodosius the break-up of the social and political order was not as cataclysmic as in the preceding century, but proceeded rather with the measured tempo of a steady transformation. However, it also becomes clear that the structure of the ancient world was undergoing profound and continual alteration. There are two aspects of the process which merit particular attention during the later decades of the fourth century: the opening of the lower Danube frontier and the establishment of a Christian State-Church, two momentous decisions belonging to the reigns of Gratian and Theodosius.

The personalities of these two rulers are of importance in these events, if at first only in the sense that officials of the central government and military command were more than ever taking the initiative. Gratian, the pupil of Ausonius who became ruler of the West in 375, kept books in his tent alongside his weapons; as the church historian Rufinus remarks, he had more piety than was healthy for the empire. Gratian was sixteen when he first began to rule and at nineteen was for a moment virtually sole ruler of the empire, so that his entourage acquired a disproportionate influence. It is true that his younger step-brother, Valentinian II, bore the name Augustus, but at first he was restricted to Illyricum; dominated by his mother and kept in the background by his ministers, Valentinian never attained full independence, even when the whole West fell to his share on the death of his brother. This leaves us with the emperor Theodosius as the one man whose personality could directly have influenced the decisions taken in these decades. Theodosius came of a Hispano-Roman family with estates in Gallaecia, in the north-west of the peninsula. A staunch adherent of the Catholic faith, he had his share of that religious fervour which seems inseparable from people of his native land. Theodosius entered on a military career and for a time served under his father, an army commander who won successes on many fronts, and notably in Africa where he suppressed the rising of Firmus, the Berber prince. On his father's death Theodosius retired to his Spanish estates, but in 378, in the hour of mortal danger following the defeat of Valens at Adrianople, he was recalled to be commander of the army and in January 379 was raised to Augustus, to rule the East and the Balkan territories as co-ruler with Gratian. Certain traits in his personality remind one of Constantine; he was volatile in temperament and inspired affection, he was given not infrequently to tempestuous fits of rage and was capable of cruelty; he was open-handed to a fault, and delighted in the pomp of imperial residences, wherever he lingered on his long journeyings, above all in the court of Constantinople. He added several new buildings and monuments to the city, including a spacious forum with a lofty imperial column dedicated to himself. In the conduct of war he was cautious, at times even timid; he reinforced the headquarters staff, and by multiplying the numbers of commanders increased the danger of internal strife. Uneven though our material for the different years of the reign may be, it nevertheless becomes clear that all the great decisions in military and religious policy go back to Theodosius himself.

First and foremost in this category must be placed the revolutionary change in Roman policy towards the Goths, or perhaps one should say towards alien peoples in general – after the reign of Valentinian I no-one could claim that the Gothic front was still the only serious danger! The Persians, admittedly, were quiescent, but in Britain there was continuing warfare against the Picts and Scots, as also against Saxon pirates; when in 383 part of the army in Britain departed with the usurper Magnus Maximus to the mainland, Hadrian's Wall had to be abandoned and the north of England completely evacuated. The Rhine frontier, whose fortifications had actually been strengthened under Valentinian I, was still under attack from the Franks and above all from the Alamanni; in 378 Gratian dared to cross the Rhine at Basel and make a sortie into enemy territory, an act of boldness quite remarkable at this period. The Sarmatians were still advancing on the middle Danube, with the result that on the death of Gratian the province of Pannonia lapsed into chaos. Yet along all these sectors of the front the only measures taken were the usual ones, evacuation of a small district here, strengthening of frontier forts there, enlistment of yet more foreign soldiers and settlement of alien farmers on imperial soil.

It was only on the lower Danube that these measures proved entirely useless. It is true that about the year 369 the west Goths (Visigoths) pledged themselves to respect the river as their boundary, but a few years later these same Goths were faced with the onslaught of powerful tribes coming from Asia. For the first time the true source of the unrest which plagued all the peoples of eastern Europe stood revealed. The Alans, an Iranian tribe, had long since advanced from central Asia to occupy the land between the Caucasus and the Don. They were now followed by the Huns, nomads from the Turkish group of tribes, who about 370 reached the territory of the Alans and forced them to join their ranks. Thanks to their decided superiority in armament (due to their experience in working iron and producing steel), and the impetus of their nomadic drive, which terrorized all their neighbours, the Huns swept westward, poured over the Don, occupied the kingdom of Hermanric the east Goth (Ostrogoth) and confronted the Visigoths on the Dniester. At this time leadership of the Visigoths was disputed between two rival chieftains, Fritigern and Athanaric, who headed the section of the tribe which had gone over to Christianity. Fritigern, who had recently found favour with the empire, now entered into negotiations with Valens, and was promised lands in Thrace, in accordance with the traditional policy of settling a neighbouring tribe within the boundaries of the empire to provide additional farmers and fighting men. As a result, in 376 a great crowd of Visigoths, led by Fritigern, crossed the Danube. The reception of this horde – it contained about ten thousand fighting men, so one may postulate a total of some fifty thousand people – created difficulties, and the rapacity of corrupt governors and officers goaded the Visigoths into war. Reinforced by sundry groups of Ostrogoths, Alans and Huns, they pressed through the Balkan range in the direction of Adrianople. This was the moment to call on the imperial reserve. Valens advanced with his own army, sent an appeal to the emperor of the West for help but then, without waiting for Gratian, in September 378 decided to offer battle at Adrianople. The Visigoths won a resounding victory over the numerically superior Roman army, two-thirds of the Roman levies were destroyed and Valens himself was killed. This was a military catastrophe and the Goths moved on through the countryside with no-one to check them. In this desperate situation Gratian called on the proved military experience of Theodosius, appointing him first to the supreme military command and then raising him to co-ruler. Theodosius created a new army from a levy of peasants and workers, with an increased complement of foreigners, and achieved some small successes over the next few years; in 382 he concluded what was to be an epoch-making treaty with the Visigoths. The Germans were allocated settlement land between the Danube and the Balkan range (in the northern part of modern Bulgaria); their tribal organization was left intact and they were free to live according to their own laws under their own chieftains; as federates (*foederati*) of the Roman empire they undertook to provide auxiliary contingents, which would serve in their own national formations, in return for high pay and an annual tribute from the Romans. The policy of the empire towards the Germans was thus set on a new course. Hitherto *foederati* had been tribes living outside the frontiers, and any foreigners admitted into the empire were settled in detached groups; but now a tribe had been received as a whole, a self-contained unit. The Visigoths were members of the empire, but not citizens; the new allies were a foreign body implanted in Roman territory. Although Adrianople came to contemporaries as a great shock, it was soon overlaid by comforting illusion. Public orators began to talk of Goths living in bondage to the Romans, making not the slightest reference to the treaty of alliance. Themistius praised the conscription of the Scythians – as the Goths were frequently called – as a great act of imperial philanthropy, and opined that through enforced settlement the 'barbarians' would advance on the road to improvement. Not taken in by these panegyrical flourishes, Theodosius pushed his hazardous plan to its logical conclusion. He increased the proportion of Germans in the army, allowed many more German officers than formerly to rise to the higher commands and imposed heavier taxation to meet the greatly enlarged public expenditure entailed by his course of action. He was successful in attaching Germanic tribal chieftains to himself by ties of personal friendship, as a guarantee of peace. In the end Theodosius came to be known by the paradoxical-sounding title 'friend of the Goths and of peace'.

However, voices enquiring into the deeper causes of the disaster were not wanting. The historian Ammianus laid the blame on the decay of the old virtues of self-sacrifice and discipline, bishop Ambrose of Milan held that Valens' defeat was a divine punishment incurred by the Arian heresy and that emperors would not be victorious until they were orthodox. It is a fact that the imperial decision to impose the Catholic faith on the whole empire was taken in the epoch-making year 378–9. When Theodosius was raised to be co-ruler with Gratian soon after the death of Valens, he did not assume the office of Pontifex Maximus; Gratian, who until this date had held the office, like all his predecessors before him, followed suit and relinquished it. This gesture, which signified the empire's total dissociation from paganism, must plainly be attributed to the personal religious convictions of Theodosius himself, who was concerned to fulfil his duty as emperor and Christian without being disturbed by inner conflict. Throughout the ensuring complications, he showed himself at once anxious to secure his own salvation in the faith and to discharge his responsibility for that of his subjects.

Pagan resistance was by no means the only complication; still greater difficulties arose from confusion among the Christians. Theodosius first addressed himself to the restoration of Christian unity. It was just about this time that Epiphanius, bishop of Salamis in Cyprus, revealed the existence of eighty heresies and in his *Panarion*, or 'Medicine Chest', prescribed an antidote for all who had been bitten by those evil serpents, namely heretics. The fierce controversies aroused by Arianism, particularly in the East, have already come to our notice. As it happened, some prospect of a rapprochement between the doctrinal opinions and parties represented in this theological dispute, which had such a deep effect on the population at large, was already emerging in the time of Valens. The Nicene doctrine had found distinguished defenders in the great Cappadocian Fathers. As part of the process of theological clarification, the doctrinal formula of Nicaea was widened by definition of the third Divine Person, the doctrine of the Holy Ghost. Basil, from 370 Metropolitan of Caesarea, embarked on negotiations with the churches of Alexandria and Rome. So much progress was made that in 370 a synod of oriental bishops meeting in Antioch could accept the Nicene formula and in so doing subscribed to the statement of the faith sent them by Damasus, bishop of Rome. Theodosius immediately made this the basis of his attempt to reconstruct the unity of Christian belief. On 28 February 380, at Thessalonica, he issued a constitution which made the Nicene formulation of the faith generally binding: 'All peoples whom the rule of our gracious benevolence directs shall, as is our will, steadfastly adhere to the confession of faith which the divine apostle Peter delivered to the Romans, which tradition has preserved to this day as the faith he preached, and which is now clearly professed by the pontifex Damasus and by Peter, bishop of Alexandria, a man of apostolic holiness. That is to say, that we believe, in accordance with apostolic teaching and the message of the gospel, in a Deity of Father, Son and Holy Ghost, in equal majesty and holy trinity. Those who follow this law shall, as we ordain, have the right to be called Catholic Christians; and as we judge all others unreasonable madmen, we brand them with the ignominy of heresy and declare their conventicles shall not bear the name of churches and they shall be punished, first by divine vengeance and thereafter through the chastisement of the judicial proceedings which we, supported by Heaven's judgement, shall institute.'[10] This is certainly a remarkable constitution. The personal creed of the emperor, who invokes in its support the bishops of Rome and Alexandria, is set up as the formulary of all Catholic Christians (*nomen Christianum catholicum*); people living in the empire who reject this creed are threatened with punishment. Arrangements for putting the constitution into effect were not long in forthcoming. Once Theodosius had taken up residence in Constantinople he issued an edict (January 381) ordering heretics, some of them mentioned by name, to surrender their places of worship to orthodox bishops. In the same year the question of the creed was referred to a body with spiritual competence, to be defined for the whole empire. An oecumenical council summoned to meet at Constantinople (to settle amongst other matters a burning dispute over certain episcopal sees) agreed a formula which by including an express doctrine of the

Holy Ghost made the 'Nicene Creed' a declaration of belief in the divine Trinity. Further canons of the council brought the ecclesiastical hierarchy into still closer alignment with that of the empire : a bishop whose see was the capital of a secular diocese was to take precedence over other metropolitans ; the bishop of new Rome, Constantinople, was to rank immediately below the bishop of Rome himself. The emperor's definition of the creed to be held by all Christians was thus accepted by the Church, while the episcopal hierarchy, in disregard of the precedence formerly accorded to the old patriarchates of Jerusalem, Antioch and Alexandria, was brought into line with that of the state.

Further administrative measures to back up the parent constitution soon followed ; an order was made for the confiscation of heretical churches and Manichees were deprived of their right to make wills and receive legacies. Other problems were settled by two further councils held at Constantinople in 382 and 383 ; at the second an attempt was made to bring the heretical bishops into line. The council's effort having failed, the heretics were made to present their formularies to the emperor ; he gave his verdict by tearing up the documents in the presence of their authors – evidence that the emperor's claim to authority in doctrinal matters extended even into details. Throughout the East measures against heretics now increased in ferocity. As for the pagans, an edict had already been promulgated against them in 381, forbidding visits to temples and sacrifices for divining the future. Even the Jews had their rights curtailed. Christian unity, as adumbrated in Theodosius' constitution of Thessalonica, was being realized by action on all fronts.

But how did things stand in the West of the empire, where Gratian, although younger in years, ruled as first-ranking Augustus ? At the beginning of his reign he had shown himself tolerant in matters of religion. Ausonius commends him for this indulgence, which made it possible for men to err without putting themselves in jeopardy. But after the shock of Adrianople Gratian followed the example set by Theodosius and relinquished the office of Pontifex Maximus ; this was a gesture fraught with consequence, in the first place for the cult of Rome and ultimately for paganism as a whole. With regard to the Christian heresies, the Nicene formula, long defended by Christian Rome, was now accepted almost everywhere in the western provinces, leaving Arianism with only a few isolated strongholds, mainly in Illyricum. In carrying out his policy Gratian relied heavily on the episcopate, represented at Rome and Milan by two quite outstanding personalities. It was not for nothing that Theodosius had invoked the name of Damasus of Rome in his constitution of Thessalonica. Damasus had become bishop in 366, through a disputed election in which Rome had been disturbed by bitter strife, fought out in law-suits and accompanied by outbreaks of violence serious enough to require the intervention of the emperor and the city prefect, which ended in the suppression of the rival congregation led by Ursinus, the counter-bishop. Despite all this, Damasus (who also had connections with the educated pagan elite of the city) succeeded in imposing his authority and was astute enough to enhance his position in the Church by solicitous recognition of imperial rights. On the basis of a petition presented by a Roman synod of 378 and assented to by the emperor, it was established that while spiritual jurisdiction in matters of faith and discipline should correspond with the tribunals of the secular provinces and dioceses, the bishop of Rome had a general appellate jurisdiction in such matters, extending over the whole empire. In his letter informing the emperor of the synod's request, Damasus refers to the Roman bishopric as the Apostolic See, without qualification. The next move came from the council of Constantinople (381), which published a canon ascribing primacy to the bishop of Rome. By asserting his succession to the apostle Peter, the bishop of Rome won prerogatives for himself as incumbent of the Apostolic See. In addition to his essential contribution to the definition of Roman primacy, Damasus also revived the martyr-cult at Rome; he restored the catacombs and paid tribute in metrical inscriptions to those of the city who had witnessed to the faith with their blood. Pope Damasus – for such we may call him – was not the only western churchman to play a part in the religious policies of this period. The other great figure is Ambrose, bishop of Milan, the city where the emperor of the West had his residence. Ambrose, who came from a Christian family belonging to the senatorial aristocracy, received his literary education at Rome; he then entered on an official career and achieved the governorship of the Ligurian province, which had its seat at Milan, a city in which he was so highly regarded that in 374, although not a cleric, he was elected its bishop. In this capacity he was a devoted pastor to his flock, contributed to the shaping of the liturgy, composed hymns, and by using chants taken from the Greek churches of Syria bestowed on his congregation – and ultimately on western Christendom at large – the priceless gift of Latin hymnody. His theological writings reveal his endebtedness to the Cappadocian fathers, although his teaching on Christian morality also contains elements of the moral philosophy represented by Cicero in his treatise *De Officiis*. Until his death in 397 the voice of this commanding personality always carried great weight at court, whether the emperor were Gratian, Valentinian II or Theodosius. If the attitude adopted by the Church in the West towards the emperor came to diverge substantially from that of Constantinople, it was Ambrose, still more than Damasus, who was responsible.

When Gratian returned to the West after his meeting with Theodosius he issued an edict prohibiting heretic conventicles (August 379). The ecclesiastical authorities soon followed suit. In 381 anathema was pronounced against the Arians by a council at Aquileia. An attempt made in the following year to bring the eastern and western bishops together in a single assembly met with no success. Clearly, the oriental churches did not want direct western participation in the settlement of disputes over eastern sees, nor did they wish to make an all too open recognition of Rome's primacy; a degree of estrangement between eastern and western Christendom is already visible. In 382, therefore, the western bishops met in Rome while another episcopal assembly took place simultaneously in Constantinople. In the lands ruled by Gratian the problem presented by the heretics proved far less intractable than it was for the Greeks. When a little later the Arians of Milan again started agitating, Ambrose rallied all his forces to achieve victory in the Catholic cause.

On the other hand, the overthrow of paganism in Rome, and indeed throughout Italy, was attended by considerable excitement. Brilliant accounts of this last great battle have been given by G. Boissier and J. Geffcken, and further interesting sidelights have emerged from a volume published recently by A. Momigliano. In the autumn of 382 Gratian issued a decree depriving the Vestal Virgins of their privileges, and the Roman priesthoods of their revenues from the State; he also ordered the Altar of Victory to be removed from the Curia, the meeting-place of the Senate. These measures were a devasting blow to the senators, especially those in the circle of Symmachus. The holy flame tended by the Vestal Virgins was one of the most venerable pledges of the empire's safety, the ancient priesthoods were the prized heritage of Rome's foremost families, and the altar, at which senators burned incense on entering the Curia, was a perpetual reminder of a Roman's duty to his ancestral faith. Gratian's death in battle against a usurper in 383, together with a failed harvest which was interpreted as a sign of divine wrath, gave the champions of paganism the opening they needed. Valentinian II, whose Arianising mother Justina was always at his side, was now sole ruler of the West; Symmachus held the office of city prefect in Rome, Praetextatus was prefect of Italy. A senatorial delegation led by Symmachus presented itself at the court in Milan, to petition for the restoration of the Vestals' privileges and the return of the Altar of Victory. In a letter addressed to the court Symmachus is most persuasive in stating the reasons for their request.[11] The old religion, he says, brought the world under Roman dominion, 'vouchsafe to us that we may bequeath to our posterity what we ourselves received as children'. He argues, moreover, that religion takes many forms, that the supreme mystery is not to be attained by one road alone; and the failed harvest and general want are signs that the gods are angry. It was Ambrose, as champion of the rising faith, who acted in response to this moving appeal. He secured its rejection by sending an admonitory letter to Valentinian and as soon as he had Symmachus' statement in his hands composed a written refutation, dealing with each point in turn;[12] Rome has been protected not by the gods but by the strength of her armies; now that Christians have received the truth from the mouth of God, it is error to believe that God can be reached by many roads. Full of confidence, Ambrose claims that the course of the world is tending towards the Good; men should not cleave to the past, Rome is not too old to make a fresh start. Christianity is thus presented as the source of what is new, the agent of progress; the pagan Senate was given written confirmation of its defeat.

In the years which followed Theodosius carried his campaign against heretics and pagans to its logical conclusion and was able to extend his legislative activities to the West, where he was twice called on to overthrow usurping emperors, and on both occasions enhanced his power and authority by military success. After his defeat of Maximus he spent the best part of three years at Milan, where his brushes with Ambrose showed the position of the emperor within the Church in a surprising light. It was reported to Milan that as a result of a quarrel between Christians and Jews at Callinicum on the Euphrates, the bishop of the locality had ordered the synagogue there to be burnt. Theodosius sent an order commanding that the ringleaders be punished and the bishop made to rebuild the synagogue: and was censured by Ambrose for his action. In making his accusation, Ambrose invokes both that freedom of speech which a princeps is bound to indulge and also the priest's duty, as the representative of things which are of God, whose voice in church the emperor must if necessary heed. At first Theodosius abode by his order; but when he came to church, Ambrose charged him from the pulpit to repent and delayed starting the sacrifice of the mass until the emperor had solemnly engaged to revoke his command. The priest prevailed against the emperor. More serious was the collision which occurred in 390. The army commander at Thessalonica had thrown into prison a very popular charioteer, on the grounds that he deserved punishment for infringing an imperial law against unnatural practices. A riot then broke out, in which the commander was lynched. Enraged at hearing the news, Theodosius ordered the populace to be penned in the amphitheatre and massacred. He quickly repented of his horrifying command and revoked the order, but this second instruction arrived too late: thousands of men must have been slaughtered as a result of his initial order. Ambrose regarded the emperor's action as a grave offence on the part of a Christian and informed him that he was not to be present at mass without doing penance. Theodosius presented himself at church for a while as a penitent, and on Christmas Day 390 was finally readmitted to the Lord's Table. The masterful bearing of Ambrose has been contrasted with the docility of the eastern bishops and interpreted as proof of a specifically western spirit in the Church : some indeed, have wanted to conclude that Ambrose demonstrated the Church's formal superiority to the temporal power. This would be a misreading of the bishop's conduct. Admittedly, in these two episodes Ambrose successfully made clear that the Church was not the servant of the State, but in both cases the issue at stake was not political power but spiritual authority : the Christian emperor bowed to a religious command. Even on this interpretation the affair is significant enough : a pious emperor submitted himself in humility to the spiritual might of a bishop, and by his posture of penitence proclaimed what a profound transformation had overtaken the ancient world.

Towards the end of the reign Theodosius' measures against paganism became noticeably harsher. A constitution of 391 forbade pagans to offer sacrifice, to enter temples or worship images ; apostates – Christians who lapsed into paganism – were condemned to perpetual disgrace. Some famous sanctuaries were destroyed, including the temple of Juno Caelestis at Carthage, and the temple of Sarapis at Alexandria, where bishop Theophilus was winning a reputation as a zealot. This urge to destroy vented itself to the full in the events which followed the death of Valentinian II in 392. The Frankish general Arbogast had set up Eugenius, formerly a professor of rhetoric, as a rival-emperor, a gesture which gave fresh heart to the pagans of Rome. Theodosius replied with a drastic pronouncement, in sermonizing vein, prohibiting all forms of pagan cult. Everything was forbidden: offering to images, lighting lamps, burning incense, hanging up garlands. Divination from entrails was classed as treason. All pagan places of worship were annexed to the fisc. Any breach of these orders was threatened with dire penalties ; judges, chief citizens and town councillors were made responsible for implementing the law. At the time this law was issued in the East, the senators of Rome, encouraged by Eugenius, had reverted to the ostentatious celebration of pagan cults. The religious question thus once again depended on the outcome of a civil war. In 394 Theodosius and his eastern army advanced against Eugenius, who had seized the passes over the Julian Alps, and both Christians and pagans awaited a judgement from heaven. At the battle of the Frigidus (now the Vippacco) Theodosius won the day, thanks to a sudden wind-storm from the north ; Eugenius and Arbogast both lost their lives. Public opinion interpreted the result as the verdict of heaven. The cause of paganism was now irretrievably lost, although traces of paganism survived in the belief in Rome. Nicomachus, appointed prefect of Italy by Eugenius, died while the war was in progress; his son, who had become city prefect took refuge in a church, was pardoned and became a Christian.

Theodosius entered Rome as a victor, showed mercy to the survivors and placated the Senate to the extent of appointing his younger son Honorius to succeed him in the West, having already raised Arcadius, the elder, to be co-ruler with him in Constantinople.

In January 395 Theodosius died at Milan. Through his life's work he had made Constantine's choice of religion a reality for the whole empire. But what Constantine had begun in caution and cunning was finally accomplished with radical thoroughness. Paganism was banished from public life. Even if a few Roman nobles still held to their ancestral religion, even if inhabitants of wide tracts of the countryside still followed the customs of their fathers, the state as such was now Christian. The unity imposed on the Church itself was just as complete; the Catholic faith was prescribed by law, heresy ranked with treason. The empire had assumed the theocratic aspect it would retain in Byzantium for a thousand years. In the west, on the other hand, despite all efforts at uniformity, the first signs had emerged that the Church was capable of resisting imperial domination.

If we now ask whether the elevation of Christianity into the state religion was accompanied by any inward transformation of the ancient world, we are exploring a territory where the all-important question is not the power of the State, however all-embracing, but that of the faith itself: that is to say, whether the gospel's power as the message of salvation reached out to men and transformed them, whether lives could be changed through the manifestation of Christian love, whether examples of holiness were to be found in men of all degrees.

We must first notice that in the second half of the fourth century the Christian faith was winning new ground within the empire. In addition to reaching urban centres in northern Italy, the Rhineland, Gaul and Spain, missionaries were now carrying the gospel into regions which were wholly rural. In the countryside primitive magic was still a potent force, men worshipped sacred trees and springs and went in terror of demons. In the fourth century such fetish-worshippers were described as *pagani*, a name which first occurs in an official document dated 370. It seems that originally this word did not denote inhabitants of the *pagi* or cantons, it is more likely to have been treated as synonymous with *gentiles*, in its sense as the equivalent of the Greek *ethnikoi*, tribesmen, worshippers of tribal gods, non-Christians – in fact pagans. Sanctity worked miracles in combating these rural cults, as we know from accounts of missionary activity relating to this period. For example, there was Martin, the divinely-inspired monk who became bishop of Tours about 370 and whose miracles, it is said, broke down the stiff-necked opposition of villagers in the remoter *pagi* of Gaul. We are indebted for this account of the saint to his biographer Sulpicius Severus, who on Martin's advice himself became a monk and left a moving exposition of the ascetic ideal. In his view, doubting the saint's miracles was tantamount to a denial of the gospel itself – an utterance typical of the belief in miracles characteristic of his generation. But this is not to say there was any lack of careful planning in St Martin's mission. A system of country parishes was set up alongside the urban sees, evidence that in some places an episcopate based on towns was already felt to be insufficient. Other bishops and monks were acting in similar fashion to bring the gospel into remote areas, thus Victricius of Rouen in Flanders, Vigilius of Trent in the Julian Alps and Jonas in the mountains of Thrace; later activity included the British Isles.

The thorough evangelization of urban society is most clearly evident at Rome. A few noble families had already turned Christian by the middle of the century. The Anicii led the Christian minority in the Senate; when the male line died out, the house continued in the female line, with the same religious complexion. The rejuvenator of the dynasty was Sextus Petronius Probus, who held the office of praetorian prefect on at least four occasions, under Valentinian I, Gratian and Valentinian II; he was baptized shortly before his death and was buried close to St Peter's. In another family, the Ceionii Albini, the men for the most part remained pagan while the women practised Christianity in its ascetic form. The monastic ideal was in fact invading Roman high society – and what a society it was! Its salient features are familiar from the writings of Ammianus and other contemporaries: the wealth and luxury of the aristocratic elite, the passion for the circus and arena, the ostentatious progresses with attendant hordes of slaves and eunuchs, the extravagant banquets, the ornate hairstyles and jewelry flaunted by the women. Amid all this worldly racket there were not a few who resolved on a total renunciation of property and sensual pleasures. This was not merely a withdrawal from all the temptations and vices of a decadent society; it was also a protest at the official Christianity which from Constantine to Theodosius had made the capture of the secular world its main objective. In this movement the lead was taken by women who were either members of the Ceionii Albini dynasty or had close connections with it. From 365 Marcella, niece of the praetorian prefect Lampadius, presided over a convent of pious women in her house on the Aventine. News which now reached Rome of the ascetic life led by eastern monks aroused great interest. When the elder Melania, daughter and grand-daughter of consuls, was widowed at the age of twenty-one, she set off for Syria and Palestine to see the lives of the hermits for herself; she reached Jerusalem and founded several convents, living there in rigorous asceticism for several decades. Melania's spiritual adviser was the learned monk Rufinus, who undertook the task of translating authoritative works of Greek theology into Latin. This is the first instance of Latins turning to the East, and others soon followed. Another monk, Jerome, who returned from the East in 382 to enter on a period of friendship and collaboration with Pope Damasus, held a magnetic attraction for women of aristocratic birth and won them over to the ideals of poverty and chastity. His circle included Paula, whose family traced descent from the heroes of the Trojan war. On the death of her husband, Paula seized the new ideal as her own; and when Jerome went east again in 385 she followed him, together with her daughter Eustochium. She used her fortune to build religious houses in Bethlehem, three for women, over which she herself presided, and a fourth for men, directed by Jerome. The writings of Jerome and Rufinus have left a vivid impression of these individuals who gave a new look to the image of Christian womanhood in their own century and social circle. The recognition, established from the early days of Christianity, that women were of equal value with men in martyrdom and works of charity, was now extended to the fields of learning and asceticism.

During the second half of the fourth century Christians made some spectacular advances in the whole field of education, culture and literature. Reconciled to the classics, they branched out in new forms of eloquence and erudition. Study of the Bible entailed exegesis of the Old and New Testaments, the sermon in many respects came to occupy the position once held by public oratory, and theology replaced philosophy. Marrou has recently summed up for us the historical importance of this heyday of the Church Fathers. In East and West there were now learned theologians who by their words and deeds acquired the utmost authority in the world around them: the great teachers of the East, the three Cappadocians, Basil, Gregory of Nazianzus and Gregory of Nyssa, to whom must now be added that great master of eloquence, John Chrysostom, and their contemporaries in the Latin Church, Ambrose, Jerome and Augustine, whom we shall meet again. These individuals had certain features in common, which helped to give the spiritual stamp of this century its particular cast. Middle class by origin – apart from one or two aristocratic exceptions such as Ambrose and Chrysostom – they had studied literature and rhetoric, taught at the universities and then, out of sincere conviction, embraced the ideal of Christian perfection; some were active as preachers, writers and bishops in the great cities of the world: all presented Christian scholarship to their contemporaries and succeeding generations as a new spiritual value.

There is a certain phase in the life-story of some western Fathers which merits particular attention from the historian, the phase in which recovery of Christian belief occurred while the subject was immersed in his literary and philosophical studies. Although these men came of Christian families, they were Christians without inward assent, until such time as their search for truth brought them to a formal self-scrutiny. We might prefer to interpret this process as inversion, turning inward, rather than conversion: it represented a metamorphosis of something not previously understood, a new awareness of Christian values and their deeper significance. For many educated Christians of the fourth century this inward journey was the crucial event of their lives. It is no wonder that some who were so smitten described the experience in literature which has become the prototype of the Christian soul's experience in the world. In the forefront stands Augustine, whose *Confessions* recount the history of his soul during the period running from Julian to Theodosius. This book has attracted the interest of many generations of scholars, and has recently been interpreted for us above all by P. Courcelle. Even its name has a double significance: it is a confession of error and sin and at the same time praise of God; human confession becomes prayer, self-awareness is the result of the dialogue with God. Augustine was baptized in 387 and began the *Confessions* ten years later. It is possible that their composition was prompted by certain extraneous circumstances; it may be that Donatist allegations persuaded the bishop of the need for making some personal apologia; the decisive factor was that as a theologian Augustine was at that time occupied with the question of how divine grace operated to effect man's justification. The wholly personal tone of the book thus becomes explicable. Its literary form is also unique. Pagan and Christian philosophers before him had left accounts of their quest for truth, tales of conversion, reports of visions, grateful acknowledgments of grace divinely bestowed; with Augustine autobiography becomes at once the history of a soul in continuous confrontation with Divinity and a self-examination which touches the reader closely, so that he, like the author, is stirred to the depths of his being. In this book we have the great example of a soul becoming aware of Christian existence.

Augustine describes for us his parents' house at Thagaste in Numidia, a region where Catholics and Donatists co-exist, a town which has both its pagan and its Christian element. We meet his pleasure-loving father Patricius and his deeply Christian mother Monica, who devotes all her thought and energy to the salvation of her son. The boy starts his study of rhetoric at the high school in Madaura; Homer, and indeed everything Greek, is distasteful, but Virgil and his wisdom are taken earnestly to heart. He speaks openly of his sensual indulgences, particularly during his time as a student at the university of Carthage (370–74). We are introduced to the life of this predominantly pagan cosmopolitan city, and to student life in particular, with its literary cliques and love affairs. It is here that Augustine meets the woman he will live with for so long; we never learn her name, but Augustine's son Adeodatus is born of their union. In Carthage Augustine experiences his first shock, which comes from reading Cicero's *Hortensius*. Although it is only transitory, he feels the yearning for a settled intellectual and spiritual position and makes a tentative effort to find it in the Bible and the Church; but the Bible falls short of his literary standards and the Church is too institutionalized by far. Now he turns to Manichaeism, seeking redemption through wisdom, aspiring towards personal union with the higher power. But since he is only a 'hearer' in the Manichee congregation, he can continue to savour life in all its aspects. On returning home he falls out with his mother and goes again to Carthage, this time as teacher (375–83). Despite a stimulating circle of friends, we find him now beset by serious doubt: he is sceptical about pagan superstition, Manichaeism is offensive because of its fantastical element and he is not taken in by Faustus, the Manichee bishop, whom he describes as a prattler. Greatly disturbed, he leaves Carthage, deceiving even his mother over his departure, to spend a difficult year in Rome, where the Manichee hearer becomes a philosopher of the sceptical school, a still flourishing branch of Academic philsophy. Without a job, he decides to apply for a recently vacated chair of rhetoric at Milan. He delivers a trial lecture, makes use of his personal recommendations and is appointed to the professorship by Symmachus, the city prefect. In 384 the newcomer to Milan pays a call on Ambrose, occasionally hears him preach, and feels attracted to his allegorical exposition of the Bible. For the rest, Augustine is fully occupied, if not entirely satisfied, with the teaching and official oratory demanded by his position. Friends have arrived from Africa; they include his mother who now takes charge of his household. She scores a notable success in detaching her son from his mistress, since his betrothal to a girl of good family is intended only to advance him in his professional career and carries no moral obligation. Now he conceives the singular idea of withdrawing from the world to establish a communal brotherhood with his philosophical friends, but this plan for a secular monastery founders on opposition from their womenfolk. In 386 Augustine is hearing sermons from Ambrose, who was at this juncture leading his congregation in the last battle against Arianism. Augustine is now deeply impressed by his readings among the neo-platonists, including Plotinus himself, admittedly in the translation of Marius Victorinus. To one so long a captive of Manichaeism and its dualist conception of the world, neo-platonism comes as a liberation. In this system the unity of the cosmos has its basis in the One, who is pure spirit; the evil in the world is understood as an absence of the Divine, the way for man to become spirit is open and wickedness appears as a perversion of the free will. This turning to philosophy is followed by further shocks. A Christian priest, Simplicianus, tells him of the conversion of Marius Victorinus from neo-platonist philosophy to Christianity. Now Augustine starts to read the Bible, in particular the Pauline epistles, and asks himself whether this message can be reconciled with the teaching of Plotinus. His perturbation increases with a visit from Ponticianus, a native of Africa and an officer in the army, homeward bound from Trier. He tells of the holy hermit Antony and of the conversions which have resulted from reading his life-story. In rebellion against himself, Augustine goes out into the garden, where all his temptations and passions rise up to taunt him. Overcome by weeping, he hears a child's voice saying '*tolle, lege*', 'take up and read', and seizing the sacred book lights on St Paul's words: 'Let us behave with decency as befits the day: no revelling or drunkenness, no debauchery or vice, no quarrels or jealousies! Let Christ Jesus himself be the armour that you wear; give no more thought to satisfying the bodily appetites.'[13] Although this episode has so frequently been debated, it remains difficult to say what really happened, whether children were really playing there. Probably Augustine was intent not on reporting a miracle but on giving a symbolic discription of the process which produced his inner enlightenment. What is certain is that this was his moment of self-discovery. With his mother, his son and his students, he now withdraws to the estate belonging to his friend Verecundus at Cassiciacum. Here philosophical discussions take place which he will later revise and publish as Dialogues, whose theme is as follows: the philosopher who searches his heart comes to a new understanding of the ascetic ideal, since the sought-after wisdom is God himself, and this has the effect not only of providing a new way of thinking but also of bringing order to the soul. Philosophizing at this level has a religious and moral connotation and is no longer an obstacle to belief. And so it is done. Augustine resigns his professorship, applies for baptism and receives the sacrament from Ambrose on the vigil of Easter, 387.

Whatever degree of literary artifice has gone into the shaping of Augustine's account, which fills the first nine books of the *Confessions*, the main turning-points in his life have a secure historical foundation: his reading of the *Hortensius* provoked his first revulsion from worldly ambition, the Manichaean recipe for salvation was tried for many years and found wanting. Augustine was not attracted to Ambrose as a person, but listening to his sermons introduced his mind to the possibility of lifting neo-platonic thought into Christian exegesis. The writings of Plotinus carried him one stage further; but the final impetus came from St Paul: it was St Paul who provided the final detonator which opened the ears of the questing Augustine to the voice from his own depths, which led him to the word of God. Such was the inward turning of a Christian who had been led to self-discovery by way of Manichaeism and neo-platonism, to be brought face to face with God, so that now faith was what reason directs and the final step of joining the fellowship of the Church could be taken.

Alongside these *Confessions* of a Christian philosopher we have the self-revelation of a poet, Paulinus of Nola, who was grappling with the Christian ideal at the same time as Augustine. For Paulinus, the struggle turned not on any conflict with ancient philosophy but on renouncing the beauteous world of gods and muses, at the cost of creating unbearable tension between himself and a beloved teacher and friend. He belonged by birth to the nobility of Aquitaine, and in his youth had attended the university of Burdigala, sitting at the feet of the great Ausonius, whose lectures were little occupied with the Christian faith, since the course was taken up with exercises in ceremonious rhetoric and in pedantic games with traditional poetic forms. Paulinus became the distinguished teacher's favourite pupil, but one day – in which year is unknown – he felt called to a religious life of the monastic type, as it was then being introduced from the East. Although he had already reached the consulship, Paulinus abandoned his political career and from 389 resided with his Spanish wife Therasia on their estates in Spain. During this period his resolve to renounce the world ripened. To put it into effect, he had not only to sacrifice his rich estates but also to turn his back on the literary diversions of his student years and on his revered master. By a lucky accident, rare in ancient literature, we possess the poetic correspondence in which the two friends revealed to one another how widely their paths had diverged. This correspondence is not only arresting testimony to the rift in a deep friendship but records the inward-turning of the younger generation, in its quest for Christian faith and Christian love. Let us try to reconstruct this episode, with the help of certain passages from these poetic confessions.

It appears that although Ausonius wrote every year to his friend in Spain, his first three letters all arrived together, so that Paulinus was without news for three years at a time. Only one letter of this first batch written by Ausonius appears to have survived, and with it we are plunged straight into the older man's griefs.[14] I had hoped, he says, to talk you round with the reproaches in my last letter and by cajoling reproof to win some word from you. But you remain silent, as though after swearing an oath. Are you ashamed of this friend who claims a father's rights? Or are you afraid of some informer, or some censor in your midst? If this is the case, resort to cunning, which has guarded many a secret – or so the stories tell us. So write your letter in milk, I will sprinkle the paper with ashes and the writing will then be visible again.

> Countless ways of the ancients can I show you,
> Paulinus, for disguising your secrets in writing,
> If you fear a betrayal and dread a reproach for our love,
> Keep Tanaquil out! Heed nothing from others!
> But disdain not to speak with your father.
> I am the teacher who taught you first,
> I was the first to win you honours,
> The first to lead you among the Muses.

When this letter too remains unanswered, Ausonius gathers himself for a fourth, and becomes even more outspoken.[15] This fourth letter brings you my complaint and by cajolery will force you to speak. Why this long proud silence? Even an enemy greets an enemy on the battlefield. Rocks and forests, meadows and brooks, nothing in nature is dumb, the animals have their language, men delight in the sound of cymbals and clashing brass. But you are silent as though your lips were sealed. I understand your shyness: for long delay fosters its own defect. But who prevents you from sending me a brief word of greeting or farewell, a yea or nay? For my part I cannot keep silence, for affection between friends must be free, it cannot bear a yoke, neither can it place flattery before truth. Dearest Paulinus, have you changed? Is Spain perhaps to blame, and forgetfulness of our native skies? Who is the impious wretch who reduces you to so long a silence? May he lose all power of speech, all power of hearing sweet sounds, and wander mute in the wilderness!

> This is my prayer, O divine Muses of Boeotia,
> Receive my voice and call back your bard with Latin strains.

It is only now, four years after his departure for Spain, that Paulinus answers, in a lengthy poem of 331 lines composed in a number of different metres.[16] In the first section, in distich form, he explains that four years have passed without a letter reaching him. Then came the happy day which brought three together: but these are at once sweet and bitter to him. He is more touched by his father's goodness than by his strictures as a critic. The reproaches will be answered shortly, in heroics; for informal conversation he prefers the iambic measure. What good will it do, he asks, to recall the Muses? Hearts which belong to Christ want nothing of Apollo and the Muses, whose pleasantries are things of the past. The poet is unequivocal in proclaiming his conversion:

> Now another power drives my spirit, a greater God,
> Claiming from man the gift he gave, so that we live only for life's Lord.

Under this law, he continues, poetry, philosophy and rhetoric are but idle chatter, useless in the pursuit of salvation and truth. Man must see truth and goodness in Christ alone, in Christ who demands our all, our thoughts and understanding, our belief and reading, our fear and love, and will return it all in overflowing measure. If I live for this faith, do not call me impious, for piety is the very hall-mark of a Christian. If I can attain such piety, I owe it to you, my patron, my teacher, my father, who set me on the path of eloquence and learning, office and fame.

> Pardon me, as you love me, if I do what is
> Best, and let me live as I will.

Now follows the central section of the poem, Paulinus's justification of himself to his beloved teacher, executed in hexameters. It is useless for Ausonius to recall his protégé to the Muses. For without God, answers Paulinus, the Muses are nothing. God is lord of all, through Christ he rules the world. He alone has changed Paulinus' heart, so that it can never again be what it was.

> My spirit is new, I confess, not mine as once it was,
> But mine through the gift of God;
> And if in my mind or heart he sees anything worthy his gift,
> The glory is yours, who made me what Christ could love.

Paulinus thus maintains that even as a Christian, he still belongs to Ausonius. He recounts in detail the change of heart, the inversion, which has turned him from the empty affairs of the world to face eternity. He protests at the idea that his wife is blameworthy: she is no Tanaquil but Lucretia. He repudiates any suggestion that he has forgotten his homeland or that he has become a savage through living in a Spanish wilderness – Spain is a delightful country, well-endowed with cities. In any case, Ausonius himself is living in the country, some distance from Burdigala and remote from Rome, although he too once was consul. Towards the end Paulinus becomes more emphatic still, reproaching Ausonius for his inappropriate levity and again affirming the seriousness of his conversion and the sureness of salvation in a life lived according to the law of Christ. He concludes with a haunted description of the Second Coming and the Last Judgement, asserting that in belief lies hope of eternal life:

> If you think thus, then rejoice in your friend's rich hope.
> If it be otherwise, well and good; leave me to Christ.

This is truly a bitter pill for the great man of Burdigala, who feels his life drawing to its end and yearns for a sign of affection! But Ausonius answers like a true poet[17]: Paulinus, we are shaking off the yoke we two bore so well together. This yoke, which our fathers carried to the end and left us as their legacy, was so easy that no words, no complaints, no anger, no error, no suspicion could dislodge it. It endured as long as the faith between us partners made it light. But now, Paulinus, we are shaking it off, and the blame is yours. For myself, I would gladly bear it still. It is hard when the burden falls only on the one who is constant. But I take it on myself, even if I am crushed, I keep faith in our friendship until kind memory brings back again my errant comrade. – Truly, you are impious ! Think what joy there was among the people, what expectations seized the nobly born ! Our names were already being linked with the great friendships of the past, men marvelled at our constancy, all the more since we were so unequal in age. Plainly we spoke a presumptuous word and so provoked the avenging goddess – but Nemesis should turn rather against Arabs and Persians. Paulinus and Ausonius, men who have assumed the sacred purple of Quirinus and been clad in golden raiment should not have to submit to persecution from an alien goddess. – But let us return to ourselves ! The thought of Tagus' shore fills me with anguish, the Pyrenees separate us, and all the wide lands between Emerita and the Garonne. Your home is now Caesarea Augusta, not far from Tarraco on the Tyrrhenian Sea, I am remote from Burdigala, on my estate in the Noverian canton. It is pleasant to be here, but without you every season loses its savour. – Beloved friend, do you recognize your fault ? For my part, I keep faith, venerating still the Paulinus of former days. Why, then, these sorrowful lines, whence my reluctance to pray for better things ?

> This confidence remains,
> If God the Father and Son accept this holy plaint,
> My prayer may once again restore you to me.

For I cannot hear news that the house of old Paulinus has been destroyed and plundered, that his royal possessions are divided up and he himself a homeless wanderer in Spain. O come back, my pride and my sorrow, while you are yet young and I have strength in my old age ! When shall I hear the message sounding, See, your Paulinus comes, already he sets foot on his brother's neighbouring estates, already his boat is launched downstream,

> Yea, he is already sighted, his bark is already turned for home,
> He alights at his haven, where joyful men foregather,
> He walks through his people, who crowd around him,
> He passes his house and knocks at my door . . .
> Is it true ? Or do lovers simply dream what they desire ?

This is the last poem we can be sure of from Ausonius, a poem which has perhaps more feeling in it than all the rest of his works combined, as

F. Leo once remarked. Deeply troubled, he lays all the blame on his arrogant young friend and affirms his eternal loyalty. He accuses Paulinus of cheating the expectations of nobility and people by destroying what has already become the image of a classic friendship; this is *impietas*, impiety towards his fellow-citizens and his forebears. This impiety is entirely his own fault. Pagan thoughts and feelings are equally responsible for Ausonius' fear that they have both provoked the avenging goddess. He then gives way to the anguish of an afflicted heart, speaks of the great distances which separate them and comforts himself with the picture of Paulinus as he was in the old days. Tossed this way and that by his emotion, he is prepared to believe that Nemesis could have been responsible for the rift in their friendship; but scarcely is this said, and he recovers himself with a prayer to God the Father and the Son – what abasement for a worshipper of the Muses! – coming a long way towards his friend, whom he conceives to be in danger. For the thought of winning back the prodigal brings in its train reproof of Paulinus as he now is, for contemplating the dissipation of his Spanish estates: and a warning against embarking on the monastic life. At the end feelings of longing are again uppermost. Ausonius believes the friendship will endure and allows the poet to take full charge again, indulging in a dream picture of his friend returning.

Paulinus' answer has survived. It offers no promise of a return, but places the relationship on a new footing.[18] Paulinus deals first with the accusations contained in Ausonius' letter: the long silence, his retreat into private life, his neglect of their friendship, his being afraid of his wife. He beseeches Ausonius to refrain, assures him that loyalty and devotion have always been and remain his constant aim. In my attitude and conduct, he protests, I have always sought your goodness and never given my indulgent father cause for any suspicion. My household has held you in the same veneration, and still does; we are united in our love of you, just as we are one in worshipping Christ. After this moving declaration of friendship, Paulinus refutes some of the specific charges. He asks what rancour is at work, what wicked gossip has inflicted wounds, and vehemently protests the sincerity and innocence which make him undeserving of any false accusation. As for throwing off the yoke, he maintains that in learning he is so far below his master that they could never be a balanced team. But in friendship, which recognizes equal striving between loving and being loved, he remains at his side:

> No evil gossip has prised from off my neck
> This yoke; no parting has deprived me of it,
> Nor ever shall; were I removed from you in space and time,
> Still would there be no separation of our spirits; my life itself
> Shall be expunged sooner than your image from my heart.

This conception of an indivisible friendship is again reiterated in the concluding iambics, where it is supported by a final declaration of faith. Paulinus sees his friend ever-present through all changes of time and space. And when his body dies, his love will still live on:

> For the soul survives, though the body dies,
> Secure in its heavenly birth,
> Preserving its senses and heart's affection
> As surely as its life:
> And so admits forgetfulness no more than death
> And ever loyalty keeps.

Soon after this last salutation, Paulinus was consecrated priest and took the final step into the ascetic life. Together with Therasia, he removed to Nola, which contained the grave of Felix, a martyr he greatly revered, and there erected a majestic basilica, capable of receiving a large throng of pilgrims; for himself he built a noble dwelling close to the hospice he had already established for the sick and the poor. While the empire was crumbling before the Goths and the Vandals, Paulinus continued in his monastic household, dedicated to a life of prayer and the care of the sick and occupied with his duties as bishop of Nola, which he shortly became; he composed odes for the annual feast of his saint and corresponded with eminent personages throughout the Mediterranean world; a monk entirely devoid of fanatacism, a cultured ascetic who rejected, but did not despise, the world.

CHAPTER 3

THE ROMAN WEST AND THE NEW PEOPLES IN THE FIFTH CENTURY

1. *The west Roman empire and the Völkerwanderung – social, economic and legal aspects*

The emperors from Diocletian to Theodosius performed an astonishing feat in keeping the empire firmly together in face of the new world situation. The extended system of military defences long remained intact. Along their entire length, the frontiers were guarded by *limitanei*, a militia partly settled on the land and commanded by frontier generals (*duces*); particular sectors of the frontier were covered from the rear by reserve attacking forces, *comitatenses*, composed of legions and auxiliaries and led by the Masters of Infantry and Cavalry; the emperor had his personal corps, the *scholae* or imperial guard. We happen to possess a list, intended for official use, of all the military and civil offices of the empire, the document known as the *Notitia Dignitatum*. This manual, a source of quite exceptional value both for the military system and for the court and administration of the late Roman empire, has long been the object of searching scrutiny, especially from the time the latest edition of the text was published, by Otto Seeck in 1876. On the basis of penetrating observations by F. Lot and the rigorous examination of the text by A. H. M. Jones, it seems fair to say that the *Notitia* was drawn up shortly after 395 for the administrative head of the western division of the empire, although certain details about officials and troops were revised in subsequent years. The section on the East reflects the situation as it was not long after 395. On the other hand, many items in the section dealing with the western division of the empire have been brought up to a date *c.* 425, although there are admittedly some omissions and discrepancies. With certain reservations, one may calculate a total combined force of about 352,000 limitanei and comitatenses for the East and of 248,000 for the West, to which must be added a few thousand men of the scholae for each half of the empire. Compared with the figure of 10,000 fighting men traditionally ascribed to the Visigoths on their invasion of the empire, this total armed strength appears to indicate a good margin of superiority over the potential aggressors.

Yet it is here, if anywhere, that the figures are deceptive. The information contained in the *Notitia*, intended primarily for use by the financial administration, is an insufficient guide to the exact effective strength of the units. It must also be borne in mind that the frontier troops were tied to their posts and that in course of time even the reserves (the comitatenses) lost much of their original mobility. Hence by the end of the fourth century it was already difficult to free a powerful army for a specific task, whether defensive or offensive. A further difficulty, experienced throughout the empire, was that of finding suitable military replacements. Since the urban population was by now as good as useless for the purpose, recruits were drawn largely from the coloni ; but labour was also very scarce on the estates, so that proprietors were allowed to discharge their obligation to supply recruits by making a money payment. These payments were then used for hiring foreigners in large numbers, the so-called barbarians. From the time of Constantine, and to an even greater extent from the reign of Theodosius, whole regiments of the mobile army were made up of Germans, Franks, Alamanni, Saxons, Goths and others. These included foreigners settled on the soil of the empire and contingents supplied by neighbouring chieftains under treaty ; but the majority were volunteers from outside the empire, now being recruited in ever-increasing numbers. We occasionally hear of Germans living beyond the frontiers who refused to serve under the Roman banner. For example, it is said that Athanaric was made to swear an oath to his father that he would never tread on Roman soil. But in general there was a distinct movement among neighbouring tribes in favour of service under the Romans. Many of these volunteers engaged to serve for only a specified number of years ; they were given periodic leave to visit their homes and when their term of service expired were allowed to return to their tribes. Now and then even greater concessions were made, as for example when Theodosius allowed German volunteers enrolled in the army to withdraw at any time, provided they supplied a substitute. Many of these Germans attained officer rank, germanic names crop up in the records and even Roman names may often conceal foreigners : Silvanus, hailed as emperor by the Rhine army in 355, was a Frank. We cannot know for certain whether such foreigners in the Roman service, who as a rule were required to fight against German tribes, who may well have been their close kinsmen, were disturbed by a conflict of loyalties and emotions ; ancient authors certainly at times accuse them of treachery, either actual or potential. But remarks of this kind are in keeping with the general view that the Germans as a whole were inspired by feelings of national loyalty and that all barbarians were faithless – a bookish prejudice, widely held and deeply rooted. It is a fact that some foreigners reached high-ranking positions and from the middle of the fourth century were penetrating the supreme commands. Many German generals fought with devotion in the Roman cause and exerted considerable political influence, whether through their advice on general questions of strategy or as the decisive voice in emperor-making. We know of Frankish commanders playing an historic role, Merobaudes under Gratian, Bauto under Valentinian II and Arbogast under Eugenius. A few generals were even given the distinction of a marriage link with the imperial house. It is true that a constitution of Valentinian I prohibited *conubium* between Romans and barbarians under pain of death,[1] but exceptions were made for emperors and germanic chieftains. Bauto's daughter Eudoxia became the wife of Arcadius, Theodosius honoured Stilicho, the Vandal who did him such great service, by granting him the hand of Serena, his niece and step-daughter. This marks the highest point reached by Germans in the service of Rome; the death of Theodosius produced a serious and immediate crisis.

The arrangements Theodosius made for the succession brought about a significant cleavage both in the imperial régime and in the administration of the empire. In appointing his sons to follow him, Theodosius had been guided by purely dynastic considerations; but at his death in 395 Arcadius was eighteen, Honorius only eleven. Unsuited – and often disinclined – to assume the burden of government, they made no attempt at exercising their supreme military command; in the East of the empire two centuries would pass before an emperor again appeared at the head of his army. The fact that there were two co-equal emperors meant that there were now two distinct imperial domains; the East was presided over by Arcadius, the rest, comprising the prefectures of Gaul and Italy, together with the Balkan territories, by Honorius (plate 73). This dual monarchy, in no way a return to the collegiate system which had been tried on so many previous occasions, had the effect of dividing the empire into two independent parts (*partes imperii*). From this time forward there was one government in Constantinople and another in Milan; the ministers and councillors whose task it was to guide their feeble masters contributed not a little to widening the rift still further. The government of the West was for many years controlled by Stilicho, Master of both Infantry and Cavalry and generalissimo of the army; in the East a praetorian prefect, a grand chamberlain and the empress Eudoxia followed one another in swift succession as the dominant voices. It was not so much the existence of two emperors but of two groups of ruling magnates which produced lasting rivalry and made it difficult to reach agreement over questions affecting the empire as a whole. There are indications that Stilicho, motivated less by personal ambition than by the desire to continue the policy of Theodosius, aimed at controlling the whole empire, a design in which he was successfully thwarted by the regents of the East. In both capitals court life continued to develop along lines already laid down: the emperors who had lost much of their political power were set on a pedestal, like larger-than-life palace statues; ceremonial and protocol became rituals of the utmost solemnity. When high officials took the oath of loyalty, they laid their forefingers against the emperor's head; Jovius, prefect of Italy under Honorius, made the flattering remark that while the breach of an oath sworn on the name of God might still receive divine pardon, this could never be so of an oath sworn on the head of the emperor, but such avowals of courtly devotion did not prevent magnates from spinning intrigues against their masters. The Senates of East and West also became embroiled in this antagonism. The Senates of Rome and Constantinople, parliaments of the imperial aristocracy, were hierarchical in their composition. The lowest rank, the *clarissimi*, embraced inferior provincial governors, regimental tribunes and numerous officials who had been raised to senatorial rank as a mark of distinction; next came the *spectabiles*, mainly provincial governors of higher rank and the heads of the imperial chanceries; and finally the *illustres*, who comprised the highest dignitaries of all, for example the prefects, the masters of the army and former consuls. Since in both parts of the empire the senatorial order represented the top layer of society, the rift between East and West showed up very clearly in these upper chambers. The western notables, even when they hailed from outlying provinces, adhered to Latin ways of life and cultural traditions and continued to see Rome's civilizing mission in a practical light. In the East, where the senatorial order was drawn from the bourgeoisie of the old Greek cities and the governing class of the hellenized parts of Asia Minor, Syria and Egypt, Greek language and civilization was still a living reality and the leading spirits were conscious of their superiority over the west in scientific knowledge and philosophical talent. With the advance of Christianity, the divergence between the cultural traditions and ethnic characteristics of East and West was already very marked even in the third century. Thus the two now opposed divisions of the empire also represented two distinct cultural worlds: Byzantium and Rome, Hellas and Hesperides.

In the situation which arose after the death of Theodosius, the tension between the eastern and western governments showed up with particular clarity in their attitudes towards Germans serving under Rome. Apprehensions concerning the role of these germanic upstarts were common enough in bourgeois and senatorial circles, whether expressed in terms of Roman patriotism serving as a cloak for jealousy of the intruders or as dark premonitions of the outcome of a policy of friendship towards the Germans, fears which refused to be allayed even by the thought that barbarians who served Rome were fighting other barbarians and so in the end inflicted damage on the whole enemy world. But in Constantinople feeling against the Germans now had a keener edge. A foremost representative of the movement favouring their expulsion was Synesius of Cyrene, who in his life history and writings (rhetorical-philosophical works, hymns and letters) typifies the Greek elite of his day. Born about 370, he occupied his youth with aristocratic sports and philosophical studies and embraced a neo-platonist form of Christianity. In 399 Synesius was sent as an envoy from his own town to Constantinople, where he stayed for three years; about 410 the people of Ptolemais chose him as their bishop, which made him metropolitan of the province of Cyrenaica. In this spiritual office he also intervened in the secular affairs of his city and proved a very perceptive observer of the contemporary scene. In 400, during his sojourn at Constantinople, he delivered a great oration at court, taking the imperial office as his subject. Starting from the philosophical image of the true ruler, he sets out to show how greatly the reality has declined from this ideal, chiding the emperor for his pomp-encrusted seclusion within the palace. 'You hide in your apartments lest men discover you too are human'. He then prescribes his remedies: the emperor should break loose from all the stultifying ceremonial and the palace clique, he should show himself to the public, join his soldiers in military exercises and lead them into battle – as in the days of his predecessors. Next he turns to the Goths: the Goths are traitors, just as dangerous in the field as in the council chamber, a threat even to families whom they serve as menials. They should be expelled from the army, none but Romans should be entrusted with the defence of the father-land, in keeping with the principle that citizens should win their own victories. Barbarians, he says, are born to slavery; it is a scandal that skin-clad Scythians – again he means the Goths – should parade as army captains: let all fair-haired men be banished from the seats of the mighty! In contrast with those earlier orators who praised the emperor Theodosius for conciliating the Goths, Synesius denounces the policy of granting them land: the Romans should force them to work the soil, as the Spartans did the Messenians. Here speaks the voice of a Hellene whose literary studies have inspired him with the citizen spirit of the classical age, leading him to make drastic demands on his own generation while giving no hint of how the ideal of a citizen body in arms was to be realized in the changed situation. The orator's attack on the Goths sparked off feelings already highly combustible. The fate of a Visigothic general named Gainas illustrates just how deeply the urban population was pervaded by hostility towards the Germans. Gainas was at this time lodging with his troops in Constantinople, oppressing the capital by his presence and embroiling himself in the intrigues of the court. Bishop

John Chrysostom tried in vain to reduce the tension between the citizens and the foreign troops, whose Arianism gave further cause for offence. In an outburst of popular frenzy the Goths were surprised and massacred just as they were withdrawing from the city. Another officer named Fravitta, also a Goth, was commissioned to destroy the fleeing Gainas, and in the end both foreign generals fell victim to the executioner. However much popular feeling and the machinations of the court may have contributed to this anti-Gothic demonstration, the episode leaves us in no doubt that the tradition of *Romanitas* was still being cultivated in the East, and with good reason: the men who ruled the East called themselves Rhomaioi, and Constantinople was known everywhere as the New Rome.

In the West, on the other hand, Stilicho (plate 5) showed great adroitness in continuing Theodosius' policy of friendship with the Germans. The Vandal had his enemies in the Roman Senate, but as a skilled tactician he found ways of dealing with the aristocracy, treating paganism with deference and granting landed proprietors relief from taxation. Honorius made some concession to Roman patriotism by attempting to curb the growing vogue in Rome for German fashions, sleeveless brightly-coloured jackets, wide trousers and long hair. But the Germans still held their dominant position in the army; Stilicho, an energetic and far-sighted general, won numerous further victories over the germanic tribes still invading the empire and so retained the confidence of the court. In 398 Honorius married Stilicho's daughter Maria (plate 71) and after her death took her younger sister Thermantia as his wife. But this same year, 408, was one of disaster for the German generalissimo. Alien tribes who stormed the Rhine frontier wrought such havoc in the provinces that Stilicho's reputation was shattered. Nevertheless, on the death of Arcadius, he was commissioned by Honorius to go East to act as regent for his nephew, the youthful Theodosius II. But just at the very moment when Stilicho must have hoped that control of the whole empire was within his grasp, the long gathering opposition to him as a foreigner finally broke. Through the stratagems of his personal enemies, Stilicho was discredited with the emperor and lost his support in the army; he was eventually taken prisoner and beheaded. But even this tragic ending to the Vandal's career brought about no total reversal in the German policy pursued at the western court; all that happened was that for half a century no German officer was entrusted with supreme command of the army. Stilicho had his successors as commanders-in-chief and chief ministers to the emperor, but they were eminent Romans. The first was Constantius, a Master of the Soldiers who in 417, at the height of his career, married Galla Placidia, the emperor's sister. The son of this marriage, Valentinian III, reigned as emperor of the West for thirty years, starting in 424; but during the fateful years 434–54 the supreme military command and conduct of the state was in the hands of another Master of the Soldiers, Aetius. Romans though they were, these powers behind the throne still kept to the old procedure of filling gaps in the army with Germans and other foreigners and thought it clever tactics to set German tribes in occupation of imperial territory at each other's throats.

Soon after the death of Theodosius, the initiative in the long drawn-out contest between the empire and the hostile world outside, between the ancient world and the new peoples, passed to the close-knit leagues of German tribes; whether they were still outside the frontiers or had already advanced into Roman territory was immaterial. The elemental drive and will to freedom of these peoples now descended on the Romans in full spate. As we trace the advances made by the various groups down to the middle of the fifth century, our concern will not be with specific questions of warfare and policy but with the general aspects of German activity and the Roman reaction to it. The forefront of the picture will be occupied by the empire of the West, virtually the sole target of German attacks. For a number of reasons the eastern empire remained essentially unaffected by the Germans. In the first place, the geographical starting-point of the chain of aggression made it inevitable that tribes pressing in from eastern Europe would push against the Rhine and the Danube, that is to say the western empire. In addition, the diplomats of Constantinople repeatedly showed their skill by deflecting migrating tribes away from Thrace and sending them on to the West. But the decisive factor was that the political, military and economic systems of the eastern empire suffered no material damage. The capital city of Constantinople, a fortress protected by the sea, was impregnable, while the eastern government found ways of adapting the provincial government to the new situation and by its financial policy ensured that there was no fall in the value of money. The cities of Asia Minor and Syria continued to prosper from their industrial activity and active pursuit of trade. In view of their success in keeping the alien tribes at bay, it is no wonder that the men who ruled in Constantinople came to feel that whereas old Rome had abdicated her responsibilities they were the true representatives of Rome's world-wide mission.

Numerous references to the germanic peoples themselves in the first decades of the invasions are to be found in poems, sermons and lives of the saints; this literary history of the German migrations has been reconstructed for us by W. Capelle and P. Courcelle. But in these sources the Roman side of the picture overwhelmingly predominates. We hear much of the sufferings of inhabitants of the empire, of the atrocities committed by the barbarians – often deplored in the platitudes usual in ancient literature – and the plight of refugees who fled from Italy, Gaul and Spain to north Africa and the East. We hear something of the strong penetration of the Roman army by germanic elements and are told of the suspected or actual treachery perpetrated by individual officers and even by citizens of beleaguered towns. There are references to bishops who organized resistance to the foreigners and to churches used as places of asylum. In Christian writers detached observation of the foreign invaders is often hindered by the author's excessive reliance on divine protection, secured through the intercession of the saints and the miraculous deeds of holy monks. Even military leaders could fall back on miracles, as for example the general named Jacobus whose cult of the saints inspired the poet Claudian to an ironic epigram. We thus cannot expect these contemporary witnesses to give us any definite information from the German side, even about matters of the first importance. The figures suggested for the numerical strength of the tribes are often pure fantasy; the results of modern scholarship suggest that in numbers the German fighting forces were far inferior to the Roman armies and that the total number of aliens introduced into the empire by tribal settlement was minute compared with its existing population. We are no better informed about the weapons available to the invaders. E. Salin and others who have investigated graves and their weapon deposits, using new archaeological techniques, have concluded that in this respect the Germans were superior to the Romans; it seems that their outstanding skill in making offensive weapons – lance, sword, javelin and throwing axe – was derived from the metal-working Celts of central Europe. If we ask how the tribes moved about, we discover that no author has described them on the trek, that no relief depicts their wagon trains or temporary encampments. Opinions vary as the objectives of the invaders. It is often assumed they were in search of booty, but we know that these Germans were not strictly speaking nomads but dispossessed cultivators: in need of sustenance, they halted when they came to state granaries and had to move on again when the supply was exhausted; it was not long before they felt the urge to possess land for permanent cultivation. Often the political aims of the germanic princes also remain obscure. Many fought with dogged determination to achieve their ambition of high office under the empire; yet they shrank from seizing the imperial dignity itself – even at the height of his success, when he had won the emperor's daughter as his bride, the Visigothic king Athaulf preferred to set up an insignificant Roman rather than himself as rival emperor. At a certain juncture, though just when is often difficult to say, some chieftains were struck by the idea of achieving complete independence for their own peoples within the boundaries of the empire. There are many further questions we should like to ask: how was contact made between the strangers and the emperor and his emissaries, what relations did they have with the local urban and rural populations? Were there interpreters? We hear only seldom of Romans and Germans who could speak both languages. Our sources often allude to the conflict of religious belief, to tension between the Catholic inhabitants of the empire and the Arianized Germans. But these Greek and Roman writers make no comment on the way these tribes and peoples, uprooted as they were from their traditional way of life, endured the hardships of migrating with their wives and children, they tell us nothing of the poetry by which the Germans transfigured their heroic feats, nor of the religion which sustained them in their plight. When so much must remain obscure, it is all the more essential to bear constantly in mind that the phenomenon we are observing is a migration of peoples, not merely an invasion of 'barbarians'.

In describing the assault of the Germans on the Roman empire it is difficult to keep the various peoples sharply distinct, since the movements of Visigoths, Vandals and Burgundians were often closely interwoven, and other migrant groups were also involved. Unrest started among those Visigoths who had settled in Moesia following the treaty of 382. After the death of Theodosius, this tribe broke out in rebellion, led by Alaric, the chieftain who afterwards became their king. With their first onslaught (395–7) the Visigoths ravaged the whole Balkan peninsula and, being at the mercy of the rival governments of Constantinople and Milan, were first granted settlement land in Epirus. Having gathered strength for a new attack, the Visigoths directed their second onslaught against Italy (401–3) but were eventually expelled by Stilicho, who had summoned all available Roman forces including troops from the Rhine and Britain, and made to settle on the Save. It was during this war that the decision was made to transfer the imperial government, which had been besieged for a while in Milan, to Ravenna, a small town protected from surprise attack by its surrounding swamps. In earlier days the imperial fleet had been stationed here; the move to Ravenna gave Honorius' government an outlet to the sea, although the actual harbour, Classis, was silted up and much labour had to be expended before it could be re-opened for maritime traffic. Ravenna, difficult of access from the landward side but open to the sea, made a superb refuge for the imperial government in its hour of need. In the fifth book of his history Zosimus paints a vivid contrast between the land of Italy, for so many years an almost defenceless prey to its conquerors, and the court of Ravenna, pursuing its ceremonies and intrigues as though playing out some ghostly game.[2] The many churches and tombs which came to adorn Ravenna over the years complement this impression of a cloistered monarchy, turned in on itself in anchorite seclusion.

While Alaric's Visigoths spent a few years recuperating, other tribes invaded the empire by way of the weakened Danube and Rhine frontier. Fleeing before the Huns, in 405 a migrant host composed largely of Ostrogoths and led by Radagais forced a passage over the Danube and the eastern Alps into Italy, to be annihilated by Stilicho only when they reached Faesulae in Etruria. The invasion which followed at the end of 406 was more serious still: Alans, Vandals and Sueves reached the Rhine by way of Pannonia, Noricum and Rhaetia and on 31 December crossed the river, probably in the region of Mainz. This group was led by the Vandals, who in the early days of the empire had settled in Poland and Silesia. There the tribe had divided into two, the Asdings and the Silings. From the second century the Asdings had been infiltrating the plain round the river Theiss, but the advance of the Huns now forced them to migrate, and together with Alans, Sueves and, in particular their tribal kinsmen the Silings, they swept towards the middle Rhine. After crossing the river these tribes spent three years ravaging Gaul and then crossed the Pyrenees into Spain; here they split up into groups which settled in the north-west, the west and the south of the country; because their units were small, they were able to come to a temporary accommodation with the Hispano-Roman population. However, the weakening of the Rhine frontier in 406 provided opportunity for yet another east German tribe to enter the empire. These were the Burgundians, who from the middle of the third century had occupied the area round the Main, a base from which they advanced slowly towards the Rhine which they now crossed. Once in Gaul, the Burgundians were at first used by Roman commanders to protect the empire against other invaders, but in 413 the Roman Master of Soldiers, Constantius, as representative of the west Roman government, granted them recognition under treaty as *foederati*. The area they then settled was not the lower Rhine, as has often been asserted, but a region west of the middle Rhine in the neighbourhood of Worms. Archaeological finds made here confirm the tradition handed down in medieval German heroic epic.

Now that Stilicho was dead, the Visigoths once again started on the move. In this their third onslaught they drove deep into Italy and turned against Rome. Three times Alaric laid siege to the eternal city. The first blockade, in 408, was raised on payment of a hefty ransom by the Romans; as a result of his second blockade Alaric succeeded in imposing a rival emperor on the Senate, whose role was to open the way to Africa for the Goths; at the third assault, in 410, the city was captured and ransacked and the emperor's sister, Galla Placidia, carried off as a hostage. The news of the Gothic conquest of the city sent a momentary thrill of horror through the provinces, but the court in Ravenna, inaccessible to the Germans, stood firm, cutting off supplies from the invaders and frustrating Alaric's plan for crossing into Africa. When Alaric died, his successor Athaulf led the Visigoths into Gaul, where they occupied the fertile band of country between Narbo and Burdigala, including Tolosa. The Roman counter-offensive was slow in getting under way: but it succeeded in making the Visigoths attack the germanic tribes which had settled in Spain. Having wiped out the Silings, the Visigoths negotiated a settlement treaty under which they received part of Aquitania, namely the tract of land bordering the Atlantic coast between the Loire and the Pyrenees; this marked the beginning of a régime of coexistence with the Gallo-Roman population, which will later be discussed in more detail.

In Spain the Suevi still held Gallaecia in the north-west corner, while the Alans and their Asding allies were firmly entrenched in the extreme south, in the province of Baetica. In 428 leadership of this southern group passed to Gaiseric, king of the Vandals and Alans, a man of great strength, not to say violence, who knew how to add to his royal stature and in his dealings with Ravenna discovered ways of backing armed force by clever and often unscrupulous diplomacy. He conceived the plan of transporting his entire people to Africa; here they could feed directly from this 'bread basket' of the western empire, and break the resistance of the imperial government by cutting off the export of grain. Roman rule in the provinces of north Africa had for a long while been ineffective. Firm support for the empire came only from the landed aristocracy and the Catholic Church, with its numerous episcopal sees in the cities of northern Algeria, Tunisia and Tripolitania. Most of the Berber mountain tribes had made themselves independent, and the widely scattered Donatists and Circumcellions were still in constant rebellion against the governing class. In 429 Gaiseric landed in Africa with his people, to a reported strength of eighty thousand, marched east through Mauretania without meeting any resistance and was only challenged by Roman defence forces when he reached Numidia. The Romans met with no success in the open field, but some cities stood firm, for example Cirta and Carthage and also Hippo Regius, where in 430 Augustine died during the siege. Once again German invasion resulted in a settlement treaty, agreed in 435: against a promise of military help, the Vandals were granted specific territory in Numidia. But when this was followed by the capture of Carthage, the capital city, in 439, their independence was recognized and the first sovereign germanic state to exist on Roman soil had come into being.

This survey of the incursion of new peoples into the Roman empire would be incomplete without a glance at the later activities of the Burgundians. Their settlement in the region of Worms was followed, thanks to the exertions of Aetius, by a consolidation of the Roman position in

Gaul. In 435, when the Burgundians attempted to break into the neighbouring province of Belgica, they were massacred by an army led by Aetius and containing a strong contingent of Huns. The death of the Burgundian king Gunther and his sworn companions forms part of the historical kernel of the German *Nibelungenlied*, in which the figures of Aetius and Attila have been conflated. According to one chronicle, the remnant of the tribe was settled in 443 in south-eastern Gaul, in the province of Sapaudia (Savoy), south of Lake Geneva. However, the evidence of place names and archaeological finds seems to indicate that this original settlement area extended northwards as far as Lake Neuchâtel. From this base the Burgundians were able to expand north of the line Geneva–Lyons to found a germanic state.

We shall later have occasion to trace developments in the different parts of the empire as a result of the German contact with ancient civilization. Our immediate concern is with the effect of the German invasions on the inhabitants of the empire, as it affected their thoughts and feelings, their beliefs and hopes. The disturbance to the existing order was undoubtedly tremendous. Alien peoples had established themselves in many provinces, including some of the most fertile in the empire, the left bank of the Rhine was settled by Germans along its entire length, Britain had been abandoned to its fate. The emperor was left in firm possession only of Italy and part of Gaul, where Arles now became the seat of the prefecture and the centre of Roman authority. The city of Rome had been humiliated, the government lingered on in Ravenna, its city of refuge. Here Galla Placidia, whose destiny was so closely interwoven with that of the empire, continued to assert her sway as army commanders and ministers jostled one another for power; even when her son Valentinian III married in 437, she still had her title and dignity as *piissima et perpetua Augusta mater*. How did contemporaries, pagan and Christian, view this decline in the empire, what did they envisage for the future? Many voices make themselves heard, and when we listen to those who bear the leading part in this stately chorus of agents and patients we may well wonder at what we hear. It is surely strange that the tottering Roman world of the late fourth and early fifth centuries could still produce significant Latin poetry, and what is more, Latin poetry which takes belief in Rome as its theme. Even the short-lived success of Stilicho was enough to loosen men's tongues. Thus on the one hand we find a poet once again invoking the traditional pagan image of Rome's universal dominion, on the other a poet offering a Christian interpretation of the age-old vision of Rome, an interpretation clothed for the first time in classical dress: Claudian and Prudentius.

Claudius Claudianus, an immigrant from the Greek East, won office and renown at the court of Honorius. Of all Greeks who adopted the

Roman tongue, he was the most thoroughly imbued with the Latin spirit. A master of poetic diction, he was completely at home with his classical exemplars, from which he also drew his images of gods and mythical figures. Although the name of Christ occurs in one of his smaller poems, in the full-dress works he composed for ceremonial occasions the poet presents himself as a spokesman for the traditional religion. He found inspiration for his epic verses in the events of his own day: the consulships of the emperor Honorius and the emperor's nuptials, the assumption of the consulship by Stilicho and by sundry members of the old aristocracy, the feats of war accomplished by the Master of Soldiers in his campaigns against the African rebel Gildo and against the Goths. When called for, the court propagandist could also inveigh against internal enemies, for example Rufinus and Eutropius, ministers of the eastern empire; on such occasions, adulation is combined with unrestrained abuse. This poet uses his mastery of words and richness of imagery to speak for all those who could not live without the old sustaining faith in Rome. With his glorification of the eternal city and the universal empire, Claudian is reverting to the basic position of the classical poets and historians. Eulogies of the good old days – and there can be no doubt that he means the pagan good old days – are linked with praise of the mighty city whose protection came from the gods; the high virtues of self-denial, frugality and obedience are extolled, the roll of heroes, stretching from Horatius Cocles through the Decii and the Scipios down to Cato and Brutus, is once again rehearsed. The poet remains convinced that Rome's conquest of the peoples was a noble deed. The universal dominion it achieved is a reality still, Stilicho has won willing service from the nations, Rome has only to threaten and the Rhine is pacified. Rome's imperium rests not on force of arms but on the truth of her law and justice, as already proclaimed by the orators and poets of the age of Caesar and Augustus. The enduring service of Rome has been to establish justice among men and friendship among the nations.

It is astonishing that anyone could entertain such illusions twenty years after Adrianople and only ten before the sack of Rome by the Goths. But Claudian, panegyrist that he is, insists that the present generation is shouldering its inheritance, that the empire is a guarantee that *virtus* will remain the fundamental principle of life. The poet becomes quite intoxicated as he describes the splendours attending grand occasions of the day, for example one of Honorius' consular processions: he shows us the city of Rome thronged with people, the fêted ruler received by the august Senate, the victor mounting on his chariot and flanked by armoured cavalry making his way to the forum and the Palatine, all set against a carnival background of chariot races, wrestling matches, animal contests, pantomimes, concerts, comedies, tragedies, not forgetting the water organs and rope dancers, the fire-works and theatrical sea-battles – in fact all the vanities which Augustine castigates as *pompa diaboli* ! Admittedly, Rome has its enemies, but Claudian contends that the barbarians are savages, bent only on war and brigandage; their habit of dressing in skins is sufficient proof of their lack of culture. Stilicho has succeeded in making them beat their swords into ploughshares, they gain no admittance to the Roman world unless they bow to the Roman yoke. There must be no miscegenation; he comments with disgust on the consequences of union with African barbarians, 'a coloured bastard besmirches the cradle'.[3] But it is not only blood that makes men barbarians; men become estranged when they deny their Roman heritage, for example the rebel Gildo who had been an officer in the Roman army. As the partisan of Rome, Claudian directs the full force of his invective against the rulers of the eastern part of the empire, the 'Greek Quirites'. The iniquity which once made the Hellenes resist the Persians, the vice which was the ground of Augustus' charges against Antony, has made its home in Byzantium: the tyranny of its rulers has generated a spirit of slavery among the subjects; the eastern court is under female domination, but more nefarious still is the power of the eunuchs, tantamount to a perversion of the world itself. East Rome is thus held up to scorn as the epitome of everything asiatic. Moments of candid self-scrutiny are rare; there is the usual sermonizing over the decline in morals, but the emphasis is mostly on negative features in the Roman historical record, which exonerates from blame the world of Honorius and Stilicho. On one solitary occasion Roma is made to recognize her own impotence and shadowy existence, and to ascribe her failing powers to the empire's inflated size:

> This weight oppresses me! O would that I could return
> To the bulwarks of the fathers, to the walls of humble Ancus ![4]

This is perhaps a fleeting intimation of the danger inherent in the prodigious expansion of the empire, a danger already perceived by Florus some centuries earlier. But although the poet speaks of Rome's senility, depicting Roma as a lady advanced in years, he also assumes that Rome is coeval with the world and will fall only when nature herself is undone. It is clear that Claudian the panegyrist has succumbed to the drug of his own poetry and eloquence. Noble senators, and German generals whose long years of service identified them with Rome, were still eagerly swallowing these archaic ideas and images whilst Alaric was invading Italy and the Vandals were crossing the Rhine.

When we compare this resuscitation of the old belief in Rome's mission with the message of a contemporary Christian poet, we find that the old gods are firmly rejected and that the Christian religion is advocated as the specific for Rome's rejuvenation : but even the Christian poet subscribes to the traditional values of victory and dominion, and shows himself just as optimistic as the pagan in his assessment of the contemporary situation. Aurelius Prudentius Clemens, who belonged by birth to the senatorial aristocracy of Spain, held high office under Theodosius I but in later life devoted himself exclusively to poetry. He had no difficulty in using the lyric and epic forms of classical literature, but chose to make the Christian faith his central theme, thus becoming the first significant poet produced by Christianity. He wrote odes, but fashioned them into a prayer-book for the Christian's daily round ; he opened up a new field for didactic poetry with his poems on the divinity of Christ and the origin of evil ; his epic on the warfare of the soul (*Psychomachia*) celebrates heroic contests in the manner of Virgil, his book of hymns entitled *The Crowns* honours martyrs who deserted the banner of Caesar for that of the cross. These works probably already lay behind him when in 402–3 Prudentius set himself to compose a poetic answer to the famous memorial in which Symmachus had defended paganism, with the noble intention of winning over the senator, who was still alive and held in high respect at Rome. Written in hexameters, *Contra Symmachum* adopts many of the arguments advanced by earlier apologists, including points made by Ambrose in his reply to Symmachus, and makes great play with Christian patriotism, thus giving the belief in Rome a new twist. In the first book Prudentius relates how Rome renounced error at the call of Theodosius ; still capable of learning, even in her old age, she cast aside her own past and embraced belief in Christ. Theodosius was the bringer of salvation, the bloodless victor, the empire he initiated will have no end. The second book is taken up with refutation of pagan arguments : The Romans owed their past victories not to the gods but to the true God, who was preparing a united world to be ruled by a Christian Rome. If Roman civilization was allowed to spread over lands and continents, it was to smoothe the way for Christ. Now that Rome is Christian she stays young and strong, indeed she is filled with a sense of complete rebirth. Roma herself addresses the young emperors :

> O let me greet you, far-famed princes, noble sons
> Of that great victor, with whom my impotence
> Was vanquished in rebirth, and I beheld
> My grey hairs gold again ! Let all that is mortal age
> According to the law : for me time has ushered in another century
> And a long life taught me scorn of death.[5]

This Christian Rome has its own heroes ; the emperor takes the burden of the salvation of his subjects on himself, by uniting all its peoples the empire fulfils a dispensation of providence ; Church and State rule the world in partnership, their work spills over into eternity. This Christian conception of history, which had such a powerful influence on poets who celebrated Rome in later centuries, contains some unmistakeably pre-Christian elements. The poet's vision of the emperor and Christ riding together in the triumphal chariot owes not a little to old Roman imperialism. Again, in Prudentius we come across the traditional derogation of the barbarians, whom the Christian poet places on a level with four-footed beasts. His sense of triumph is really quite extraordinary, considering that his age was one of dire peril. So far as we know, Prudentius did not live to see the sack of Rome by the Goths. But how did his voice fall on men's ears in this year of catastrophe?

We have seen how both the pagan and the Christian image of Rome survived, despite the turmoil and misery produced by the invasions. For all their groaning over the tribulations brought by war and barbarian brutality, the chroniclers still entertain hopes for the future. The author of a poem on providence, written at this period, may enlarge on the sufferings of his native Aquitaine, but he still clings to his conviction that order will yet prevail in the world: the present distress is at once God's punishment for sin and a scourge sent to bring men of false beliefs or none to Christ. The pagan poet Rutilius Namatianus, who lived through the sack of Rome, on returning to his native Gaul could assert his confidence in Rome's continuing and peculiar faculty for self-renewal (*ordo renascendi*), which has never yet deserted her: Rome will rule so long as earth and heaven endure. We hear again the familiar complaint that Rome has brought disaster on herself by deserting the old gods, the saints are derided for failing to save her. This was the last outburst of patriotic pagan sentiment; as we shall see later, the Christian answer was given by Augustine, in his universal conspectus of the world.

These literary voices from the early fifth century, so confidently asserting that the Roman world order would continue, exemplify the baleful traditionalism which governed the thinking of this late period and cast its blight on every effort at making a clear appraisal of the actual situation. Against this deceptive picture we must set the facts of economic, social and legal life in the western provinces at the turn of the fourth century, the existing structure which provided a framework for the German successor states and determined their future. When we look at the evolution of the social and economic order as a whole, we find no succession of revolutionary shocks but rather a continuous development, along lines already laid down by the reforms of Diocletian and Constantine. We have a number of texts to guide us, the most important being the numerous imperial constitutions which were issued from the time of Constantine onward and assembled in 438, on the orders of Theodosius II, in the compilation known as the *Codex Theodosianus*. Aided by this exceptionally rich material, A. H. M. Jones has been able to piece together a magnificent mosaic portrait of the late Roman world, which is now supplemented by J. Gagé's study of class structure.

In the West of the empire, as in the East, the bureaucratic state set up by the absolute monarchy, although often shaken, remained firmly entrenched. The central government in Ravenna and the system of prefectures, dioceses and provinces weathered many storms. The army was still organized along the lines projected by Diocletian and Constantine, both as regards disposition of troops and the relationship between the commands. But great difficulties were experienced in finding sufficient man-power. In the second half of the fourth century recruits were being demanded from the coloni working the estates, but proprietors often found ways of evading this levy and there was such widespread resistance to the call to arms among the conscripts themselves that there is frequent mention in the sources of self-mutilation by recruits and desertion on the part of soldiers. In this serious situation the rule was established that sons of soldiers were bound to follow their father's profession, a rule now imposed on other trades as well. Despite these measures, there were still wide gaps in the army which had to be filled by increasing the number of foreigners, above all Germans. Volunteers from outside the empire were recruited in droves; defeated Germans continued to be forcibly enlisted in Roman units, for preference in the palace troops, where they appear under the heading *gentiles*. However, the other method by which Germans were settled within the empire and bound to serve in the army was also followed, as evidenced by frequent references to the *Laeti*, who occupied land chiefly in eastern Gaul. In addition to this system of military recruitment by coercion, compulsory duties were demanded of civilians. The higher classes were made responsible for heavy undertakings at their own expense, tradesmen as a body discharged arduous works (*munera*) on behalf of the state. From time to time oppressive imposts were levied, either in cash or kind, to ensure the sustenance and supply of the army and bureaucracy. Strenuous exertions were expended to keep the tax-system in working order; the land tax *capitatio-iugatio* was the state's largest source of income, followed by the *collatio lustralis* (a tax on manufacturers much complained of during the fourth and fifth centuries), supplemented by indirect taxes and customs duties. A whole army of tax officials was at work, assessing liability, collecting what was due and chasing the increasing number of defaulters. Complaints of the venality and rapacity of the tax officials are legion, yet through all manner of crises, it was still found possible to amass the enormous sums needed for the maintenance of the court, for the stipends of soldiers and officials and above all for the conduct of the never-ending wars.

The fisc was also fed from other sources, chief among them the enormous estates under cultivation as crown property and the emperor's private demesne. In addition there were the mines and quarries, almost without exception in state-ownership and worked largely by men condemned to forced labour. The gold mines in the western part of the Balkans were still giving a good yield, gold and silver was coming in from Sardinia and Spain, zinc and lead from Spain and Britain, while the extraction of iron in Noricum was still in Roman hands. The state controlled not only the supply but also to a large extent the processing of this raw material. The large towns of the frontier provinces had publicly owned arms factories in which workers on the army pay-roll produced helmets, shields, armour, spears and bows. The State also operated weaving mills for linen and woollen fabrics, in which state slaves and also some free artisans were employed. The vital needs of the army and bureaucracy could thus be met, even if war became a permanency. Demands on men's purses and bodily labour inevitably increased the longer the invasions continued and the deeper they penetrated within the empire, but the state system established by Diocletian and Constantine long withstood the ravages of the times. Recent research has in fact shown that the fourth century was a time of partial economic recovery. To arrive at some general conclusion about the process of social and economic change, we must first look closely at the state of the various social classes and of the various branches of the urban and rural economy.

The organization of the later Roman empire has often been described as a system of state-socialism. But it must be realized that as a political régime it recognized no equality between citizens and the longer it continued, the more flagrant became the differences between the classes as regards power, prestige, property and legal status. The senatorial order, always pre-eminent, was now raised to a still higher plane. We have already seen how the ranks of the old senatorial families were enlarged by the addition of many new members, chiefly holders of high military and civil office, who owed their elevation to imperial favour. Which grade he entered depended on the size of a man's fortune. Membership of the nobility conferred not only the utmost prestige but also specific privileges, for example exemption from municipal taxes and the right to have law-suits heard before a specially constituted court. The political magistracies attached to the Roman senate were now devoid of content. The city prefecture was the only one which still carried great weight, as the authority responsible for maintaining public order in Rome and the judiciary for an extensive area round the city; to this was added responsibility for the welfare of the urban population of Rome, an almost impossible office to discharge at a time when overseas communications were frequently interrupted. The meetings held in the Curia, normally attended only by senators domiciled in Rome and a few Italians, were rarely given the chance of making an authoritative pronouncement, but the senatorial order as a whole, as a continually expanding imperial aristocracy, were still in some sort a counter-weight to the absolute monarch. In general, such political opposition as existed germinated among the ranks of the *clarissimi* and in the new order which was now asserting itself – the clergy of the Christian Church.

Economically speaking, the fortunes of the senatorial class rested on their possession of land. The pre-eminence and expansion of the order was linked with a concentration of landed property in the hands of senators so complete that in all essentials the history of agrarian development at this period is that of the senatorial estates. The richest senators had at their disposal houses and land in many provinces of the empire. The family of Symmachus, as we know from his letters, possessed three houses in Rome, altogether twelve villas in the surroundings of Rome, in Latium and on the gulf of Naples, and large estates in southern Italy, Sicily and Mauretania. The contemporary biographer of the younger Melania, the most conspicuous of all noble Romans in her ascetic zeal, tells us she possessed estates in Italy, Spain, Sicily and Africa which she systematically sold, devoting most of the proceeds to the endowment of churches. These senatorial estates, whose exploitation was entrusted either to agents (*procuratores*) or leaseholders (*conductores*), varied appreciably in size. From a poem by Ausonius we might infer that an estate of medium size ran to about six hundred and forty acres, but there were much larger estates, known as *fundi*, and really gigantic blocks of *fundi* are described as *massae*. Cultivation of cereal crops, vines and olives continued in the old style, but the exploitation of the soil was now supplemented by a number of manufacturing crafts. To avoid the heavy outlay in money entailed by large-scale purchases of clothing and equipment, the proprietors and their agents arranged for all essential goods to be produced within the estate. The villages where the land-workers lived thus had their own potters, weavers, smiths, carpenters, bakers and butchers. The fundus was not only required to send a maximum of its produce to the market; it also had to be self-sufficient. Finding labour to work these large estates presented enormous difficulties. Wage labourers, hired only for seed-time and harvest were now a rarity; the main burden fell on slaves and coloni. We find that on estates in Italy and Spain slaves predominate, although they are less numerous in Africa. The supply had once been kept up by prisoners of war, but this source had long since started to dry up, and now became scantier still, since so many captives were absorbed into the Roman armed forces. In consequence the number of slaves reared on the estates appreciably increased, in comparison with what it had been formerly. Their numbers were augmented by tragic victims of the class-state, infants who had been sold or exposed immediately after birth and the many children who, contrary to all legal provision, were sold into slavery in time of famine. There were thus many slaves still available for agricultural work or employment as masons, carpenters, spinners and weavers. On one huge estate belonging to Melania, in the neighbourhood of Rome, the unfree workers lived in twenty-six hamlets, each containing four hundred slaves. Admittedly the generalization that under the late Roman State the condition of the unfree was approximating more and more closely to that of the free proletariat, also holds good for agricultural slaves. In towns the rights of masters over their slaves were being restricted, slave marriages were recognized and indeed free and unfree were intermarrying to such an extent that the nomenclature of inscriptions is often no longer a safe guide to the personal status of individuals named. Agricultural slaves were allowed a small parcel of land in return for rent and could build up a modest property (*peculium*). There was thus no longer any sharp line dividing them from the coloni, who were indeed finding their freedom so much curtailed that their status was almost indistinguishable from that of slaves. Broadly speaking, the institution of the colonate still followed the old pattern ; landlords granted out a significant portion of their property to cultivators on lease and exacted in exchange part of the yield and compulsory services on the home farm. On smaller estates the constitution of Constantine which bound coloni to the soil was not rigorously observed, but on larger properties a register was kept of the coloni and the estate to which they belonged ; these men, known as *coloni originales*, retained only a vestige of freedom and under a constitution of Valentinian I were even required to seek their lord's permission before selling any scrap of land they might still have in their possession. A hereditary class of serfs was thus slowly being formed. The constitutions of the period make frequent reference to the flight of coloni, and to the efforts of landlords and tax officials to bring them back. But despite all exertions, no way of overcoming the shortage of agricultural labour on the estates was found. In the last analysis it was this desperate situation which produced the deserted lands (*agri deserti*), of which we hear so often. It is true that a combination of circumstances was responsible for the loss of cultivated land, on large estates often as much as a fifth of what was available. The insecurity induced in many parts of Gaul and Spain by the barbarian invasions and in north Africa by Berber attacks obviously played a large part. Where forests had been cut down and not replanted, heavy rainfalls brought down scouring torrents, to the ruin of the plains. Lastly, a system of taxation which took little note of the quality of the soil and the size of the yield, combined with the dearth of labour, forced many proprietors to abandon cultivation on the less fertile portions of their estates.

It is characteristic of the fifth century that the government's greatly increased financial exactions should in many ways have augmented the power of the landed proprietor. There was still a class of freeholders whose properties were only small, and in the fourth century their numbers even increased here and there, as veterans were settled on the land. For a time these small farmers were actually protected by the government, in so far as the freeholders of a village (*vicus*) were recognized in law as forming a type of association (*consortium*) : members enjoyed the right of pre-emption if an inhabitant of the village was obliged to abandon his property. This was a frequent occurrence, since the small farmer was much less well-equipped than the large proprietor to withstand the ravages of war, the misfortune of a failed harvest and the rapacity of tax collectors. With the connivance of corrupt officials, the land magnates (*potentes*) found ways of bringing even free peasants under their control. One result of this often singular collaboration between a government bent only on the collection of taxes and an upper class motivated essentially by class egotism was that proprietors laid claim to powers of protection (*patrocinium*) over the free peasants living on their estates and in the surrounding country. The earliest evidence for this development comes from the provinces of the East, for which our information is fuller than for those of the West. Egyptian papyri show small farmers already subjected to proprietors in this fashion around the year 360 ; Libanius describes a similar development in Syria. In the provinces of the West the process was now carried one stage further ; peasants anxious to avoid charges of tax evasion, and the corporal punishment which often ensued, were placing themselves under the protection of large proprietors, here and there even choosing as their patron some military commander who happened to be prominent in their region : they surrendered their property and received it back on a temporary basis (*precario*), thus becoming clients of their patron. Several emperors, recognizing that the lordships so created represented a threat to the state, prohibited transactions of this kind and appointed special officials to deal with the hardships of the poorer classes of the population. Valentinian I and Valens, in particular, initiated a number of measures aimed at improving the lot of the lower orders (*plebeii*). It is quite possible that the exceptional rigour of these rulers in prosecuting members of the senatorial nobility is to be explained by the spread of *patrocinium* among senators : so great a usurpation of public rights came close to underground revolution. Valentinian I created the special office of *defensor plebis*, charged with the protection of the oppressed peasantry and indeed of poor people in general. Wherever the need seemed urgent, some trustworthy imperial official was appointed; armed with the necessary judicial powers he was commissioned to protect the plebs against unjust tax demands. But this counter-stroke failed to prevent a steady accretion of power to the ruling class. In some places great magnates brought whole villages under their control. At times of extreme financial stress the emperors again found themselves obliged to allow landlords to collect taxes due from their coloni. In this way tax officials could be completely excluded from the domain of the great estate. As early as the reign of Theodosius I, there were already landlords who were not only collecting taxes on their own initiative and levying recruits from all their estates, but who also sat in judgement on their subjects and built their own gaols to house those convicted. The instability of the central government made it possible for the great estate, already well on the road to self-sufficiency as an economic unit, to become a separate enclave, subject in every respect to the dominion of its master. Feudalism was being born on the soil of the empire; soon it would also penetrate the states founded by the Germans, where its progress was further assisted by the already existing class structure.

It is surprising that in general the rural populations seem to have acquiesced in the increasing misery of their lot and in particular in their descent into serfdom. Nevertheless, there were still instances of open resistance and rebellion. At the turn of the fourth century brigandage was such a menace in certain regions that subjects had to be allowed to carry arms in self-defence. The worst hit provinces were those affected by the German invasions. In Gaul, the year of the great break-through (407) also witnessed a recurrence of the peasant unrest which towards the end of the third century had erupted in the rising of the 'Bagaudae', the name also used to describe the peasants involved in this new revolt. Some sparse information about the rebellion, which lasted a long time and also spread into Spain, can be gleaned from the chronicles and from the history of Zosimus. Even during the first period of activity, 407–14, coloni and slaves are to be found forming themselves into military units, to resist both the Roman government and the foreign invaders. The second rising in 435 was led by Tibatto, who appealed to all the slaves in Gaul and succeeded in harrying the Roman levies sent out by Aetius until he was finally captured in 437. It is possible that some of the rebels escaped to Spain; at all events, from 441 detachments of imperial troops had to be sent to combat Bagaudae in the north-east of the peninsula. Further disturbances then broke out in Gaul, instigated by a physician named Eudoxius. When in 448 he was forced to flee, he took refuge with the Huns and incited Attila to undertake the invasion of Gaul. At much the same date Bagaudae were responsible for acts of violence in northern Spain, a region already disturbed by inroads of the Suevi, and were crushed only in 454, by a Visigothic army despatched by Aetius. Although much about this whole episode is still obscure, these wars must surely be interpreted as despairing efforts at self-defence on the part of peasants caught between the coercive state of the late Roman empire and the germanic kingdoms which were slowly coming into being.

In the hierarchy of the empire, the urban middle class occupied a social station midway between that of the nobility and the lower grades of half-free and unfree. As we have seen, in the third century urban prosperity was already declining while state intervention was severely curtailing the freedom of municipal self-government. There followed the long period of stress brought about by the invasions: new walls had to be built, many public buildings were in ruins, the ownership of much municipal land was transferred to the emperor. The decurions, drawn from families whose birth and financial standing obliged them to serve as civic officials and town councillors, showed astonishing powers of endurance in face of the general distress. They were now saddled with the full responsibility for returning the taxes due from the entire area within their town's jurisdiction and for carrying out essential services. It seems there were still men who took pride in belonging to the order, as evidenced by inscriptions in which office holders are listed (*album decurionum*), as for example the tablet from Timgad in which they appear in descending order of rank: first the patrons, that is to say honorary members of the order, then the incumbents of the many priesthoods, next the municipal officials and former holders of these offices and finally their sons, as future notables of the town. But much more frequently we hear how powerless the decurions have become in face of the public tax officials, or indeed that they themselves are hated in their area on account of their fiscal exactions. It signified little that the imperial government had appointed a *defensor civitatis* vested with petty judicial powers to protect the interest of the poorer population, since what the state gave with one hand it took away with the other. The pressure of taxation continually increased, while profits from modest landed properties and urban professions were falling. In consequence many curiales sought admission to the imperial service, others took refuge on the land, becoming leaseholders or even labourers; there were even some who, from dire necessity, became soldiers or clerics. But since the state needed the curiales as auxiliary agents, transference to another career was forbidden, permits were required for every absence from the town and finally even their right to dispose of their own property was restricted. The decline of this once proud class of citizens was made plain for all to see when threat of enrolment in the curial order was held out as a punishment to evil-doers. With the decay of municipal office, in time of emergency the bishop often took the lead, performing the secular functions required by the urban community, actively co-operating in the defence of the town and maintaining the link with the imperial government.

Even at this period, when municipal government was so perceptibly declining, many branches of the urban economy were still in a healthy state. Although the state exercised complete control over the production and consumption of all goods vital to the army and the bureaucracy, there was still scope for independent commercial and industrial activity. The men who pursued it were called plebeians and did not belong to the urban upper class, but personal success in industry and commerce still carried prestige. Many small craft businesses were carried on by the proprietor with the help of his family and a few slaves, for example potteries and carpenters' shops, bakeries and butcheries. Weaving flourished in many towns of the West; if expensive garments were still being imported from the long famous workshops of Antioch, Alexandria and Tarsus, simple inexpensive clothing made from wool and linen was produced locally in private establishments and Mutina, Trier and Poetovio were renowned for the quality of their woollens. Craftsmen who supplied the court and nobility with luxury articles (as also architects and doctors) had already been exempted from obligatory works under a law issued by Constantine: the list includes painters and sculptors, workers in mosaic, goldsmiths, wood carvers, producers of fine glass, fullers and furriers. Most of these craftsmen were enrolled in trade guilds, in which the son was bound by law to succeed his father; it was thus easy for town or state to commandeer their services for larger undertakings and at the same time exercise some control over the market. The guilds essential to the needs of the city of Rome are known to us from numerous imperial laws and inscriptions, for example that of the pork butchers (*suarii*), whose members were expressly precluded from holding office and from taking clerical orders, and the guild of bakers (*corpus pistorum*), which according to a fourth century survey, drawn up district by district, possessed 274 bakeries in the various quarters of the city; the members of this guild were bound to devote themselves and their financial resources wholly to the community and could not obtain release even to join the army. Apparently this was the only way to ensure that the grain unloaded on the quays at Portus, stored in the great Roman granaries and ground in the city mills – water mills were gradually coming into fashion – would finally be distributed as loaves from the door-steps of the bakers' shops (*panis gradilis*).

The exchange of goods was effected in town markets and by long distance trading over land and sea. As a calling, commerce was no more highly regarded by senators and curiales than manual work, but many a merchant was sufficiently successful to be elected to the curia. The greatest profit came from trading in high quality goods which were in demand at imperial residences and in large cities frequented by the aristocracy. Oriental luxury articles were eagerly sought after and commanded high prices; engraved silver tableware from Syria, myrrh and frankincense from Arabia, spices, in particular pepper from the Malabar coast, silk from China. Even in the West, the trade in objects of eastern origin, or which had reached the empire by way of the East, was often handled by oriental merchants, Greeks and Syrians, the latter being particularly conspicuous. Slaves were another much sought-after form of merchandise. It is not known whether slaves were still needed in large numbers for employment in workshops, since in fact the general role of slaves in the industry of the Roman empire is still in need of clarification; but there was still a big demand for household slaves, senators were used to having large staffs of slaves at their disposal and poor people liked to have at least one menial. It appears that the theatres of war were also the scene of many private forays against the 'barbarians', whose object was to acquire more goods for the slave trade. Slaves with special talents, for example musicians, theatrical performers and drolls, were still being imported from the East, and since castration was prohibited in the Roman empire eunuchs had to be imported at heavy expense from Armenia and Persia. The transportation overseas of all this material and human merchandise was in the hands of shippers (*navicularii*), who were often also dealers (*negotiatores*). To ensure the movement of essential freight, in particular shipments of grain, the shipowners had already for some time been compulsorily enrolled in guilds and in effect formed a state-controlled merchant navy, which kept communications open between Italy and Africa and also with the eastern provinces. Despite the division of the empire into two, the Mediterranean remained a single trading area, the network of roads continued to link lands and continents, the imperial postal service took no account of diocesan boundaries and coins issued by the emperor, wherever they might be struck, were still accepted everywhere as legal tender. The economy as a whole benefited from the adherence to the gold standard introduced by Constantine as the basis of exchanges and from the continuing stability in the value of the solidus. It has been shown that during the fourth century there was even a fall in the price of such vital commodities as grain and meat. Apart from the government, the main beneficiaries of these deflationary measures were people of superior social standing who had the valuable gold coins in their pockets. The great mass of subjects had to pay their land tax in kind, and an appreciable portion of the empire's salary bill was met from contributions paid directly into the state granaries. There was thus a growing trend in the direction of a natural economy.

This survey of the various departments of social and economic life suggests that the most important effect of the changes at work was in the formation of closed social classes, sharply differentiated as regards property, political influence and legal status. Men of the senatorial class reaped most advantage from the confusion of the age; the most powerful, the *potentes*, were setting up their own lordships in formal competition with the imperial régime and administration. With the marked decay of urban life and the bourgeois middle class, these territorial lordships would in future become the chief centres of activity. Side by side with the senatorial aristocracy we find the higher clergy of the state Church: a now numerous corps of bishops, arranged in a hierarchy which to all intents and purposes followed that of the empire's division into provinces and dioceses and in the West culminated in the see of Rome. As a result of imperial benefactions, legacies from well-to-do Christians and gifts from the whole body of the faithful, the episcopal churches were in control of appreciable wealth which often included extensive landed property. It is no wonder that the higher ranks of the clergy, which in the third and fourth century had been filled by men of the middle class, were now also attracting men of senatorial descent, or indeed that the pagan senator Praetextatus could say in jest to Pope Damasus, 'make me bishop of Rome and I will become a Christian tomorrow'. However, the higher clergy also created something of a precedent in late Roman society in setting aside perhaps a fourth of episcopal revenues for the relief of the poor, the distressed proletariat of day labourers and artisans in the towns and the half-free and unfree of the countryside. If senior magistrates, notably at Rome, kept up the time-honoured custom of regaling the plebs with bread and circuses, if the old idea of poverty as a natural phenomenon which could be disguised from rich and poor by the illusory gaiety of folk carnivals still persisted, nevertheless there never was a time, even in the stormy period of the invasions, when at least some Christians were not prepared to renounce riches and dedicate their lives to the care of the poor. Paulinus of Nola, formerly a landed magnate, became a monk and a bishop, the younger Melania gave away her princely possessions, Pammachius, a student friend of Jerome, used his wealth for the relief of poor men and strangers. The influence of the Christian ethic on legislation, which we have already noted in the time of Constantine, became still more pronounced. Some alleviation was brought to the slave's lot, in that manumission was encouraged and churches opened as places of asylum. New laws gave assistance to needy debtors, new regulations introduced a touch of humanity within the grim walls of the prison. The law now extended the protection it afforded to the married state and the family to include the menages of the unfree. Valentinian I's prohibition of infanticide was a landmark, since it restricted the sovereign right of the paterfamilias. While the social teaching of the Church Fathers admittedly wrought no revolutionary transformation in society as a whole, theologians and councils were unanimous in their condemnation of extravagence and their disapproval of usurious transactions. There was no dearth of preachers to interpret wealth as a debt to be discharged to the community, a God-given responsibility. But the claims of communal ownership were urged only by a handful of ascetics and were heard less frequently as monasteries became richer.

In any case, the social aspects of imperial legislation cannot be attributed wholly to Christian influences, since they are already in evidence even before the recognition of Christianity by the state. Some of the credit must go to the emperor's secular advisers, to the officials in the ministries and academic lawyers. Modern research which has dug deeply into the history of Roman law in the post-classical period has made it clear that Roman law survived in the germanic successor states and in the Byzantine empire under a variety of forms. Undeniably, the jurists played an essential role in the consolidation of the class-state and in making occupations hereditary; they were also partially responsible for an increasing brutality in the criminal law and in forms of punishment. As in earlier times, the penalties exacted under criminal law varied with the class of the accused. Torture, which from the time of Marcus Aurelius could be used on free men as an instrument of judicial examination, was now applied also to curiales and even senators. Numerous crimes were subject to the death penalty, often carried out in hideous fashion. But in addition to displaying these harsh features, legislation and jurisprudence show an increasing social and humanitarian concern. Apart from its Christian inspiration, this trend owed something to hellenistic influences, and its effects were also felt in the West of the empire. Admittedly, western jurisprudence suffered appreciably during the fifth century from the loss of professional precision, due as much to the absence of state law schools as to the fact that the imperial chancery, where laws were formulated, was now staffed by men trained in literature rather than law. Yet it was perhaps precisely this schooling in rhetoric and classical literature which enabled Hellenistic and Oriental conceptions of law to survive. Lawyers with a literary education not only gave imperial legislation its moral foundation but also upheld the principle of equity, *aequitas*, as against strict justice and tempered the law with humanity. The tendency of legislation and jurisprudence to show indulgence towards regional and tribal customs must certainly be accounted a departure from classical law. From the fourth century West Roman law exhibits just such a trend, and from this point of view can be said to merit the description 'vulgar law'. However much we may regret the disappearance of specialist legal terminology, vulgarization of this kind at least meant that jurisprudence was bringing within its scope the older popular elements, which would survive the ruin of centralized government in the West, and also the new nations who were establishing their own kingdoms on the soil of the empire.

2. *Western Christendom – education, theology, missions*

Christianity did not arrest the process of social change during the fourth and fifth centuries. However important the role of the Christian faith and of the Church in the late Roman world, neither governments nor peoples underwent a total moral regeneration. Augustine and other Christian authors admittedly speak of 'this Christian age' (*Christiana tempora*), but what they chiefly mean is that a Christian government has stamped out active paganism within the empire – though naturally they are also thinking of the established position of the Christian churches with their organization and settled divine worship. There is no denying that the age which saw secular institutions disrupted and enfeebled was also the very times at which Christian leadership gathered strength. So far as concerns the authority of the pope, we find Siricius, who succeeded Damasus in 384, expending in word and deed the practical significance of the legacy of St Peter and the rank of Apostolic See as it affected the Church as a whole. From the papal chancery, now organized along the lines of the imperial chancery, there issued numerous communications claiming for the bishop of Rome a supreme oversight over the Church. Siricius ordained that the instructions he addressed to individual bishops be made known to all other bishops of the province and preserved for the future. In form and style these documents, now known as decretals, resemble synodal constitutions; but they also begin to echo secular official phraseology. Innocent I, pope from 402–17, progressed still further in shaping the Roman claim to primacy. Undeterred by the capture and sack of Rome, he proceeded to set the papal supremacy on a sure foundation – not, indeed, by any revolutionary action but by applying and expounding his existing rights in numerous decretals. In the matter of ecclesiastical jurisdiction he went further than his predecessors, since he claimed that all important disputed issues (*causae majores*) should be brought to the papal see for decision. Questions of this nature were thus no longer to be adjudicated by the synods of provinces adjoining the scene of the dispute; instead, the pope would be supreme arbiter. The documents issued by Innocent, couched in language which speaks in the unmistakable and measured tones of superior authority, proclaimed to the world that the unity of the Church now had its custodian in the successor of St Peter.

In the field of education and learning, Latin Christianity gradually grew to a stature commensurate with its heavy responsibilities. The schools maintained by the state and the municipalities withstood the initial shock of the invasions. The study of rhetoric and letters, which remained the essential prerequisite for an important official career, was still cultivated in aristocratic families. Even Germans who had risen in the service of Rome showed some interest in literary culture. We know from Claudian that Stilicho arranged a traditional education for his daughter Maria, and that she was familiar with the mythological world of the poets. Christians were becoming increasingly caught up in this cultural tradition. The rhetorical skill deployed in their sermons and literary writings by Church Fathers of the fourth and fifth centuries was learned in the public schools: for them, too, eloquence was one of the indispensable attributes of eminence. Christians also took to imitating the social habits of the literary elite and we find many bishops, even some anchorites and women vowed to asceticism, careful to conduct their literary correspondence in accordance with the conventions of high-brow society. Christians grew so used to the prevailing system of education that there seemed really no need to provide a special system for the instruction of the new generation of young Christians. The fifth century in fact produced only one institution that was new, and this catered not for Christians in general but for a particular group: the monastic community which had its nucleus in an episcopal household, as set up by Paulinus of Nola and others. In the rules Augustine proposed for clerics who followed this common life, he insists that they should renounce their private possessions, either in favour of the Church or their own families, and devote themselves to academic study. This particular combination of theological training, monastic discipline and pastoral activity was characteristic of Augustinian Rules.

But what did the education provided in these secular and religious institutions offer by way of academic content? Received tradition recognized a curriculum for higher education consisting of seven subjects, (*artes liberales*): grammar, rhetoric and dialectic, arithmetic, geometry, astronomy and music. The four subjects in the second group, which provided instruction in specialized disciplines, had for some time past been either neglected or totally abandoned. Other disciplines which led to the acquisition of professional knowledge and skill, for example medicine and law, continued to occupy a place apart. In the period under discussion, the general education provided in the universities offered the student nothing more than a grooming in the art of rhetoric, knowledge of the classics and a certain facility in philological party tricks, in the manner of Macrobius. The decline in scientific knowledge is especially marked : all that the authors of the period have retained is a remnant of rudimentary information and a conventional interest in natural and human marvels, as exemplified by Ammianus' excurses on earthquakes and planets and Augustine's numerous references to *mirabilia*. The growing lack of familiarity with Greek, among Christians and educated people in general, also had serious consequences. The families of the social upper crust for a time remained unaffected : the schooling Ambrose received in his father's household enabled him to read and understand the works of Greek theologians. On the other hand, Augustine in his state school acquired neither mastery of the language nor familiarity with the literature and it was only in later life that he was able to improve his knowledge. There was thus a crying need for translations from the Greek : Marius Victorinus translated Plotinus, Evagrius introduced the *Vita Antonii* to the Latin West and Jerome made accessible one or two of Origen's writings. When Latins and Greeks met to discuss controversial issues, the party often included interpreters. This was so on the occasion when the Pelagian doctrine was being debated before Bishop John of Jersualem : but Orosius, who was present on behalf of Augustine, complained of the incompetence of one of the interpreters, to which he attributed a great deal of the theological misunderstanding. In a wider field, the Pelagian dispute once again brought to light the deep divergence between western and eastern Christendom in matters of theology and forms of worship. In the East the Christological question was once more a great and burning issue ; fresh doctrinal formulations were arrived at, which in turn led to the formation of new Churches ; the Nestorian and Monophysite movements, whose influence extended into places beyond the boundaries of the empire, were forces to be reckoned with throughout the century. In the West, theological passion continued to centre on man's place in the Christian order and on questions of ethical teaching. The collision between Pelagius, who held that even after the Fall man was still capable of acting righteously – indeed of remaining sinless – and Augustine, for whom man's justification was grounded solely on the grace of God – grace undeserved and unrequitable – posed questions which would leave the Latin Church no peace.

It is undeniably typical of the state of learning as a whole in the ancient world of the fifth century that scientific work was no longer being undertaken with the object of achieving any specific advance. The activity which went under the name of science was not a matter of methodical observation and experiment but of deploying information culled from books. Revered antiquity was now accepted as authoritative for the standard of learning, and knowledge received from the ancients, however fragmentary it might be, was considered sufficient. As Marrou has shown, men who thought thus had reached a late staging post along a road the ancient mind had long been travelling. It seems as though in the Greeks, whose genius for enquiry was such a dynamic force until early in the hellenistic period, a powerful speculative drive was combined with a certain impatience in the accumulation of experimental data. The neglect of empiricism led in turn to the stagnation of scientific research, already noticeable in the early days of the Principate. From this it followed that the subjects of the curriculum (*artes*) came to have no function apart from those of training the minds of the young and providing writers and orators with examples from history and nature. The structure of thought erected to deal with the problems peculiar to Christianity was built on this same foundation. Christian scholarship (*doctrina Christiana*) inherited the classical education of the pagans, although Christians were less in awe of its merits. For Augustine, the spell of classical literature and eloquence, still greatly respected and admired by the Cappadocian fathers, has already lost much of its aesthetic charm. Even so, literary education could supply material for sermons and tracts and here and there might offer something in support of the faith; it was not required to stimulate scientific research. The supreme task of Christian scholarship was to apprehend and deepen the truths of revelation; hence its main object of study was the Bible, the book of revelation. This source supplied the questions which agitated Christian thinkers: metaphysical questions concerning the essential nature of divinity and the fate of human souls. Dogmatic theology had as its province the formulation and interpretation of the creed for the whole Christian church; it was also required to dispute with heretics and rebut such pagan polemics as still appeared. Ultimately, Christian scholarship should lead to the knowledge of God, it should unlock man's inner nature and make accessible to him the bliss of contemplation, the new *vita beata*. Some discussion of the works of Jerome and Augustine will show how the possibilities and limitations of the *doctrina Christiana* manifested themselves in the outstanding achievements of this period.

Jerome's voluminous writings show him an exemplary representative of Latin biblical scholarship at the turn of the fourth century; his stormy career is an indication of the many stresses felt by Christian scholars as they lived and worked. At the conclusion of his student period Jerome experienced an inward conversion to the faith; and from that time forward he took as his ideal a life in which asceticism and literary work could combine. He became acquainted with the monastic life in the desert of Chalcis in Syria, and for a time practised it himself (376–8), but even in his cave Jerome still could not live without books; by writing the lives of holy hermits he contrived to make authorship a penitential exercise. After the Roman interlude we have already noted, he spent thirty-three years (386–419) as a hermit in his monastery at Bethlehem; but even here he was surrounded by an impressive library, scribes and readers were always at his disposal and he kept up a literary correspondence with cultivated men and women all over the world. The man who achieved this synthesis possessed a temperament which placed many obstacles on the road to sanctity. High-spirited and sensitive, his contacts were many and various and he became the confidant and spiritual adviser of pious matrons. As secretary to Pope Damasus he found scope for his powerful streak of self-assertiveness and even had a fair chance of becoming his successor; once he had overcome the temptation and returned to the East he still insisted, even at this distance, on playing his part in theological controversy, always on the side of ecclesiastical orthodoxy. Vain and contentious as he was, he traduced his literary and theological opponents in quite unseemly fashion, and introduced a sharply satirical note into his descriptions of personalities and social cliques, not even refraining from a cruel rupture with Rufinus, the friend of his youth. The littérateur was so puffed up in his self-conceit that he could console Paula, grieving over the death of her beloved daughter, with the assurance that his books would make her famous throughout the world. This man, to whom books were everything, was the author of a number of dogmatic-polemical treatises; but his scholarly labours were devoted not to speculative theology but to establishing and interpreting the text of the Bible. Just as Donatus, his instructor in grammar, made Virgil his life's work, so did Jerome devote himself to holy writ. He brought to the Christian study of philology, still a novelty in the Latin West, a knowledge of classical authors and a feeling for good classical style; yet he vehemently rejected the current vogue for classicism: 'our Athens is Jerusalem'. A revealing dream, to which he frequently refers, shows the effect this renunciation had on him.[6] The first time he was in the East he fell ill of a fever; in his delirium he found himself suddenly translated in spirit before God's judgement seat. Smitten by the blinding light, he fell to the ground and dared not raise his eyes. On being asked his condition, he replied 'I am a Christian'. 'You lie', said He who sat upon the throne, 'you are a Ciceronian and no Christian'. Thereupon he was soundly beaten and began to beg for mercy; those who stood round suggested that he should receive leniency on account of his youth and be given opportunity to make amends. Having sworn an oath to read no more worldly books, he was set free. By and large Jerome honoured the oath taken in his dream: yet he remained a classicist. He might make the Bible the central object of his endeavours, but in speech and style he was a Christian Cicero, in theological controversy he felt himself always a Latin, *homo Romanus* in the eastern world.

Pope Damasus was responsible for arousing his scholarly interest in the Bible. In this field the Latin West had much ground to make up, since the Latin text of the Bible, in the various transmissions known today as *Vetus Latina*, was already in a glorious confusion. Jerome set himself to produce a reliable Latin text and turned his attention first to the four gospels. Here what was required was a revised text rather than a new translation, but Jerome already found himself attracted by the general problems of translation. During his initial sojourn in the East he had perfected his knowledge of Greek and embarked upon Hebrew; he regarded learning this language, to which he devoted untold exertions, as a form of mortification. As a man now of three languages (*vir trilinguis*), he acquired a deep insight into the problems of reproducing a foreign language text with accuracy and elegance. He was thus ideally qualified for the great task which would be his major claim to fame: the new translation of a substantial part of the Old Testament, undertaken in the years 390–406. The Latin translations hitherto in use were based on the Greek version of the Old Testament, the Septuagint. This was the text Jerome started from, but realizing that it departed in many places from the original he decided to go back to the basic Hebrew text, the *Hebraica veritas*. Jerome's translation, exemplary for its method, is admittedly more successful in some books of the Old Testament than in others; nevertheless it displays a remarkable feeling for the original language, even to the extent of imitating its musical rhythms, which Jerome particularly admired in Psalms. The fruit of these stupendous labours, the Latin Old Testament, was at first cold-shouldered in the West and two centuries passed before it was recognized as of equal value with other current texts; it gained general acceptance only in the Carolingian period, and again several more centuries passed before the name Vulgate became attached to it. The other great interest of the Bethlehem circle was biblical exegesis. Jerome himself concentrated mainly on the Old Testament, writing commentaries on individual books, letters dealing with specific problems of interpretation and sermons on various texts. His approach to the texts was essentially that of a philologist, but he also attached importance to archaeology as a source of illumination and points out that the Bible becomes alive when people see the places and monuments of Palestine with their own eyes. True, he did not neglect allegorical interpretation of the text, though he valued it chiefly as a means of edification; moreover, he held that allegorization should only begin when the work of philological and historical exposition was complete. Jerome worked at great speed, with the result that his commentaries often lack finish, but his great achievement in the translation and exposition of biblical texts earned him veneration in the Latin West, where he was regarded as the father of this new and Christian learning. It is astonishing to find him still immersed in his scholarly activity even when more and more alarming tidings of invasions by alien tribes reached him in his isolation. Jerome was cut to the heart by the catastrophes of his age and he bitterly lamented the capture of Rome by the Goths: to Jerome the Latin, Rome was the 'light of the world'; to Jerome the biblical scholar, it was a new Jerusalem, symbol of eternal peace. He appears to have been one of the tiny minority of his contemporaries to realize that the position of the empire had drastically changed. As early as 409, in a letter to Geruchia,[7] he has brought himself to recognize the incredible, namely that with the breach of the Danube frontier, the whole territory of the Roman empire between the Black Sea and the Julian Alps is itself in jeopardy. 'Who would believe it possible, what work of history could relate in temperate language, that Rome should be fighting within her own boundaries not for fame but for existence, nay, not even fighting but buying her life with money and household goods?'

If, by way of contrast with Jerome's life work, we look for a work by Augustine to exemplify the creative power of Christian scholarship, our choice must fall on his book *On the City of God*. Here we have an essential piece of his theology, set squarely in the intellectual situation of his age, which has influenced succeeding generations down to the present. The twenty-two books of this work were conceived and written between 410, the year of the sack of Rome by the Goths, and 430, the year when Hippo was besieged by the Vandals: telling indication of its actuality, as has often been pointed out. Augustine had been Bishop of Hippo for fifteen years when the terrible news arrived of the sack of the eternal city. As a scholar he had already clashed with Manichees and Donatists, going so far as to condone the imperial authorities' use of force against pagans, heretics and schismatics; it would not be long before he took up the cudgels against the doctrines of Pelagius. His book *De civitate Dei*, which started to appear in 413 and was issued in instalments, was written concurrently with numerous tracts on dogma. The disaster to Rome created great panic in Africa, which had received many refugees from Italy. As was only natural at this period, men were quick to see a religious significance in the catastrophe, especially since in the years 405 and 408 government policy had been so decisively pro-Christian. Was Christ then powerless? Or was it indeed true that this evil had befallen Rome from the neglect – nay the suppression – of her former tutelary deities? Everywhere it was said that the bodies of the apostles, the relics of the martyrs, had failed to save the city. Augustine set out his views on these questions in a sermon preached as early as 410: the terrible privation was a visitation, a punishment inflicted on men, the disaster to Rome was not a condemnation but a test. In letters and sermons he frequently returns to deal with the complaint, still loudly voiced, that this evil should have struck in the very epoch which was called Christian (*Christiana tempora*). It is true, he says, the world was growing old, but in its time of senility and decay Christ appeared and made it new again: 'Let us lead a good life, and the times are good. *We* are the times. As *we* are, so are the times'. Increasingly this question leads him on to consider the general problem: where, in this time of trouble, would what is lasting and permanent be found, what society could one point to as eternally secure? Thus he braces himself for the comprehensive work which was to be at once a scholarly apologia for Christianity and a moral interpretation of history, founded on the Christian conviction that God does not exist for the sake of increasing man's worldly benefits and that human life cannot be understood if its fulfilment is expected in any one day and age. Deploying his great learning, he starts by dowsing the latest flare-up of pagan recrimination. The first ten books are occupied with a critique of polytheism, whose object is to show that even in the past the pagan religion did not lead to happiness in this life and could never, quite rightly, have led to eternal life. The traditional Roman pride in historical achievement is subjected to a searching examination, in which the arguments used are primarily those of the historian. In his attack on this pagan concept of Rome's mission, Augustine adduces criticisms voiced by pagan authors, in particular those of historians – Sallust above all – who gave forcible expression to the idea of Rome's decline. Relentlessly, Augustine reviews the entire Roman past, from the fratricide of Romulus the city's founder to the abomination of the last decades of the Republic. The gods of Rome were no obstacles to wickedness, they were indeed in themselves a cause of moral depravity; so powerless were they in face of external evils that the pagan centuries were literally filled with wars and civil strife. These idols were no gods, but figments created by human megalomania! The old claim that Rome's greatness was achieved through just wars is also dismissed as untenable. Roman policy is characterized by injustice, for justice has been ousted by wicked pride (*superbia*), the sin which brings out all that is worst. True, there is no denying the vastness and long duration of Roman rule; but its wide extent cannot by itself be regarded as an advantage and a blessing. Certainly, the empire has done good service in keeping the peace; but its dominion was no gift from the gods but the dispensation of the one true God, a work of providence. The Romans possessed a few political virtues: their sense of freedom and longing for fame, which, if they achieved nothing good, were at least a bar to still greater evils. Even these qualities remain somewhat dubious, but at least they have served to hold in check the base vulgarity of naked avarice. Pagan Rome is thus exposed as a creation founded on pride, and as such a power of evil. But Augustine also has reservations when he comes to judge the state of Rome under its first Christian emperors. He does not accept Eusebius' interpretation of Constantine as the representative of the Logos and rejects the view that a Christian Rome is assured of secular success. Only Theodosius receives unqualified praise, which also includes endorsement of his constitutions prescribing the beliefs to be held by Christians. The cardinal point is established that even the Christian state has imperfections. True, it is fortunate to have a Christian on the throne, since the thought of God will restrain him from abusing his power. Yet however powerful the effect of Christian belief on men's moral conduct, the world as a whole cannot become Christian. There can be no identification of the *civitas Romana* with the *civitas Christiana* in the way suggested by the poet Prudentius; with Augustine this line of political theology came to a full stop.

These ten polemical books use as their only yardstick the faith contained in biblical doctrine. All Augustine's judgements proceed from the fundamental insight that God is the lord of history. God is working out a plan of salvation for all mankind, just as he did with Israel: all great crises prepare the way for a community of citizens, for a commonwealth of God (*civitas Dei*). Human existence has its being in time, it pertains to the good but at the same time is exposed to what is evil: through humility man can co-operate in God's saving plan, through pride he falls victim to the opposing power and serves the terrestrial commonwealth (*civitas terrena*). There is no simple identification of these two citizen bodies with the Church and the secular state; when he is speaking of the state in its ordinary sense Augustine usually employs the terms *respublica* and *regnum*. The contrast goes deeper and wider than the conflict between Church and state: to the *civitas Dei* belong all good spirits and good men, past, present and to come, while the *civitas terrena* is made up of all spirits who have turned away from God. The antithesis is between God and Satan, humility and pride, belief and unbelief. The whole history from the creation to the last judgement is now explained and expounded in the light of this concept, rooted in revelation. The second section of the work (books 11–22) deals with the origin, continuation and termination of these two opposing commonwealths, whose paths continually cross. The story has a supernatural beginning in the creation of the world, the origin of the human race and the Fall. It continues with the events of history proper: the happenings from the time of Abel to Noah, the age of the patriarchs, the working out of the redemptive process from Moses through David Christ, and the concurrent secular history. Then follows an account of history after Christ, the comparison of the two commonwealths and finally a description of their appointed end at the last judgement, when the wicked will be brought to book and the good received into bliss. Augustine thus presents us with a purely biblical concept of history, which stands out in contrast with all the interpretations offered by ancient historians. We hear nothing of that cyclical pattern of events which dominated men's outlook in the ancient world and was so often linked with a certain fatalism. The divine plan of salvation leads through all ages to a final goal; jeopardized by sin, it is reaffirmed by the incursion into history of the Divine Word and by that communion of saints, the mystical body of Christ, which the Word brought into being. It is in this manner, as a continuous building up, that the commonwealth of God achieves completion. The drama of history, a unique performance, is only comprehensible in the light of God and his plan of redemption. Stage by stage, mankind is led towards his goal. Salvation can never come through purely secular action, all states and kingdoms are subject to decay, the works of men have merit only in the context of eternal goodness. Even a temporal state may contain some element of goodness; one must not assume that a state bent on political self-assertion is necessarily unchristian. Secular progress, even technical progress, can be used to serve the ultimate goal. But the history of mankind does not therefore become a triumphal progress; the earthly course of history is typified rather by defeats and disasters, but always in union with advances on the spiritual plane. The counterplay of the divine and terrestrial commonwealths gives history a double aspect, a duality which because it is based on empiricism owes nothing to dualism of the Manichaean type. Marrou has taught us to understand Augustine as a philosopher of being, not of becoming. In Augustine's thought – and here one may describe him as a Platonist – suffering and failure, old age and death pertain essentially to time, which is something fleeting and insubstantial. Time is ambivalent and brings both advance and decline, both hope and despair. In any case, this applies to historical time. For in the beginning there is the cosmic time of the day of God's creation; then only human existence is altered through sin; it is since the Fall that time has become linked with ageing and death. Time can still have positive value, but only through divine redemption and grace. From these same sources springs the Christian hope of all who work together to build the commonwealth of God.

In his theological interpretation of history Augustine offered both pagans and Christians a universal conspectus of world events. He not only exposed the emptiness of the patriotic Roman idea of history but also demolished the short-sighted Christian view that the Christianization of the empire guaranteed its permanence. In reaching this theological position, Augustine returned to the early Christian vision of men and mankind as pilgrims on a journey through present time, whose vocation is to help shape the eternal city. Their watchword must not be withdrawal from the world, nor must there be moaning over the vale of tears, any more than exultation over progress; what they must realize is that the citizens of God are continually on trial and accountable, their wills and actions aspire beyond the present world. The goal has been marked out, both for individuals and for all mankind; hence it may be possible to discern the general meaning of the drama, even though individual episodes and their possible bearing on the whole still remain obscure. The two commonwealths are so intertwined that no human eye can separate them. History thus still guards her secrets. Augustine makes the drama of history a symphony: its significance as a work of art will only be apparent at the end.

Through this fundamental distinction between the divine and terrestrial commonwealths, Christianity acquired theological liberty, which was already an asset in Augustine's own day: the Christian faith, the Christian church could now break loose from the fetters of the Roman empire. Certainly, the State still had its importance and the Roman empire continued to receive its due. No objections were made to the peace-keeping machinery which held intruders in check and ensured that justice was dispensed at home, nor was any doubt cast on the validity of dependent relationships which were preserved in the household and in the class structure of society. Political thinking, in fact, remained markedly conservative in aspect. But if Christians entertained no thoughts of actual separation from the Roman empire, they nevertheless achieved a degree of detachment towards it. In his later writings Augustine himself voiced the thought that the world might continue even after the Roman empire had come to an end. He did not, as is sometimes alleged, go so far as to anticipate the rise of the germanic states. True, in one place he makes passing reference to the desirability of several small states existing side by side (*regna plurima gentium*), but he is not thinking of the Germans, whose settlements he certainly would not wish to describe as states. If severance from the Imperium was conceivable for Augustine, it was only at the most fundamental level.

Others who were close to Augustine, or followed after him, took to the same path almost as soon as he had pointed the way, although with some hesitation. Thus Orosius, an Iberian cleric who had fled from the Vandals in Spain to Africa, where he assisted Augustine in his theological work, was set by his master to compose a universal history reflecting the guiding principles of Augustinian thought. Orosius' *Historia adversus paganos* was composed in the years 417–8. He draws on earlier Christian chronicles but also incorporates pagan views on universal history; the result is a history of world events which follows the fortunes of successive world empires as they dissolved into one another in a sequence, already familiar to the ancient world, which starts with the Assyrians and continues through the Medes, Persians and Macedonians down to the Romans. This Christian universal history, the first of its kind, sets out to prove that the sufferings of mankind were greater under the former dispensation which still acknowledged the pagan gods than they have been in the Christian epoch; for with the advent of true religion, man's blood-lust could be kept in check. The turning-point came with the rule of peace inaugurated by Augustus, the empire into which Christ was born. The empire of Orosius' own day also has merit, since it is an all-embracing unity which enshrines the noble virtues of justice and religion: 'Wheresoever I come as a stranger, even though I am displaced person I need fear no act of sudden violence. A Roman among Romans, a Christian among Christians, a man among men, as a citizen I am sustained by the order upheld by law, as a man of right conduct by religion, as a man pure and simple by the nature I have in common with other men. On the temporal plane, every country serves me as a fatherland.'[8] The faults one could find with this picture of the contemporary situation were present in the author's mind: he had himself experienced the trials of foreign invasion. His reply to doubters is not always wholly consistent. Throughout the work there are frequent references to the aliens and to the Germans in particular, above all in the seventh book, which covers the period since the time of Christ. On occasion he tries to make light of the sufferings endured by his contemporaries: the Goths spent but three days in Rome, Alaric can be dismissed as a fugitive brigand, and now the Goths have actually entreated the emperor for an alliance, although in their strong position they could have made the sky the limit. The Burgundians, he says, treat the Gallic population as brothers in Christ; and he believes that even the Vandals who remained in Spain suffered a change of heart after making peace with Rome, so much so that they are exchanging their spears for ploughshares. This is a rose-coloured picture, painted to sustain the apologist in his optimism. Here and there, Orosius makes passing reference to what he conceives to be the future of the Germans: he envisages, apparently with approval, some form of co-existence between the germanic states and the Roman empire and realizes that at some future date the Germans may well make a positive contribution to culture. His general estimate of the Goths is that they are hostile to the Roman world (*Romania*), but he admits the possibility that they may one day create order where now they sow discord. Did not Alexander, did not the Romans themselves, first perfect themselves in the destructive art of war, in order as conquerors to establish law and order throughout the world? It is clear that in Orosius' view this was an action with two distinct stages, which could not take place simultaneously. In an often quoted passage he puts into the mouth of Athaulf, the Gothic king, a speech declaring that although his original aspiration was to extinguish the Roman name and set up a Gothic empire (*Gothia* in place of *Romania*), when he realized that his people were too lawless to be restrained he made it his ambition to win renown as the restorer of the Roman empire, having failed to effect its destruction.[9] J. Straub, who has gone deeply into the historical thinking of this period, justifiably remarks that the words attributed to Athaulf can have no factual foundation; the king's actual plans were nothing like so ambitious. The sentiment is in fact much more in keeping with the Roman idea of the natural urge which drove great nations and individuals to seek mastery of the world. Even Seneca once observed that the Germans who could fight with such passion wanted only discipline to rival the Romans as conquerors. Furthermore, Orosius perceived that the Germans settled in the Roman provinces showed signs of an incipient culture; and he was forced to admit the existence here and there of Romans who chose a life of freedom and poverty under the barbarians in preference to the tax-ridden burden of life under the empire. This admission is scarcely made before he plunges deeper still, to make a positive connection between the invasions and the spread of the Christian religion – a feat entirely consistent with his intent as a Christian apologist to understand and interpret great events from the Christian standpoint. 'If the barbarians were sent into the Roman empire with this sole purpose, that everywhere in East and West the churches of Christ might be filled with Huns, Sueves, Vandals, Burgundians and countless other tribes of believers, then should man indeed praise and exalt the mercy of God, since through these events so many peoples – although this may involve the crumbling of our empire – could be given knowledge of the truth, which otherwise they would certainly not have attained.'[10]

Orosius was thus bold enough to give the folk migrations a Christian interpretation, and in so doing found a solution to the great riddle of the century. It is not long before other voices are raised to ascribe the sufferings of the present generation to one first cause, the providential dispensation which was using the wanderings of the peoples and the devastation of the provinces as an instrument to bring about the salvation of all mankind. The idea is strikingly expressed in a work written before the middle of the fifth century and entitled *De vocatione omnium gentium*. Taking issue with later adherents of Pelagius and their doctrine that the will to salvation may proceed from man himself, the author poses the following question: if it was the intention of Providence to lead all men to blessedness, why did God not call the pagans to him earlier? His answer is to make grateful recognition that in recent times the fulness of grace has been poured out on all peoples, so that the Church has spread far and wide: 'these same weapons which destroy the world do but promote the grace of Christianity'.[11] Theology thus took another step forward along the Augustinian road, as the old antithesis between Romans and barbarians began to be swallowed up in the unity of Christendom.

It is time now to turn our attention to the conversion of the Germans to Christianity. Even if we limit ourselves to those tribes which had some connection with the Roman empire, the process to be described was one of long duration, played out in a variety of settings. The literary sources for the period down to the end of the western empire are often scanty in the extreme; fortunately they can be supplemented to some extent by archaeological finds and by the evidence of linguistic history and folk-lore. But there is much that remains puzzling and still more that is controversial.

We begin with those Germans who were already living on Roman territory in the early days of the empire. There is evidence of the presence of Christian communities in the Rhineland provinces from the end of the second century; from the time of Constantine church buildings are attested at Bonn, Cologne and Xanten and, above all, Trier, where a large double church was erected on the remains of an imperial palace. Fourth century bishops of Trier and Cologne are mentioned in connection with the Donatist controversy and as adherents of the Nicene profession. By this time episcopal sees had also been established on the middle and upper Rhine, at Mainz, Worms, Speyer and Strasbourg. True, these Christian congregations in the Rhineland cities were predominantly Roman, but from the evidence of philology it seems there were already some German Christians at this period. The origin of a number of words in the German language can be traced back to this early Christianization of the Rhineland, words which later passed into general use, for example *Almosen* (alms), *Opfer* (sacrifice), *Bischof* and *Kirche* (meaning the actual edifice). This confirms what really needed no proof, that Christian congregations in the Roman provinces admitted Germans to membership and carried out missionary activities among the native population. A similar situation is found in other northern frontier provinces. From hagiographical and archaeological indications, it seems that in Switzerland and parts of southern Germany the Christianity established there in Roman times continued without interruption throughout the period of the migrations. Augsburg and Regensburg had church buildings at an early date; in the second half of the fifth century St Severinus was working in the province of Noricum Ripense, chiefly in the northern part of present-day Austria. All the same, southern Germany contained only isolated groups of Christians, which meant that the Alamanni could long remain undisturbed in their paganism. We know from chance references that neighbouring bishops were starting to convert other smaller germanic units admitted to the empire. Amantius, bishop of Jovia in Pannonia, was preaching to Germans settled in the vicinity; around the year 400 Niceta, a friend of the poet Paulinus and bishop of Remesiana (east of Niš in Serbia) converted the Goths of this region to the Christian faith.

The question of when and how the germanic peoples settled outside the empire were converted is more difficult to answer. E. A. Thompson has suggested that neither the emperors nor the Roman Church assumed or recognized any responsibility in their direction. After a rapid review of the historical testimony, he concludes that prior to the year 476 none of the great germanic tribes living beyond the frontiers had been converted to Christianity. Now there is no denying that at the turn of the fourth century the emphasis in missionary work was all on the conversion of the pagans of Rome, that patriotic elite which figures so largely in the literary sources, and of the rural populations of the provinces. Neither Ambrose nor Augustine could yet see any end to missionary labours in this field. But preaching the gospel was a responsibility which devolved not only on bishops but on all the baptized. And there are numerous indications that Christianity was in fact being carried beyond the borders of the empire. Admittedly, this extension of the Christian mission followed no systematic plan; but even so its effects were very great. Roman exiles and fugitives played their part, as did Romans whom the Germans captured in war. It is said that German mercenaries serving under Rome often adopted Christianity, and one may assume that some remained loyal to their faith even after they returned home. Another group to bear in mind are the Romans who traded with the Germans. It was probably from a Christian merchant that the Marcomanni heard news of the great bishop Ambrose, with the result that their queen Fritigil asked the bishop, now in his declining years, for instruction in the faith. More is known of the beginnings of missionary activity among the Goths, to which brief allusion was made in an earlier context. The Goths had been in contact with Christianity before Ulfilas appeared on the scene. Their initial encounter was with Christians in the Greek cities of the Black Sea littoral, notably in the Crimean peninsula and what was formerly Dacia. In the second half of the third century the Goths extended their pirate raids into the Aegean, ranging as far as Asia Minor, and not a few among their captives were Christians. The probability that there were Christians in the Gothic entourage even before the year 300 is confirmed by coin finds and by the report that

Theophilus took part in the Council of Nicaea as bishop of Gothia; all the evidence suggests that he held his see among the Goths of the Crimea. Ulfilas began his work among the Goths on the Danube; consecrated bishop about 341, he followed the Arian persuasion – or to be exact the Homoean creed which was produced as a tentative effort at reconciliation with the Nicene. After seven years among the Goths he was forced to migrate and with his tribal group was admitted into the empire; he was probably settled in the province of Moesia, a region for which there is evidence of settlement by 'little Goths' in the succeeding period. Just as Christian missions habitually adopted the speech of their hearers, thus making an active contribution to the history of spoken and written language among many peoples, so did Ulfilas; he preached the gospel in the Gothic tongue and made a profound impact with his Gothic translation of the Bible. In order to write down the sacred text he invented an alphabet from germanic runes, creating a national script and paving the way for the development of a literary language among the Germans. In his Gothic version he adapted certain features of biblical life and thought to bring them closer to German understanding, and made the gospel so congenial to his fellow-tribesmen that his particular Goths always remained loyal to their Christian belief. By now, however, the message of the gospel had reached the whole people of the Visigoths, bringing with it disturbance and conflict. When Athanarich, one of the tribal chieftains, started persecuting Christians in 369 he was attacked and beaten in the field by Frithigern, aided by imperial troops. A little later, as a result of the Hunnic advance, Frithigern and a large part of the Visigothic nation was admitted to the empire. These Visigoths who settled on Roman soil were already Christians before Alaric led them in rebellion against the emperor, and they remained Christians throughout the whole period of their wanderings and settlings in the Balkan peninsula, Italy, Gaul and Spain. It was not a matter of compulsion; no authority existed which could have compelled them to profess and adhere to their belief.

Although our information about the other eastern germanic peoples is very incomplete, it seems probable that the tribes of the great federations were already Christian at the time they entered the empire. The Vandals are described as heretics throughout their sojourn in Spain, and in Africa they appear from the first as professors and champions of Arianism. Within the empire the Nicene faith had been imposed by law from the time of Theodosius, so that the Vandals could not have acquired their new faith on Roman soil; their conversion must have taken place outside the empire. The case of the Ostrogoths is similar. They were indisputably Christian by the middle of the fifth century; as Ennodius tells us, the great Theoderic was born of Christian parents.

Since the Ostrogoths professed the Homoean creed, it seems likely that the Visigoths were instrumental in their conversion. Socrates, in his ecclesiastical history, claims that the Burgundians were Catholics from the first, but today it is considered likely that their original conversion, which probably took place between 406 and 451, perhaps through Visigothic missionaries, was to the German form of Arianism. The Suevi, who migrated with the Vandals without entering into a close relationship with them, were still pagans when they reached Spain; towards the middle of the fifth century they adopted Catholic Christianity, but tended to fluctuate between the Catholic and Arian creeds, the decisive factor being the personal position of the king.

The pressing question of what motives the eastern germanic peoples had for their adoption of the Christian religion is still left unanswered. Since contemporary accounts are silent on the subject, our only course is to investigate the state of mind prevailing among these peoples as a whole at the time they were coming into closer contact with Rome. Conclusions may also be drawn from a comparison with the conversion of the west Germans and still more of the Scandinavians, about which we have fuller information.

It is essential to bear in mind that the east Germans found themselves continually on the move. Although they might pause for a time, in southern Russia, on the lower Danube or on the Rhine, their archaic way of life was shattered. Uprooted from their primitive prehistoric existence, individual groups came into contact with the world of civilization, whether on short raiding forays or as mercenaries serving under the banner of Rome. Whole tribes were driven to fight for land to grow their crops, wresting it either from Romans or from a neighbouring kindred tribe. Adventuring, the habit of setting out into the wide world, was another trait which impressed some contemporary observers as characteristic of these strangers. The Anglo-Saxon poem *Widsith* may perhaps be mentioned in this connection: here we find an account of the tribes and peoples of the migration period which is shot through with the longing for space characteristic of the generations who, whether as warriors or singers, felt themselves 'wanderers over the earth'. This state of mobility clearly produced an unparalleled fluidity in political and religious institutions. Powerful chieftains came to the fore in times of emergency and as the leaders of hazardous enterprises, monarchy was introduced. The traditional religious order was shaken, the annual cycle of primeval festivals no longer corresponded to the new mode of life. The deities Tiu, Donar and Woden now became personalized figures dominating the whole range of religious thinking. This tendency to personalize the major deities may have been strengthened by influences from the ancient world. The Germans were becoming familiar with the gods of the Greeks and Romans, and in the period of crisis a degree of syncretism is evident. It was not only that Celtic and Roman deities were infiltrating the regions closest to the Germans; there was also a growing interchange of religious symbols among the Germans themselves, so that Woden, for example, now appears as Odin among the Scandinavians. In time of emergency there was a general readiness to try something entirely new. The church historian Socrates tells us how Frithigern only decided to transfer his allegiance and that of his following to the more powerful God of the Christians in his hour of victory over Athanarich, champion of the old gods.

It is at this point that one may look to Scandinavian literature for guidance, although naturally with all possible caution; it must be stressed that it is adduced merely by way of analogy. The Norse sagas, which took shape several centuries later, contain passages with an important bearing on the changing aspect of personal religion in an era of religious crisis. We find that individuals are frequently linked with a god by ties of formal friendship: a man has what is described in Icelandic as his *fulltrui*, that is to say, a god to whom he devotes himself entirely. He is on intimate terms with his god-friend, and his offering elicits a counter-offering from the god. Now that men were thus less in awe of the gods, religion in the north became appreciably more human. If the friendship wore thin, it could rapidly be dissolved: a trusted friend who failed to fulfil his expected share of the bargain was cast aside. The sagas abound in descriptions of such testing moments: a foreign missionary arrives, destroys the image of the god or hews down the sacred oak; and the conclusion to be drawn is that the new god is more powerful, white Christ mightier than Donar. But one also comes across an opposing view, namely that experience proves all gods to be impotent and points plainly towards atheism. Thus the case of a priest of Frey who dedicates his all to the god, builds him a sanctuary, and then enters on a feud with his rivals, who burn the sanctuary. Now he breaks with his god, convinced 'it is folly to trust in gods' and henceforth relies solely on his own energies and strength. We do not know what personal experiences of this kind the Goths, Vandals and Burgundians had to face. But we can well imagine that their old beliefs were severely tested in the course of their bold and hazardous enterprises. At such times of crisis, it is probable that the belief in destiny, as it appears in what remains of German heroic poetry, assumed overwhelming importance. Life was ruled by war, to fight like a hero became the highest good. But what happened when the hero fell? The answer, given in a spirit of sturdy resignation, might be that everything is ruled by fate, gods as well as men, even Woden himself. There can be no doubt as the east Germans drew closer to the empire there was a loosening of the old religious values and some acceptance of alien gods. In these circumstances, when chieftains transferred their allegiance to the new religion which had its origin in the civilized and coveted empire, they carried their people with them. This was admittedly but the first step into the Christian faith; bringing the reality of the faith home to the Germans, making them true Christians, was a long drawn-out process, in which Christianity itself acquired certain germanic features. It may well be that the Christian message of the God who was both creator and controller of the world, the news of the Redeemer and Lord who relied on the loyalty of his following, and lastly the promise of the judgement day, which would see the powers of darkness put to rout, all combined to break the hold of fate. The strong ethical teaching of the new religion must in many ways have appealed to the German mind, despite fundamental differences between the German and the Christian ethos, and despite the enduring link between moral conduct and clan loyalty. Salvian, whom we shall meet again, in his account of the Roman empire in the fifth century contrasts the depravity of Roman cities with the exemplary life of the Germans, a life characterized by purity, deep respect for marriage and the family, and piety. This moral habit made acceptance of Christian standards all the easier. But it is also obvious that the conversion of the Germans put fresh heart into Christianity. Instead of running up against the jaded intelligence of latterday Greeks and Romans and the privileged morality of a ruling class, for whom the ideal of humane conduct applied only to social equals and compatriots, the Gospel was here breaking fresh ground among new peoples. By its message, the new faith proclaimed that all men were of equal value, instead of relegating the Germans to the inferior degree of barbarism.

A word must be said of the form of Christian belief embraced by the east Germans, their Arianism. While the Vandals accepted the formula of Arius, the other peoples adopted the Homoean creed preached by Ulfilas, which seems to have been roughly as follows: Christ is God, but subordinate to God the Father – the Goths may have linked this article of faith with the germanic father-son relationship. Even in the Catholic world of the empire, the east German peoples long remained loyal to their profession and the Vandals kept it to the end. It can scarcely be presumed that this Arianism corresponded in some special fashion to the germanic nature. We have no detailed information about the theology taught by German clerics of the Arian persuasion; in general they relied on the text of the Bible which is not saying much. It was only in the liturgy and in ecclesiastical organization that the germanic churches developed some distinctive features. Church services were – and continued to be – conducted in the germanic tongues, in the same way that national languages came to be used in the eastern churches, and this alone must have helped to separate the germanic peoples from the men of the Romania. Ecclesiastical organization was adapted to suit the germanic way of life: each tribe had its bishop, there were no metropolitans, no link existed with Rome. There are further problems about this period of German church life which still lack definite solution. Did the priests, who retained their germanic vestments, remain attached to their kindred? Was the spiritual authority of the princes so great that when they endowed a church they controlled not only its revenues but also its direction, creating thereby what is known as an *Eigenkirche?* This much is certain; the germanic churches, separated from the empire and its theological culture by reason of their creed, liturgy and organization, gave firm support to tribal cohesion. Moreover, it had been established – and here the implications extended far beyond the immediate issue of the Germans – that a man could be a Christian without becoming a Roman citizen and without adopting the Catholic creed.

3. *The early German kingdoms and the Roman cultural tradition*

The establishment of germanic states on the soil of the Roman empire brought ancient civilization into continuous and searching contact with germanic nationhood. The conditions under which this encounter between Roman tradition and the new peoples took place varied with the different tribes and provinces, as did the outcome. The Roman provinces which were the theatres principally affected – Gaul, Spain and Africa – differed appreciably from one another in their social and economic organization and intellectual activity. It must be borne in mind that on the German side there was no over-arching unity binding all the separate peoples. Certainly, Goths, Vandals and Burgundians felt a sense of kinship, while their external appearance kept them all equally distinct from the provincial population, but in their dealings with the Roman empire they followed very different and often opposing courses, their kings oscillating between accommodation with the imperial régime and total rejection of Roman supremacy. This initial experience of coexistence between Romans and Germans therefore took different forms in different provinces. It will be convenient to consider the major new foundations one by one, tracing their history and cultural development down to the beginning of the sixth century.

As an example of the encounter between Romans and Germans, the Vandal kingdom in Africa is in every respect an extreme case. Geographically, it lay on the edge of the Roman empire, separated from its central territories by the sea and having as its neighbours on the other side mountain and desert tribes, almost untouched by romanizing influences. King Gaiseric, the founder of the kingdom and leader of his people for almost half a century (428–77) laid down the lines governing relations with the Roman empire once and for all, showing exceptional enterprise and a rare combination of cunning and savagery. His decision to cross from Spain into Africa in 429 seems to have been reached with a clear understanding of the prospects Africa offered as the seat of an independent German power: the provinces were torn by internal dissension and would be an easy prey; he could force Italy to acquiesce by cutting off the export of grain and his position vis-à-vis the west Roman emperor, who had long ceased to command a navy, would be impregnable. As soon as they landed in north Africa and the Roman army had been routed, the Vandals made a concentrated attack on the landowning aristocracy and the Catholic clergy, the chief props of Roman rule. Many members of this ruling class who failed to escape were reduced to slavery, just as many slaves who deserted their masters to join the invaders were set free. The old tensions resulting from the diversity of ethnic descent, social status and religious persuasion among the provincial population were still so strong that the mass of people was either indifferent or actually sympathetic towards the invaders. The first treaty Gaiseric made with the Roman government, in 435, did not satisfy him for long; in 439 he made a surprise attack on Carthage, adopting it as his seat of government and evicting the Roman governing class; and this was followed by a bold foray against Sicily, unchallenged either from Ravenna or Constantinople. A new treaty made in 442 precisely delimited the areas of German and Roman occupation. The Vandals were assigned the eastern part of Numidia including Hippo Regius, the province of Africa Proconsularis around Carthage together with Byzacena lying to the south, to which a small part of Tripolitania was still annexed; the Romans were left with the rest of Numidia, including Cirta, and the provinces of Mauretania; the remaining north African territories were allowed to go their own way.

King Gaiseric made no further additions to his African dominions; he did, however, attack islands in the western Mediterranean, some of which he occupied. After the fall of Aetius (454) and the death of Valentinian III (455) he became the key figure in the grand diplomacy of the period as it was played out between Ravenna, Constantinople, the kings of the germanic states and the Huns. From this position of strength he was able to conquer firstly the Balearic Islands and Corsica, then Sardinia and finally even Sicily; at this period he was also mounting attacks on the coastal regions of Italy and the Balkan peninsula. His descent on Rome in 455 brought him an immense booty. Although Pope Leo, as protector of the city, negotiated an agreement that there would be no bloodshed or burning, after a ransack lasting a fortnight the Vandals bore away some priceless treasures and numerous captives, among them the widow of Valentinian III and her two daughters and some experienced metal-workers, required by the king for his Carthaginian workshops. As a result of these plundering expeditions, the ruinous state of the western empire, as indeed the weakness of the empire as a whole, stood so clearly revealed that in 474 the Emperor Zeno, ruler of the eastern empire, was forced to grant Gaiseric recognition in due form as an independent ruler in full possession of his kingdom; two years later Gaiseric also came to terms with Odoacer, the new ruler of Italy. Vandal expansion in the western Mediterranean has often been set on a par with the policy of the Carthaginian empire, but the essential features which would justify such a comparison – possession of a navy and organized trade – appear to be lacking. All the Vandals did was to seize the Roman grain fleet and build some additional freighters; thus equipped, they carried off booty as they pleased and commandeered the Sicilian and Sardinian grain harvests for the use of Vandal Africa. As C. Courtois has aptly remarked, their empire was an *empire du blé*, a unit which served Vandal agrarian needs.

When we come to investigate the impact made by these Germans on the world of late Roman civilization, we can concentrate on one area, the provinces settled by the Vandals in eastern Algeria and Tunisia. Here the Vandal kingdom (*regnum Vandalorum*) embraced both Germans and Romans and for a time still included a number of Moors. The Vandals found themselves in a terrifyingly small minority. Admittedly, there was some initial increase over the number of 80,000 tribesmen who made the crossing, but the Vandals probably never amounted to more than one twentieth of the romanized population living in the territory they occupied. The extent to which this minority remained distinct from the indigenous population is further emphasized by the fact that the Vandals were not quartered on properties belonging to Romans, as in the case of other germanic settlements, but occupied areas set apart. In the proconsular province the most productive Roman properties were confiscated and distributed among the Vandal warriors as tax-free, heritable estates; in the neighbouring provinces the Roman latifundia became crown lands. All these expropriations were effected under the law laid down by the victor, ordaining that the proprietors be expelled, usually to be sent into exile, while the tillers (coloni) remained on the estates. This drastic proceeding meant that lordship passed into the hands of a warrior class. Intermarriage between Vandals and Romans was forbidden, although political considerations permitted one great exception, the union between Eudocia, daughter of Valentinian III and Huneric, son of Gaiseric. This exclusiveness on the part of the ruling minority had serious consequences. The Vandals suffered permanent losses in man-power as a result of their maritime expeditions; but even in peacetime, their exceptionally privileged position was so enervating to their vital energies that even before the death of Gaiseric their strength as a nation was already on the wane. When after the lapse of two more generations the east Roman empire gathered itself in 533 for decisive action, the Vandals could put into the field only a small army of cavalry, which was swiftly annihilated in a series of short-lived engagements.

The instability inherent in the foundation of the Vandal state was further exacerbated by the particular nature of the monarchical rule exercised over Germans and Romans. We possess no written laws applicable either to Vandals or Romans, but it is clear from the literary sources and archaeological discoveries that in matters of private law both people retained their existing codes. Interesting light has been shed recently on the law concerning property and labour, as it affected the Roman population, by the discovery of the so-called Albertini tablets. These consist of thirty-two deeds of sale scratched on wood, executed during the years 493–6 on a Roman estate lying on the Algerian-Tunisian border. They show that the social and economic order continued unchanged, particularly as regards the collection of dues in kind by the proprietors and the labour services owed by the *coloni*. Public law, which was the same for both peoples, emanated from the monarch, in his capacity as king of the Vandals and lord of the Romans. Gaiseric's autocratic temperament raised the rights of the monarchy to a level far above what was usual among the Germans. In matters of war and peace, leadership of the army and external policy, the king was absolute master. The Vandal nobility, whose effectiveness was seriously impaired by plots which miscarried, could only retain some vestige of its status by entering the royal service. There is no mention in the sources of the popular assembly of ordinary free men as a living political organ; Gaiseric's division of the tribe into eighty groups of thousands had clearly weakened the old ties of kindred, introducing the leaders of these new units (*millenarii*) in place of the old clan chieftains. Gaiseric also took arrangements for the succession entirely into his own hands. By means of a dynastic law, which remained in force as long as the kingdom lasted, he ordained that the succession should devolve on the eldest of his living descendants in the male line; only after the death of the last male of the first generation could the kingdom pass to the eldest male of the second. This rule of seniority, which recalls Celtic arrangements in the British Isles, was designed to prevent any partitioning of the kingdom. This augmentation of royal rights and the fore-ordained succession met with no resistance from the Vandal people; the subject Romans had been excluded from any voice in political matters right from the start. Gaiseric also gave formal expression to his independence vis-à-vis the Roman empire, and in diplomacy and war conducted himself in his dealings with the emperors of Ravenna and Constantinople, as indeed with all other princes, as an equal. While other germanic kings displayed the head of the reigning emperor on their coinage, Gaiseric suffered neither the name nor the image of the emperor to appear on his silver and copper coins. He emphasized his secession from the empire still further by introducing a new form of chronological reckoning. The day on which Carthage was captured, 19 October 439, was declared the beginning of a new era, from which the king's regnal years were reckoned; the names of Roman consuls ceased to appear. But even this rugged aloofness from the ancient world was no complete barrier against the incursion of Roman influences into public life. In court and administration alike, Romans were to be found in influential positions side by side with Vandals, while the regulation of the affairs of the Roman population still living in urban communities or on landed estates was left wholly to the existing bureaucracy. In these Roman territories, stringent application of the old system of *capitatio* continued to produce the taxes which, together with confiscations and the fruits of raiding expeditions, formed the most important sources of public revenue.

Right from the beginning, the opposition between Vandals and Romans was sharply evident in the sphere of religion. The Vandals were Arians of an extreme type, the Romans were Catholics; and there were still some surviving remnants of Donatism. The Arian and Catholic churches were both subject to the royal authority, but even so Gaiseric carried out a deliberate plan for weakening the Catholic Church, whose numerous episcopal sees and extensive landed estates made it an important power in the land; his son Huneric, whose intention was to make Arianism the sole religion of the state, embarked on a campaign of actual persecution. This led to serious conflicts and the issue of harsh decrees, brutally enforced. These events are described for us in a work entitled *Historia persecutionis Africanae provinciae*, written by Victor, bishop of Vita in Tunisia, probably with the aim of stirring up Constantinople to intervene on behalf of the oppressed inhabitants of Africa. The impassioned tone of this work, whose protestations become overemphatic, is clear enough indication that the religious conflict had a political and nationalist connotation. The Catholic bishops, Romans through and through, combined resistance to Arianism with opposition to the barbarian conquerors; since they not infrequently exploited their external connections, they came under suspicion of conspiring with the enemy. But there can really be no doubt that Gaiseric himself had the intention of exterminating the Catholic religion in all territories occupied by the Vandals. After 454 Catholics were deprived of all their churches in Carthage, and the confiscation of liturgical vessels and books made celebration of divine service impossible throughout the pro-consular province; many bishops were sent into exile. When individual Arians resorted to violence, the Catholics had their martyrs, both clerical and lay. Branded as Anti-Christ, Gaiseric had to reckon with opposition from the Roman population, especially the upper class, throughout his reign. In 482 his successor Huneric proceeded to a systematic suppression of the Catholic religion. Having dismissed all Catholic officials from his court, he then debarred all non-Arians from holding public office; thousands of clerics and laymen were banished and forced to make a long weary trek – its rigours are vividly described by Victor – to the Moors of the desert. When an attempt at agreement by a synod of Catholic and Arian ecclesiastics failed, the king ordered the confiscation of all Catholic churches and the transfer of their properties to the Arians. A decree of 24 February 484 required all Catholics to embrace the Arian faith and to publicize their action by receiving Arian re-baptism before the 1 June; any who refused were threatened with corporal punishment, impoverishment and exile. This attempt at imposing the state religion by law, made by an alien ruler supported by only a tiny minority and lacking even the undivided allegiance of his own people, was more drastic even than that of Theodosius. The decrees were put into force. Priests were banished, monks dispersed and many forced baptisms effected; but there were martyrs and confessors to set against the many who apostasized. The sudden death of Huneric brought no reversal of policy; his two immediate successors admittedly refrained from blood-shed, but their politico-religious objective was the same, even though one was the high-minded and cultivated Thrasamund, who carried on a theological discussion with the learned bishop Fulgentius of Ruspe, and himself formulated the ten theses of his creed. It was not until Hilderic, son of Huneric and Eudocia, who had passed much of his life in Constantinople, came to the throne in 523 that the bishops were recalled and toleration for the Catholic religion proclaimed. This bitter religious conflict was largely responsible for hardening the Romans in their hostility and helped to prevent Vandal rule from striking permanent root among the indigenous population.

Towards the end of his book Victor of Vita addresses himself to the small band of Vandal sympathizers: 'You few who love the barbarians and are always singing their praises, condemning yourselves out of your own mouths, do but consider their name and reputation! Could any other name but that of barbarian, which signifies savagery, cruelty and terror, fit them so well? One may coddle them with kindness, woo them with assiduous service, all they think of is their envy of the Romans. Their design is obvious, all the time they are trying to besmirch the glory and honour of the Roman name. Their desire is that no Romans shall survive. If they spare their subjects in one or another case, it is to exploit them as slaves. For they have never had any affection for Romans, even as individuals.'[12]

With his tales of violence, this pugnacious theologian provided more fuel than all the chronicles of the period for that denigration of the Vandals as a band of destructive brigands which is found in historical writing from the seventeenth and eighteenth centuries, and which in the time of the French revolution gave rise to the word Vandalism as signifying a sheer lust for destruction. Impartial critics of our own day, above all C. Courtois and F. Lot, have pointed out that pillage, arson and slaughter cannot fairly be regarded as peculiar to the Vandals. What distinguished the Vandals from other germanic peoples was their use of force in questions of religion, which was the basic obstacle to any appeasement between the Roman population and their masters. In fact there is evidence that in the Roman provinces of the kingdom the Vandals made some contribution to art and culture. In the first decades of the occupation, the overthrow of the Roman governing class brought intellectual life almost to extinction but in the period after Huneric, once the worst storm was past, we again hear of schools providing instruction in grammar and literature. The grammarian Felicianus had both Romans and aliens among his pupils, as the late fifth-century African poet Dracontius is witness. Kings such as Thrasamund and Hilderic kept Latin poets at their courts, who excelled in highly mannered epigrams after the fashion of Martial. Thrasamund was complimented by Fulgentius – high praise indeed – for propagating culture even among the Vandals, a people otherwise distinguished by their ignorance. Admittedly, the fates which overtook Dracontius and Fulgentius are eloquent testimony to the hazards which continued to threaten educated Romans. When Dracontius paid tribute in verse to a foreign ruler – it must have been the emperor of Constantinople – this was accounted high treason; he was arrested and put to the torture. While in prison he wrote a poem entitled *Satisfactio ad Gunthamundum*, in which he acknowledges his fault in having celebrated a foreign ruler instead of the native dynasty, and begs for mercy. Bishop Fulgentius, descended from an eminent Carthaginian family and hence well grounded in Greek and Latin literature, belonged on the evidence of his letters and other writings to the class of theologians who kept up a literary standard throughout the period of religious conflict. Twice exiled to Sardinia and twice recalled, his life exemplifies the difficulties of a scholar concerned to maintain the Augustinian religious tradition while living under foreign rule. All classes of the Roman population were thus made to suffer; but on their side the kings failed to preserve the ancestral tribal customs of their own people and to carry the development of germanic institutions a stage further. Latin, not the Vandal language, was used in the administration; bilingual Vandals existed, but there is no record that Romans learned to speak the alien tongue. No trace of Vandal literature has survived; however, some modest archaeological finds testify that germanic art was kept alive in the form of craft work. Salvian of Massilia praised the Vandals of the time of Gaiseric for the purity of their morals; they were not only contemptuous of Roman corruption, they also put an end to prostitution throughout their kingdoms and forbade unnatural intercourse. But even this moral strength seems to have deserted them. The sources are unanimous in stigmatizing the Vandals of the last decades as an effete ruling class, with a passion for baths and spectacles, indulging themselves in the good life in the fastness of their castles; the Vandals, says Procopius, historian of the Vandal war, are the softest-living of all the peoples who have come to our notice.

The Vandal adventure was thus a failure both for the germanic and for the Roman world. After a century spent living in isolation, in a dangerous form of apartheid, the whole tribe was so debilitated, both physically and morally, that it fell an easy prey to its Byzantine conquerors and the work of generations in Africa was wiped out. The ancient world as a whole suffered severe damage from the period of Vandal domination. Economic decline was accelerated by the replacement of Romans by still less competent Vandals as proprietors of the soil in once flourishing provinces; no fresh impetus was given to education and culture. The Vandal pirate raids not only revealed, but also appreciably increased, the weaknesses of the empire; and the Moorish tribes were now completely beyond the orbit of Roman power and civilization, sunk back into the anonymity of what has been called 'forgotten Africa'.

The encounter of the Visigoths and the Burgundians with ancient civilization followed an entirely different course. These two peoples can be considered together, although their relations with the empire were very different. In the first place, what they had in common was the Celto-Roman basis of their settlement areas in Gaul, with ancient cities and landed estates to act as channels of continuity in social, economic and cultural life. Further, the two kingdoms experienced a similar initiation into a life of peaceful co-existence between Germans and Romans. Lastly, both kingdoms were in contact with the Alamanni and the Franks, the western German tribes whose incursions into the Roman empire never cut them off from the old area of germanic settlement. Relations with the Franks are of particular importance, since from the sixth century they assumed the leading role in the second act of the drama in which Germans confronted Romans. The Visigoths and Burgundians thus became intermediaries between the Imperium Romanum and the Frankish empire.

First we must look at the terrain occupied by the states in question. Under a settlement treaty agreed in 418 the Visigoths received the territories bordering the ocean south of the Loire, including Burdigala (Bordeaux) and Tolosa (Toulouse). In principle, the way the settlement was carried out followed the rules laid down for the billeting of Roman soldiers, under which they were assigned a third of their host's house. In the case of the Visigoths this apportionment was extended to include all the householder's immovable property and probably amounted to more than a third right from the start; at all events, half a century later two thirds seems to be the norm of occupation. The Goths had acquired a fertile land, but were deliberately cut off from the Mediterranean. The kings of the succeeding period made it their aim to expand in the direction of the province of Narbonne and become completely independent of the Roman empire. Even so, Aetius long remained as the stalwart champion of the Roman cause in Gaul and in 451 contrived to enlist the Visigoths as allies against the Huns: King Theodoric I was killed in the battle of the Catalaunian Fields. Theoderic II was also inveigled into furthering the policies of the Gallo-Roman aristocracy and in 455 was present at Arles when Eparchius Avitus, one of its foremost representatives, assumed the purple. But after the overthrow of this emperor and of his successors, the Goths made a successful thrust towards the Mediterranean and in 462 the city of Narbonne and its adjacent territory came under their control. King Euric, an energetic ruler and zealous Arian, who ruled from 466–84, made open war on the now completely enfeebled emperors; he enlarged Gothic territory to include the whole area between the Loire, the Rhône and the Pyrenees and by the end of his reign had even occupied the Auvergne, the last redoubt of the Gallo-Roman aristocracy. At the same time he also conquered the greater part of Spain, driving the Sueves into the extreme north-west of the peninsula. Under the peace treaty of 475 the emperor Nepos was forced to confirm the Goths in possession of all their conquered territories and recognize the independence of the kingdom of Toulouse. The last remnant of Roman dominion on the soil of southern Gaul, namely Arles and the coastal strip running from the lower Rhône to the Alps, was surrendered to the Goths by Odoacer, the new ruler of Italy. However, the Visigothic kingdom was unable to sustain this powerful expansion for very long. In 507 the Franks advancing from northern and central Gaul under the leadership of their King Clovis seized southern Gaul from the Visigoths, who from now on made Spain the chief basis of their state; only the western part of the Mediterranean zone, the region known later as Septimania or Gothia, continued to be Gothic. Since we are here concerned with the fifth century, our survey of the Goths' encounter with ancient civilization will be confined to what took place while their state was still planted on Gallic soil. To turn now to the Burgundians. We have already traced their progress down to the time they settled in the province of Sapaudia and the adjoining territory to the north, in western Switzerland. Defending themselves all the while against Alamannic expansion, the Burgundians continued to enlarge their own territory, and were at the same time careful to preserve good relations with the Roman emperor. Several Burgundian kings were appointed to the office of Master of Soldiers and received the honorary title of Patricius; a Burgundian auxiliary troop also took part in the great battle against the Huns. As allies of the Gallo-Roman aristocracy, the Burgundians were allowed to take possession of Lyons, an ancient Roman colony which they made the capital of their dominions (461). Further expansion brought them to the Durance in the south and to Langres and the Burgundian Gates in the north; their eastern frontier ran along the upper and middle Aare, passing through Solothurn. King Gundobad (490–516) was skilful in preserving the traditional good relations with the Roman emperor in Constantinople and in winning the diplomatic support of Theoderic, king of the Ostrogoths, which made it possible to avert the threat of Frankish aggression against his vast domain. Indeed, Romans were already being enlisted for service in the Burgundian army, the first step towards a society in which the Germans and Romans in the population were placed on an equal footing.

Initially, the position of Germans settled on imperial territory was governed by the Roman law concerning billeting. According to this, the Visigoths and Burgundians were 'billeted guests' (*hospites*) in the Roman provinces and as such wholly dependent on what the institutions rooted in the land could provide. The numerical inferiority of the foreigners was itself a reason for reaching a considerable measure of accommodation with the native population. In the relatively small areas where the Visigoths and Burgundians first had their settlements, the German as compared with the Roman element in the population was of respectable size, and in the neighbourhood of the royal residences remained so over a longish period; but in the newly conquered territories the germanic warriors dwindled to a small minority. In the extended kingdom of king Euric the Visigothic element amounted to perhaps two per cent of the total population. The Burgundians were more strongly represented in the north, where they had to defend themselves against the Alamanni, particularly in the region around Besançon and

Langres, than they were in the south; but it was precisely in the southern portion of their domains that the aliens' encounter with the ancient world was to produce really fruitful results. It was very difficult for these German minorities to withstand the pressure of Roman influence. Moreover, the solidarity of the germanic peoples was to some degree impaired by their own social organization. The distinctions between the various grades of property-owning and status which were the legacy of the pre-migration period, were now reinforced by the even harsher inequalities which arose from settlement on Roman estates. The Visigoths had an upper and a lower stratum (*potentiores-inferiores*), each with its own law, while the Burgundians were divided into the three strata of nobility, medium-free and low-free. Upon this shaky foundation the two peoples proceeded to erect a state which comprehended both Germans and Romans, two elements which were required to live side by side and yet preserve their identity. The most important binding ligament was the monarch; for the Germans he was *Rex Gothorum* or *Rex Burgundionum*, endowed with the traditional royal authority, to his Roman subjects he was made acceptable by the offices and honorific titles conferred by the emperor or a fictitious kinship with the imperial house. The germanic aspect of the monarchy was most apparent in the king's command of the armed host, but in its new setting royal authority tended to increase among the Visigoths and Burgundians, although it still fell short of the Vandal autocracy. The assembly of germanic warriors was rarely consulted before important decisions, and the germanic aristocracy had to content themselves with serving the king. The monarchy was the repository of all public authority: government, administration, supreme jurisdiction and ecclesiastical control over its Roman and German subjects all fell within its sphere. From the beginning, Romans had access to high positions in the central government, and in the royal household with which it was closely associated. The chancery retained its Roman stamp, the structure of the provincial government was left untouched and there was no interference in economic affairs. There was one modest German contribution, the practice among the Visigoths and Burgundians of giving combined military and civil functions to the men appointed by the king to administer a city (*comites civitatum*), even if in practice they were drawn from the native aristocracy. Latin was adopted as the administrative language, the tax system remained in being and the coinage followed the imperial pattern.

Such were the main outlines of this Romano-German experiment in co-existence. The exercise was not without difficulties; on the one hand was the Gallo-Roman population, in possession of ancient civilization but politically dependent, on the other the handful of germanic warriors and masters, the intrusive beneficiaries of long-established institutions.

Moreover, prohibition on intermarriage long remained in force, while the retention of the both germanic and Roman codes of private law ensured that the distinction between the two elements in the population would remain. The idea that a man's juridical affiliations were determined by his tribal origin rather than his membership of a state was a concept already familiar under old Roman law; the Germans were so wedded to this principle of the personality of law that the Visigoths and Burgundians, when they later came under Frankish rule, still claimed the right to live under their own laws. The Roman population thus continued to live under the law of Rome, though this was no longer the law of the classical Roman jurists but a provincial version of it known as vulgar law, the law for the common people of the provinces. Thanks to the efforts of the kings and their advisers, this Roman law was codified for use in the Visigothic and Burgundian kingdoms. Alaric II, finding himself in need of support from the Gallo-Roman population in face of the Frankish threat, arranged in 506 for the publication of the *Lex Romana Visigothorum*, the law valid for Romans living in the kingdom of Toulouse; this code became known as the *Breviarium Alaricianum*. At much the same time King Gundobad brought out the *Lex Romana Burgundionum*, for the benefit of his Roman subjects. These two codes drew on Roman vulgar law; in fact, two products of late Roman jurisprudence are officially annexed to Alaric's code, namely an epitome of the text-book written by Gaius and a collection of interpretations of the *Codex Theodosianus*; so it is not surprising that this *Breviarium*, which later found acceptance in the Merovingian kingdom, was for centuries regarded as providing an authoritative and sufficient statement of Roman law. Both kingdoms also produced Latin codifications of their germanic tribal laws. Euric led the way for the Visigoths with his *Codex Euricianus*, issued in 475; Gundobad followed suit in 501 with the *Lex Burgundionum*. These germanic legal codes, which bring together the customary laws and the laws made by the kings, are significant testimony to the meeting of the two worlds, German and Roman: not merely because germanic concepts and institutions are given professional legal formulation in the Latin tongue, but still more because even here the influence of vulgar Roman law is unmistakable. Euric's code, which had a strong influence on the development of medieval law in the West, contains more that is Gotho-Roman than pure Gothic, particularly in the sections dealing with mercantile law. All the same, both codes retain many of the rules found in old germanic law. For example, there is the characteristic idea that a man metes out justice for himself, even though this archaic principle survives only in fragmentary form. Thus under Visigothic law, in cases of adultery the faithless wife and guilty man are handed over to the husband for punishment, just as a wronged wife is left to deal with her rival. Even some features of the old kindred law survive, and this is all the more remarkable in that during the migration period the tribal organization by kindreds was already giving way to a system of division into hundreds and thousands, following the model of the Roman army. Among the Burgundians an accused man swears to his innocence supported by eleven 'oath-helpers' belonging to his family, including his wife, children and parents; among the Visigoths a man guilty of kidnapping a child is handed over to the parents or relatives of his victim, who can kill him, sell him, or indeed claim damages. The continuing strength of the kindred is implicit in the great emphasis the *Codex Euricianus* places on the legal responsibility of the individual, insisting – obviously by way of contrast with earlier received opinion – that the father is not responsible for his son, nor the son for his father, that the wife is not answerable for her husband, nor the brother for his brother; punishment is reserved for the one who has earned it. A number of provisions expose the gulf separating the Germans from the Roman population: the Germans still recognize the old custom of bride-purchase, divorce is much harder for them than under Roman law. Penalties for misdemeanours and felonies vary substantially under the two systems. Romans guilty of raping and abducting a virgin are threatened with the death penalty, Burgundians escape with a fine. Under Roman law heavy penalties, extending even to banishment, might be incurred by cutting down fruit trees standing on a neighbour's land; Burgundian law demanded only the payment of a solidus for each tree.

The co-existence of these parallel codes of law certainly sustained the co-existence of the two elements in the population. In both kingdoms, even where the germanic minority was very small, it was self-contained and long continued to be so. The Visigoths and Burgundians kept to their own language, whereas the men thronging the towns and markets spoke vulgar Latin; and both peoples continued to create their own poetry and song. Sidonius Apollinaris mentions that heroic lays were being recited at the Visigothic court, and it seems likely that it was at this period, when the Burgundians settled on the Saône and Doubs were in contact with the Franks and even with the Bavarians, that the various sagas which make up the *Nibelungenlied* were brought together. In many ways these Germans were still strangers to their surroundings, and they certainly tended to strike the Romans as bizarre. Their physical appearance and dress alone was enough to rouse the excited interest of their contemporaries, the men because of their long hair, trousers and pelts, the women on account of their clothing and ornaments. For a long time craftsmen and artists succeeded in retaining the purity of their germanic style, as is shown by vessels and ornaments worked in precious metals which have been unearthed in many places, fibulae, pins, brooches, finger-rings, arm bands and neck chains. Goldsmiths' work shows clear evidence of the continuing influence of Graeco-Pontic techniques, and as time goes on we find late Roman forms contributing to the decoration of ornamental ware. These minorities found the effort of maintaining their identity in the states they themselves had founded increasingly difficult. The longer their kingdoms lasted, the more marked became the influence of men of Roman descent and of Roman ways of life, whether in the kingdom of Toulouse or in the state founded by the Burgundians. Cemeteries which have recently been submitted to thorough investigation make it clear that the fusion of peoples and cultures was proceeding apace as the generations succeeded one another.

Admittedly, the Roman culture which for centuries past had had a firm foot-hold in the provinces in question could boast of no new startling achievements; but it continued without interruption. The workshops of the potters and weavers appear to have suffered little interference from the storm; the late Roman style could still find expression in works of architecture, sculpture and painting. It is established beyond doubt that in the provinces of Gaul, as in Italy and Africa, schools of rhetoric survived with no break in continuity into the fifth century, and here, as elsewhere, offered the sons of the upper class the usual grounding in classical literature and eloquence. Latin was the only language used in diplomacy and legislation, educated Romans reached high positions, they acted as counsellors and tutors at the royal courts. King Gundobad promoted Latin schooling among his Burgundians, just as his great contemporary Theoderic did among the Ostrogoths in Italy; Gundobad had Laconius to advise him and Heraclius as his court poet. The Visigothic King Theodoric I and his sons were endebted for their initiation into Latin literature and Roman law to Avitus, who has already been mentioned; in the succeeding reigns Sidonius Apollinaris, whom we shall meet again as a key figure in the Roman aristocracy, managed to make at least fleeting contact with Theoderic II and even with Euric. Euric's chancellor was Leo, who was complimented by being compared with Tacitus and Horace. Although Euric had only an imperfect command of Latin and often had recourse to interpreters, other Visigothic kings, and even some of the Visigothic aristocracy, could speak both languages. It seems very probable that Ragnahild, Euric's queen, could understand Latin for on one occasion a friend of Sidonius Apollinaris, named Euodius, anxious to solicit her intervention in a personal matter, brought as a gift a large shell set in silver on which was inscribed a Latin epigram composed by Sidonius, a tribute to the queen written in a high-flown and elaborate style:

Shell of Venus, drawn by Triton on the backs of whales,
The goddess at once retires when she finds herself beside such an one.
Incline, a little, we beg you therefore, your princely head
To accept, O mighty protectress this little gift;
Be gracious not to spurn Euodius' friendly plea:
Make him great, and you will be loftier still.
You have kings for father, father-in-law and husband,
May your son be king with his father and remain so after him!
Fortunate water, surrounded by the metal's sheen; you capture
The still higher gloss of this lady's countenance.
When it pleases her to bedew her cheeks from this vessel,
The silver reflects back again the light of her countenance.[13]

Speaking quite generally, it can thus be said that the Roman aristocracy maintained its position, even under germanic domination. As K. F. Stroheker has recently shown, the senatorial aristocracy of Gaul had progressed further towards becoming a hereditary class than was the case even in other provinces. Once a member of an old Roman family had reached senatorial rank, through holding high office in the civil service or in the army, his house was permanently ennobled. Senators were the proprietors of extensive landed estates, especially in central and southern Gaul, with magnificent palaces, baths and colonnaded halls; the home farms of large properties were worked by slaves and serfs, while the remaining land was handed over to dependent tenants who had to render compulsory dues and services. These Roman proprietors often had armed retainers in their service, just as from the end of the fourth century some high-ranking officers in the Roman army had their own private soldiers, the so-called *buccellarii*; in some of the regional fighting there were actually occasions when Gallic landowners sent their own contingents into the field. So long as this senatorial aristocracy remained in being, the Roman tradition lived on and the hard core of the old culture survived.

Lastly, the difference in religious persuasion worked to the advantage of the Romans and the detriment of the Germans. True, there was no religious warfare, as in the Vandal kingdom, although in his newly conquered territories Euric sought to reduce isolated pockets of Roman resistance by leaving episcopal sees vacant over long periods and seeing to it that Catholic places of worship were desolated. With the two Churches existing side by side, the Germans were at a disadvantage in that Arianism failed to develop any drawing power. There is evidence that theological literature made a tentative beginning among the germanic Arians, but this soon petered out. A theologian anxious to make his voice heard in controversies which harked back to Arius and Pelagius had to be versed in Latin. The Catholic Church numbered among its theologians men of the calibre of Claudianus Mamertus of Vienne, who even at this date had reached his Christian philosophy by way of neo-platonism. The episcopate was firmly entrenched, indeed its ranks were appreciably enlarged as the century progressed. When the western empire collapsed, and with it all prospects for the Gallic aristocracy of a career in the imperial service, many sons of these families aspired to episcopal office, a position from which they could also exert an influence at the courts of the germanic kings; it was thanks to Avitus, bishop of Vienne, that the Burgundian royal family was converted to the Catholic persuasion. The link with the Papacy was maintained. Caesarius, who occupied the see of Arles for a long period in the sixth century, succeeded despite many difficulties in strengthening the attachment of the Gallic bishops to Rome; he was also very influential as a preacher, especially since he introduced the practice of preaching in vulgar Latin instead of the literary language which had hitherto been the fashion. In both germanic kingdoms the Catholic Church thus brought additional strength to the forces of *Romanitas* and was a firm ally of any move tending towards the romanization of the alien minorities. For the Burgundians, the decisive step marking their entry into the Roman world was the conversion of Sigismund to the Catholic faith in 516. But well before this date, the vital energies of the Germans had become so exhausted that this alone would have made it impossible to maintain their separate position. Prodigious demands were made of the warriors – particularly in inter-tribal warfare, for the germanic states formed no unitary block. Once the Burgundians were obliged to enlist Romans in their army, the prohibition of intermarriage went by the board. The Visigoths in Spain were able to retain the ban over a longer period and were only converted to the Catholic persuasion towards the end of the sixth century.

Latterly there has been a tendency to regard the historical phenomenon of these germanic states as part of that process of provincialization which had begun in the western Roman empire well before the migration era; in individual provinces local resistance to the centralizing authority of the emperor was developing as early as the third century, several of the fourth century rival emperors proclaimed on Gallic soil were candidates promoted by members of the governing class who had a stake in the land. At this period, too, we find changes creeping into the Latin of the western provinces, Latin literature written in Gaul and Spain becomes distinctly regional in flavour – witness Ausonius and Prudentius – and the plastic arts become more emphatically provincial in character. The first 'barbarians' to arrive in provinces which were already becoming more and more remote from Rome settled only in small groups and retained their former way of life, forming as it were enclaves in the northern parts of the empire. Ultimately these germanic territories became independent states and thus set the final seal on a process of provincial differentiation which had lasted for centuries. It may well be that certain features of the germanic states become clearer when seen in this light. But one must not fail to recognize that the Visigoths and Burgundians made a wholly distinctive contribution to the metamorphosis of ancient civilization. These peoples injected new and vital energies into the provinces of the collapsing Roman empire, energies which were still potent even after the German elements had mingled with the Roman. For us, the most striking indication of this vigour is the linguistic legacy which the Goths, Burgundians, and later also the Lombards, bequeathed to the romance languages in the shape of numerous place and personal names and a significant array of commonplace expressions: in short, the germanic imprint on *Romania*, which will later be described in detail. Other mental and moral stimuli provided by the new peoples, which affected the social life of the provinces, the concepts of friendship and marriage, family life and the Church, are difficult to reduce to institutional terms; their importance however, is established beyond doubt, since contemporaries were already remarking on and praising their effects.

Of the writers who help us to form a picture of fifth century culture we shall here mention only two, whose account of Romano-German co-existence in the western provinces, notably Gaul, is exceptionally penetrating: Salvian of Massilia and Sidonius Apollinaris. Salvian ranks first, for he saw most clearly what was new and important for the future in the rise of the germanic peoples. Salvian started to write only a few decades after Orosius had already brought some degree of historical insight to his treatment of the Germans in the first phase of the migrations; but he speaks not as an historian but as a Christian critic of the contemporary scene, unrivalled in his acuteness of observation and discerning judgement. Salvian was born shortly after 400, probably in the Rhineland, where Romans and Germans had already long been living side by side; in his youth he followed a course of rhetoric and perhaps also studied law. After a brief marriage, he entered the ascetic community of Lérins, whose influence, partly through its monastic foundations but still more through the priests and bishops it sent out as missionaries, at that time extended deep into Gaul. Salvian became a priest and spent many years (from before 440 until perhaps *c.* 480) working in this capacity in Massilia (Marseilles) – a city on Roman soil but with Germans in the vicinity. In his two theological works and the handful of letters which have survived, he shows himself a writer in the old tradition, who was nevertheless not too proud to experiment with linguistic forms derived from the regional Latin of this late period. In s first work, written under the pseudonym Timotheus, the priest-scete advances ideas for reforming the Christian life. Christians, he says, are God's debtors and as such should divest themselves of material goods; monks and clerics should live without possessions, laymen should make their property over to the Church in their last testament, if not before. We shall keep in mind these radical proposals, which point towards ecclesiastical communism, as we consider Salvian's major work, the *De gubernatione Dei*, which was completed not later than 440. Starting from the question why God should have allowed Christians and Romans to be conquered by the foreigners, Salvian expounds a theodicy in which the disaster is interpreted as a merited divine punishment. The grace of belief demands from Christians a transformation of their ethical code; the rich had to prove themselves by their conduct towards the poor, the Romans by their attitude towards the alien invaders. The higher a man's status, the greater his obligation, and the greater his guilt if he fell short. Measured against this standard, the nobles had acquitted themselves worse than slaves and the Romans worse than the aliens; men had thus brought down God's punishment on themselves by their moral guilt. It was not Christianity that led to the fall of Rome, as some people still insisted, but the unchristianity of the Romans.

This fundamental proposition is made the basis for an attack on the social and economic order, which runs through the entire work. In unmasking the sinful and criminal features of the world around him, the preacher becomes the spokesman of the oppressed class, the *humiliores* of the later Roman empire. 'The richer the greater' is the maxim of the powerful, who have no scruples about using it to justify theft and extortion. The landed proprietors unload their taxes on to the poor; officials of all grades, in particular the curiales or town councillors, are rapacious in collecting taxes, especially from widows, orphans and monks, to whom they show no mercy: there are as many tyrants as there are curiales! Because of the greed of the great, the venality of financial officials and the unjust dealings of curiales, the weak must bear the burdens of the strong. Such is their distress that the poor find themselves obliged to give up their freedom. Some surrender their small property to magnates living in the neighbourhood in order to win their protection and become their clients. As we know, there were villages where many or indeed all the smaller farmers took this course, which meant that the landlord acquired a tutelary lordship (*patrocinium vicorum*) over the whole class of *plebeii*. The others, says Salvian, leave their homes and find themselves work in some foreign place as dependent labourers, *coloni* or *tributarii;* but it may well be that they are reduced to complete slavery. It was the wickedness of judges and officials which turned the Bagaudae into rebels – a reference to the peasant revolt which dragged on in Gaul for so long. Again and again, Salvian contrasts this corrupt Roman society with the better world of the 'barbarians'. Admittedly, his attitude smacks somewhat of the idealization of the foreigner, above all the primitive foreigner, which occur in the works of Stoics and Cynics and spill over into ethnographical and historical writing. But Salvian has made his own careful observations of the Vandals, Goths, Franks, Alamanni and Saxons, and can even make some remarks about the Huns and Alans. Among these foreigners there is no oppression of the poor, which explains why Romans living on Gothic territories have no other wish than to remain outside Roman rule. There are many Romans, even eminent and cultivated men, who take refuge with the 'barbarians.' Despite the difference in manners and language, despite the repellent stench of barbarian bodies and clothing, they prefer the freedom and humanity of life among the foreigners to the restrictions and inhumanity they experience under the Romans. Even those who remain behind acknowledge in their hearts that they no longer wish to be Romans. The faults and failings of the foreigners are not glossed over: they are entirely lacking in culture; unable to read, they know their Christian faith only from hearsay, but even as heretics their conduct is superior to that of Catholics. While the Romans are always squabbling amongst themselves, the 'barbarians' have affection for their fellow-tribesmen; Goths and Vandals are chaste, humble before God and therefore successful. 'It stands to reason how God judges between us and the Goths and Vandals: they increase from day to day, we decrease; they prosper, we are humbled, they flourish, we wither away.'[14] The Vandals are singled out for quite exceptional praise – admittedly at a time when the persecution of African Catholics had not yet started. It was to punish the Romans that the Vandals were set on the course which led them through Belgica, Gaul and Spain to arrive finally in Africa, the land where all wickedness was at home. In Africa the contrast between germanic virtue and Roman moral degeneration was plain for all to see: the Vandals not only kept themselves pure, they also made the Romans chaste.

As a Christian, then, Salvian passes harsh judgement on the world around him. Yet even he feels a last flicker of Roman pride, and leaves the reputation of at least the early Romans untarnished. In time-honoured fashion he praises the Curii, Fabricii and Cincinnati, extolling Roman antiquity as the blissful time when citizens dedicated their poverty to the state and so became valourous and strong. Thereafter, indeed corruption set in, whose effect was to make men 'more like Greeks than Romans', and with this moral decay came tribulation – Salvian here combines the views of Sallust and Augustine. Now the state is dead or at its last gasp. People do nothing to arrest its demise; on the contrary, through their dissolute amusements and wanton sins they are killing it before it is dead, as for example the inhabitants of Trier, who still clung to their games although their city had thrice been plundered. Misery and merriment go hand in hand, 'the Roman people are dying and laughing'. But however trenchant his accusations, however emotive his rhetoric, the preacher does not resign himself to the corruption he sees around him; he continually calls on men to reflect and repent. True, he has no concrete advice to offer on the conduct of the patriotic struggle or on social reform; as a critic, the road he advocates is the road of Christian regeneration, just as it was when he wrote as Timotheus. He dismisses as unwarranted the Christian claim that because Christians are ostensibly more pious than other peoples they must also be more successful. Even if the emperors are now Christians, even if there is no longer any religious persecution, the name of religion is being used to cloak despicable actions, Christians are false to their profession, love of neighbour has become rare among them. But the fundamental evil is still private wealth. Contempt for riches, which the exemplary Romans of earlier days achieved despite their ignorance of God, is the great and immediate duty of those who follow Christ. To sum up, Salvian's book is evidence of a will on the part of Christian *Romanitas* to reform. Salvian's references to the plight of the oppressed and the flight to the 'barbarians' are often quite unspecific and hence difficult to relate to any particular place and time; yet his conviction that the Germans offered a fresh source of moral energy to the Roman world still remains suggestive. One wonders if Germans and Romans could not together have made a fresh start, if only this voice crying in the wilderness had been heeded by the Roman upper class.

This is not to say, however, that the Gallo-Roman nobility were in general as corrupt as Salvian would have us believe. It is only fair to give a hearing to one of the *potentes*, the governing social class, Sidonius Apollinaris, whose poems, speeches and letters brightly illumine the decades following the middle of the fifth century. His life-story is itself an indication of how wide a field of activity was still open to the Roman aristocracy. Sidonius was born in Lyons about 430, into a highly aristocratic and Christian family – though in common with most other aristocratic houses in Gaul, its Christianity was of the kind left untouched by the asceticism preached from Lérins. His study of grammar and rhetoric gave Sidonius only a general literary education, his knowledge of geography and history was slight and with philosophy he had only a nodding acquaintance. His marriage with the daughter of the great Avitus brought him the property of Avitacum in the Auvergne, a beautiful estate in a countryside remote from the great highways; here, as he remarks, he found his second home. Although the decline of imperial authority must have made the outlook for Romans uncertain, Sidonius nevertheless played an active part in Gallo-Roman politics. When his father-in-law assumed the purple as the choice of the Gallo-Roman nobility, it was Sidonius who spoke his panegyric in Rome, in 455; when Avitus fell, Sidonius celebrated the new emperor, Majorian, a man of the Italo-Roman aristocracy (458); and his final panegyric was delivered on behalf of Anthemius, the Greek emperor sent from Constantinople, for which he was rewarded by the city prefecture of Rome (468). But for all his panegyrical fervour, he did not allow himself to become wholly wrapped up in politics. There were more tranquil years which he could spend with his friends in the Auvergne or at Arles, and he was not above fostering relations with the germanic courts of Toulouse and Lyons, so long as they served the interests of his class. Finally, to his own surprise, in 470 Sidonius became bishop of Clermont, an office he filled with sincerity and dignity until his death in 488. The change cut deeply into his habit of life, and it was not merely that he no longer wrote secular poetry; far more telling is his close identification of himself, as bishop, with his flock and his acceptance of concern for the distressed populace as a duty. When the Visigoths launched their attack on the Auvergne, Sidonius the Roman patriot, together with his brother-in-law Ecdicius directed the defence of his city; when this last Gallic stronghold fell, Sidonius was for a time expelled. On his recall, he set himself to cultivate better relations with the Germans, and at the end of his life was able to pass on the ideals for which he had lived to his son.

In his style, language and versification Sidonius observed the traditional rules; as a poet, he took Lucan, Statius and Claudian as his models, as a letter-writer the younger Pliny and Symmachus. He had a predilection for artificial modes of expression, played prettily with words and was a master of mythological imagery; among his circle of friends, as A. Loyen aptly remarks, he had the reputation of an *esprit précieux*. All the same, he could observe closely and write a vivid narrative; this enabled him, particularly in his letters, to portray to perfection the aristocracy which lived under the shadow of the Goths and Vandals, and yet basked in the last rays of the Roman imperial sun. To belong to this order, it is not enough to flourish a noble genealogy and extensive landed estates; even a refined literary education is insufficient. The aristocrat concentrates his ambition on reaching a high rank in the imperial service, not so much for the sake of the financial advantage but for the honour; more highly regarded still, however, is the life he leads on his country estate in social intercourse with his peers. We hear of some truly magnificent country residences, a few of them walled and turreted. The proprietor has no thought of setting his own hand to the plough – as

Sidonius remarks, only an old veteran would even consider it; he supervises his olive groves and vineyards, superintends the construction of handsome new buildings, delights in ball games and the chase and frequently entertains guests. Men read Terence, puzzle over the meaning of Virgil; works by Augustine and Prudentius are to be found in the library. There is much coming and going of one's social equals, on extended journeys one puts up at a friend's estate, long periods of separation entail writing letters to exchange the latest social gossip. This network of acquaintance covers a wide area of Gaul, running from Massilia and Narbo through Lyons and Clermont to points north; it has been reckoned recently that the senatorial families of Gaul known to have existed at this period numbered about one hundred. As regards the exclusive nature of this class, Sidonius' description of it as an all-embracing community of the nobility (*nobilium universitas*) seems apt enough. On the other hand, the men of the middle class and the lower depths have no significance for the orator and letter-writer, and even coloni and slaves who work the estates are dismissed as of no consequence, peasants who in their ignorance once dug up the grave of one of Sidonius' forbears are severely punished. Here we have the *grand seigneur*, touched as little as possible by the course of the world, his style of life modelled on that of his ancestors. It is not immoral if a young nobleman from this social stratum takes a slave-girl as his mistress, so long as he ultimately makes good through marriage with a daughter of one of the leading families.

The uncultured foreigners, among whom one is forced to live, are kept at arm's length, even if political considerations often make it necessary to keep on good terms with germanic princes. But Sidonius himself is familiar with 'barbarians' of every shade. Proud of his knowledge, he sums up their characteristics in brief sketches: the skin-clad Goths, noisily gregarious, the Burgundians, who smear their hair with rancid butter, the fair-haired, clean-shaven Franks, the blue-eyed Saxons with their keen sight and sea-faring skill. In one famous letter he gives a character sketch of Theoderic II, the Visigothic king who helped Avitus, Sidonius' father-in-law, to become emperor.[15] He describes his subject's appearance from top to toe, without however mentioning the colour of his eyes or hair, although he does say that his moustache had a daily trim. A typical day at court begins with worship, after which the king, surrounded by his retinue, attends to affairs of state and then goes hunting; the midday meal, which is simple and accompanied by serious conversation, is followed by a board game, played quietly and without loss of temper, until the time when petitioners start arriving again and court officials seek audience; the evening meal is sometimes enlivened by jesters and drolls and the music of the lyre is also appreciated. Despite his familiarity with the Germans, Sidonius differs from Salvian in that he fails to recognize that the Romans have any duty to cultivate good social relations with them. In his panegyric on Avitus he makes the facile comment that since the Goths and Romans are now friends they have common interest in saving the empire, but this sentiment was as short-lived as the reign of Avitus. Soon afterwards we find Sidonius repudiating the idea of intercourse with the aliens, chiding one acquaintance for learning their language and remarking in a letter to another of his peers 'you avoid meeting the barbarians because you think they are bad, I do so even though they may be good'.[16] This is what convention demands. Roman tradition was still strong enough to produce new material for the glorification of Rome and her empire, and it was not beyond the skill of the public orator to adjust the Roman idea to fit the policies of reigning emperors. In his speech on Avitus, Sidonius expresses his assurance that the city which has survived so many misfortunes will even now emerge triumphant; for the benefit of the youthful and martial emperor Majorian, Rome is likened to an embattled queen, while the Greek emperor Anthemius is suitably offered the flattering thought that the city of Rome must now seek her fortune through an alliance with rulers coming from the East, through which harmony between East and West may be restored. It was apparently only when he became a bishop that Sidonius reached a more realistic view of the Roman and germanic world. The crowd of petitioners thronging his house opened his eyes to the social distress of the age and broadened the horizons of the aristocrat who had so long been obsessed with his own social class. The failure of the patriotic defence of the Auvergne and the bitter experience of his expulsion taught him a lasting lesson, namely that it was in the interests of the Gallo-Roman population to foster good relations with the Visigothic court. Full of foreboding, the bishop believed the day would come when the Goths ruled the whole of Gaul, and to the end of his life he held to his conviction of the superiority of Roman culture over all that was non-Roman. His last observations on the subject are contained in a letter to John the Grammarian : the social classes can no longer be distinguished by their place in the scale of official dignities, since these offices have ceased to exist; only his knowledge of literature marks a man out as an aristocrat[17]. Many others appear to have thought the same, even while, like Leo, they took service in Gothic chanceries.

We are led to the surprising conclusion that the Gallo-Roman aristocracy survived their exposure to germanic rule without suffering any great material or cultural damage. These *possessores* emerged as beneficiaries from the crises of the fourth century, and having contrived to keep their estates intact even during the period of germanic occupation, were still there to preside as landlords over the beginnings of feudalism, a system which they introduced into the germanic world. The class as a whole still prized Roman culture as a precious legacy, even if poetry, rhetoric and letter-writing had become lost in trivialities. Mannerism of this type was no medium for reshaping the world in the way Salvian desired. But by merely existing these cultivated aristocrats acted as the custodians, or perhaps we should say missionaries, of Roman culture in the germanic world. The tribute Sidonius paid to the half-destroyed city of Narbonne may perhaps serve as an apt description of the civilization of these latter-day Romans:

> Proud midst your ramparts half in ruins,
> You flaunt the scars of battles long ago,
> Witness to blows which struck you to the heart:
> Such glorious ruins make you precious in our sight.[18]

4. *Rome and Romania – The Ostrogothic state and culture*

Although much was destroyed by the foreign invasions, ancient civilization continued to show powers of endurance on the soil of the first germanic states and in Gaul there were already indications that the Germans would assimilate with the Roman population. But what of Italy, Rome, the empire and the imperial office during this century? For all that new peoples were continually appearing on the scene, the Imperium Romanum was still the framework for all the political and cultural activity of the Mediterranean region. In the first half of the fifth century even the west Roman emperors found it possible to steer the Germans in their course and to keep their kings in check. Valentinian III (424–55) was indeed neither a general nor a statesman, but Aetius, his Master of Soldiers, was capable of grasping the imperial authority with a firm hand. Once again, we find the harmony between the imperial house and the office of generalissimo being extolled in the literature of the day: from the extant fragments of his verses and orations Flavius Merobaudes appears to have been a second Claudian. Merobaudes was rewarded with high office and the honour of a statue in the Forum of Trajan, that shrine of ancient fame. While such accord reigned between the emperor, the general and the poet, while the city of Rome continued to provide a rostrum for patriotic displays, many contemporaries may well have believed that the empire Augustus had created still stood firm.

One thing is certain beyond any doubt. By the outstanding genius of his personality, Aetius rescued the west Roman empire, and the germanic states within its borders, from the greatest storm to threaten the western provinces, the hurricane of the advancing Huns. After destroying the Gothic kingdom on the Black Sea, the Huns had become even more aggressive and at the beginning of the fifth century broke out of southern Russia, to fall first on Rumania and Hungary and later on Poland and Silesia. Their prime objective was the broad, fertile land in the plains of the Danube and the Theiss, which in earlier centuries had already attracted the nomadic Scythians and Jazyges and later would attract the Avars and Magyars. As the Huns advanced they brought under their sway, in a loose form of association, a number of Sarmathian tribes and germanic peoples: first the Ostrogoths and some of the Heruls, later the Gepids of the lower Danube, the Rugians on the Theiss and the Lombards in Bohemia. The methods by which the Huns added to their power were in keeping with the outlook and habits of the northern Eurasian steppes. To mounted nomads a defeated enemy quickly became a friend, a conqueror annexed not territory but peoples. Thus the tribes they subdued entered a great federation, whose unity was personified in the king of the Huns; within this association they enjoyed a measure of independence. The exhaustive researches of E. A. Thompson, J. Harmatta and F. Altheim have exposed the distinctive features of the Hunnic empire, both in general and during the brief period of its deep impact on the Roman world. By means of warfare and diplomacy the Huns had already secured the upper hand over east Rome and Persia when king Attila made himself sole ruler around the year 446, having done away with Bleda, his brother. As with so many other leaders of the steppe peoples over the centuries, Attila's kingship took on a semi-divine character: whatever the king did, the people accepted as a fulfilment of the divine plan for the world. The Byzantine historian Priscus, who in 449 spent some time as an envoy at Attila's court, claims to have heard of the recent rediscovery among the Huns of the long-lost sword of God, symbol of universal dominion! Attila obviously aimed at extending his sway over all the four quarters of the world. Priscus also gives us a character sketch of Attila and his court. The king himself was of a deeply serious disposition and lived in utmost simplicity, surrounded by numerous advisers and friends, among them men from the tribes he had conquered; ambassadors came from all over the world, from the Persian and Roman empires and from remote germanic tribes, to marvel, as Priscus did himself, at the glittering luxury of the court, the richness of the clothing and ornaments, the lavish banquets and entertainments. As J. Werner has demonstrated, archaeological evidence testifies to the massive diffusion of this affluence. Warrior and feminine graves, which have come to light throughout the whole region dominated by the Huns, but especially in the region between the Theiss, the Save and the Vienna basin, have yielded up weapons, ornaments, metal mirrors and bronze hollow-ware exhibiting artistic features typical of a style of workmanship which had its origin among the mounted nomads of the eastern steppes. The glittering furniture of princely graves from the first half of the fifth century shows an exceptional wealth of gold and precious stones, presumably acquired as tribute or as the booty from extended forays. Nomadic-style weapons and ornaments also appear to have made some headway among the satellite German tribes. Even the Hunnic custom of flattening infants' heads by artificial means was for a time imitated by individual Germans; it is found, for example among the Gepids, Lombards, Thuringians and Burgundians. After the collapse of the Huns as a great power, the Germans found such habits, geared to the life of mounted nomads, less and less appropriate; they retained only the broad sword, which had proved especially well-adapted to their own methods of fighting.

The Huns' first target was the east Roman empire, which was forced to pay tribute and, more serious still, prevented from enlisting Roman soldiers from any of the tribes acknowledging Attila as their king. The next prize to attract the notice of the conqueror was the west Roman empire. The ties of friendship with Aetius, who had grown up as a hostage among the Huns, were growing weaker, the year 448 brought Eudoxius, the fugitive leader of the Bagaudae, to Attila's court, bearing news of the latest situation in Gaul, envoys reported that differences, indeed open hostilities had occurred between the germanic peoples, notably the Visigoths and Vandals; finally, and it was this that tipped the scales in favour of a large-scale attack, there was provocation on the part of the Roman court at Ravenna. The Asiatic flood which poured over central Europe in 451 presented a severe challenge to the stability of Romano-German society. Attila and his horde of Huns, together with some of his federated allies, notably the Ostrogoths, advanced upstream along the Danube as far as the Middle Rhine, crossed the river and invaded Gaul in the direction of the Loire. It took time for Aetius to organize resistance. First the Roman imperial army was assembled in Gaul, to be joined by a contingent sent by Aetius' Burgundian allies, next King Theoderic I appeared with a strong force of Visigoths and even the Franks and Alamanni were roped in. With this concentration of power behind him, Aetius stood firm before Orleans and forced Attila to retreat. There followed the great battle of the Catalaunian plains, west of Troyes in Champagne, in which Aetius won the day. The allies suffered heavy losses and Theoderic was killed, but Gaul, the heart of the empire, was saved. It was this battle, fought as it was by an alliance of peoples, which gave contemporaries their first understanding of the historic tie binding the Roman empire to the Germans. Even before the battle, the imperial envoys who were sent to solicit Visigothic help against Attila had stigmatized him, in the words of the

Gothic history of Cassiodorus-Jordanes, as a world tyrant, the common enemy of all mankind : a hundred years later a chronicler would remark on the solidarity of the peoples who defeated 'the brigand of Europe'. All the same, Attila was still strong enough to invade Italy in the following year. Without meeting any resistance, he captured Aquileia and ravaged the Po valley, while the emperor, with his court and government, fled from Ravenna to Rome. Milan and Pavia were sacked, and still no imperial army appeared in the field. Instead, Attila received Roman ambassadors led by Pope Leo, in view of the emperor's inertia the highest responsible authority, who negotiated the Huns' departure on terms of which we are ignorant. Pope Leo was fêted as the saviour of Rome ; according to later legend, the meeting between the Pope and the king was graced by the appearance of the apostles Peter and Paul, armed with swords, about the pontiff's head, a scene perpetuated in a famous mural among the cartoons of Raphael in the Vatican. Yet it was only Attila's death which removed the danger of a further onslaught on Italy. He died in 453, at the height of his power and full of plans for new conquests ; with his death the empire which for a brief moment had seemed to fulfil Hunnic dreams of universal dominion started to fall apart. The kingship was divided among Attila's sons, the germanic peoples rebelled and won a decisive victory, and the Huns retreated to southern Russia. Germans were now advancing along the middle Danube, the Ostrogoths established themselves in Pannonia, around Lake Plattern.

While the resistance against the Huns marked the last appearance of the west Roman empire as a leading power, for the Papacy it inaugurated an era of world-wide influence. The concord between the emperor and his generalissimo was fated to be destroyed : in 454 Aetius fell by the emperor's own hand, in the following year Valentinian was assassinated by the soldiers of Aetius. In the years which followed the extinction of the Theodosian dynasty, the Roman empire in the West entered on a precipitate decline. Whilst the court was the scene of perpetual contests with the military leadership, centrifugal tendencies gained the upper hand in the provinces. The feudalism of the senatorial aristocracy produced further disintegration, the germanic states were bent on expansion. All these competing factors came into play as emperors swiftly succeeded one another. The initiative over the succession was seized in turn by the Gallic aristocracy, the Senate of Rome, and the east Roman emperor, but for some time yet the man who held the office of Master of Soldiers still had the upper hand. Of the emperors who reigned from 455–76, only one died a natural death, two were deposed and the remaining six came to a violent end. For more than ten years (461–72) these puppet emperors were dominated by a Master of

Soldiers named Ricimer, son of a Suevian prince. Although he had no intention of destroying the empire, his unbridled ambition nevertheless totally undermined the authority of the emperor. The names of the rulers in question are of no importance here; what matters is to observe how the disintegration of the west Roman empire came to pass. While the Vandals continued their plundering raids in the Mediterranean unchecked, the Visigoths conquered Spain and the greater part of southern Gaul, the Burgundians established themselves in Lyons, and the Franks and Alamanni occupied fresh territory west of the Rhine; northern Gaul was the only place where a Roman governor, Syagrius of Soissons, still held out. The ending of this sorry tale had fateful consequences for the imperial monarchy, for the empire and for Italy. In 475 Orestes, the Master of Soldiers, who was a Roman, instituted his infant son as Augustus, with the intention of once again combining imperial majesty with military leadership. But the last Roman army decided otherwise. It was by now composed predominantly of Danubian Germans – Heruls, Scirae and Rugians, and its commander was an imperial officer named Odoacer, the son of a Scirian prince. This army now claimed for itself the privilege which had been accorded other germanic national entities within the empire: recognition as an allied power and a share of Italian land. When this claim was rejected by the imperial government, Odoacer was acclaimed by his troops as their king, forced his way into Ravenna, deposed the emperor and granted his soldiers a third share of Italian estates in the neighbourhood of their garrisons (476). Thus after a protracted and miserable prologue, the Empire in the West was finally extinguished, almost without any fitting notice of the occasion from contemporaries. The epilogue which followed may perhaps have disguised the gravity of the event. An embassy of the Roman Senate conveyed the imperial insignia to the emperor Zeno in Constantinople and prevailed on him, as the sole remaining imperator, to confer on Odoacer the title of a patricius. Italy, together with the neighbouring territories still annexed to it, was now ruled in the name of east Rome by a German vice-regent who was acknowledged by his troops as king. Odoacer claimed no right of legislation, struck no coins which did not bear the image of the emperor, kept the whole administrative apparatus in being and filled his office with such tact and circumspection that the Imperium Romanum continued as a unitary framework for the western provinces and their culture.

It was at this period that the name Romania was first used to designate the whole area embraced by Roman culture and the Latin language. On its first emergence in the fourth century, the term was used of the Roman empire in its political sense. This was the meaning it still held for Orosius when he set Romania and Gothia – a Roman and a Gothic empire – in opposition, holding that either must be universal in scope. Thereafter, however, the expression changed its meaning in the West, and when men spoke of Romania they were thinking of the heritage of Roman culture as still displayed in the Latin speaking provinces. All men whose lives were governed by cultural forms created and disseminated by Rome now called themselves Romani; so deep was their sense of a common allegiance that Sidonius Apollinaris could describe them as forming from the cultural point of view a widespread *civitas*. Anyone outside this cultural community was a barbarian, inhabiting the world of *Barbaria*. We have already traced the fortunes of this Romania, which had to accommodate a host of foreign guests, in Italy, Gaul, Spain and Africa; it was seen that the old culture still survived among the upper classes of the population and that Roman law, albeit in a vulgarized form, retained its validity. Even economic life went on in much the same way, men still proclaimed themselves Romans by their style of dress and dwellings, by their sports and amusements. The strongest bond of unity, however, was the Latin language. Even so, the Latin of the provinces had long since started to diversify, both in vocabulary and pronunciation. From the turn of the second century there were places where pre-Roman expressions again became current and the social stratification of the provinces was also starting to leave its mark on language. When the Germans appeared on Roman soil they helped to carry this linguistic differentiation a stage further. Thanks to the researches of E. Gamillscheg and E. von Wartburg, the germanic contribution towards the formation of the romance languages is now much clearer. First to be affected was the vocabulary of warfare, through the influence of Germans who served the Romans as soldiers or coloni: if a romance language substitutes *werra* for *bellum* and *marka* for *finis*, in the last analysis it is these men who were responsible. With the germanic states firmly established, we find a number of germanic expressions invading the language of commerce; some are found only within the region covered by these kingdoms, others became current in Latin generally. When we look at this process as a whole, bringing the Ostrogoths, Franks and Lombards as well as the special case of Rumania into the picture, it becomes clear that germanic borrowings in the romance languages are evidence of material borrowings: hence the words for shirt, trousers, pocket, stirrup and spur. In addition, numerous place names are known to have been formed from germanic personal names. In the region settled by the Burgundians these are the place names ending -court and -ville, among the Visigoths -ingos or -ens, Romanized forms of the germanic -ingen. Place name research has made a vital contribution to our understanding of the history of the settlement, especially as regards the density of germanic and Roman elements in any given region. With the Burgundians, place names of germanic origin are thicker on the ground in the portion of their territory which was occupied before 460, with the Visigoths they are most frequent in the neighbourhood of Toulouse and the zone bordering the Mediterranean. Yet despite such borrowings, Latin still held its own throughout the Visigothic kingdom and nearly everywhere in the Burgundian, and so became the most effective of all the bonds cementing the Romania.

Nevertheless, from the fourth and fifth centuries there is already evidence that the appellation 'Romanus' carried the special implication 'adherent of the Catholic persuasion', that is to say, the description was applied to Christians who accepted the credal formula of the bishop of Rome, as opposed, say, to that of Arianism. This common membership of the Catholic Church was of decisive importance for the meaning of Romania. Not only were Roman Christians of the western provinces united in holding the Catholic faith, they had also all adopted the ecclesiastical organization evolved during the Church's association with the Roman empire. While much of the secular apparatus of government had been damaged by the storms of the migration period, the number of bishoprics actually increased and monasticism made further advances. Holders of episcopal office frequently assumed political leadership in their cities and adjoining countrysides, organizing resistance to the intruders or negotiating with the enemy. Tradition has it that bishops Anianus of Orleans and Lupus of Troyes took such action in 451; the salutary influence of St Severinus, whose life was written in 511 by the presbyter Eugippius, was to become more celebrated still. This *Vita Severini* gives a graphic account of events which took place between the years 453 and 488 in Noricum Ripense, in a frontier region on the Danube which lay between either Regensburg or Passau and Vienna. At a time when the Rugians, who had invaded the province in company with the horde of Attila, were making life hazardous throughout the region, Severinus, monk and miracle-worker, made himself both the religious and political leader of the Roman population and was not afraid to deal with the Germans who came within his sphere of influence although they were still pagans.

In historical importance, the role played by pope Leo I far outshone that of these spiritual leaders in the provinces. This Roman pontiff, who in the course of his long period of office (440–61) confronted Attila and persuaded Gaiseric to moderation, has left behind a body of letters, decretals and sermons from which he emerges not only as a teacher of the Church and pastor but also as a far-sighted and methodical politician. It was Leo who finally set the Roman primacy on a biblical foundation. His doctrine proceeds from the assumption that through his steadfastness in believing St Peter attained *consortium* with Christ, that is to say a formal partnership in His authority, and that he mediated this authority to the other Apostles; as the successor and representative of Peter, the bishop of Rome, like his predecessor, transmits his authority to other bishops; thus all bishops are subordinate to the representative of St Peter, who possesses a universal episcopate. The doctrine was put into practice. In a long drawn-out conflict with Hilary of Arles and other Gallic bishops, in which he enlisted the support of the emperor Valentinian III, Leo frustrated attempts at setting up an independent patriarchate in Gaul. A rescript addressed to Aetius by the emperor expressly enjoins that no-one shall attempt anything in contravention of the authority of the Roman see, declaring that the bishop of Rome is leader of the whole Church. Leo even succeeded in persuading the eastern bishops to accept his claim. The Greek East was still torn by Christological controversy, made all the more bitter by the fact that doctrinal opposition between the schools of Antioch and Alexandria was bound up with their competing claims to precedence in the eastern patriarchates; moreover, the position of the bishop of Constantinople, the capital city, still awaited final definition. These disputes dragged on in the East for centuries and led eventually to the secession of Syria and Egypt from the official Church of the eastern empire. In 449, a year in which Christological controversy was at a peak, Leo intervened with a dogmatic epistle in which he set forth his doctrine concerning the nature of Christ and in so doing made explicit the Roman teaching with regard to Petrine authority in matters of faith. The credal formula imposed by the oecumenical council which met at Chalcedon in 451 was based on Leo's epistle: as the victorious Fathers declared, 'Peter has spoken through Leo'. All the same, canon twenty-eight of this same council accorded the bishop of New Rome the same honorary precedence as was enjoyed by the bishop of the old imperial city, a decision Leo did not allow to go unchallenged.

One of Leo's successors, Gelasius I (492–6) seized his opportunity, at a time when the political disintegration of the West was still further advanced, to secure the Roman primacy against all possible contenders. In a screed addressed to the emperor in Constantinople, Gelasius expounded the relationship between episcopal and secular authority as follows: in matters within the secular sphere, priests and bishops are subordinate to lay rulers; nevertheless, their's is by its very nature the overriding authority, since at God's judgement seat they will have to account even for kings. The concept of Sacerdotium and Imperium as two co-ordinate but contrasted authorities thus started on its momentous career. Gelasius also claimed for the Roman see, against all other bishops, the right to decide cases affecting any church, a judgement from which none might appeal. A few years later, when Pope Symmachus, who owed his see to a disputed election, faced senatorial charges alleging irregularity, a synod of Italian bishops declared that there was no man who could judge a Pope, that a Pope could not be deposed. Ennodius of Pavia justifies this position in detail, pointing out that the Pope's invulnerability is derived from the merits of St Peter: 'Who could wish to doubt the holiness of one who holds so high a dignity?' Later on this would become the corner-stone of the formal sanctity of the papal office and with it of the unassailable position of the head of the Roman Church.

The Roman primacy fortified the unity and moral strength of the Catholic Church during the period which witnessed the eclipse of the western emperor. Contemporaries were quick to appreciate the contrast in imperial and papal fortunes. The lay theologian Prosper Tiro, in his earlier years the author of verse and prose works championing Augustinian theology, makes some suggestive observations in his poem *De ingratis*, composed about the year 430, in which he compares the two Romes, imperial and ecclesiastical:[19] now that Rome, as the seat of Peter has become chief pastorate of the world, Rome possesses through religion what she failed to conquer through force of arms. Just as Tertullian had asserted that the kingdom of God extended far beyond the Imperium, so the Roman see was now credited with a power which spanned the entire Christian world. Tiro, who later composed a world chronicle in continuation of Jerome, was a close observer of the events of his own time; he was employed for many years in the chancery of the great Pope Leo, with whom he clearly had a spiritual affinity. In one of his sermons for the Feast of St Peter and St Paul, Leo himself dilates on the antithesis between ecclesiastical and secular Rome.[20] Rome, as the foundation of the Apostles Peter and Paul, is a sacerdotal and royal city, as the seat of Peter it is head of the world, indeed, the sway of Rome founded on religion stretches further than the terrestrial rule of earlier days. The preacher goes back again to declare that St Peter, first in the order of the Apostles, was destined for the capital of the Imperium so that the light of truth might stream from this head over the world; he trod his appointed way undeterred by the mistress-might of Rome. It thus appears that around the middle of the fifth century the new Christian conception of the Roman idea was already gaining ground, in a version which went far beyond that of Prudentius. From this only a small step was needed for the Church itself to be described as the new Imperium Romanum.

Even when Romania, the Roman primacy and the Christian idea of Rome are considered all together, our picture of the historic role of Italy in the metamorphosis of ancient culture is still incomplete. If we look at Rome, we must also look at Ravenna, and with it the kingdom of the Ostrogoths. In Ostrogothic Italy, to a much greater extent than in Gaul and in contrast with what happened in Africa, efforts at consolidating the old cultural tradition and at gathering together in enduring form the last articles of inherited wisdom met with some success. At the same time, we are here confronted with the grandeur and tragedy of the germanic kingdoms more starkly than in all the other states. In the *Gothic History* of Cassiodorus (admittedly extant only in the epitome made by Jordanes) we have a source which, for all its confusion of narrative, provides a guiding thread through the path of Ostrogothic history; as evidence of cultural change, the twelve books of Cassiodorus' *Variae* are more rewarding still, containing as they do a wealth of official documents, notably the letters and decrees he himself drafted on behalf of King Theoderic. In the *Variae* the world inhabited by Romans and Ostrogoths in common stands revealed in all its colours.

When the Hunnic empire collapsed, the Ostrogoths were settled as federates in Pannonia. To guarantee the permanence of the treaty, Theoderic, a king's son from the house of the Amals, was in 461 sent to Constantinople as a hostage. The east Roman army of the day also contained many Ostrogoths serving as mercenaries, and the policy of the Byzantine court was to play the two groups, federates and mercenaries, off against each other. In pursuit of this aim, in 471 the emperor Zeno sent the youthful Theoderic back to his people, equipped with a knowledge of Greek and Latin and deeply impressed by what he had seen of ancient civilization. When on his father's death Theoderic succeeded him as king, he was expected to fight on the imperial side to crush the rebellious Ostrogothic mercenaries. From an early date, Theoderic had a clear appreciation of the significant role fate had assigned to his people. After many years, during which the Ostrogoths fought now for and now against the emperor, he led them on a trek through the Balkan provinces and in 483 obtained permission for them to settle in Lower Moesia, the north-western part of modern Bulgaria, himself receiving the office of Master of the Army and the honorary title Patricius. Eventually Theoderic was commissioned by the east Roman emperor to reconquer Italy from Odoacer, who had become too powerful for the Byzantines' liking. In 488, hoping that the Ostrogoths would at last find a plenteous and permanent home, Theoderic and a large part of the tribe set out from Moesia. The whole assemblage, including women and children, moved up the Save and reached the frontiers of Italy; early in 489 Theoderic appeared at the Isonzo, defeated Odoacer and invaded the Po valley. A fresh victory at Verona brought about the surrender of Milan and Pavia and gave Theoderic opportunity to shut Odoacer up in Ravenna. The struggle for the capital, celebrated in epic tradition as the 'battle of the ravens', dragged on for more than two years, since Odoacer commanded the channel to the sea and Theoderic had no fleet. Eventually an agreement was reached whereby Odoacer and Theoderic were to exercise a joint rule, and in 493 Theoderic entered Ravenna. It was immediately obvious that the plan of a shared rule was impracticable. Only ten days later, Theoderic repudiated the agreement and stabbed his colleague to death in the palace of Ravenna. This act of violence may also have been an act of vengeance, since in annihilating the Rugians in 487 Odoacer had killed some of Theoderic's kinsmen. Be that as it may, the deed was certainly premeditated, since Odoacer's troops too were massacred and his family liquidated. Having made himself ruler of Italy in such brutal fashion, Theoderic met no further resistance and even the Roman Senate submitted. The government in Constantinople, unprepared for the king's rapid success, long remained aloof and it was only in 498 that the emperor Anastasius recognized the Ostrogothic régime by despatching the royal insignia to Theoderic. Theoderic, king of the Goths, as Master of the Army and Patricius was now also regent of the Romans, acting on behalf of the emperor. His territory embraced the prefecture of Italy together with Sicily and part of Rhaetia, to which was added Noricum and Dalmatia. He had command of the army and supreme administrative and judicial powers; but he lacked the right to issue laws of general application and had no authority to confer Roman citizenship.

If the trek from Moesia to Italy had revealed Theoderic as a man of ambition and decisive action, his thirty-three years of royal rule in Italy would prove to be the accomplishment of a great statesman, a work of pacification which even the Romans admired. Here, as in the other germanic states, Germans and Romans were living side by side, in a numerical ratio not very different from that of the Visigothic and Burgundian kingdoms; the Romans probably outnumbered the Ostrogoths by twenty to one. But king Theoderic, whose youthful experiences had convinced him of the superiority of ancient culture, was quick to appreciate the limitations of his own people. In his state the two peoples were to occupy two orders: the Romans would devote themselves to the works of peace, the Goths would protect their productive labours by their armed might, and both peoples would live together in harmony under the rule of the king. There was no intermarriage; the Romans lived under Roman law and went for justice to Roman judges, the Goths had their germanic customary law, while in mixed suits an authority on Roman law sat with a Gothic *comes*. There was no codification of the two laws; the so-called *Edictum Theoderici* has no connection with this Theoderic and should probably be ascribed to Theoderic II, the

Visigothic king. Thus both peoples preserved their traditional mode of life, even though they were living side by side, even cheek by jowl. The Goths received a third of the houses and estates belonging to their Roman 'hosts', together with the labour force attached to these properties, and were made responsible for paying the land-tax. Their settlements were concentrated in the region of Ravenna and Verona and were also numerous near Milan and Pavia; further south they were much sparser. Excluded from work on the land, which was still left to coloni and slaves, they had only their skill as armourers to occupy them; they were not allowed to learn to read and write, since their king held that boys who had once trembled before the school-masters' rod would never have the stamina to become good fighting men. For the mass of the Roman civilian population, the organs of government and of economic life functioned as before; Latin remained the language of Italy and of the regions annexed to it. At the royal residence in Ravenna there was no alteration in the organization of the court and the composition of the central administration, in which ministers and the praetorian prefect continued to collaborate. Even Rome retained its privileged position. The city prefecture and the other traditional offices continued, the Senate still had its prerogatives and the populace was deprived neither of its corn dole nor of its circus entertainments. The provincial divisions remained as they were and every town still had its active curia. To demonstrate the continuity of the political order, the years continued to be named for the consuls appointed by the emperor and the coinage to bear his name; the initials of the king appeared only on the gold solidi.

Theoderic showed great delicacy and magnanimity in carrying out his plan for the co-existence of the two peoples and the two orders; there are countless witnesses to his humanity and social sensibility. He was fortunate in that for many years even religion was in a state of equilibrium. The Ostrogoths were Arians, their ecclesiastical system was established and well endowed, they had four churches of their own in Ravenna and two in Rome. But Theoderic also extended toleration to the Catholic church and to other faiths. On one occasion, with reference to the Jewish community, he explained the principle underlying his attitude: 'religion is not something we can command; no-one can be forced into a faith against his will'.[21] It is possible that the king's relations with the Pope gained considerably from the tension existing at the time between the Roman and the Byzantine churches. In 484 east Rome had come down on the side of the Monophysites over the long-debated question of the nature of Christ and broken the link with the Roman Church, which held strongly to the credal formula reached at the Council of Chalcedon. For a time this tension within the Catholic

Church had a chilling effect on relations between the Romans and Constantinople, which made it easier for Theoderic to pursue his irenical policy in Italy. The harmony between the peoples united under his rule was strikingly demonstrated when the king visited the eternal city in the year 500 – his only appearance in Rome. Having been received by the Catholic clergy, with the Pope at their head and by the Roman Senate, he went first to St Peter's to pray, then addressed himself to the Senate in the Curia and spoke in the Forum to the populace, making a solemn promise to uphold the laws issued by the emperors. He spent six months in residence on the Palatine: a germanic king who thus penetrated the imperial sanctuary is indeed worthy of commemoration between Alaric, the first German to take Rome by force and Charlemagne, the Frank who would receive the imperial crown in the eternal city.

The continuance of the Pax Gothica was a fruitful stimulus to creative activity in the cultural field. Theoderic's personal attachment to the culture of antiquity led him to arrange a classical education in the Latin and Greek languages and literature for his daughter Amalasuntha and his nephew Theodahad. Goths who achieved high office mastered the Latin tongue, whereas few Romans became familiar with the Gothic speech. As a patron of architecture and the fine arts, the king did much to rebuild cities which had been destroyed or had fallen into decay and to renovate the monuments of his imperial predecessors. In Rome the theatre of Pompey and the Colosseum were restored, new buildings arose at Pavia and also at Verona, where Theoderic occasionally resided. The artistic activity of the period found its fullest expression at Ravenna, now aspiring to become a second Byzantium. The church of Sant' Apollinare Nuovo and the Arian baptistery came to join the Catholic sanctuaries; the royal palace, built on the imperial model, has not survived, but a mosaic in Sant' Apollinare Nuovo depicts the impressive entrance to the residence. Literary life revived at Rome, Ravenna and Milan. The universities resumed their activities, grammarians, rhetoricians, jurists and doctors working in Rome received annual salaries from the state, poets and scholars vied with one another, as in classical times. Better known to us is Ennodius of Pavia, who from 496 was active in Milan as a writer and rhetorician, and devoted several years to the composition, in the verbose style of this late period, of poetry and prose works which attempted to combine pagan and Christian themes. At an important juncture he formed a connection with the court of Ravenna. It so happened that a disputed papal election had given rise to a disturbance which lasted for several years, until in 507 Theoderic by his intervention at last restored harmony to the Church in Rome. Ennodius addressed a panegyric to the king, in which he hailed the Gothic ruler as saviour of Italy, bringer of healing to the land, the central point of an expanding world created by his own peaceable endeavours. Even after becoming bishop of Pavia in 514, Ennodius still maintained contact with the court and made it his constant concern to defend the king and his people against the false and deeply-rooted imputations of barbarism.

The most significant representative of Gotho-Roman collaboration is Flavius Magnus Aurelius Cassiodorus. He came of an aristocratic family which belonged not to the city of Rome but to Bruttium in the extreme south of Italy; as the son of a praetorian prefect he had received an excellent literary education and while still a young man was appointed *c.* 507 secretary to the king's cabinet of advisers; in later life he was honoured with the consulship and towards the end of the reign became *magister officiorum*, that is to say, chancellor to the king. As secretary, Cassiodorus imparted an elevated tone to the royal decrees he drafted, interweaving much of his own historical and philosophical knowledge, so that the *Variae* become a mine of information concerning cultural history. These decrees and letters show the monarchy in a most favourable light: head and shoulders above the other kings thrown up by the migrations, the monarch rules with justice and wisdom, rivalling the imperial régime in his efforts to revive the unity of the empire and restore the peace of the emperors; the Gothic nation has been called to rejuvenate the ageing world by its youthful vigour. Cassiodorus' high estimation of the Germans is also evident in the fact that in his official drafts he never uses the word *barbari* of the Goths. The government's daily duty of forging a link between Goths and Romans also gave Cassiodorus a theme for historical contemplation. As an historian, he found a way to secure for the Goths a permanent place in Roman history. Revising the chronicle of Jerome, he continued it down to the memorable year 519, in which Eutharic, the king's son-in-law and presumptive successor, held the office of consul in partnership with the emperor Justin: this year, he thought, should mark the beginning of a new era. Now Momigliano has pointed out that the idea of a peaceful co-existence of the two peoples also provided the *leitmotiv* for Cassiodorus' history of the Goths, *De origine actibusque Getarum*. Although the writing was only begun soon after 519, by 533 the book was so widely known that Athalric, Theoderic's successor, could sing its praises in the letter he addressed to the Senate announcing Cassiodorus' appointment as praetorian prefect.[22] In this letter the king remarks that Cassiodorus has placed the origin of the Goths within the mainstream of Roman history. In fact, deceived by a misunderstanding about the Gothic name, long current, Cassiodorus has included in his account the Getae of Thrace and the Iranian Scythians, claiming for the Goths all the wisdom traditionally ascribed to these peoples. Cassiodorus' history is known to us only in the epitome made by Jordanes in 551, during a momentary pause, which gave opportunity for peace and reflection, in the war the emperor Justinian had been waging against the Goths since 535. A son had just been born to the marriage between Germanus, a cousin of the emperor, and Matasuntha, a grand-daughter of Theoderic, and this event aroused hopes of a reconciliation between the two peoples. It is clear that Jordanes has to some extent slanted his epitome in order to persuade the Goths to abandon their resistance; but the same tendency seems to have been apparent in the parent work. In 538 Cassiodorus had resigned from his high office and around 550 was living in Constantinople; it may well be that he himself continued the Gothic history down to the year 551 and then commissioned Jordanes, who numbered Goths among his forebears, to make a summary version of his book. It is in any case noteworthy that a Roman historian should have taken as his subject the history of an alien people who had invaded the Roman empire bent on conquest, and moreover that he placed them on a par with the people of Rome: in this respect, Cassiodorus comes close to Polybius, the first Greek to write the history of the Romans after they had conquered Greece.

Educated Romans were not all so well-disposed towards the Goths as Cassiodorus. The city of Rome contained a circle of scholars determined to have as little contact with Germans as possible. The group included Quintus Aurelius Symmachus, a great-grandson of the Symmachus who led the Senate in the days of Gratian and Theodosius. In 485 this younger Symmachus was made city prefect, but he would accept no office at court, seeing it rather as his duty to foster the old Roman tradition, in which the Christian religion was now an integral part. He was active in preserving literary texts, wrote a history of Rome on his own account, perhaps as an appendage to the work of Nicomachus, and gathered round him a number of like-minded senators to form a neo-Symmachan circle of Roman patriots. A few of its members still had perfect command of the Greek language and literature and even studied Greek philosophy. It is thus not surprising to find them making contact with the Greek East, above all with Constantinople. Conversely, there were also some attempts at this period to interest the Greeks of the East in Rome. In the first decades of the sixth century Priscian occupied a chair of Latin grammar at Constantinople; in his major work, the *Institutio grammatica*, he gave a full account of Latin grammar and Latin usage, linking it with the teaching of the Greek grammarians; when Symmachus visited Constantinople as an envoy, Priscian made his acquaintance. Italy and the western provinces benefited greatly from the renewed contact of Roman scholars with Greek philosophy and learning. The Scythian monk Dionysius Exiguus, who was living in Rome around the year 500, translated theological and philosophical treatises from Greek into Latin. But the most illustrious figure in this academic field was Boethius, a descendant of the ancient Anician family and son-in-law of Symmachus, who in 510 was dignified by the consulship. When his two sons became consuls in 522, Boethius spoke the panegyric on Theoderic and was soon afterwards appointed to one of the highest offices in the court and administration, that of *magister officiorum*. His energies were devoted wholly to learned activities and the study of philosophy. Fully aware that at this critical juncture it was essential to preserve and hand on the legacy of the ancients, he conceived a plan for translating the entire philosophy of Plato and Aristotle, which he would interpret for his contemporaries. He was able to complete only a part of this ambitious scheme. The handful of Aristotle's writings on logic which he managed to translate would for a long time to come remain literally all that the Latin West knew of Aristotle. In addition he translated an introductory treatise on dialectic by Porphyry the neo-platonist and writings of acknowledged Greek masters in the fields of arithmetic, geometry, astronomy and music. Two of the branches which made up the encyclopedia of the seven liberal arts, grammar and rhetoric, were thus omitted, but the solid core of elementary knowledge attained by the Greeks had been salvaged for the West.

Such efforts to keep in touch with Greek philosophy, on the part of scholars who were not content merely to embalm Roman antiquity, were in fact the cultural hall-mark of Ostrogothic Italy. For a long time King Theoderic welcomed these endeavours and was careful to preserve good relations with the court in Constantinople. In one letter to the emperor Anastasius he remarks that there are two states (*res publicae*) but only one empire (*unicum imperium*) and describes his régime as an imitation of the imperial rule. A king who spoke thus could keep his reputation with the east Roman court unblemished. Theoderic also soon won the awed respect of his germanic neighbours and for a long while exerted a commanding influence. Theoderic accepted a multiplicity of germanic states as natural, but in letters to his brother kings made constant reference to the ties which unite the German rulers and to the accord among their peoples. From the outset he sought to guarantee peace through dynastic marriages, in keeping with germanic practice. In 493 he himself married Audofleda, sister of Clovis, the Frankish king who had penetrated deep into Gaul; he married one of his daughters to the Visigothic king Alaric and another to Sigismund, heir to the Burgundian throne. He attached particular importance to maintaining friendship with the Vandal kingdom and in 500 married his sister Amalfrida to King Thrasamund. Even remoter peoples, the

Alamanni, Thuringians and Gepids, were drawn into the network of Ostrogothic diplomacy. The documents collected in the *Variae* tell of the comings and goings of ambassadors and the exchange of gifts: thus we find Theoderic sending the Burgundian king a sundial and a water clock, or despatching singers accomplished on the lyre to the king of the Franks. It is possible this diplomatic activity owed something to memories of the vastness of the empire once ruled from Rome; what is certain is that there was no ulterior intention of creating a germanic block in opposition to the eastern empire. Theoderic's sole concern was clearly the security of Italy, which could be guaranteed so long as neighbouring states remained stable and none emerged as more powerful than the rest. This plan for keeping the peace was severely disrupted by the advance of Clovis. The energetic and farsighted king of the Franks made his own contribution to solving the difficult problem of Romano-German relationships: through his conversion to Catholicism, he won the sympathies of Romans throughout Gaul and ended by driving the Visigoths out of southern Gaul into Spain (507). Theoderic several times intervened to keep the Franks away from the Mediterranean; then at the height of his power, he was able to ensure that the Visigoths retained the coastal strip between the Pyrenees and the Rhône and that the region east of the Rhône, together with Avignon, was added to the Ostrogothic kingdom. But it was beyond him to make the balance of power among the germanic states permanent and so keep the peace. Relations between the Burgundians and the Vandals soon worsened, there was renewed conflict between the germanic kings and eventually Theoderic found himself in isolation.

Still more serious in its consequences was the threat to the Ostrogothic state in Italy itself. The two peoples had been slow to adjust to one another, a section of the population still looked on the Gothic warrior class as a burdensome army of occupation. It was fatal when many educated people, notably among that part of the aristocracy which had always held aloof from the court, started to turn towards the emperor in Constantinople. Political overtures of this kind became all the easier when an initiative towards finding a solution to the religious quarrel on the part of the emperor Justin (from 518, with his nephew Justinian as his chief adviser, ruler of the eastern empire) resulted in 519 in the restoration of ecclesiastical harmony between Rome and Byzantium. The harsh treatment thereafter meted out to Arians within the eastern empire made the Goths in Italy fearful for the independence of their own ecclesiastical and political order. In this tense atmosphere, it is not surprising that eminent Romans came under suspicion on account of their Byzantine connections. When the highly respected patrician Albinus was denounced for his alleged conspiracy with the emperor, Boethius appeared on his behalf before the royal council, sitting in the presence of Theoderic, and claimed that Albinus' case was that of the entire Senate. Thereupon Boethius was himself arrested, found guilty by the king without being given a hearing and condemned to death (522); he was executed in 524, after a lengthy imprisonment. When Symmachus fell in the following year, the rift between cultivated society and the Goths could no longer be disguised and all Italy was thrown into a ferment. To make matters worse, discord developed between the king and the Pope, John I. Theoderic had sent John to Constantinople in an effort to persuade the emperor to withdraw his anti-Arian decrees. When the Pope returned virtually empty-handed, ill though he was he was imprisoned at Ravenna and died in captivity (526). The religious peace between Catholics and Arians, vital if the Italian state was to have any future, was now at an end. When Theoderic died in 526 the entire Ostrogothic creation was in jeopardy. The mausoleum built to receive the remains of the great king exhibited classical and germanic styles in intrepid combination. (plate 27). But no successor appeared who was capable of sustaining this synthesis on the political plane. The Ostrogothic people finally succumbed, after a long drawn-out and heroic struggle; Justinian triumphed, but his victory also entailed the extinction of the Roman Senate and of the last venerable remnants of a Roman *res publica*.

Even so, the Pax Gothica had borne fruit in the spiritual and intellectual life of Italy and of the western provinces in general. Boethius and Cassiodorus saved ancient philosophy and learning for western Europe. Whilst he was in prison, Boethius wrote his *De consolatione philosophiae*, in form a conversation between a man afflicted by suffering and Philosophy; the deeply felt philosophical poetry it incorporates makes the exchange one of unequalled nobility. Probing the supreme question of how man, as he wrestles with the power of incalculable fortune, may yet win through to attain what is constant and eternal, the poet-philosopher discovers a way of reconciling God-given necessity with man's freedom as an agent. It is a consolation of philosophy – and if it has no point of contact with the Christian faith, neither is it incompatible with it. In this book, which for generations of Christian scholars in the West bore the authentic stamp of ancient wisdom, Boethius left behind a life-giving testament. Cassiodorus also had a further part to play. After the end of the Ostrogothic kingdom, he withdrew completely from political life into the isolation of Vivarium, the monastery he founded in his native Bruttium. Under his inspiration Vivarium became the first monastery in the West which was also a sanctuary of learning and culture: the monks of St Benedict would indeed make this true of their monasteries as a general principle, but this development still lay in the future. Cassiodorus' final aspiration was to make the received knowledge of pagan antiquity available to Christian scholarship and with this intention he made a compilation of theological and secular knowledge, the *Institutiones divinarum et humanarum lectionum.* In content the epitome is thin indeed, thinner even than the amazing work entitled *The Marriage of Philology and Mercury*, an encyclopedia written by Martianus Capella only a few years earlier. But however jejune this residue may appear, there was merit in preserving elementary knowledge and in saving books from oblivion in the midst of a collapsing political order.

5. *Frankish Gaul and the British Isles*

Through their invasions and the states they founded, the Vandals, Burgundians and Goths hastened the decay of the empire yet at the same time powerfully assisted in the metamorphosis of ancient civilization. The inroads made by the west Germans on the cultural life of western Europe were more profound still. The Franks and Alamanni who attacked the empire during the fourth and fifth centuries never strayed far from their base and so avoided exposing themselves to the threat of tribal disintegration always inherent in germanic forward thrusts into Spain, Africa and Italy. From their secure and permanent habitat they moved into the adjacent frontier regions of the empire, enlarging their area of settlement step by step, and meeting no resistance from the Roman empire of the West, then at its last gasp. On their entry into Gaul these west Germans reached first the transitional zone which had long been the meeting-point of Celtic and germanic tribes. As they pressed further into Gallic territory, this affinity with the Celts was to prove of value, in that it made the symbiosis of the conquerors with the Gallo-Roman population an easier matter than in Africa or Italy.

The same observations apply to the Alamanni, though to a lesser degree. From the middle of the fifth century they had been winning more territory on the left bank of the upper Rhine, in Alsace and the Pfalz ; there are also sporadic traces of them in cemeteries in the region north of Nancy. Further south, around the year 500 they occupied the region of Basel and crossed the upper Rhine to reach north-western Switzerland and Besançon by way of the Burgundian Gates. On both sides of the Jura they were in competition with the Burgundians, but this rivalry had no effect on the larger politics of the Mediterranean region. Here and there in their advance the Alamanni trampled roughshod over Roman civilization, but failed to destroy it completely. Even after the withdrawal of the Roman holding army and provincial administration from the frontier provinces and the flight of the upper class, the bulk of the ordinary population remained behind to perpetuate the old methods of land cultivation and craft work. Moreover, the Christian church continued to survive in places where it already had a footing. However, the Alamanni were operating in only one small corner on the periphery of the empire, so that for the purposes of our present discussion they occupy a subsidiary role in the great drama. The Franks, on the other hand, who aimed their attack at the old centres of Roman life on the Rhine and in the heart of Gaul, were destroying the last remnants of Roman authority and seeking an outlet to the Mediterranean. But by a very fateful turn of events, the Franks succeeded in expelling or absorbing the older germanic foundations on Gallic soil and found a way to live in religious harmony with the Gallo-Roman population. As a response to the challenge presented by the ending of the Roman empire in the West, the Frankish expansion thus had a fundamental contribution to make to the future of the west European provinces, and this was already becoming clear from the turn of the fifth century.

About the year 460, the Ripuarian Franks, whose settlement was on the middle Rhine, took over Mainz and Cologne, occupied the Moselle region and pressed on to reach the Meuse. A letter written about 475 by Sidonius Apollinaris to the *comes* of Trier makes it clear that Latin was no longer being spoken in those parts. Yet even though the land had been seized by the Germans, there was still no complete break in continuity with late Roman culture. Archaeological finds, in particular, reveal that in the more lowly spheres of social and economic life everything continued much as before, to say nothing of the Christian church, whose basic institutions were faithfully preserved. The Salian Franks, coming from the lower Rhine, pressed much further into Gaul, establishing colonies as they went. In the third and fourth centuries these Franks had already advanced north of the Roman garrison town of Vetera to occupy land on both sides of the Yssel (in the Netherlands). The emperor Julian settled Franks in Toxandria, in the region south and west of the lower Meuse (chiefly in Dutch Brabant). Further acquisitions were made, and in the fifth century the Salians had several petty kingdoms in Belgium and northern France, among them that of Childeric, a descendant of the house of Merowech, whose troops served under the last Roman commander in Gaul. Childeric's grave, uncovered at Tournai on the middle Scheldt, was furnished with weapons and gear of the finest Roman workmanship and contained in addition a Roman robe of state and a seal-ring – sure indication of his federate status. Childeric was succeeded (probably in 482) by his young son Clovis; and it was Clovis who, with elemental force and great cunning, made the Franks masters of Gaul.

The greater part of Gaul was at that time under Visigothic and Burgundian rule although in the north Syagrius still held out as Roman governor of Soissons. In 486 Clovis overthrew this last pillar of the empire and brought the area between the Somme and the Seine, with an extension as far as the middle Loire, under his rule, settling his Franks in varying degrees of density and paying no attention to the Roman law governing military occupation. This success alerted his German neighbours; even Theoderic the Ostrogoth sought an alliance with the Frankish conqueror, requesting his sister's hand and inviting him to join the circle of germanic Arians. The Franks were still pagans; their king, who now stood at the centre of Gaul and ruled over a Christian Gallo-Roman population, was faced with a difficult religious decision. He became friendly with Remigius, Bishop of Rheims, and in 492 married a Catholic Burgundian princess, Clotilde; the sons of this marriage were baptized with Clovis' consent. Gregory of Tours, in his *History of the Franks*, tells us – and here his testimony should be reliable – that Clotilde tried to win her husband for Catholicism. But Clovis hesitated; unlike almost every other germanic king, he was free to choose which persuasion he would follow when he made his entry into Christendom. Avid for still more power, Clovis fell upon the Visigoths and the Alamanni. Gregory of Tours relates that in 496, in the heat of a crucial battle with the Alamanni, Clovis vowed himself to Christ in the event of being granted victory. He won the battle, made his decision for the victory-giving God, and at the shrine of St Martin at Tours announced his intention of seeking baptism, enlisting his whole people as recruits to the Catholic faith. In 498, together with three thousand of his warriors, he received the sacrament at the hands of Remigius of Rheims. This was the great turning point in Frankish history. There were even one or two contemporaries who perceived its significance for the future. For example, we have the remarkable letter sent by bishop Avitus of Vienne to Clovis after his baptism.[23] By his freely exercised choice, says Avitus, the king has taken a decision binding on all; since Clovis has so far surpassed the morality demanded of his forebears, the claims of clan and ancestral custom can no longer debar the rest from deciding for religion. The Greek world, the bishop continues, has the emperor for its luminary, but now the light of the ancient sun shines also on the West, streaming from this king; the ruler is already invested with every virtue, there is nothing more to be desired in him. The passage which follows merits special attention: 'There is but one aspect we would like to see enlarged upon. Now that God through you has made your people wholly his own, from the riches of your heart may you spread the seed of the faith to the peoples outside who are still in their natural ignorance and have not been corrupted by the germ of perverted doctrines. After God has raised your land so high, no doubt or dismay should deter you from despatching emissaries to accomplish the work of increasing the territories of God. So may the heathen peoples living outside, who will serve you first under the title of religion, in future come to be known by their tribe rather than their ruler, although until now they seem to acknowledge another as their chief.'

In suggesting that the rule of the Franks and the empire of religion were one and the same, the bishop was ahead of his time. But even as he wrote, the conversion of Clovis was already having its effect in Gaul. There are indications that Gallo-Romans living under Frankish rule pledged their sympathies to the Catholic king. Sigismund, heir to the throne in the neighbouring kingdom of the Burgundians, which was allied with the Franks in a common enmity towards the Alamanni and the Visigoths, deserted Arianism for Catholicism. The Visigothic king Alaric tried to avert the Frankish threat by making overtures to his Roman subjects, but in 507 Clovis joined forces with the Burgundians and declared war; at the battle of Vouillé (in the neighbourhood of Poitiers) Alaric lost both the day and his life and his son fled to Spain. Clovis could now extend his rule as far as the Pyrenees; at this juncture it was only the intervention of Theoderic which prevented the Franks from reaching the Mediterranean. The status of the Frankish kingdom as a new major power received formal recognition when the Byzantine emperor conferred an honorary consulship on the Frankish ruler and sent him a royal robe of state. Clovis now removed the petty Salian kings, the last encumbrances to his exercise of sole rule over the Franks, extended his power as far as the lower Rhine and took up residence in Paris, at the centre of his kingdom. At the time of his death in 511 he may well have been entertaining plans for further conquests; his successors made further advances at the expense of both the Roman and the germanic worlds, annexing the Burgundian kingdom, winning access to the Mediterranean and not neglecting to subjugate even the Thuringians and Bavarians. Theudebert was shortly able to boast, in a manifesto to the emperor Justinian, that his kingdom was bounded on one side by the ocean and on the other by Pannonia.

The way in which the Merovingian empire came into being meant that the Franks encountered the ancient world on an entirely different footing from the Goths and the Burgundians, to say nothing of the Vandals. There was no longer any Roman emperor in the West and east Rome made no attempt to reconquer Gaul, so that the king of the Franks was left an exceptionally free hand. His vast territory, well-endowed by nature, gave him ample scope for the pursuit of power politics so that the historical scene was now invaded by the energies of a new people. Admittedly, the Germans and Gallo-Romans formed separate entities within the Frankish empire, markedly distinct from one another. To understand the cultural evolution of Frankish Gaul it is first necessary to take note of the way the land was occupied and of the density of germanic settlement on the soil of the former empire. Drawing on a variety of material – literary sources, archaeological finds, philological indications and above all place names – modern scholarship has succeeded in laying bare the essential features of this process. The early stages of this work were enlivened by a vigorous debate over the extent of cultural continuity in the Rhine frontier provinces. A. Dopsch, in his *Wirtschaftliche und soziale Grundlagen der europäischen Kulturentwicklung aus der Zeit von Caesar bis auf Karl den Grossen* tried to demonstrate that the invasions were not as catastrophic as ancient reports, and later humanist scholars who followed them, would have us believe. Exact research on specific points has to some extent invalidated the statements Dopsch offered in support of his thesis of cultural continuity. It can now be taken as certain that the departure of the Romans was at first followed by an economic decline in the Rhinelands. The considerable business which for centuries had flowed from the central regions of the empire into this frontier region now fell away; the large industrial undertakings had already fallen into decay for the same reason, since demand had perceptibly shrunk. Admittedly, the sites of Roman towns were still occupied, but in the early germanic period even urban land exhibits a rural type of settlement, as, above all, at Trier. The superstructure of Roman life disappeared, but 'whatever was rooted in the soil, – vines, boundary marks, town walls, solid buildings in stone, – together with many amenities of everyday life, withstood the storm of the invasions and had their effect on the germanic conquerors.' (H. Aubin). In addition it can be shown that Christian congregations continued in being and preserved their diocesan structure intact; and there was no complete disruption of the higher cultural life which went hand in hand with Christianity. The permanency of the link with ancient culture was ensured by the continuing connection between the Rhinelands and central Gaul, where the upholders of tradition were more firmly entrenched than on the periphery.

This brings us to the wider problem: just what was the extent and strength of germanic, more specifically Frankish, settlement in Gallic territory? Investigation of the areas in question, particularly the Walloon country and northern France, has shown that the density of germanic settlement was distinctly uneven. In the zone west of the Rhine germanic settlers for a long time lived alongside the Roman population. At first this region was bilingual, but little by little the germanic tongue established itself on one side of it and the romance on the other. By the year 1000 at latest the linguistic frontier was as it is today: a line running east from Boulogne to Brussels, to continue in the same direction until it takes a southerly turn at Liège, passing between Diedenhofen and Metz to the Vosges ridge and thence west from Basel to the Swiss Jura, to climb by way of Fribourg in Uechtland to the Alpine crest. North and east of this line germanic settlement was numerically so preponderant that it left its mark on the national character of the entire region. But the central portion of the Frankish kingdom, the area between Metz, Rheims and Paris, which lay on the other side of the linguistic boundary, also had a strong complement of German immigrants, even if they no longer formed the majority of the population. Finally, the many cemeteries found even between the Seine and the Loire, point to germanic immigrants in so far as they are furnished with weapons, but here we are dealing with outposts of the Frankish occupation. When speaking of the germanic immigration into Gaul, it must constantly be remembered that the Germans were taking their place alongside romanized Celts. The German influx brought a new wave of Indo-Europeans into the country, to strengthen the indigenous Gallic core.

The Frankish empire resembled other germanic states in being composed initially of two different peoples, each possessing their own language and culture and living under their own personal laws. The *Lex Salica*, the customary law of the Franks, was probably first put into shape as early as the time of Clovis. For the Gallo-Romans and for all matters affecting the Church, the valid law was Roman law, in the form of the *Breviarium Alaricianum*. Even so, throughout the kingdom legal proceedings were conducted in Frankish fashion, and certain rules applicable to germanic law also met with acceptance among the Roman population. For example, the idea gained ground that when blood was spilled the crime was to be purged not by punishment meted out by the state, as Roman law required, but through the blood-feud or by private treaty: the ill-doer was obliged to pay a wergild, but if a Roman were the victim the price was only half what it would be for a German. This provision emphasizes the superiority of the conquerors; yet within the nation as a political unit the men of both languages were on an equal footing. Over the years the rights of the kindred were restricted by royal legislation, intermarriage between Germans and Romans was permitted right from the start, Romans were enlisted along with Germans for service in the armed host. Unlike the states of the east Germans, the Frankish state made a deliberate effort at merging the two peoples. The success of this policy was soon demonstrated. The grave goods in the cemeteries gradually acquire a Roman stamp, even though in many places the germanic form of *Reihengräber* is retained well into the period after the conquerors had become absorbed by the native population.

In the time of Clovis and his immediate successors, the constitution and government of the Frankish state shows both germanic and Roman elements. The Merovingian kingship kept the sacral character of its heathen days, as evinced above all in belief in the divine descent of the royal clan and the thaumaturgic powers of the ruler. On the other hand, the tendency for the royal authority to make itself absolute, at the expense of the assembly of warriors and over the opposition of the nobility, was Roman, Untrammelled control of the army and possession of large estates already assured the king a large measure of independence. The estates belonging to the Roman fisc all fell to the king, as did mines and quarries; he received the revenues derived from the taxes and customs taken over from the Roman system and even the technique of constructing land-registers was not lost, while the minting of coins continued, to the best of men's ability. The king's chief judicial adviser was the *referendarius*, whose title is again borrowed from the provincial administration. The royal diplomas drafted in the chancery were modelled on imperial documents; though it must be admitted that the late Roman custom of using documents to record all important legal transactions had now largely fallen into disuse. Latin made headway as the language used for legislative and administrative purposes, and this too gave further scope for Gallo-Roman influence. In regional government there was less reliance on Roman institutions, since here certain germanic ideas were introduced by way of simplification. The provincial divisions of the late Roman empire were discarded almost completely; on the other hand, the small administrative units, the *civitates*, were retained. In appointing an official, the *comes* or count, to administer such units for a given number of years, the king was following Roman precedent; but when he gave these counts a combined military and civil authority, so that they were at once army commanders and superior judges, he was acting in accordance not with the Roman order but with germanic custom.

After only two generations, the symbiosis of the two peoples led to the formation of a germano-roman aristocracy, in which Frankish 'ethelings' took their place beside the descendants of old senatorial families, important officials beside bishops. Members of this aristocracy possessed large estates which, since they were worked by slaves and half-free peasants, in every respect resemble the self-contained economic units centring on a household which had developed on the soil of the Roman empire. Where Roman methods of exploitation survived they continued to be used, with far-reaching effects on the economy of the Frankish kingdom. Roman practice was followed in the choice of cereal crops for cultivation, the implements employed and the organization of the estate; moreover, horticulture and viticulture were now introduced into more northerly regions. But – and this is a specifically Frankish characteristic – a class of independent cultivators flourished alongside the great estates. It was not merely that villages already established from Roman times as the settlements of petty farmers continued to exist; villages and hamlets populated by independent cultivators were also springing up in regions where Germans were in the majority. The *Lex Salica* gives us a very vivid picture of such villages, where the community was a self-contained unit and the individual cultivator relied on the resources of his own property. Village life stimulated the Germans to divert their energies into new channels: they were now cultivating the land they had occupied. As they intensified their labours, new villages were founded to accommodate the increasing population. The indigenous section of the population was also spurred to fresh endeavours, freed from the fiscal oppression of the late Roman administration.

To a certain extent, what has just been said applies also to the towns. Admittedly, they became neither larger nor more numerous; since the Franks, like all Germans, chose as a rule to live in villages, the superiority of urban over rural communities could no longer be taken for granted. But towns continued to be of great importance in economic life. Once the new state had stabilized lines of communication, manufactured goods were again in demand and held out prospects of a good return. As the finds show, the old techniques were still applied to the production of earthenware and bronze vessels, germanic forms started to affect the style of bronze ornament and new workshops were established. It was in keeping with the enterprising spirit of the age that water-mills, a Roman invention which the Romans themselves had been hesitant to exploit, now became much more widespread. Literary sources testify to the continuance of long distance trade. In support of his great thesis that it was not the advent of the Germans but the Arab conquests which marked the end of an epoch in European history, Henri Pirenne laid great stress on the survival of maritime trade in the Mediterranean during the sixth and seventh centuries. It is now clear that he overemphasized the cultural influence of the Mediterranean as a single trading area, but there can be no doubt that even in Merovingian times there was a steady flow of oriental wares into the western provinces, to gratify the tastes of the upper class or to serve the liturgical needs of the Church: spices and precious stones, fine linen and papyrus. The Rhône delta and valley were still arteries of traffic, still frequented by the Jewish and Syrian merchants whose trading was conducted on the basis of a money economy. It is indicative of the general movement in the economy that a lively trade now developed from Gaul to the north-east. The continuous stream of goods which found their way from the

Romania into the interior of Germany shows that in this respect, as in others, Frankish Gaul was following in the steps of the Roman empire.

The conversion of Clovis to Catholicism meant that life at all levels – popular, cultural and political – was diverted into new channels, especially after the Burgundians, and later the Visigoths, had followed the Frankish example. If Gaul enjoyed stability of culture as well as stability of settlement during the migration period, the ultimate credit lies largely with this religious move. First and foremost, the adoption of the Catholic faith gave definition to the ecclesiastical structure of the Frankish kingdom. Bishops, frequently descended from the old senatorial aristocracy, were the heads of their dioceses and episcopal synods remained the forum for the discussion and decision of all questions affecting the Church as a whole. One synod, summoned by Clovis himself, took the fundamental step of decreeing that all instructions as laid down in ecclesiastical canons and contained within Roman law, were to be observed, which meant that the Catholic order was accepted in its entirety. Latin, from now on the language of the liturgy throughout Frankish territory, in this clericalized form penetrated to new peoples and new places, to become at once an instrument of romanization and a vitalizing force of international scope. Most important of all, however, the decision to adopt Latin for church purposes gave access to the store of spiritual and religious energy locked up in Christian antiquity. Yet for all their respect for Roman tradition, Clovis and his successors knew well enough how to subdue the Frankish church to their royal will. It is unnecessary to assume that their model was the Arian church; more likely, what we see here was the working out of an old germanic idea, namely that the king was the representative of his people even in the eyes of God. Clovis ordained the agenda for the synod summoned to meet in 511 and confirmed its decisions; later, the kings would also arrogate the right to appoint bishops.

In view of this political direction of the Church, it is surprising that the Christian religion was so slow to penetrate public life. In its earliest version the *Lex Salica* contains nothing specifically Christian (and nothing specifically heathen, either), nor did the kings draw on Christian ethical teaching in framing their laws. It was left to the clergy, whose power soon greatly increased, to establish the superiority of ecclesiastical over secular authority in matters of faith and morals and to draw attention to the obligations of a Christian ruler. But the first aim of the Church was to exterminate paganism, a long and wearisome labour since the pagan cults showed great tenacity, especially in country districts. The numerous amulets in many shapes and forms which have been found among grave goods testify that in the sixth century men still clung to their former beliefs about the after life, and it is only in the seventh century that Christian symbols start to increase. Engaged thus in the conversion of its own flock, the Merovingian church took no initiative in sending missionaries to the Germans on the right bank of the Rhine; the impulse for this had to come from outside. Within the Frankish kingdom, day-to-day life gradually took on a more Christian complexion. By royal decree, Sundays and Church festivals became public holidays and church buildings were granted the right to provide asylum. Veneration of the saints and their relics developed on a large scale. From certain anecdotes related by Gregory of Tours, and much other testimony, it is clear that Frankish popular piety had its pagan side. Almsgiving and grants for the endowment of churches were often stimulated by business-like calculations of the benefit to accrue in the life to come. Religion appears to have had little influence on morals, if the crimes and passions of the Merovingian royal house are anything to go by. The kings from Clovis onwards encouraged monasticism, not infrequently, it would appear, because of the rôle monks could play as intercessors for important sinners or as a counterweight to their misdeeds. The synods were fully occupied with the task of bringing Christianity home to such men and upholding the rules of Christian discipline against royal – and even clerical – violators. More effective was the influence of great saints, of which even this century had its share.

In the wider field of education, literature and art, the Christian Church did succeed in preserving at least something of value from the ancient tradition. Nethertheless, men who still read the classical authors no longer did so with any thought of emulating their achievement through new works of equal merit; they looked to their literary authorities to provide them with a certain linguistic facility and a body of elementary knowledge. Even at this date, there were still public schools in Gaul capable of satisfying these modest demands. Recent re-investigation of the literary tradition has shown that municipal schools of grammar and rhetoric continued to function in Gaul throughout most of the fifth century, thus at Lyons, Vienne, Bordeaux and Clermont. Moreover, many families of the Gallo-Roman aristocracy sought to perpetuate the traditional form of education, in however exiguous a form, by engaging private tutors, and this practice continued even when the schools eventually closed. Latin remained the language in general use not only for legislation but for all types of literature, ecclesiastical, historical or secular. On the other hand, a few rare exceptions apart, no-one in the west had any knowledge of Greek. With the final disappearance of the municipal schools, the Church took steps on her own account to ensure that at least a minimum of knowledge and culture survived, since without it the Bible and the Church Fathers would remain inaccessible. Schools for the education of the clergy were being set up at episcopal seats of residence as early as the first half of the sixth century, and the country clergy were running elementary classes in their villages to instruct the lectors needed for church services and, above all, to ensure a future supply of clerics. These church schools were to be found everywhere throughout the western provinces and for a long time formed the normal road of entry into higher education. The laity by and large held aloof from these educational opportunities, and hence from education in general, with the result that cultural life was radically transformed. The extent to which learning and culture were now a matter of class is reflected in linguistic usage: the Latin word *clericus* now becomes the designation not only of clerics but of educated persons in general. This new-style education bore little fruit in literature during the Merovingian period. Such authors as there were belonged to the Roman stratum of the population; what they produced reveals just how great was the gulf separating them from the knowledge and intellectual power generated by antiquity. As for the Franks of the sixth century, it is hard to say whether they were making any contribution to germanic heroic poetry. In the plastic arts and in architecture, the romanised south of Gaul was clearly in the lead. The design and decoration of the Christian basilicas of this region and period, as of Spain and Italy, testify that late Roman architecture and sculpture were still developing forms. In the germanic contribution to art, for the time being still restricted to ornamentation and the production of decorative objects, two influences can be detected: the so-called 'migration style', whose repertoire of forms is to a large extent derived from the art of the Asian steppes; and Mediterranean art. It was only by degrees that the Germans reshaped the motifs and forms reaching them from these two directions to produce an art in keeping with their own genius.

Viewed as a whole, these beginnings of Frankish culture confirm that the cultural heritage of antiquity was accepted and handed on. 'The house which the Romans had built on the soil of ancient Gaul lost its roof, but the foundations and walls stood firm'; such was the conclusion of E. Salin after his thorough-going examination of Merovingian civilization. But in the setting of the new germanic world, with its different social structure and spiritual aspirations, the heritage took on a new function. Citizen communities inhabiting free cities were no longer the custodians of knowledge and creators of art; the elements of the traditional culture had been taken over by the Christian clergy and subordinated to different ends. The process already gestating within the womb of the Roman empire during the third and fourth centuries was thereby materially advanced. It would be decisive for the shaping of cultural life in the future that the Frankish empire succeeded in fusing its Roman and germanic populations and that this synthesis was not destroyed by any fresh invasions, whether of the Lombards or of Islam. Thus, in the end a way was found to link the germanic world as a whole with the Imperium Romanum and its culture. Disturbed, the tribes came first as plunderers, continuing their raids over a long period ; next, tribal units found admission to the empire as federates and tried to set up their own germanic kingdoms ; but these creations, cut off from the ancient world by reason of their Arianism, resulted in a dangerous multiplicity of alliances and rivalries. Now the Franks and Gallo-Romans together had created an empire which embraced many of the former germanic foundations and reached out to the tribes beyond the Rhine and Danube, an empire which through its alliance with the Catholic Church contained the germ of a universal polity. For with the end of the Roman empire in the West, the Catholic Church became the standard-bearer of unity throughout the western provinces which the Byzantine emperor failed to recover – and of a unity which allowed for a plurality of peoples and states. We can thus recognize the creation of the Frankish kingdom as one of the cornerstones of what we know as the Christian West.

Roman writers showed little hesitation in equating the Roman empire with the circle of the earth itself, surrounded by the ocean, *orbis terrarum;* Britain, lying actually within the ocean, appeared to them *extra orbem*, out of the world. In the course of its history, this insular position on the margin of Europe had frequently cut Britain off from European events ; but there were times at which Britain became an Archimedean point, from which the whole continent could be moved. Such a moment occurred in the age of transition from ancient to medieval civilization ; and this becomes especially clear when Ireland is also brought into the picture. Hibernia never formed part of the Roman empire and no Roman legionaries ever landed there, but the Christian religion took root and its influence spread back to Britain and the continent. It thus came about that at a later date the British Isles played a unique rôle in the transmission of the Christian religion and the civilized learning of antiquity inside the Frankish empire.

The Romans never succeeded in occupying even the whole of the British mainland. The Antonine wall, built on the Forth-Clyde isthmus and the furthermost Roman fortification in Britain, left the north of Scotland unconquered, and Hadrian's wall, between the Tyne and the Solway, which was defended down to the end of the fourth century, did not shelter even the whole of England : eloquent testimonies to the difficulty of advancing in northern mountainous country and to the sustained resistance offered by the Celtic Picts and Scots. The British lowland, however, which for four centuries formed part of the empire, was exploited economically by the Romans and shaped by Roman culture. The province was protected against the tribes living in Wales and along the Pennine Chain by three Roman legions, garrisoned at Eburacum (York), Deva (Chester) and Venta Silurum (Caerleon). Agriculture and mineral exploitation received a powerful impetus and the country was covered by a network of roads. As the Celtic population became partially romanized, flourishing towns grew up, colonies were founded and even places serving as the headquarters of a tribe took on an urban aspect, with broad, encircling walls. The Celtic languages held their own in country districts, but in towns gave way to Latin ; however, unlike Gaul and Spain, Britain produced no Latin authors. Even though the process of urbanization soon came to a halt, in the third and fourth centuries the economy of Britain was still in a flourishing state. From the end of the third century the province was menaced by the plundering raids of Frankish and Saxon pirates, but in the time of Diocletian and Constantine the south-east was provided with a special coastal command (*Litus Saxonicum*), linked with the defence of the coastal regions on the opposite shore in Gaul, the *Tractus Armoricanus et Nervicanus,* running from Aquitaine to lower Germany. In consequence of these measures, economic prosperity continued into the fourth century. In fact archaeological evidence points to this period as the heyday of the Roman villa – that is to say, of the large farms, economically independent, which lay scattered throughout the province. These impressive estates were probably largely in the hands of indigenous chieftains, who exploited them in the Roman fashion and occupied the luxurious mansions. While urban populations were becoming impoverished under the weight of oppressive Roman taxation, the landed proprietors, with their dependent peasantry, were acquiring wealth and power. In many ways private initiative also seems to have succeeded in trade and industry, where the coercive efforts of the late Roman state had failed.

From the middle of the fourth century, however, the threat to Roman Britain grew to alarming proportions. At the very time when the Picts were storming Hadrian's Wall and the Scots of Ireland were invading the western shores of Britain, Saxon pirates intensified and increased their raids on the southern part of the province. The west Roman emperors, fully engaged on the Rhine and the Danube, could no longer provide the province with an adequate defence. During the empire's most critical years, the Roman army in Britain had repeatedly set up officers from its own ranks as rival emperors, and these in turn had withdrawn troops from the island to consolidate their bid for power on the continent. When the usurper Magnus Maximus crossed over to Gaul in 383, Hadrian's wall had to be evacuated. Still worse consequences followed the removal of the Roman army in 407 by the usurper Constantine III, to help him repel the invasion of the Vandals, Alans and Sueves on the continent. There was now nothing to stop the Saxons from returning year after year on their plundering raids; in fact, after the year of catastrophe, 406–7, there was no longer any regular official intercourse between Britain and Gaul. It was only in the south-east of England that there was still some semblance of Roman rule, and within their now shrunken territory the Romans and their dependents were left to fend for themselves, with no hope of reinforcements, from the central provinces of the empire. While Aetius was concentrating all his effort on the defence of Gaul, Spain and Africa, Britain was being lost to the empire. The year 441 can probably be taken as the beginning of the German conquest of Britain. Saxons, accompanied by their wives and children, invaded the country from Holstein, the Angles and Jutes left the Danish peninsula in search of wider and better fields to cultivate in Britain. The germanic occupation of the country took many years to complete, but at no time did the Romans venture to offer battle in a last ditch stand; little by little, Roman life in the English lowland became extinct. Around the middle of the fifth century part of the British population fled southwards over the sea to Armorica on the north-western coast of Gaul, to settle in particular in the peninsula which took its name from these immigrants, Brittany; there they reinforced the existing Celtic population, as yet little romanized. Such Celts as remained in the former province of Britain were forced by the conquerors back into the mountains, taking refuge in Cornwall, Wales, Lancashire and Cumberland. The Germans, who were continually making fresh additions to their territory, lived under their own laws, spoke their own language and kept to their old religion. It seemed that the work of romanization was completely annihilated.

Yet here we have a classic example of a process which can also be seen at work in other parts of the Roman world: what the Roman Imperium lost, the Catholic Church recovered. In our sketch of the romanization of Britain it was possible to ignore the advent of Christianity, since while the country was still firmly under Roman rule, the new religion played no appreciable role. The beginnings of British Christianity are shrouded in darkness; the earliest Christians to reach Britain probably arrived during the second century, as a result of the island's trading and military contacts with the mainland. Tertullian and Origen are the first to mention the existence of Christians in Britain, and their testimony is borne out by archaeological finds and inscriptions. Next there is a reference, in the collected canons of the Church, to the presence of three British bishops at the Council of Arles (314). But the Celtic and

Roman deities still had many worshippers, as altars and other places of worship built in the provincial Roman style testify. However, it is known that in the fourth century the Christian hierarchy supported the orthodox party in the struggle against Arianism. Even in the fifth century, there was still a link between the churches of the British Isles and the continent. The British-born monk Pelagius studied in Rome and Carthage and then went to the East; his thesis that man could free himself from evil by the decisive act of his own will was contested by Augustine and condemned by the African synods, but it won adherents in the East and in a modified form – Semi-Pelagianism – also found sympathisers among monks in Gaul, from where it actually spread into Britain: Pope Celestine felt obliged to send bishop Germanus of Auxerre to Britain to strengthen the country in the faith. The Roman Church thus found it possible to intervene in Britain, whereas no help for the beleaguered province was forthcoming from the emperor.

In 431 this same Pope sent a cleric named Palladius as bishop to Ireland. This is the first news we have of the existence of Irish Christians. It seems clear that the gospel had reached the island at an earlier date but that the Christian mission had met with little success; nor is anything known of the activities of Palladius. Untouched by Roman rule, the pastoral Irish Celts retained their old kindred and tribal organization and remained true to their belief in the gods celebrated in bardic song, whose strictly prescribed worship was conducted by the druids. It was only with the arrival of Patrick, at much the same date as Palladius, that Ireland was opened up to Christianity. The life-history of this saint soon became embroidered with legend and poses many riddles; but two writings which can with certainty be attributed to Patrick himself give us something definite to work on. These are his *Confessio* and his letter to Coroticus, a British chieftain whose subjects had plundered the Irish coasts and carried off Christian captives. These documents, written in a mediocre school Latin, give us a clear picture of the main traits of the personality and achievement of the Apostle of Ireland. Patrick was born in Britain about the year 380, the son of a deacon who belonged to the town council of his community; he was abducted by Irish pirates and made to serve six years in Ireland as a herdsman's slave, during which time he experienced an inward conversion to the Christian religion of his childhood. He then escaped to Gaul and received a rudimentary education; it is noteworthy, however, that he describes himself in his *Confessio* as an uneducated man. On his return to Britain, Patrick was ordained priest (432) and resolved to make preaching the gospel to the Irish his life's work. By his sermons and miracles he converted the tribal chieftains and through them their clans, he founded churches, set up a bishopric at Armagh in northern

Ireland and spent the last years of his life in solitude, dying probably in 461. In its language, liturgy and constitution this first Church in Ireland followed the Roman pattern – and this at a time when Roman rule in Britain was on the point of collapse.

However, even on the mainland the end of Roman provincial government did not entail the complete extinction of the Christian religion. Although the Church organization ceased to function throughout the territory now populated by the Anglo-Saxons, it continued in being in the Celtic redoubts of the west, above all in Wales. The Celtic Christians of these parts were in lively communication with the refugees who had settled in Brittany; it seems, indeed, that their contacts extended as far as Aquitaine and Spain, and through these intermediary links even reached the East. It is very probable that around the turn of the fifth century new forms of religious and ecclesiastical life travelled by this route to reach the extreme north-west of Europe, Wales and Ireland. This new mode of Christianity had two essential features: asceticism, which gave man access to a higher, more spiritual form of Christianity, and a monasticism in which a basic acquaintance with academic knowledge formed an integral part. The Welsh Church of the sixth century – the century of St Gildas – thus became a monastic Church; monasteries were founded, with schools attached to them. At this same period monastic Christianity was also transforming Ireland. In the *Catalogus Sanctorum Hiberniae* a new era starts with the year 544. Monasteries sprang up, at first in the south, from which we may conclude that influences from Aquitaine and Spain were at work, and these monasteries became the focal points of religious and intellectual life. The abbot had jurisdiction over his monastery and the surrounding countryside, whereas the bishop, as an inmate of the monastery, was subordinate to the abbot and restricted almost entirely to his ritual functions. The monastic church of Ireland, which combined strict asceticism with learning, introduced the art of writing into the country and thus made an essential contribution both to the conservation of the native heritage and to the transmission of the culture of antiquity. The Gaelic script was joined by the Latin alphabet, the old heroic tales were written down, and even if the texts were soon pervaded by Christian motifs, the kernel of the great saga, which has affinities with the German-Norse saga, remained intact. But educated monks were interested chiefly in texts relating to the Christian life: they eagerly wrote out and composed monastic rules, penitential books, lives of the saints. The Latin they used in the liturgy gave them access to a few isolated works of classical literature, above all the poetry of the Augustan age. In Ireland men found this literature completely new and strange: it was not, as in Italy and Gaul, a piece of their own pagan past and therefore able to be received with open arms.

Christian learning and the understanding of classical culture were alike in demanding a certain grounding in school-work, first and foremost in grammar. During the sixth century, the monastic Church of Ireland thus acquired a basic stock of culture derived from ancient civilization. In this same period there was also a new flowering of the Irish art whose beginnings reach back into remote Irish antiquity; its main characteristics are an abstract style and a preference for linear ornamentation, a stylistic language which had also survived among the Celts in Britain during the centuries of Roman occupation. In Ireland this artistic tradition now combined with Syrian and Coptic influences to transform the abstract style of the north into an instrument for the expression of Christian feeling, seen at its most perfect in the masterpieces of book illumination contained in Irish manuscripts.

These remarks have led us beyond the chronological limit set for this book, the turn of the fifth century. It is worth taking one further small step into the future, in order to observe by what astonishing paths the influence of *Britannia extra orbem* was reflected back to the continent. One characteristic of the Irish monastic Church was that abandonment of homeland, to wander among strangers and lead the religious life in voluntary exile, was reckoned an act of supreme piety, a surrogate, indeed, for martyrdom. This idea of the *Peregrinatio pro Christo* turned the Irish pilgrims into missionaries of the Christian faith. When the Irish crossed the sea they came first upon the Picts in Scotland. During the second half of the sixth century Columba founded a monastery on the island of Iona (Hy) off the west coast of Scotland, which was to become a centre of missionary activity and intellectual life for the whole country. Towards the end of the century Columba set out for the lands of the Franks and Lombards; through his monastic foundations, at Luxeuil in Burgundy and Bobbio in Lombardy, he inspired fresh vigour into the churches and a new interest in classical learning, which in the Frankish kingdom had sunk to a low ebb. Other missionaries, from Scotland and Northumberland, brought the gospel to the Anglo-Saxons. They were already at work when in 596 Pope Gregory sent the Benedictine monk Augustine and his band of missionaries to convert the Angles. The Celtic evangelists from the north were thus brought into contact with a Roman mission. The subsequent and surprisingly rapid conversion of the Anglo-Saxons to Christianity brought to a close the circle which had started with a Roman initiative to convert the British Isles to Christianity, and in so doing released new religious and intellectual energies for work on the continent. Over a long period the Irish and Anglo-Saxons acted as custodians of the heritage of classical culture and learning, so sorely jeopardized in the later Merovingian kingdom. It was a fortunate day when Anglo-Saxons, in their dual role as missionaries of the Roman Church and upholders of the ancient cultural tradition, directed their attention and their zeal towards this same Frankish kingdom, in which the unity of the European West was taking shape.

CHAPTER 4

CULTURAL CHANGE REFLECTED IN ART

FREQUENT reference has been made to buildings and items of painting and sculpture, where it seemed opportune to adduce visible witnesses to the feelings about life and conception of the Divine among men of these centuries. Various phases in the metamorphosis of ancient culture have thus been brought to notice. If at the conclusion of this exposition we now endeavour to sum up these changes in artistic form, it is in the hope of affording a deepened insight into the process of transformation as it worked among men as a whole: artists, patrons, and the urban and rural groups in the population who gathered in these buildings and were confronted by these images.

At one time, certain exponents of art history defended the thesis that the new stylistic phases encountered in the Graeco-Roman world of this period were importations from the East, and thought this showed how the classicism of Hellas was being choked and stifled by the Orient. Penetrating investigations, however, have shown that in all the continuous interchange of art forms taking place within the empire we should recognize as the driving force behind the development the alteration in men's spiritual outlook, their new artistic purposes. We have heard the poet Paulinus exclaiming 'My spirit is new, yea is no longer as once it was.' This was an experience shared by many in these sorely-tested generations, even though they felt no call to give it poetic or artistic shape. We have found clear enough indications of the estrangement of the bourgeoisie and the great mass of the population from the state and its values, we have seen how overwhelming was the surrender to new divine powers which bound men inwardly, and how crucial, even for leading spirits, was the revelation of a suprahuman and supraterrestrial reality.

As we now review the surviving artistic monuments of the age, we shall keep the political and social upheavals already traced constantly in view. The urban bourgeoisie, whose taste determined the architecture and statuary of the classical age, was now completely supplanted as patron by the emperors, by religious communities, and above all by the Christian Church. Even in these altered social circumstances, there was still a variety of artistic groups and schools, whose individual characteristics can be identified even if we no longer know the artists by name. Nor, too, were attempts lacking to give currency to still not forgotten models of the past age. Classicism experienced a renaissance. Pagans and Christians participated alike in these divergent movements. But whatever the twists and turns of artistic intention, the overriding direction is so plain that art history was the first of all historical disciplines to recognize this epoch as a period in its own right, bestowing on it the name Late Antique, to distinguish it from the Early Empire on the one hand and Byzantium and the so-called Western Middle Ages on the other. It has been shown that the art of the third century can be regarded as a phase in preparation for that new art form which confronts us in the gigantic creations of the age of the Tetrarchs, finds its clearest expression in the decades of the Theodosian dynasty and comes to an end in Ostrogothic Italy. From the fourth century, a certain cleavage between the eastern and western halves of the ancient world is as noticeable in art as in literature and the stamp acquired by Christianity. Our attention will focus primarily on the West, on Italo-Roman stylistic intentions and the art of the western provinces. For us, the city of Rome, whether imperial or papal, retains its importance, Trier carries greater weight than Palmyra and at the end of the road stands not Byzantium but Ravenna.

The age of the Severi saw Roman architecture at the height of its creative power. Whatever, over the generations, this architecture may have taken in the way of architectonic solutions from the East, it reached its peak through the mastery of strictly Italo-Roman methods of construction and ideas of composition. Among the essential features of this architecture must be reckoned the deployment of all its technical resources to surmount physical obstacles and the shaping of the interior space at the expense of a grandiose external finish to the fabric : brick-building, mortar techniques and vaulting are its old and well-tried methods. The Severan emperors paid homage to the city of Rome as the centre of the empire by commissioning works there on the grand scale. Septimius Severus built a palace for the new dynasty on the Palatine, to which the massive substructures extant on the south-western side of the hill still bear witness. In his reign work also started on the public baths development in the south of the city on the Appian Way, a huge undertaking which was continued by his son and successor Caracalla. This, too, followed a precedent set by former emperors, of providing the inhabitants of the capital with luxurious bathing facilities at an admission price which made them accessible even to the poorer classes. When completed, the baths of Caracalla were more extensive than any existing thermae and were afterwards surpassed in size only by those of Diocletian. There was a clear separation between the main building and its surrounding enclosure. The main building, containing three chambers, hot, tepid and cold, together with numerous dressing rooms, gymnasia and facilities for cures of every description, forms a symmetrical complex based on a rectangular ground plan; the only projection from the right angle is the circular construction containing the hot room, a domed hall in the manner of the Pantheon. The most significant member of the entire complex – its exact form has been ascertained from the ruins – was the central hall, roofed with massive cross-vaulting. Invented in Italy and tried out in numerous buildings, this technique of gathering the load of the vault on to four pillars which support the terminals of the arches made possible the creation of a vast interior space, cut out, as it were, from infinity. We have here before us the construction which descended, by way of the imperial basilica, to the great circular edifices of the Christian Church. The thermal hall was a necessary precursor of San Vitale at Ravenna and of St Sophia at Constantinople.

The provinces also felt the benefit of the Severan urge to build. Syria, where Heliopolis (Baalbek) received an extension to the sanctuary area, and the city of Palmyra, whose colonnaded streets and tomb-reliefs show Hellenistic-Oriental art forms developing down to the time of Zenobia, are outside our purview here. But the buildings erected in Africa, the native land of the Severan dynasty, are of crucial importance in the development of western art. Thanks to imperial patronage, several towns in the region acquired at this period new temples, basilicas, thermae and theatre buildings. The temples (to the Capitoline deities but also on occasion to native divinities, for example Dea Caelestis at Thugga) were often concentrated in a sanctuary precinct. The new forum at Lepcis Magna provides an outstanding example of this specifically Roman urge to relate the layout of an area to the eye of the beholder, by means of its positive alignment and optical axes. For the first time in a complex of this importance the columns of the halls surrounding the forum are linked by balancing arches. Here we have the rows of arcades which became an established feature of the architecture of late antiquity, both sacred and profane; it recurs in the colonnaded promenades of the palace of Diocletian, the so-called peristyle (plate 17), as also in the principal naves of many Christian basilicas (plate 19). Other monumental structures built in Africa are further testimony that urban prosperity continued there into the third century, and in some instances reveal the far-reaching change in forms which was taking place in Roman art. This province, which supplied many of the beasts in such great demand for animal contests, is well-provided with amphitheatres: that at Thysdrus (El Djem), indeed, is the most imposing of any from this period. In towns where they were lacking, men sometimes went so far as to convert their theatres for animal performances. Several theatres, at Sabratha in Tripolitania, have survived. In this instance the high wall of the structure containing the stage has been given a three-tiered formal facing of superimposed columns. Even libraries and thermae occasionally received this grandiose treatment, often with the further refinement of statuary placed in the wall-niches. The use of statuary in combination with architecture becomes a characteristic of late Roman building style. It is characteristic of the sense of form and space prevailing among men at this period that free-standing statues set up in the open are a rarity; for preference, statues are placed against a wall or incorporated as members into a column order. The autonomous sculpture, the glory of the Greek classical style, is undergoing attenuation in the Roman world and in early Christian art has almost wholly disappeared.

Portrait sculpture, on the other hand, shows a powerful development. The imperial image was now an object of ritual adoration, in provincial towns and the army encampments of legionaries and auxiliaries just as much as at Rome. As soon as a new emperor was installed, his portrait was circulated to the provinces, the official version of his features became familiar to every citizen from the coinage. The wide currency thus given to the imperial portrait had a profound effect on portraiture in general. Even so, the numerous heads and busts surviving from this century evince a lively diversity in stylistic trends. Hellenistic classicism persists alongside the Roman realism whose insistence on an exact, realistic rendering is in such contrast. From mid-century, the tendency to emphasize facial expression at the expense of the organic construction of the head becomes stronger; new methods of moulding are tried out, to seize a look and capture a subject's inner experience. Success in categorizing personality is thus achieved in a variety of ways. We have the neurotically disturbed portrait of the emperor Caracalla, which brings out the violence and brutality of the despot; we have the bust of the emperor Philip the Arab, a stereometrically formed head which expresses a profound scepticism (plate 34); and we have some moving portraits of Gallienus, notably the head in the National Museum (Terme) at Rome, the portrait of a man with a philosophical cast of mind, soft and sensual in feature, his gaze scanning the far distance. Towards the end of the century spiritualization of the expression becomes even more marked; caught up, perhaps, in the wake of neo-platonism, artists are searching for new ways of portraying the transcendental reality underlying material things.

In the art of historical relief, the Severan era also shows the beginning of a departure from the classical style. In erecting his triumphal arches at Rome and in a number of African cities, Septimius Severus adhered to the traditional mode of the official monument, glorifying his deeds through cyclical reliefs to leave a record of them for posterity. The arch standing at the northern corner of the Roman forum depicts on its faces, with a wealth of detail, the great event of the Parthian wars. The battle-scenes follow one another in continuous sequence, the figures emerge in full relief, elements of landscape are incorporated. In this pictorial record, which continues the painterly style of earlier arches and columns, the concluding scene which shows the emperor addressing the army is worthy of special remark. The emperor, flanked by his sons, is here presented frontally, an artistic device which makes the majestic, imperial figure stand out from the lengthy cycle. In the relief on the arch at Lepcis Magna, the imperial trinity is also made to appear frontally in the centre of the composition, but here the continuity of the central group with the flanking profile figures has been broken. There is a flatness in the disposition of all the figures in this relief, corporeality has depreciated, the drapery has frozen into sharp-cut folds. Plastic sensitivity has been sacrificed, which reveals afresh the distance travelled from Greek art; the figure is in process of becoming a pointer to something transcendental, of becoming a symbol – a transformation which prepares the way for the language of form in early Christian art.

As part of this change in forms, mention must also be made of the renunciation of unity of spatial vision often encountered in mosaics of this period. Mosaics which formed the pavement covering in the main apartments have survived in some numbers from the villas of great proprietors, especially in the north African provinces; the mosaic technique was often used also for the decoration of roof vaults, and appears to have made headway largely because of its faculty for preserving colours in all their freshness, in contrast with pure paint. Scenes from country house and estate life are favourite subjects in villa mosaics, although often executed at the expense of perspective. Thus, for example, one may find hunting scenes occupying a bottom strip, next another distinct band showing beasts being watered at a draw-well, further along still the cattle-shed and the homecoming herd and finally – right in the background as it were – a ploughman with an ox-team. The lower portion is thus reserved for remote objects, the upper for those near at hand: a form of inverted perspective. It is possible that folk art has exerted some influence here. But since the grand art of the period also in many respects abandons perspective, and with it the means handed down by classical artists of combining all the separate parts of a composition into a harmonious whole, it has been suggested that the philosophy of Plotinus has had its effect on the language of art forms. When Plotinus says that the eye must take in the exact dimensions of the object and attach equal significance to every detail, it remains for the intellect to reconstitute in all its fullness the picture presented to the eye shorn of its third dimension.[1]

Furthermore, there can be no doubt that those provinces which under the later empire found it possible to develop a life of their own were also evolving their own artistic language, in a sense which ran counter to that of classical art. Among these provincial art-dialects, the style of the celto-germanic border zone deserves special mention, since in this late period it managed to hold its own against the official style of the empire, and in medieval times, to all appearances, again played an active role in the art of this region. During the first centuries of Roman occupation Italo-Roman influences penetrated even northern Gaul and the Rhineland, but after the middle of the second century indigenous workshops started up, to provide an outlet for the increasingly powerful artistic urge at work among the new peoples. Numerous second to fourth century reliefs from Belgian Gaul and lower Germany have survived, many of them originally part of funerary monuments; they take a real delight in depicting events of everyday life, and thus mark a departure from the thematic repertoire of classical art. The well-known Neumagen reliefs already mentioned (plates 36–8) perpetuate scenes which have no historic significance yet are rich in intimate charm: a schoolroom, a lady at her morning toilet, peasants paying their dues, wine transports on the Moselle. Through skilful characterization of the heads and a subtle capture of expression, the artists succeed in conveying the full flavour of the scene. This folk-accented art language, which embraces the workaday world and extends sympathetic human feelings to new social classes unknown to classical art, continued to flourish in the north-west until the end of Roman rule; during the ensuing period of confusion its voice becomes mute, but thereafter rings out again in all its purity.

In the provinces of ancient Greek civilization, as afterwards in Italy, from the second century the art of relief found scope in a new field, which affords us some insight into the changing view of life among the upper class. Inhumation, long the prevailing form of burial in the East, now also became the custom of the West. The awakening belief in human survival after death – which may have been connected with the spread of oriental religions – perhaps did much to promote this practice of depositing the corpse in a grave. In Italy, a revival of ancient Italo-Etruscan conceptions may also have helped to give inhumation precedence over cremation. In affluent circles it became usual to place the dead in a relief-decorated sarcophagus within a burial chamber. Asia Minor and Greece played an important role in originating and developing the marble sarcophagus as an art form; the sarcophagus whose four sides are decorated with columned façades has its provenance in Asia

Minor. But Roman workshops also started up, and at Rome it became usual to make the front of the sarcophagus a show-piece or to confine the relief decoration to this side alone. The motifs employed in this new form of relief, which was by now widely diffused, include scenes from Greek mythology, notably themes from the cycle of Dionysus, which were readily accessible to sepulchral interpretation. But festal civic occasions and incidents recalling the earthly deeds of the dead man in his prime were also acceptable. The Ludovisi battle sarcophagus, which belongs to the middle of the third century, is an outstanding monument to this sarcophagus sculpture and its artistic language. The relief is a powerful rendering of the tumult of the battlefield: we see the conquering Romans surging down upon the mangled mass of the barbarian underworld, while in the centre of the composition, at the point where the masses dissolve, the general leaps up with a gesture of triumph, emancipated from the toils of the action and confronting the beholder. This purely formalized presentation of the victor is novel; but the rules of classical composition are further contravened in that most of the defeated are made to appear as dwarfed figures, and the pathos of the picture as a whole, with its disturbing rendering of the pain-twisted features of the barbarians, might be described as baroque. We observe a quite different departure from classical style, and also a change in subject matter, in the fragment from the 'philosophers' sarcophagus', thought to be a generation later (plate 39). Here the centre is occupied by a seated philosopher, expounding the text of a book-roll; two women, in their attitude and bearing reminiscent of the Muses, face towards him, while in the background and apart stand three men whose heads are typical of philosophers. The figures – in contradistinction to those of the battle sarcophagus – retreat into the flat plane. The governing mood of this philosophical reading is one of contemplation, the spectator – so the decoration of the tomb asserts – is caught up in that spiritual world which has opened up for the man who has died. This is a fundamental conception, since contemporary Christian sarcophagi also approach this composition and reflective treatment.

From what date were there Christian sarcophagi? What is the position generally regarding the origin and specific character of Christian art? Extensive investigations, which have now come together in the discipline of Christian archaeology, have thrown considerable light on these questions. The earliest generations of Christians inherited from the Synagogue the Old Testament prohibition of images, and we know from Origen that temples and images were still abhorrent to Christians of his day. Among isolated groups and in certain regions this early Christian repugnance towards art persisted even longer, and has never been wholly absent from Christianity at large. But there can be no doubt that as congregations started to grow, as the liturgy and the idea of venerating the dead took shape, a specifically Christian art came into being, at latest from the beginning of the third century. We know for certain that it did not originate with sacred architecture; Christians of this period still met to celebrate the Eucharist in private houses adapted for worship, the so-called house-churches. The excavations at Dura-Europus have brought to light one such house-church, probably dating from 232, in the neighbourhood of the renowned synagogue with its wealth of pictorial decoration; annexed to it was a form of baptistery, whose frescos include the earliest representation of Christ. During the second half of the third century purpose-built churches were erected in major towns, only to be demolished during the Diocletianic persecution. Christian burial-places, however, go back as early as the second century, as is established in the case of Rome by literary testimony and archaeological finds. In such burial-grounds, as among the pagans, the first tombs were set up on plots in a delimited area; but subsequently passages were dug in the tufa below the plots, to leave places free for sarcophagi on either side of the alley-way, chambers were laid out here and there and many of the passages were linked by flights of steps. One such cemetery, *coemeterium*, lay to the south of Rome on the Appian Way, close to a meadow which bore the name *ad catacumbas*; much later, the word catacombs, derived from this name of a meadow, was applied to any subterranean Christian burial place irrespective of its location, which might be at Rome, Syracuse or some other city.

The Roman catacombs, the great majority of which post-date the official recognition of Christianity by the state, furnish an exact guide to the beginnings of Christian art. Sarcophagi for the reception of Christian dead are at first more modest than their pagan contemporaries, although they follow them closely in form and decorative design. Whether a simple box or a sarcophagus in architectural form, as a rule the frontal and both side walls are decorated with reliefs. Gravestones give the name of the dead man and the day of his death, often adding the formula *in pace* (in peace), and through simple pictures – of a fish, a basket with bread, a cup with wine – make allusion to the religion's mysteries. Paintings start to adorn the wall and roof surfaces of the burial chambers: a network of lines is drawn, in the spaces between, on bright surfaces, figures and scenes appear, terse figures and briefly sketched scenes which seem to hint at an underlying symbolical meaning. Just as there is reliance on pagan exemplars in the design of the sarcophagi and the decorative scheme of walls and ceilings, so too the motifs of the sarcophagi and wall paintings show no lack of contact with the art of antiquity in the preceding age. Importations from the image-world of antiquity include not only masks and garlands, flowers and birds (plate

42), grapes and olive branches but even some erotic themes, while the pastoral scenes which earlier provoked thoughts of the Elysian fields now give the Christian beholder intimations of Paradise. T. Klauser has shown that even figures which were long regarded as the earliest authentic creations of Christian art had their pagan prototypes: the Good Shepherd (plate 49) comes to replace the herdsman shouldering a ram, the figure which hellenistic and early imperial art had already made a symbol of man's love and solicitude for his fellows; the standing figure with hands and arms uplifted in prayer, the Christian 'Orans' figure, follows the representation of Pietas as established through the coinage and also, indeed, by pagan sculptors; the book-reading scene in which the shepherd and the praying-figures both appear could also be interpreted by pagans as an illustration of philosophical teaching, instruction in virtue. Christians permeated all these motifs with the truths of their own faith, giving them as it were formal baptism: the ram-bearer becomes the Good Shepherd of the gospels, the praying figure comes to symbolize the soul standing face to face with God, the reading is understood as initiation into the gospel message.

Christian eyes saw a symbolical significance in all the pictures adorning their cemeteries and places of worship, and this was also true of the biblical pictures which from the outset took their place alongside the motifs already mentioned and would soon predominate. It was here that Christian art became fully independent. None of the artists concerned can be named, since among Christians of this period, as for the most part among men of the ancient world in general, sculptors, painters and mosaicists ranked as craftsmen, who neither needed, nor indeed deserved any fame. Stories were now taken from the Old and New Testaments, never in any detail but reduced to their essential content, to be used, as symbols of revealed truths, in the decoration of sarcophagi and burial chambers. The following subjects from the Old Testament have been shown to occur even in the pre-Constantinian era: Adam and Eve, Noah's Ark, the sacrifice of Abraham, Moses and the miraculous spring, the young men in the fiery furnace and Daniel in the lion's den. New Testament subjects include the baptism of Jesus, the adoration of the Magi, the healing of the man with a palsy, the raising of Lazarus and one or two other miracles of Jesus. It is only from the time of Constantine that New Testament motifs increase in numbers and variety. These pictures have as their theme rescue from misery and the miracles wrought by God, they bring to mind the redemption, the mysteries of the faith and the promise of eternal life. The didactic function of the reliefs and paintings is brought to fullest effect by the style of these earliest works of Christian pictorial art. The artists succeed in imprinting these figures on sarcophagi, disjointed though they may be, with dignity and composure, in impressing their faces with the peace of an interior life; the possessed gaze of the painted figures stares out at devout visitors to the tombs. The world as it lies in wickedness is overcome through knowledge of salvation – such is the message of these pictures, but the experience is shared by all men of this century who have found peace through belief in a divine redemption. In the first half of the third century a certain Aurelius prepared an underground burial chamber outside the city of Rome, on the Via Labicana, whose walls and ceilings he adorned with paintings in lavish abundance. Very delicate in line and colouring, the pictures present figures of the philosopher type, pious assemblies and various scenes of rural life – but Adam and Eve and the Good Shepherd also make their appearance. This was probably the catacomb of a gnostic sect of Roman Christians. One of the larger murals in the vault introduces us into the world of ideas and at the same time the prevailing mood of this community of believers. We see a bearded man, in the setting of a pastoral mountain landscape, pointing to the text of a book-roll, while sheep graze around and below him. All the figures and objects, beasts and trees, are complete in themselves, each is separately anchored in the ground and has its shadow, yet the holy man imparts a marvellous unity to the whole, a unity which the bow framing the scene only serves to emphasize. It may be that the teacher and shepherd is the preacher of the Sermon on the Mount; what is certain is that this simple and graceful scene symbolizes the security found in divine knowledge. A second picture from the underground Rome of this century may bring home how strong was the Christian faculty for appropriating pagan conceptions. The excavations under St Peter's have brought to light an extensive pagan necropolis, whose tombs range in date from the second to the early fourth century and are in part decorated with frescos, mosaics and stucco-work. One of these pagan mausolea, the Julian vault, was converted in the third century into a Christian burial chamber. The interior is richly ornamented with mosaics depicting Jonah, the Good Shepherd and the Fisherman. But on the ceiling of the vault we see Christ as sun-god (plate 53), in the act of ascending the four-horsed chariot, his head encompassed with the radiate crown; green vine-tendrils on a gold background frame this picture of the light-bringer, who also leads the dead into eternal life.

At the time this picture was made, Christianity was still far removed from official recognition. The serious political and economic troubles which disturbed the third century increased men's spiritual unrest and set the various religious groups and forces in opposition to one another. The emperors were absorbed in their external and internal struggles, public architecture was at a stand-still; after Septimius Severus, nearly a century went by without producing a politico-historical relief of any importance. All men's energies were taken up with military constructions, for example the reinforcement of defensive positions and forts on the frontiers and the walling of cities in the interior of the empire. The most imposing achievement of these decades was the circular fortification thrown by Aurelian round the city of Rome. This gigantic brick construction, which boasted fifteen main gates flanked by semi-circular towers, encircled the capital for twelve miles, reached a height of about 25 feet and was provided with rectangular turrets spaced at 100-foot intervals – a fortification many other cities would imitate. Only with the establishment of the tetrarchy did emperors and the artists they patronized feel free to fashion buildings and sculptures which expressed in concrete form the self-assurance of the revived empire. The personal initiative of the rulers, who well-nigh exhausted themselves in dedication to their life's work, is apparent throughout the artistic creation of the age of Diocletian and Constantine. A larger than life marble head unearthed at Nicomedia and with good reason held to be the portrait of Diocletian (plate 5) gives some inkling of the serious disposition of these true fathers of mankind. Deep creases in the forehead and above the mouth, the expression in the eyes, which seem lost in the far distance, confer on this physiognomy, formed in a good Greek tradition, a look of anguished resignation. We have no such fully-moulded and informative portraits of the co-regents, although we know that their exertions in the tasks of war, as of peace, were no less stupendous. The residencies, palaces and villas the tetrarchs created were considered earlier, in the context of the great reforms. Here our concern is to elucidate the importance of one or two of these structures in the history of architecture and to consider certain of their constructional elements and methods of decoration in relation to the productions of Christian art which approach them so closely in time and space.

Rome itself can for the present be ignored, since Diocletian's rebuilt Curia and the vast, palatial baths he erected show little originality when compared with the buildings of his predecessors. It is at Trier, more than anywhere, that the historical significance of the systematic layout followed for the new imperial residencies is made manifest. This city, equipped from now on with its fortifying wall and ceremonial gateway, the Porta Nigra (plate 57), at this period acquired a new centre of life in the imperial residency established in its north-eastern sector. In the ancient world, the norm was for every city to have the forum as its undisputed centre of civic life and public display. In the imperial city of the late period, the complex containing the residence, the basilica and emperor's baths came to form an independent block. At Trier it was not long before the residence was converted into a Christian church. Here, then, we see taking place before our eyes the transition to the town of the Western Middle Ages, in which there were several centres of communal life : the residency and the church in addition to the market. Of the individual buildings in the imperial quarter at Trier, the basilica merits special attention. This is an undivided hall, whose long sides are furnished with a duplicated row of arched windows and which has a semi-circular apse opposed to the main entrance; the simplicity and strength in the construction of walls and ceiling made it a dignified setting for imperial appearances in full audience – an Aula Palatina classical after its fashion. It will become clear that in hall-buildings of this type the structural elements of the Christian congregational basilica are already present. In our forward glance to Christian architecture, one feature of the truly commanding complex of Diocletian's palace at Split which catches our eye is the so-called peristyle, placed along the axis of the whole layout (plate 17). As one contemplates these arches swinging from column to column, one is tempted to speak of an arcaded street leading up to the portals of a shrine; impressed by the concentrated direction of this space contained by rows of arches, the mind moves forward to the central nave of many an early Christian basilica, aligned on apse and altar. But there is also the domed space of Diocletian's mausoleum, in ground plan and elevation an octagon encircled by a colonnaded hall, and this strikes us as an anticipation of the round churches.

Some notion of the decoration of these imperial buildings can be gathered from the ceiling paintings of the palace of Trier, recently restored with such great success. The embellishments of the imperial villa near Piazza Armerina carry us a stage further. In the numerous apartments contained within this extensive complex – which departs in astonishing fashion from the rule of axial symmetry, elsewhere so rigorously observed – the art of pavement mosaic shows a brilliant blossoming. Here we have pictures illustrative of myth and ritual, sporting and hunting scenes, presented not just in the basic black and white predominant in the African estate villas but in a glorious and iridescent variety of colour. Definition of the pictures comes from the colouring, drawing takes second place. Here again one may perhaps be permitted to see the effect of Plotinus' theory that light determines form and colours are a kind of light, making form manifest. This tendency on the part of painting to drive out drawing found its consummation in the church mosaics which glorify Christ as Light.

In the city of Rome no buildings and sculptures exhibiting any stylistic innovations were produced until Diocletian's tetrarchy came to an end. Maxentius during his brief rule achieved great things as master-builder to the eternal city. Here we shall pass by his restoration of the temple of Venus and Roma, his memorial building for his deified son and the grandiose circus on the Appian Way, to halt before the basilica close to the Forum, built by Maxentius and refashioned by Constantine. This hall-building, which in monumentality surpasses all previous constructions, had three naves, the central one roofed with cross-vaulting; in Maxentius' design the entrance was on the east side, with the apse confronting it on the west. Constantine gave a transverse direction to the building, in that he placed the entrance on the south front and created a second apse opposite to it on the north side; what had been the central aisle thus became a transept, but acquired special prestige from the colossal statue of the emperor now placed in the old apse, just as in Roman temples the cult-image was on occasion lodged in a apse-like enlargement to the rear wall. This mighty edifice, flooded with light, its two spatial extensions meeting in a cruciform complex, thus acquires a semi-sacred appearance. This effect must have been further enhanced when the seated statue, by its dimensions and moulding, brought overwhelmingly before the eyes of people assembled in the hall the superhuman majesty of the ruler. In the colossal head which has survived (plate 70) we see not so much the portrait of an individual but rather the visage of sublime imperial majesty, compelling veneration. With this invasion of the sphere of the transcendental, Roman sculpture found its way towards a new assertion of religious faith.

The same insistence on the majesty of the ruler meets us again in the pictorial ornament on the Arch of Constantine. The plan admittedly follows that of the Severan triumphal arch, and several reliefs from the time of Trajan, Hadrian and Marcus Aurelius have been incorporated – an early example of the wholesale lifting or, as some art historians would have it, spoliating of such portions. It must also be mentioned that in subject matter and style the reliefs which display mythological motifs are careful to preserve continuity with the artistic tradition of the triumphal arches, as we see, for example, in the medallions on the narrow faces and in the spandrels of the arches. But in the frieze running across and above the side apertures, which presents a complete narrative of the war down to the concluding scenes in the Roman forum, we find evidence of a conscious departure from the classical style. The emperor, supernaturally large, towers above his soldiers, while in the acts of state in the forum he confronts us full-face from the centre of the scene, a majestic and god-like image. By contrast, the uniform mass of marching soldiers is composed of dumpy equal-sized figures, while the populace hanging on the emperor's words is represented by packed rows of ungainly bodies and plebeian heads (plates 63, 64); the moulding of the bodies is imperfectly realized, the clothing is indicated in summary fashion by schematic lines, the movements are uniformly repetitive. It is obvious that the style of folk-art, thoroughly at home with such portrayals of the humdrum and familiar, has here found a niche for itself in a political monument of the first importance. The style reappears in the reliefs of many contemporary sarcophagi and makes an essential contribution to the transformation overtaking the antique language of form.

We have seen earlier that Constantine, who accomplished in his own person the conversion of the Roman state to Christianity, promoted the building of Christian churches and was their most lavish patron. Christian sanctuaries now became public architectural monuments, whose function was to serve not only as places for congregational worship but also, with complete openness, as emblems of the new religion in the eyes of an empire in process of becoming Christian. It is now necessary to consider the place of these churches in architectural history and the link between profane and sacred buildings. G. von Kaschnitz-Weinberg has rightly drawn attention to the practical problems inevitably created by the demand from now populous congregations for large and speedily erected meeting-places. If the pagan temple had nothing further to offer as a model, there lay at hand a building which had long since established itself for secular purposes, the basilica in all its many modifications. Clearly the Maxentian type of basilica was thought altogether too extravagant; the solution hit upon was to construct the roof out of wood. But the length of the beams imposed such severe limitations on the width of the interior that it was decided to add low side aisles, leaving the central nave, which rose clear above them, to carry the windows. This ingenious solution to a problem of construction almost at once received treatment according to artistic principles. In the Lateran church, on which work started in 313, the long-nave basilica, the congregational church, took the form it would assume throughout the empire: rectangular ground plan, with the apse placed on the short side opposite the entrance; elevation in three, or as with the Lateran, in a central nave flanked by four aisles, with large windows in the central nave; a transverse space interposed between apse and central aisle and containing the altar; an arch, the so-styled triumphal arch, resting on two projecting columns, to separate the congregational area from that of the altar; a bench for the priests in the apse, with the bishop's cathedra in the middle. Whatever may have been the contribution of the basilica in its various manifestations and details of construction, the shaping of this church is wholly dictated by the make-up of the congregation and the demands of the liturgy. The immense elongation of the structure draws the congregation irresistibly towards the altar, at which the sacrifice is offered, and towards the bishop, who proclaims the word of God. The result is a gathering-place pure and simple, externally so ordinary that it has the appearance of a building erected for some practical purpose. All the creative effort of the artists is reserved for the interior. Mosaics soon start to adorn the walls of the central nave, the surfaces of the triumphal arch, the semi-circle of the apse and, on occasion, the pavement as well, as in the oldest church at Aquileia. By such means, the church is made a fit setting for ceremony, the liturgy comes to resemble the forms of imperial ceremonial, the triumphal arch appears to proclaim the victory of Christ. In the east of the empire, where liturgy was most closely connected with the court, galleries are added and even the dome will find a place in the basilica.

From the earliest days of Christian architecture cemetery churches existed alongside those built for congregational use. With the ending of the persecutions the cult of martyrs experienced a marked revival, which resulted in a demand for places of worship built directly above the tombs of these blood-witnesses, in which commemoration of the dead man and prayers for his aid could be combined with celebration of the liturgy. Constantine established an important precedent by building a church over the grave of the apostle Peter at Rome. Even this commemorative church (*memoria*) took the form of a long-nave basilica, and the example so set was followed in other martyr-basilicas, both at Rome and in other cities of the empire, which were built in cemeteries located outside the residential areas. The general rule, almost everywhere observed, was to position the church so that the altar stood directly above the altar-table (*mensa*) of the tomb. A ciborium-like structure resting on four columns and surmounted by a baldachin was often set up above the altar in the church. The commemorative churches built by Constantine and later emperors over the holy places in Palestine for the most part followed the martyr-basilicas in their basic form.

We still have not exhausted the structural ideas which Christian architecture took over from the ancient world. The mother church of each Christian congregation had its baptismal chapel (*baptisterium*), in which the large number of people now turning to the Christian faith could take their baptismal plunge ; this was a small and usually octagonal domed structure surrounding the pool, which was entered by a descending flight of marble steps. The pavement and walls were decorated with mosaics, whose symbolism and imagery related to the sacrament in question. It appears that in all essentials the construction of the baptistery corresponded to that of a Roman domestic bath. What is even more striking, however, is the adoption of older constructional devices for the basilica of the central type, another innovation of the age of Constantine, which was designed primarily as a Christian burial place. Looking at these round sepulchral buildings, one is reminded of the long series of tumulus graves which starts in Etruscan Caere and continues down to the mausolea of Augustus and Hadrian. To the third century, though probably not until the time of Diocletian, belongs the the monumental sepulchre of Tor' de' Schiavi, which stands a few miles from Rome on the Via Praenestina. Here a massive cylinder encloses an undivided space, surmounted by a dome. We have already noted the mausoleum Diocletian built for himself, an octagonal structure surrounded by a colonnaded hall. This is the architectural tradition to which the Christian central basilica belongs. Here the central structure is enlarged, in that it is pierced by an arrangement of columns and encircled by an aisle, a kind of ambulatory; the windows were carried by the upper wall of the central structure. This solution is perfectly realized in the church of Santa Costanza (plate 24). Constantina, the daughter of Constantine, erected a church in commemoration of St Agnes on her estate on the Via Nomentana north of Rome. The area surrounding the memoria became crowded with sepulchral monuments, and of these the mausoleum the foundress of the sanctuary built for herself has survived, to be known to this day under the name Santa Costanza. The central structure is roofed with a dome, the annular ambulatory has a barrel-vault, access to the circular structure is by way of apertures formed by double columns: Santa Costanza marks the inception of an architectural arrangement for a sanctuary area which led later to the creation of San Vitale. The vaulting of Santa Costanza is decorated with magnificent mosaics, in which the motifs found in sepulchral paintings recur, including some of pagan ancestry: tendrils, emblems of the seasons, vintage scenes in the annular hall, pictures from the Old and New Testaments on the faces of the dome.

The assimilation by Christian art of its antique heritage is further evident from the sepulchral relief and statuary produced during the fourth century. It is true that thematically speaking the subject matter of the new religion becomes all-pervasive, leaving very little space for traditional motifs of neutral connotation. But in the language of form the two sides converge. The figures of profane sculpture are no longer subject to the rigid physical laws which for so long held sway, but instead, as will appear from reference to specific examples, strive for an expression of transcendental spirituality, thus making contact with the image of man presented by Christian sculpture and painting. Conversely, among the rich material presented by the Christian sarcophagi, we find not only an inclination to replace plastic materialization of the figure by a flat picture verging on the ornamental, but also classicism coming again and again to the surface. This antiquizing trend is seen at its most impressive in the sarcophagus of Junius Bassus, who according to his epigraph died at the age of forty-two as city prefect of Rome, in the year when Eusebius and Hypatius were consuls, that is on 25 August 359 (plate 43). The side designed for show presents two tiers of reliefs arranged one above the other, each tier comprising five pictures of episodes from biblical history. The individual scenes contain only two or three figures and are framed by columns, which means that the pictures deliver their message with unaccustomed succinctness. In the upper row we have the sacrifice of Abraham, St Peter being taken to prison, Christ throned in heaven delivering the Law, the arrest of Jesus and his hearing before Pilate; the lower sequence brings us Job in his afflictions, Adam and Eve, the entry of Jesus into Jerusalem, Daniel in the lions' den and St Paul on his way to martyrdom. The thematic scheme is unambiguously Christian, leading from the fall of the primeval pair through the sacrifice and suffering of Old Testament exemplars to the Passion journeys of Jesus and his apostles, and culminates in the magisterial act of the delivery of the Law (shown in the centre of the upper tier) in which the figure of Christ in glory is presented completely full-face. Nevertheless, this didactic affirmation of the faith is executed in a style which does not ignore classical precedents. The figures moulded in the round are liberated from their background and care has been bestowed on the full realization of the heads, which are differentiated to fit their subjects. Jesus is invested with the magic of youth, even the old men are handsome, all the figures are engaged heart and soul in what is happening, yet the movements are tranquil, emotions are contained, the Passion stops short with Pilate, and death is only hinted at from afar. F. Gerke has described this as the '"beautiful style" of Christian antiquity'. This category covers a whole series of Christian works of art; indeed, one can say that in the sculpture of the fourth century the portrait of Christ is transformed into the figure of the youthful teacher and wonder-worker. The statuette of Christ in Majesty in the Terme Museum at Rome comes close to the type of the young Apollo (plate 52). Towards the end of the century representations of the Master transmitting the new Law to St Peter and of Christ enthroned among the apostles also become favourite themes of sarcophagal sculpture. The ivory casket from Brescia (plate 48), intended probably as a receptacle for relics, must certainly belong to this same movement, which aimed to present the ideal values of the Christian religion in the classical language of form. All four sides and the lid are covered with numerous pictures from the Old and New Testaments, in which the scenes are clearly articulated and the figures carefully modelled, while the rim of the lid has medallions showing heads of Christ, the apostles and the evangelists – a composition reminiscent of the antique practice of arranging portraits on a shield-shaped surface (*imago clipeata*). Here again the teacher is presented as a youthful philosopher. But at the end of these transformations of the Christ-figure there stands the regal lord, the stern commander, the pantocrator, whose presentation in his majesty – Maiestas Domini – becomes the great theme of mosaics placed in the apses of churches (plate 54).

With the advent in the time of Constantine of buildings designed for use as Christian churches, the output of state architecture and of imperial triumphal art appreciably diminished. During the last century of the west Roman empire no new thermae or triumphal arches were built; little trace remains of such new palaces as came into being. But the many works of plastic art surviving from the time of the Theodosian dynasty tell of the continuous change in the language of form. An exact date can be assigned to the reliefs on the obelisk of Theodosius at Constantinople. In 390 the emperor ordered an Egyptian obelisk to be set up on two enormous plinths in the middle of the Hippodrome, and further arranged for this technical feat, much marvelled at by contemporaries, to be recorded in a picture and inscription on the lower of the two bases. The reliefs on the upper plinth show sundry groups of people participating in some festivity – perhaps connected with the event being commemorated. On the east side the emperor, holding the victor's crown in readiness, is seen standing in the imperial box between his sons and chief ministers, flanked on either side by officials, behind them the bodyguard; the size of the figures is clearly determined by the rank of the individual portrayed. In the strip below we see monotonous rows of spectators and in front of them the small figures of female musicians and dancers. There is an almost total absence of perspective, the spectators' heads and bodies are nearly all presented frontally and entirely without movement, so that the hieratic style of the frieze from the arch of Constantine is here continued. The relief gives no sense of recording a unique event but rather of affording a momentary glimpse of eternal validity.

This same tendency, by which autonomous personality, that supreme subject of classical art, is replaced by a symbolical figure pointing towards the numinous and invisible, can also be observed in statuary. Statues have become a rarity. Whereas in the preceding period architecture still made considerable use of statuary to fill niches, now almost the only statues are those in honour of emperors and ministers; in religious life sculpture has given way to other arts. Such statues as were made – judging from the finds they were still more common in the east of the empire than in the west – no longer aspired to mirror personal appearance but rather to symbolize dignities and virtues. The standing statue of a bearded philosopher draped in a mantle, which is now in the Louvre, has been taken, probably with justice, to be that of the emperor Julian (plate 68); comparison of the portrait head with the portrait of Julian on coins and gems favours the identification, which has further circumstantial support from the substitution of the priestly fillet for the imperial diadem. The artist may well have had the portrait statue of classical art in mind, but the image he presents, through the suspended movement, the ornamentally patterned folds of the gown and the wearily reflective expression on the face, is that of a dignitary confronted by a changed world. The togate statue of a Roman consul in the Conservatori Palace at Rome, from about the year 400, speaks more clearly still (plate 67). The fact that such statues continued to be made must be ascribed to the sense of tradition among senatorial society, which was concerned to see that investiture with one of the ancient magistracies should still be commemorated by a statue, just as in the past. This Roman consul, whose toga is arranged most artistically over two tunics, holds high in his right hand the *mappa*, the flag with which to signal the start of the chariot races at an important moment in his year of office. The head shows us a handsome countenance with expressive eyes, but the body is engulfed in the ceremoniously draped masses of the folds and the movement lacks force; the figure seems swallowed up in ceremony. But even in this new formal language, it was still possible for plastic portraiture to make profound statements and it is in this respect that the art which will find its consummation in Byzantium can be recognized as most creative. A late marble head from Ephesus is an impressive revelation of the new spirituality (plate 33). The very narrow head shows pronounced elongation and is almost rectangular in form; this sacrifice of organic structure serves to emphasize the expression. The furrowed forehead, the huge eyes beneath high-arching brows, the extreme intensity of the gaze seems to presage the transcendental world. This physiognomy unmasks in disconcerting fashion the metamorphosis of ancient man into a prophet of God. The huge bronze statue from Barletta (plate 69) in all probability dates from the preceding century. The jewelled diadem betokens an emperor. Clad in tunic, coat of mail and cloak, he holds in his raised right arm the sceptre or labarum, in his left outstretched hand the orb, the insignia of imperial power. Every trace of beauty has been banished from the facial features, the stern gaze appears to pass into eternity, the countenance, indeed the whole figure, has become a symbol. This statue of an emperor, which has been claimed as the last achievement of Roman sculpture, is at the same time one of the great creations of the new age, in which sculpture adopts the language of symbolism.

There are other areas of artistic activity in which classical traditions held their own somewhat longer still. In prominent social circles men retained their passion for small objets d'art worked in costly material, and the draftsmen, carvers, engravers and goldsmiths who received such costly commissions have lost nothing of their craftsmen's skill. Many a feature of the fine style has been preserved in silver tableware and gold ornament, carved gems and gilded glass, ivory tablets and book-covers, those handsome witnesses to taste and luxury. The evident debt to classicism shown in the silver vessel unearthed at Augst (plate 87) can perhaps be traced back to the emperor Julian, to whose entourage this costly treasure may have belonged. But the silver platter (*Missorium*) of the emperor Theodosius, from the year 388, can also be accounted a work of exquisite beauty (plate 88). This salver formed part of a service for special occasions, and was in all likelihood a present from the emperor to the minister seen in the picture. The scene is the throne-room, shown as a gable-crowned miniature temple; the emperor, his head adorned with the pearl diadem and encircled by the nimbus, is seated on his throne and extends to the minister, who approaches him with awe, a small tablet which is the record of his appointment; the co-rulers are enthroned on either side of the emperor, on the margins stand long-locked body-guards, in the lower segment of the salver lies Tellus with the horn of plenty and erotes playing around. In elegance this composition takes it sustenance from the splendid exemplars of the past age, yet the scenes as depicted here have become purely representative images, in keeping with the spirit of this late period, and are made so by the frontality of the figures and the formality of their bearing and expression. The same applies to the imperial couple shown on a cameo now in Paris (plate 71). The pearl diadem of the emperor exhibits the Christian monogram on the central stone, the hair-style of the empress is of the Theodosian period; the figures are probably to be identified as Honorius and Maria, the daughter of Stilicho. The courtly mannerism of the style is strikingly at odds with the melancholy expression of the personages, entirely withdrawn into themselves. In the fourth century, gilded glass figured with portraits (plate 72), and later with biblical scenes, is not uncommon. The gilded glass from Brescia, a piece of quite outstanding quality, also belongs properly to this series of noble ornamental pieces, even though it might be considerably earlier in date. Here the busts of a mother with her son and daughter have been traced with a fine gouging tool on the gilded glass and transparent glass subsequently affixed over the picture. The subjects are arrayed in ceremonial raiment, their faces, rendered like portraits, face the spectator with wide-open eyes, in their solemnity and intensity they resemble images of saints. It is not surprising that this gilded glass was later set into a cross ornamented with gems and polished stones. But there is no indication whatsoever that we have here to do with Christians and no explanation has yet been found for the inscription superimposed in Greek characters.

The fourth and fifth centuries are especially rich in ivory work. Ivory was used in the manufacture of tablets and boxes, for the decoration of furniture and for honorific documents; workshops are known to have existed in most of the residencies down to the end of the sixth century, when this costly material becomes scarce. A large number of ivory diptychs has survived. From time immemorial, diptych was the name given to a writing tablet formed from two wooden boards joined by a hinge or a cord. The two surfaces of the tablet were covered with wax on which the writing could be scratched and afterwards erased. As a practical device for school-teaching, the diptych held its own even in the centuries when for other purposes men preferred to use writing material made from papyrus. But even in the late period, this form of writing and executing a record was adhered to for honorific documents. Eventually it became customary for high officials, on the day they assumed office or on some other important occasion, to send diptychs with artistic ornamental ivory covers to their friends. Claudian the poet and Symmachus the senator both mention this practice in their writings. Among the host of these ivory diptychs, whose sequence furnishes a precise guide to the development of style, the attention of the historian is held above all by the diptych which mentions the families of the Nicomachi and Symmachi at the upper margin of the two tablets (plate 83). On the tablet constituting the back we see the priestess of Ceres standing with lowered torches close to the altar, behind which a stone-pine rears up; the tablet on the front, which is thus the main picture, shows the priestess of Bacchus adorned with an ivy crown strewing incense on the altar, while a small serving-maiden extends to her a two-handled vessel and a basin of fruit. These figures of classical beauty, based perhaps on Augustan models, fulfilling the prescribed rituals of the ancient gods, are wonderful testimony indeed to that cherishing of the ancestral faith by these two allied families which we have already traced down to the time of the emperors Gratian and Theodosius. Certain features of this stylistic tradition are also retained in the so-called diptych of Eucherius. On the front of the diptych stands a man garbed in a general's cloak, with a ceremonial sword; his right hand holds a spear, his left rests on a circular shield decorated with the busts of two emperors. The back shows a woman, beautifully dressed and bedecked, with a rose in her right hand, and close to her a boy clad in tunic and cloak, who holds a diptych in his left hand. The subjects have been identified, with reason, as Stilicho, Serena and their son Eucherius; however this may be, the ivory is an elegant specimen of courtly art from the Theodosian period.

Works of art just as fine in craftsmanship and in their feeling for precious materials next start to appear among the possessions of churches: reliquaries of ivory and processional crosses ornamented with precious stones find their way into cathedral treasure-houses. There are also instances of sacred books furnished with handsome covers. Although it is true that to begin with Christians, too, used papyrus rolls for their books, it was not long before the scriptures were being written down in volumes put together from leaves of parchment and were in this way in advance of secular literature, which until the fourth century was still largely entrusted to rolls. This new form of book, the *codex*, also gave scope for new forms of illustration. While the roll format imposed illustration in the form of continuous narrative, the codex allowed the single picture to predominate. Thus from the sixth century onward there exists a series of codices with Christian texts, decorated with miniatures. The so-called Vienna Genesis, the earliest illuminated Bible, can be mentioned here as an example of this art of miniature which sprang from the late antique language of form.

The full-scale art of the fifth century is intimately bound up with the Christian religion, at least in the western part of the ancient world which occupies the forefront of our attention. The city of Rome, deserted by the emperors, under the leadership of its bishops surmounted the serious crises of the invasion period and at the epoch in which we have already observed the formation of the Roman primacy also received several new churches. Here we shall consider only those with the greatest artistic significance. First in time is San Paolo, built on the road to Ostia, on the site of an earlier church from the reign of Theodosius; the rebuilding of the church in the nineteenth century retained the five-aisled ground plan with its transverse space, while totally altering the decoration. The next to be built, around the year 430, was Santa Sabina on the Aventine, a three-aisled basilica whose unaltered external and internal structure are the purest embodiment of the ground plan of the early Christian church (plate 19); the sumptuous doors, with their cypress panels carved in varying style with biblical scenes, have also survived. Equally remarkable, both artistically and historically, is the basilica of Santa Maria Maggiore, erected immediately after the Council of Ephesus (431) as the first church in Rome in honour of the Virgin Mary; a considerable portion of the mosaic work, set as inlaid fields into the walls of the long nave, and the mosaics on the triumphal arch, have survived unscathed to bear witness to the stupendous unfolding of Christian pictorial art.

Following on from the beginnings at Santa Costanza, with the embellishment of the walls, arch and apse of a basilica a monumental style of mosaic painting now becomes established which proclaims both the sublimity of the faith and the sense of triumph pervading the Christian communities. Cyclical narratives from the Old and New Testaments run along the walls, themes stressing the Lord's victory and majesty are chosen for the arch and apse. The primary task of this pictorial ornament was to provide a constant and living reminder of the sacred events celebrated in the liturgy and to make them accessible to all believers. Paulinus, who at the beginning of the century, when he was bishop of Nola, had his basilica to St Felix decorated with biblical scenes, describes the rapture among the pilgrims who flocked thither from the countryside and marvelled at these pictures.[2] The picture was a language which all could understand, even the unlettered, and it was thus required to instruct men in the substance of the faith; even Gregory of Nazianzus, great orator that he was, admits that the painter is the best teacher. In addition there was the purely artistic motive of adding lustre to the courts of God through the scintillating radiance shed by the mosaics; this is the argument which was used against the iconoclast movements of later periods and which has its biblical foundation in the words of the Psalmist 'Lord, I have loved the habitation of thy house, and the place where thy honour dwelleth'.[3] In Santa Maria Maggiore the mosaics of the nave, which have survived unchanged, are entirely devoted to scenes from the Old Testament. In the composition of the pictures and the intensity of their colouring they adhere closely – probably still stemming from the fourth century – to antique painting. The thematic scheme of the mosaics on the triumphal arch is related to an important decision on dogma reached by the council of Ephesus, which answered the question, arising from the Christological debate, concerning the nature and precedence of the Virgin Mary by declaring that the mother of the Lord deserved to be acknowledged and venerated as the Mother of God. The mosaics depict scenes from the life of Mary, occasionally including episodes reported in apocryphal gospels; she is shown vested in the raiment and ornament due to a princess, the head of the child Jesus is bathed in the glow of light from which the Cross rises up – a reference to the one divine person revealed in him. As regards the language of form, in the statuesque firmness of the personages, the rigidity of their clothing and the frontality of most of the figures, these pictures reflect the sculptural style of the century. The doors to Santa Sabina, rich in biblical themes, include one scene that is new and astonishes: Jesus, his arms spread sideways, stands between two small men, placed like him flush with the wall; the nail-pierced hands and narrow loin-cloths reveal this as an early representation of the crucifixion (plate 55). The restraint of this death is in keeping with early Christian sensibility. The figures look very like men praying.

After Rome, Ravenna became the favourite setting for Christian art and architecture and by the turn of the fifth century indeed occupied first place. Raised by Honorius to be the capital city, it still continued to house the government of Roman Italy even after the ending of the western empire in the time of Odoacer and Theoderic, and in its whole lay-out took the form of a uniquely Christian residency. Ravenna was the final refuge in which the traditions of ancient art were still able to exert an influence. Although nothing has survived of the palaces of Honorius and Galla Placidia, nor indeed of the palace of Theoderic himself, the most beautiful of the numerous churches built during this period are still standing. If we look at the series comprising the most significant of these foundations, the first in order of time is the cathedral, built by Bishop Ursus after the court was transferred to Ravenna; in the eighteenth century it was replaced by a new structure, but the baptismal church of the cathedral – the so-called Baptistery of the Orthodox – remains, replendent in the beauty of its decoration, for which Neon, bishop in mid-century, was responsible. Then follow the buildings put up by the empress Galla Placidia, which fall probably in the years 416–34: the church of The Holy Cross, later remodelled, its dependent oratory of St Laurence, known as the mausoleum of Galla Placidia (plate 26) and finally the basilica of St John the Evangelist, which was destroyed in the second world war and has now been rebuilt. Around the middle of the century a church dedicated to the apostles was erected in the place where San Francesco, a complete rebuilding, now stands. To the time of Theoderic belongs the building of the church dedicated to the name of Jesus, from the ninth century known as Sant' Apollinare Nuovo, the Arian baptistery and probably also the oratory incorporated in the existing bishop's palace. The tale is completed by churches only finished and dedicated under Byzantine rule, Sant' Apollinare in Classe and San Vitale. This last-named sanctuary deviates in form from the preceding basilicas in having an octagonal ground plan and an elevation in two stages, a broad substructure and rising from it a superstructure crowned with a dome – an edifice whose peculiarity of construction betrays Byzantine influence and which was to be the model for the palace chapel of Charlemagne at Aachen.

Let us concentrate on a few buildings from the great century of Ravenna and so acquaint ourselves with this last phase in the metamorphosis of ancient art. In their layout and construction the basilicas and baptisteries follow the lead given by architecture of the imperial period. These brick buildings, whose outer surfaces are occasionally enlivened by blank arcades, renounce all attempt at external embellishment (plate 25). The impact of the interior is thus all the more intense, for here the structure and decoration work together to create a sanctuary such as the ancient world had never known. Marble incrustations and mosaics dissolve the walls, banish all restrictiveness by the splendour of their colour and transport the worshippers, as they scan these pictures, into a heavenly world. Here the art of mosaic has attained its zenith.

The technical process alone demanded a maximum of concentration and precision: the wall was first painted over, and afterwards the host of tiny, even minute, lozenges had to be fastened into place – it has been shown that about a thousand of these little stones were used for a single head in a major sixth century composition. These lustrous fields of mosaic are composed chiefly of myriads of tiny gold and enamel chips, which evoke an atmosphere of mystery and magic.

The intensification of the architecture by this means is seen at its most incomparable in the little church known as the mausoleum of Galla Placidia. The empress was very probably buried at Rome; it is only a later tradition which declares she found her last resting place in this oratory, dependent on the church of the Holy Cross and therefore given the ground plan of a Latin cross. This simple edifice is the most perfect example of a building in which the entire artistic effect is reserved for the interior. Within, the walls are adorned with marble incrustations, the vaults gleam in the brilliance of mosaic. Above the entrance is a graceful picture of the Good Shepherd, which in its landscape composition and portrayal of the shepherd-figure is in the tradition of the 'beautiful style'. In the lunette facing the entrance we have St Laurence, shouldering the cross as he advances, certain of victory, towards the red-hot gridiron (plate 81). A heaven of golden stars on a blue ground shines down from the cross-vaulting at the intersection, with the golden cross floating in the centre. The cross is the saving power which governs earth and heaven – such is the message of this holy place. In the interior of the Baptistery of the Orthodox, the dissolution of the walls by means of decoration is achieved in greater measure (plate 23). The lower sphere of the octagonal chamber is decorated with marble inlays and mosaics, next comes the window area, enlivened by rich stucco oranaments, then the band leading onto the dome in a continuous mosaic frieze, in which thrones of glory, a cross floating above, alternate with altars bearing the books of the gospels. The dome itself is partitioned by candelabra, which thrust out from acanthus tendrils, into twelve fields in which the enormous shapes of the apostles are seen in motion. At the vertex is depicted the scene which gives the house, liturgically and in artistic construction, its meaning and dedication: the baptism of Christ. In this lightly floating dome Christian architecture surpasses many of its antique models. The tall figures of the apostles with their narrow heads are contemporaries and spiritual kinsmen of the prophet of Ephesus (plate 33), whose head we have already attempted to interpret.

Sant' Apollinare Nuovo was the court church built by Theoderic, as a three-aisled basilica, close to his palace. In the lower bands of the mosaics on the walls of the centre nave we see processions of saintly men and women, bearing their martyrs' crowns, advancing towards the altar; the essential movement of the figures, which are turned to face the spectator, is defined by the positive and unitary direction of the arms. The procession of women is shown departing from the harbour town of Classis and ending beside the picture of the Mother of God, the procession of men starts by the king's palace and leads to Christ enthroned. Although the processional figures probably date only from the sixth century, the pictures of the port and palace belong to the time of Theoderic. The draftsman-like treatment of the palace shows affinity with techniques which established themselves in Byzantine art. In the middle of the composition we have the gatehouse – divided into three portals – which gave entry to the palace complex (plate 22). It is to be imagined that this magnificent and temple-like gatehouse – we are reminded of the vestibule to Diocletian's palace – was preceded by the rectangular courtyard whose seriated arcades are set flush with the gate structure: a colonnaded promenade, therefore, similar to the peristyle at Split.

We conclude our journey through Ravenna, that monumental museum of Christian antiquity, before the sepulchre the great king built for himself and his family outside the city walls (plate 27). Even this weighty edifice is no germanic foundling on Italian soil. It consists of a decagonal ground-floor and an upper storey which passes from the decagonal to the circular and is covered by a dome. The lower storey is articulated by round-headed arches, through one of which a rectangular doorway leads into the interior, a cruciform chamber which probably served as the burial place. The upper storey, which is surrounded by a gallery, can also be reached through a similar doorway, which has facing it an altar niche with a cross on the front of the arch; this space was probably the chapel used to celebrate the liturgy of the dead. The building terminates in a gigantic limestone monolith, about thirty-two feet in diameter, nearly one hundred feet in circumference and about three feet thick, which must weigh three hundred tons. In its construction the mausoleum follows the Roman pattern for such buildings; admittedly, the fact that it is built not of brick but of hewn stone marks a departure from this tradition. Ostrogothic influence is evident in the hammer ornament on the cornice which runs below the dome, and in a few technical details of the masonry, which can best be interpreted as derived from working in wood. Though the monolithic stone covering may strike us as primitive, the twelve corbels of the dome bring us back to the Christian world. For they bear the names of the apostles, apparent indication that Theoderic, like Constantine the Great, prepared for himself a tomb in the midst of memorial stones to the twelve apostles.

As we survey these beginnings of Christian art, we may agree with the assessment of its historical position made with deep understanding by F. van der Meer: Christian architecture and painting had throughout an attachment to the antique tradition, yet accomplished a decisive withdrawal from the corporeal solidity of classical art. No room is found in the place of worship for the plastic figure, decoration strives after optical effects, a sublimated art seeks to lead men into that sacred world which has become the great theme of all that is said and given shape. The mission of the Christian artist is to make accessible the truths of the new religion and the secrets of the liturgy. The artist, like the evangelist, addresses himself to all, to give living shape to the pure humanity which came into being with the manifestation of the Logos through portraying the dramatic events of sacred history. How novel was the language spoken by these places of worship, relieved of all heaviness, which became the gathering-place for the initiated! Novel, too, was the language of the pictures in the basilicas, which in the mosaics on the walls brought before men's eyes, in solemn narratives, in deeds and encounters which took many forms, the suffering of questing man and the peace of the devout who find their rest in God, while in the apse the image of Christ in Majesty proclaimed the law of life for the world redeemed. The saints address themselves with ceremony to the assembled people, their beautifully apparelled bodies an outer casing for the purity of their souls. Their faces belong to real men who have dwelt among us, the artists endow even patriarchs and prophets, martyrs and hermits with portrait-like features, still more the bishops and patrons who soon come to join them and through association with the disciples called by the Master appear as their successors. In the perfected mosaic technique, the look in the eyes, whose speaking quality owes much to the Egyptian mummy portrait, is expressive of the utmost inwardness. In his experience of the soul's salvation, the Christian of this age possesses the equanimity, the confidence, the harmony which, overriding all boundaries, links him with the antique ideal. If we think of later Christian art, it remains significant that the pictorial art of the basilicas shows neither horror nor passion but an action performed under the power of hope, a suffering in the certainty of salvation. The Lord's Passion is concluded long before the final act, the martyrs point with cross and palm to victory over death, and if for once the Crucified is brought before us, his countenance betrays no torment. Contemplation and noble moderation have become Christian virtues, the human image of Christian antiquity is characterized by a new sophrosyne.

The extent to which this disposition, coupled with humility, governed men's hearts and lives in the new era may be gathered from the epilogue which Prudentius appended to his poetic labours. Let a rendering of these lines serve as a conclusion to our disquisition:

To God the Father offers up
He who is pious, true, guiltless and pure
Gifts of conscience
Richly stored in the recesses of a blessed soul.
Another robs his wealth
To give the poor sustenance in their need.
Fleet iambics,
Swift-running trochees are all I bring,
Sanctity fails me,
Riches have I none for poverty's relief.
But God accepts
The lowly song and lends a gracious ear.
Many furnishings forsooth
In every corner of a rich man's house are found:
Gold gleams the cup,
Stands there the fine-wrought vessel bronze,
And pot of clay
And silver salver ponderous and broad,
Beside the ivories
Stand pieces hewn from wood, from oak and elm.
Each vessel has its use,
To answer for the master's daily needs.
They serve the house,
The costly and the wooden vessels both.
In his Father's house,
For me, an outworn vessel, Christ contrives
Some transitory use
And gives me leave to keep my corner place.
Service as earthenware
Is all our hope in salvation's royal court.
Low though it be,
Office performed for God means health for us.
Whatever comes therefrom,
My happiness remains, that I might sing the praise of Christ.

REFERENCES

CHAPTER I: THE CRISIS OF THE ANCIENT WORLD IN THE THIRD CENTURY

1. Cassius Dio, 76, 15, 2
2. Rutilius Namatianus, 1, 63ff.
3. *Sylloge Inscriptionum Graecarum*, 3rd ed., 888
4. Ps. Aristides, 'Panegyric to thc ruler', 21
5. Horace, *Carmina*, 3, 6, 5
6. Cassius Dio, 52, 36, 1 ff.
7. Apuleius, *Metamorphoses*, 11, 23
8. *Corpus Hermeticum*, V, 10 (A. D. Nock – A. J. Festugière, I, 64)
9. Tertullian, *Apologeticum*, 50, 13
10. Clement of Alexandria, *Stromata*, 4, 135 f.
11. *Mosaicarum et Romanorum legum collatio*, 153, 1 ff.
12. Tacitus, *Historiae*, 4, 64
13. Tertullian, *Apologeticum*, 37, 6 f.
14. Dessau, *Inscriptiones Latinae selectae*, 629
15. Lactantius, *De mortibus persecutorum*, 7, 3
16. Dessau, *op. cit.*, 642
17. *Panegyrici Latini*, 11, 18
18. Arnobius, *Adversus nationes*, 2, 5
19. Lactantius, *De mortibus persecutorum*, 34

CHAPTER 2: THE MONARCHY, THE CHRISTIAN CHURCH AND RULING SOCIETY IN THE FOURTH CENTURY

1. Lactantius, *De mortibus persecutorum*, 48, 2
2. Optatus, *De schismate Donatistarum*, Appendix VII
3. Eusebius, *Vita Constantini*, 2, 60
4. *Codex Theodosianus*, 2, 25, 1
5. Athanasius, *Historia Arianorum*, 44
6. *Corpus Scriptorum Ecclesiasticorum Latinorum*, Vol. lxv, p. 182
7. Macrobius, *Saturnalia*, 3. 14, 2
8. Ammianus Marcellinus, 19, 8, 5 ff.
9. *Anthologia Graeca*, IX, 418
10. *Codex Theodosianus*, 16, 1, 2
11. Symmachus, *Relatio*, 3

12. Ambrose, *Epistulae*, 18
13. *Romans*, xiii, 13 f.
14. Ausonius, *Epistulae*, 28
15. *Ibid.*, 29
16. Paulinus, *Carmina*, 10
17. Ausonius, *Epistulae*, 27
18. Paulinus, *Carmina*, 11

CHAPTER 3: THE ROMAN WEST AND THE NEW PEOPLES IN THE FIFTH CENTURY

1. *Codex Theodosianus*, 3, 14, 1
2. Zosimus, 5, 43 ff.
3. Claudianus, *Bellum Gildonicum*, 1, 188 ff.
4. *Ibid.*, 1, 44 ff.
5. Prudentius, *Contra Symmachum*, 2, 655 ff.
6. Jerome, *Epistulae*, 22, 30
7. *Ibid.*, 123, 16
8. Orosius, *Historia adversus paganos*, 5, 2, 5 f.
9. *Ibid.*, 7, 43, 4 ff.
10. *Ibid.*, 7, 41, 8
11. Anonymus, *De vocatione omnium gentium*, 2, 33
12. Victor Vitensis, *Historia persecutionis Africanae provinciae*, 3, 62
13. Sidonius Apollinaris, *Epistulae*, 4, 8
14. Salvian, *De gubernatione Dei*, 7, 11, 49
15. Sidonius Apollinaris, *Epistulae*, 1, 2
16. *Ibid.*, 7, 14, 10
17. *Ibid.*, 8, 2, 2
18. Sidonius Apollinaris, *Carmina*, 24, 59 ff.
19. Prosper Tiro, *De ingratis*, 39 ff.
20. Leo, *Sermones*, 82
21. Cassiodorus, *Variae*, 5, 37
22. *Ibid.*, 9, 25
23. Avitus, *Epistulae*, 46

CHAPTER 4: CULTURAL CHANGE REFLECTED IN ART

1. Plotinus, *Enneads*, 2, 8, 1
2. Paulinus, *Carmina*, 27
3. *Psalms* xxvi, 8

CHRONOLOGICAL TABLE

193–211	Septimius Severus emperor
c. 197	Tertullian's *Apologeticum*
c. 200	Clement teaching in Alexandria
203	Triumphal arch of Septimius Severus at Rome
205–212	Papinian the jurist praetorian prefect
c. 205	Philostratus' *Life of Apollonius*
212	*Constitutio Antoniniana*
213	Campaign against the Alamanni
	Baths of Caracalla at Rome
217–222	Callixtus bishop of Rome
218–222	Elagabalus emperor
222–235	Alexander Severus emperor
222–229	Ulpian the jurist praetorian prefect
226	Ardashir founds the new Persian empire
229	Cassius Dio's *History of Rome*
231	Origen moves from Alexandria to Caesarea (Palestine)
c. 232	Christian 'house-church' at Dura-Europus
235–238	Maximinus emperor
c. 240	Mani preaches his gospel; spread of Manichaeism
244	Plotinus comes to Rome; neo-platonist school
244–249	Philip the Arabian emperor
248	Millenial celebrations at Rome
	Gothic foray into the Balkans
249–251	Decius emperor
	Christians persecuted
253–260	Valerian emperor with his son Gallienus
257–260	Christians persecuted
258	Cyprian, bishop of Carthage, martyred
259	Postumus emperor in Gaul, Spain and Britain
260	Valerian captured by the Persians
260–268	Gallienus emperor
c. 260	Alamanni advance towards northern Italy; evacuation of the Decumate
263	Odaenathus *corrector Orientis*
c. 268	Porphyry writing against the Christians

269	Claudius defeats the Goths at Naissus
270–275	Aurelian emperor
c. 271	Start made on the walled fortification of Rome
	Dacia abandoned to the Goths
273	Destruction of Palmyra
	End of the Gallic 'empire'
274	Sol invictus made the official deity of the empire
283–285	Revolt of the Bagaudae
284–305	Diocletian emperor
286	Maximian co-ruler
293	Galerius and Constantius become Caesars; tetrarchy set on formal basis
296	*Capitatio* introduced
297	Edict against Manichaeans
298–306	Baths of Diocletian at Rome
	Residencies at Trier and Thessalonica
	Palace at Split
301	Edict on maximum prices
c. 302	Eusebius writing his *Chronicle* and *Ecclesiastical History*
303	Beginning of the great persecution
304–313	Lactantius' *Divinae Institutiones*
305	Abdication of Diocletian
306	Constantine and Maxentius declare themselves Augusti
308	Imperial congress at Carnuntum
	Basilica of Maxentius at Rome
311	Galerius' toleration edict
	Donatist schism
c. 311	Anthony becomes a hermit
312	Constantine victorious at the Milvian Bridge
313	New religious policy initiated at Milan
	Start on building of Lateran church
314	Synod of Arles
315	Arch of Constantine at Rome
c. 316	Lactantius summoned to Trier
318	Arius condemned by Alexandrian synod; start of Arian controversy
c. 320	Pachomius founds the first monastery
321	Sunday made an official holiday
324	Constantine defeats Licinius at Chrysopolis
324–337	Constantine sole ruler
	Further church building in East and West
328–373	Athanasius bishop of Alexandria
330	Dedication of Constantinople
335	Athanasius banished to Trier
	Church of Holy Sepulchre consecrated at Jerusalem
337	Death of Constantine; accession of his three sons
339	Death of Eusebius of Caesarea

c. 340	Church of Santa Costanza at Rome
341	Pagan sacrifices prohibited
c. 341	Ulfilas consecrated bishop among the Goths
343	Council of Sardica
from 345	Themistius teaching at Constantinople
350–361	Constantius II sole ruler
from 354	Libanius teaching at Antioch
355	Council of Milan
357	Julian defeats the Alamanni at Strasbourg
359	Hilary's polemic against Constantius
	Sarcophagus of Junius Bassus
361–363	Julian emperor; measures against the Christians
364–375	Valentinian I and Valens emperors
365	Ausonius becomes Gratian's tutor
366–384	Damasus I Pope
367	Valentinian in Trier; Alamannic wars
370–379	Basil bishop of Caesarea (Cappadocia)
	Monastic rules
c. 370	Monasticism in the West
374–397	Ambrose bishop of Milan
375–378	Valens and Gratian emperors
376	Visigoths cross the Danube
378	Visigoths victorious at Adrianople; death of Valens in the battle
379–383	Gratian and Theodosius I emperors
380	Edict of Thessalonica: Catholicism the state religion
381	Council of Constantinople: Arians condemned
382	Visigoths settled in the empire
382–385	Jerome at Rome
383–392	Theodosius I and Valentinian II emperors
384	*Relatio* of Symmachus, city prefect of Rome
386–419	Jerome living at Bethlehem
c. 386	Macrobius' *Saturnalia*
387	Augustine baptized at Milan
388	Aurelius Victor city prefect
	Ammianus Marcellinus writes his *History*
390	Theodosius does penance in church
	Obelisk erected at Constantinople
391	Pagan rites prohibited
	Destruction of the temple of Sarapis at Alexandria
c. 392	Ausonius and Paulinus in correspondence
392–395	Theodosius sole ruler
398–408	Stilicho generalissimo
394	Defeat of the rival emperor Eugenius
395	Death of Theodosius; division of the empire
395–423	Honorius emperor in the West
395–408	Arcadius emperor in the East

395–430	Augustine bishop of Hippo
400	Synesius delivers his oration on the imperial office
401	Alaric, king of the Visigoths, invades Italy
402	Ravenna becomes the capital of the West
	Claudian court poet
	Prudentius in Rome
406	Vandals, Alans and Sueves cross the Rhine
408–450	Theodosius II emperor in the East
409	Vandals in Spain
409–431	Paulinus bishop of Nola
410	Alaric sacks Rome
413–426	Augustine's *De civitate Dei*
413	Burgundians settled near Worms
416	Galla Placidia comes to Ravenna
	Rutilius Namatianus returns to Gaul
418	Visigoths settled in Aquitaine
	Pelagius condemned by the synod of Carthage
	Orosius' *Historia adversus paganos*
424–455	Valentinian III emperor in the West
	Church building at Rome and Ravenna
428–477	Gaiseric king of the Vandals
429	Vandals cross to Africa
430	Death of Augustine
431	Council of Ephesus: Nestorius condemned
	Completion of Santa Maria Maggiore at Rome
432	St Patrick goes to Ireland
434–454	Aetius generalissimo
435	Vandals settled in Africa
	Defeat of the Burgundians near Worms
from 435	Risings of Bagaudae
438	*Codex Theodosianus*
439	Peace treaty with the Visigoths
	Vandals capture Carthage
before 440	Salvian writes *De gubernatione Dei*
440–461	Leo I Pope
from 441	Angles and Saxons conquering Britain
442	Peace treaty with the Vandals
443	Burgundians settled in Sapaudia (Savoy)
446–453	Attila sole ruler of the Huns
451	Battle at the Catalaunian Fields
	Council of Chalcedon
455	Rome sacked by the Vandals
461–472	Ricimer emperor-maker in the West
466–484	Euric king of the Visigoths
	Visigoths conquer Spain
470–488	Sidonius Apollinaris bishop of Clermont
475	*Codex Euricianus*

476	End of the Roman empire in the West
476–493	Odoacer king of Italy
477–485	Huneric king of the Vandals
	Catholics in Africa persecuted
486	Clovis, king of the Franks, defeats Syagrius
488	Theoderic leads the Ostrogoths into Italy
493–526	Theoderic king of the Ostrogoths and ruler of Italy
	Palace and church building at Ravenna
496	Clovis defeats the Alamanni
498	Baptism of Clovis; Franks become Catholic Christians
500	Theoderic in Rome
c. 501	*Lex Burgundionum*
c. 506	*Lex Romana Visigothorum*
	Lex Romana Burgundionum
507	Ennodius speaks the panegyric on Theoderic
c. 507	Cassiodorus becomes Quaestor Sacri Palatii
511	Death of Clovis
	Eugippius' *Vita Severini*
516	Burgundians converted to Catholicism
522	Boethius becomes Magister officiorum
523	Cassiodorus becomes Magister officiorum
524	Boethius executed
	De consolatione philosophiae

BIBLIOGRAPHY[1]

First, a reference to the larger surveys and guides which cover the general history of these centuries or deal with particular aspects of their civilization; these works will not be mentioned again in the bibliographical notes to the separate chapters.

Edward Gibbon, *The history of the decline and fall of the Roman Empire*, 1776–1788 (new edition by J. B. Bury, 1900) inaugurated a new era in historical scholarship. O. Seeck, *Geschichte des Untergangs der antiken Welt* (6 vols., Stuttgart 1910–19) deals with the period from Diocletian to the fall of the Roman Empire in the West. E. Stein, *Histoire du Bas-Empire*, ed. J. R. Palanque 2 vols. (Paris 1949–59) and H. Dannenbauer, *Die Entstehung Europas* (Stuttgart 1959) cover the period from Diocletian to Justinian.

In the composite works which survey the whole of ancient and medieval history we have first and foremost *The Cambridge Ancient History* vol. XII (Cambridge 1939) and *The Cambridge Medieval History* vol. I (Cambridge 1911); in the *Histoire generale* founded by G. Glotz the following are the relevant volumes: M. Besnier, *L'Empire romain de l'avènement des Sévères au Concile de Nicée* (Paris 1937); A. Piganiol, *L'Empire chrétien* (325–395) (Paris 1947); F. Lot, C. Pfister and F. L. Ganshof, *Les destinées de l'Empire en Occident* 395–768 (Paris 1928). Finally, mention must here be made of L. Pareti, *Storia di Roma e del mondo Romano*, vols. V and VI (Turin 1960–61).

On the constitution, law and military organization in addition to T. Mommsen, *Römische Staatsrecht* vols. I–III (Leipzig 1887) the following may be consulted: R. Grosse, *Römisches Militärgeschichte von Gallienus bis zum Beginn der byzantinischen Themenverfassung* (Berlin 1920); H. F. Jolowicz, *Historical introduction to the study of Roman Law*, (2nd ed. Cambridge 1952); L. Wenger, *Die Quellen des römischen Rechts* (Vienna 1953); F. Schulz, *Prinzipien des römischen Rechts* (2nd ed. Berlin 1954), E. T. (from the 1st ed. of 1934), *Principles of Roman Law* by M. Wolff (Oxford 1936); M. Kaser, *Das römische Privatrecht* (Munich 1955); J. Gaudemet, *La formation du droit séculaire et du droit de l'Église aux IVe et Ve siècles;* (Paris 1957); F. Schulz, *History of Roman legal science* (revised and enlarged ed. Oxford 1953).

The administrative, economic and social history of the later Roman Empire is discussed by M. Rostovtzeff in his *Social and Economic History of the Roman Empire* (2nd ed. revised by P. M. Fraser, 2 vols. 1957) and by A. H. M.

[1] E.T.—English Translation.

Jones, *The Later Roman Empire 284–602. A social, economic and administrative survey*. 3 vols. plus maps (Oxford 1964).

Education, learning, philosophy and religion in declining antiquity are dealt with in the following general works: H. I. Marrou, *Histoire de l'éducation dans l'antiquité* (2nd ed. Paris 1950), E.T. *A history of education in antiquity* by G. Lamb (London 1956); A. Reymond, *Histoire des sciences exactes dans l'antiquité gréco-romaine* (2nd ed. Paris 1955), E.T. (from the first edition of 1924) *History of the sciences in Greco-Roman antiquity* by R. G. de Bray (1927); K. Prächter, *Die Philosophie des Altertums* (Berlin 1926); E. Bréhier, *Histoire de la philosophie: L'Antiquité et le Moyen-Âge*, 2 vols., (Paris 1948); E. Gilson, *History of Christian philosophy in the Middle Ages* (1955); J. Geffcken, *Der Ausgang des griechisch-römischen Heidentums* (2nd ed. Heidelberg 1929); K. Prümm, *Religionsgeschichtliches Handbuch für den Raum der altchristlichen Welt* (2nd ed. Freiburg 1954); J. Bayet, *Histoire politique et psychologique de la religion romaine* (Paris 1957); K. Latte, *Römische Religionsgeschichte* (Munich 1960); Nils M. P. Nilsson, *A history of Greek religion* (E.T., from the Swedish by F. J. Fielden, 2nd ed. 1949).

In the extensive field of Church history it may here suffice to draw attention to some of the more modern works: L. Duchesne, *Histoire ancienne de l'Église*, 3 vols. (Paris 1906–1910), E.T., *Early history of the Christian Church* (1909–1924); ed. A. Fliche and V. Martin, *Histoire de l'Église*, vols. I–IV by J. Lebreton and J. Zeiller (Paris 1934–7), E.T. *The history of the primitive Church* (1942–8); H. Lietzmann, *Geschichte der alten Kirche* 4 vols. (2nd and 3rd ed., Berlin 1955), E.T. *A history of the early Church* by B. L. Woolf (2nd impression in 2 vols. 1961); K. Baus, *Von der Urgemeinde zur frühchristlichen Grosskirche* (*Handbuch der Kirchengeschichte* ed. by H. Jedin, Freiburg 1962); J. Daniélou and H. I. Marrou, *Nouvelle histoire de l'Église*: Vol. I *Des origines à Gregoire le Grand* (Paris 1963), and E. T., *New History of the Catholic Church* by V. Cronin (1964). There are two publications specifically devoted to the connections between Christianity and the ancient world: *Reallexicon für Antike und Christentum*, ed. T. Klauser (Stuttgart 1950 ff.) and *Jahrbuch für Antike und Christentum* (Münster 1958 ff.).

As helpful guides to the Greek and Roman literature of these centuries the following works should be borne in mind: M. Schanz, *Geschichte der römischen Literatur* vols. II–IV (new impression Munich 1959); K. Büchner, *Römische Literaturgeschichte* (3rd ed. Stuttgart 1962); A. Lesky, *Geschichte der griechischen Literatur* (2nd ed. Berne and Munich 1963), E. T. *A History of Greek Literature*, by J. Willis and C. de Heer (1966); H. J. Rose, *Handbook of Latin literature* (1949); F. A. Wright, *A history of later Greek literature* (1932); and for the transmission of the classical literary tradition, J. E. Sandys, *History of classical scholarship* (1903). For Christian literature, see A. von Harnack, *Geschichte der altchristlichen Literatur*, 3 vols (Leipzig 1893–1904, 4th ed. with additions by K. Aland, 1958); A. Puech, *Histoire de la littérature grecque chrétienne*, 3 vols (Paris 1928–9); P. de Labriolle, *Histoire de la littérature latine chrétienne* (3rd ed. Paris 1947); B. Altaner, *Patrologie*, (6th ed. Freiburg 1960), E.T. *Patrology* by H. T. Graef (1960).

On the history of art the following may be useful by way of introduction:

W. Technau, *Die Kunst der Römer* (Berlin 1940); W. Lowrie, *Art in the Early Church* (New York 1947); G. Rodenwaldt, *Zur Begrenzung und Gliederung der Spätantike* (in *Jahrbuch des Deutschen Archäologischen Instituts* 59/60, 1944–5, Berlin 1949); E. H. Swift, *Roman sources of christian art* (New York 1951); M. Borda, *La pittura Romana* (Milan 1958); L. Crema, *L'architettura Romana* (*Enciclopedia Classica,* section iii, vol. XII, 1, 1959); D. S. Robertson, *Greek and Roman architecture* (2nd ed. 1945); H. Kähler, *Rom und seine Welt. Bilder zur Geschichte und Kultur* (Munich 1958), E.T. *Rome and her empire* by J. R. Foster (1963).

Since this book concentrates on phenomena of cultural change, mention must be made of the two great twentieth century expositions which develop a theory of history: O. Spengler, *Der Untergang des Abendlandes* (Munich 1918–22), E.T. *The decline of the West* by C. F. Atkinson (1934); and A. J. Toynbee, *A study of history,* 12 vols (London 1934–61). The problems of historical continuity and historical boundaries are given prominence in A. Dopsch, *Grundlagen der europäischen Kulturentwicklung* (Vienna 1923–4), E.T. (abridged) *Economic and social foundations of European civilisation* by M. G. Beard and N. Marshall (1937); F. Lot, *La fin du monde antique et le début du Moyen-Âge* (Paris 1927), E.T., *The end of the ancient world and the beginning of the Middle Ages* by P. and M. Leon (reimpression New York 1961); C. Dawson, *The making of Europe* (London 1936); H. Pirenne, *Mahomet et Charlemagne* (Brussels 1937), E.T. *Mohammed and Charlemagne* by B. Miall (1939). For recent work on the ending of the ancient world in relation to the history of ideas see F. Stroheker, *Um die Grenze zwischen Antike und abendländischem Mittelalter* (in *Saeculum,* 1, 1950) and S. Mazzarino, *La fine del mondo antico,* Milan 1959, E. T., *The End of the Ancient World* by G. Holmes (1966).

CHAPTER I. THE CRISIS OF THE ANCIENT WORLD IN THE THIRD CENTURY

The state and the law; economic and social history.

D. van Berchem, *L'armée de Dioclétian et la réforme constantinienne* (in *Bibliothèque archéologique et historique de l'Institut français de Beyrouth,* 56, 1952).

E. R. Boak, *Manpower shortage and the fall of the Roman Empire in the West,* (Ann Arbor 1955).

S. Bolin, *State and currency of the Roman Empire to 300 A.D.* (Stockholm 1958).

M. P. Charlesworth, *Trade routes and commerce of the Roman empire* (2nd ed. Cambridge 1926).

A. Déléage, *La capitation du Bas-Empire* (in *Annales École Hautes-Etudes,* 304, 1955).

W. Ensslin, *Zur Ostpolitik des Kaisers Diokletian* (S.B.d. *Bayerischen Akademie,* 1942, 1).

G. Forni, *Il reclutamento delle legioni da Augusto a Diocleziano* (Milan 1953).

T. Frank, ed., *An economic survey of Ancient Rome,* 5 vols (Baltimore 1933–40).

M. Hammond, *The Antonine monarchy* (in *Papers and monographs of the American Academy in Rome,* 19, 1959).

L. Harmand, *L'occident romain* (Paris 1960).
A. H. M. Jones, *Cities in the Eastern Roman Empire* (Oxford 1937).
W. Kunkel, *Herkunft und soziale Stellung der römischen Juristen* (*Forschungen zum römischen Recht* 4) Weimar 1952.
F. Lot, *Nouvelles recherches sur l'impôt foncier et la capitation personelle sous le Bas-Empire* (in *Annales Écoles Hautes-Études*, 304, 1955).
H. G. Pflaum, *Les procurateurs équestres sous le Haut Empire romain* (Paris 1950).
F. M. de Robertis, *Il diritto associativo Romano* (Bari 1936).
Ibid. *Lavoro et lavoratori nel mondo Romano* (Bari 1963).
C. Sasse, *Die 'Constitutio Antoniniana'* (Wiesbaden 1958).
E. M. Schtajerman, *Die Krise der Sklavenhalterordnung in Westen des römischen Reiches* (Berlin 1964).
W. Seston, *Dioclétien et la tétrarchie* (Paris 1964).
J. Straub, *Vom Herrscherideal der Spätantike* (in *Forschungen zur Kirchen- und Geistesgeschichte* 18, 1939).
Studies in Roman economic and social history in honour of A. C. Johnson (Princeton 1951).
F. Taeger, *Charisma*, II (Stuttgart 1960).
G. Walser and T. Pekary, *Die Krise des römischen Reiches* (Berlin 1962).
W. L. Westermann, *The slave systems of Greek and Roman antiquity* (Philadelphia 1955).

Cultural life.

A. Alföldi, *Die Ausgestaltung des monarchischen Zeremoniells am römischen Kaiserhöfe. Insignien und Tracht der römischen Kaiser.* (in *Mitteilungen des Deutschen Archäologischen Instituts*, Roman section, 49, 1934; 50, 1935.)
F. Altheim, *Aus Spätantike und Christentum* (Tübingen 1951).
L. Bréhier, *La philosophie de Plotin* (Paris 1928).
J. Carcopino, *La vie quotidienne à Rome à l'apogée de l'empire*, E.T. *Daily life in ancient Rome* by E. O. Lorimer (1941).
F. Cumont, *Les religions orientales dans le paganisme romain* (4th ed. Paris 1929).
W. Ensslin, *Gottkaiser und Kaiser von Gottes Gnaden* (S.B.d. Bayerischen Akademi 1943, 6).
A. J. Festugière, *La révélation d'Hermès Trismégiste*, 4 vols (Paris 1943–54).
Fondation Hardt pour l'étude de l'antiquité classique. Entretiens III Recherches sur la tradition platonicienne (Vandoeuvres-Geneva 1955).
H. Fuchs, *Der geistige Widerstand gegen Rom in der antiken Welt* (Berlin 1938).
P. Grimal, *La civilisation romaine* (Paris 1960), E.T. *The civilisation of Rome* by W. S. Maguiness etc. (1963).
H. Jonas, *Gnosis und spätantiker Geist* (in *Forschungen zur Religion und Literatur des Alten und Neuen Testaments*, 33 and 45, 1934 and 1954).
U. Kahrstedt, *Kulturgeschichte der römischen Kaiserzeit* (2nd ed. Berne 1958).
R. Laqueur, H. Koch and H. Weber, *Probleme der Spätantike* (Stuttgart 1930).
H. Mattingly, *Roman Imperial civilisation* (London 1959).
F. Millar, *A study of Cassius Dio* (Oxford 1964).

A. D. Nock, *Conversion: the old and the new in religion from Alexander the Great to Augustine of Hippo* (2nd ed. London 1952).

J. Palm, *Rom, Römertum und Imperium in der antiken Literatur* (Lund 1959).

U. E. Paoli, *Urbs. Aspetti di vita romana antica* (2nd ed. 1942). E.T. *Rome: its people, life and customs* by R. D. Macnaghten (1963).

G. Quispel, *Gnosis als Weltreligion* (Zürich 1951).

O. Seel, *Römertum und Latinität* (Stuttgart) 1964.

C. G. Starr, *Civilisation and the Caesars* (New York 1954).

Development of Christianity.

C. Andresen, *Logos und Nomos* (in *Arbeiten zur Kirchengeschichte*, 30, Berlin 1955)

C. Becker, *Tertullians Apologeticum* (Munich 1954).

H. von Campenhausen, *Die Idee des Martyriums in der alten Kirche* (2nd ed. Göttingen 1964).

J. Carcopino, *De Pythagore aux Apôtres* (Paris 1956).

J. Daniélou, *Origène* (Paris 1948), E.T. *Origen* by W. Mitchell, (1955).

Ibid., *La théologie du judéo-christianisme* (Paris 1958).

H. Delehaye, *Les origines du culte des martyrs* (in *Subsidia Hagiographica*, 20, 1933).

A. A. T. Ehrhardt, *Politische Metaphysik von Solon bis Augustin* (Tübingen 1959).

A. T. Geoghegan, *The attitude toward labour in early Christianity and ancient culture* (Washington 1945).

H. Grégoire, *Les persécutions dans l'empire romain* (in *Mémoires de l'Académie Belgique*, 46, 1, 1951).

A. von Harnack, *Mission und Ausbreitung des Christentums*, 2 vols (4th ed. Leipzig 1924), E.T. *The expansion of Christianity in the first three centuries* by J. Moffat (1904–5).

P. de Labriolle, *La réaction païenne* (2nd ed. Paris 1950).

J. Leipoldt, *Der soziale Gedanke in der altchristlichen Kirche* (Leipzig 1952).

C. Mohrmann, *Le Latin des chrétiens*, 2 vols (Rome 1958–61).

J. Moreau, Lactance, *De la mort des persécuteurs* (in *Sources chrétiennes* 1954).

E. Peterson, *Der Monotheismus als politisches Problem* (Leipzig 1935).

H. Rahner, *Kirche und Staat im frühen Christentum* (Munich 1961).

E. Salin, *Civitas Dei* (Tübingen 1926).

M. Simon, *Verus Israel. Étude sur les relations entre Chrétiens et Juifs dans l'empire romain* (Paris 1948).

C. Schneider, *Geistesgeschichte des antiken Christentums*, 2 vols (Munich 1954).

J. Vogt and H. Last, *Christenverfolgung* (in *Reallexicon für Antike und Christentum* II, 1954).

J. Vogt, *Von der Religiosität der Christenverfolger im römischen Reich* (*S.B. Heidelb. Akad.* 1962, 1).

W. C. van Unnik, *Evangelien aus dem Nilsand* (Frankfurt 1960).

The non-Roman world.

F. Altheim, *Niedergang der alten Welt*, 2 vols (Frankfurt 1952).

F. Altheim and R. Stiehl, *Ein asiatischer Staat* (Wiesbaden 1954).

H. Christensen, *L'Iran sous les Sassanides* (2nd ed. Copenhagen 1944).
W. Ensslin, *Germanen in römischen Diensten* (in *Gymnasium* 52, 1941).
H. J. Eggers, *Der römische Import im freien Germanien* (Hamburg 1954).
R. Ghirshman, *Iran. Parther und Sassaniden* (Munich 1962).
H. C. Puech, *Le manichéisme, son fondateur, sa doctrine* (Paris 1949).
M. Rostovtzeff, *Caravan cities* (Oxford 1932).
L. Schmidt, *Geschichte der deutchen Stämme bis zum Ausgang der Völkerwanderung* (2nd ed. Munich 1938–41).
H. Schneider (ed.), *Germanische Altertumskunde* (Munich 1951).
A. Schenk Graf von Stauffenberg, *Das Imperium und die Völkerwanderung* (Munich, n.d.).
E. Wahle, *Deutsche Vorzeit* (2nd ed. Tübingen 1952).
M. Wheeler, *Rome beyond the imperial frontiers* (London 1959).
G. Widengren, *Mani und der Manichäismus* (Stuttgart 1961).
Ibid., *Iranische Geisteswelt von den Afängen bis zum Islam,* (Bader-Bader, 1961).

CHAPTER 2. THE MONARCHY, THE CHRISTIAN CHURCH AND THE RULING SOCIETY IN THE FOURTH CENTURY

The state and the law; economic and social history.

A. Alföldi, *A conflict of ideas in the Late Roman Empire* (Oxford 1952).
M. R. Alföldi, *Die Constantinische Goldprägung* (Mainz 1963).
B. Biondi, *Il diritto Romano cristiano,* 2 vols (Milan 1952–4).
P. Bruun, *Studies in the Constantinian chronology* (in *Numismatic notes and monographs,* 146, New York 1961).
J. Burckhardt, *Die Zeit Constantins des Grossen* (Collected works II, Stuttgart 1929), E.T. *The age of Constantine the Great* by M. Hadas (1949).
N. Charbonnel, *La condition des ouvriers dans les ateliers impériaux aux IVe et Ve siècles* (in *Travaux et Recherches de la Faculté de droit et des sciences économ.* Ser.: Sciences hist. 1, Paris 1964).
A. Chastagnol, *La préfecture urbaine à Rome sous le Bas-Empire* (Paris 1960).
J. P. C. Kent, *Late Roman bronze coinage,* 324–498 (London 1960).
H. P. Kohns, *Versorgungskrisen und Hungerrevolten im spätantiken Rom* (in *Antiquitas* I, 6, Bonn 1961).
S. Mazzarino, *Aspetti sociali del quarto secolo* (Rome 1951).
G. Mickwitz, *Geld und Wirtschaft im römischen Reich des 4 Jahrhunderts n. Chr.* (Helsingfors 1932).
J. R. Palanque, *Essai sur la préfecture du Prétoire du Bas-Empire,* (Paris 1933).
P. Petit, *Libanius et la vie municipale à Antioche au IVe siècle après J-Chr.* (Paris 1955).
A. Piganiol, *L'empereur Constantin* (Paris 1932).
W. Seyfarth, *Soziale Fragen der spatrömischen Kaiserzeit im Spiegel des Theodosianus* (Berlin 1963).
J. Vogt, *Constantin der Grosse und sein Jahrhundert* (2nd ed. Munich 1960).
F. W. Walbank, *The decline of the Roman Empire in the West* (London 1946).

Christianity in the ancient world.

A. Alföldi, *The conversion of Constantine and pagan Rome* (Oxford 1948).
E. Blanchet, *Humanisme et christianisme. Ausone et Saint Paulin de Nole* (Bordeaux 1954).
J. P. Brisson, *Autonomisme et christianisme dans l'Afrique romaine* (Paris 1958).
S. Calderone, *Constatino e il cattolicesimo* (Florence 1962).
H. von Campenhausen, *Ambrosius von Mailand als Kirchenpolitiker* (Berlin and Leipzig 1929).
E. Caspar, *Geschichte des Papsttums*, Vol. I (Tübingen 1930).
N. K. Chadwick, *Poetry and letters in early christian Gaul* (London 1955).
P. Courcelle, *Les confessions du Saint Augustin dans la tradition littéraire* (Paris 1963).
H. Dörries, *Das Selbstzeugnis Kaiser Konstantins* (in *Abhandlungen der Göttinger Akad.*, 34, 1954).
Ibid., *Constantine and religious liberty* (New Haven 1960).
W. Ensslin, *Die Religionspolitik des Kaisers Theodosius des Grossen* (in *S.B.d. Bayerischen Akad.*, 1953 2).
P. Fabre, *Saint Paulin de Nole et l'amitié chrétienne* (in *Publ. Fac. des Lettres Univ. Strasbourg* 109, 1949).
A. J. Festugière, *Les moines d'Orient* (Paris 1961–).
W. H. C. Frend, *The Donatist Church* (Oxford 1953).
J. Gaudemet, *L'Église dans l'empire romain* (*IVe–Ve siècles*) (Paris 1958).
M. Guarducci, *I graffiti sotto la Confessione di San Pietro in Vaticano*, 3 vols (Vatican City 1958).
Ibid., *La tomba di Pietro* (Rome 1959), E.T., *The tomb of St. Peter* by J. McLellan (1960).
J. Haller, *Das Papsttum*, vol. I (Stuttgart 1934).
R. Hernegger, *Macht ohne Auftrag. Die Entstehung der Staats-und Volkskirche* (Olten and Freiburg 1963).
K. Heussi, *Der Ursprung des Mönchtums* (Tübingen 1936).
L. Homo, *De la Rome païenne à la Rome chrétienne* (Paris 1950).
W. Jaeger, *Early Christianity and Greek Paideia* (Cambridge Mass. 1961).
H. U. Instinsky, *Bischofsstuhl und Kaiserthron* (Munich 1955).
H. Kraft, *Kaiser Constantins religiöse Entwicklnng* (Tübingen 1955).
B. Kötting, *Peregrinatio religiosa. Wallfahrten in der Antike und das Pilgerwesen in der alten Kirche* (in *Forschungen zur Volkskunde* 33–35, 1950).
P. de Labriolle, *La correspondance d'Ausone et de Paulin de Nole* (Paris 1910).
A. Momigliano, ed., *The conflict between Paganism and Christianity in the fourth century* (Oxford 1963).
B. M. Peebles, *The poet Prudentius* (New York 1951).
A. Salvatore, *Studi Prudenziani* (Naples 1958).
E. Schwartz, *Zur Geschichte des Athanasius.* Collected works Vol. III (Berlin 1959).
K. M. Setton, *Christian attitude towards the Emperor in the fourth century* (New York 1941).
J. Vogt, *Kaiser Julian und das Judentum* (Leipzig 1939).

Ibid., *Constantin der Grosse* (in *Reallexicon für Antike und Christentum* III, 1957).
K. Voigt, *Staat und Kirche von Konstantin bis zum Ende der Karolingerzeit* (Stuttgart 1936).
D. S. Wallace-Hadrill, *Eusebius of Caesarea* (London 1960).

Cultural life.

A. Alföldi *Die Kontorniaten* (Leipzig 1942).
J. Bidez, *La vie de l'empereur Julien* (Paris 1930).
G. Downey, *A history of Antioch in Syria* (Princeton 1961).
A. J. Festugière, *Antioche païenne et chrétienne* (in *Bibl. Éc. fr. d'Athènes et de Rome* 194, 1959).
R. J. Forbes, *Man the maker* (New York 1958).
T. R. Glover, *Life and letters in the fourth century* (Cambridge 1901).
W. Hartke, *Römische Kinderkaiser. Eine Strukturanalyse römischen Denkens und Daseins* (Berlin 1951).
R. Janin, *Constantinople byzantine* (in *Archives de l'Orient chrétien*, 4, 1950).
F. Klingner, *Römische Geisteswelt* (4th ed. Munich 1961).
J. Lana, *La storiografia del Basso Impero* (Turin 1963).
R. Mayer, *Byzantion-Konstantinopolis-Istanbul* (in *Denkschrifter der Wiener Akademie*, 71, 3, 1943).
P. Petit, *Les étudiants de Libanius* (Paris 1956).
C. Singer and E. J. Holmyard, *A history of technology* (Oxford 1954 ff.).
L. Sprague de Camp, *The ancient engineers* (New York 1963).
J. Straub, *Heidnische Geschichtsapologetik in der christlichen Spätantike* (Bonn 1963).
E. A. Thompson, *The historical work of Ammianus Marcellinus* (Cambridge 1947).
Ibid., *A Roman reformer and inventor* (Oxford 1952).

CHAPTER 3. THE ROMAN WEST AND THE NEW PEOPLES IN THE FIFTH CENTURY

The state and the law; economic and social history.

H. Aubin, *Vom Altertum zum Mittelalter* (Munich 1949).
Ibid., *Strukturen und Triebkräfte der abendländischen Wirtschaftsentwicklung im frühen Mittelalter* (in *Vierteljahrschrift für Sozial- und Wirtschaftsgeschichte*, 42, 1955).
J. B. Bury, *History of the Later Roman Empire*, Vol. I (London 1923).
E. Demougeot, *De l'unité à la division de l'empire romain* (Paris 1951).
H. J. Diesner, *Kirche und Staat im spatrömischen Reich* (Berlin 1963).
P. Hübinger, *Spätantike und frühes Mittelalter* (Wiesbaden 1959).
P. Koschaker, *Europa und das römische Recht* (3rd ed. Munich and Berlin 1958).
R. Latouche, *Les origines de l'économie occidentale IV*[e]*–XI*[e] *siècles* (Paris 1956), E.T. *The birth of the western economy* by E. M. Wilkinson (1961).

A. Piganiol, *Le sac de Rome* (Paris 1964).
E. K. Rand, *Founders of the Middle Ages* (Cambridge, Mass. 1928).
L. Ruggini, *Economia e società nell 'Italia annonaria'* (Milan 1961).
C. Sanchez-Albornoz, *En torno a los origenes del feudalismo*, 3 vols (Mendoza 1942).
V. A. Sirago, *Galla Placidia e la trasformazione politica dell' occidente* (in *Univ. de Louvain: Rec. de travaux d'hist. et de philosophie* IV, 25, 1961).
K. F. Stroheker, *Der senatorische Adel im spätantiken Gallien* (Tübingen 1948).
Ibid., *Die geschichtliche Stellung der ostgermanischen Staaten am Mittelmeer* (in *Saeculum* 12, 1961).
F. Wieacker, *Recht und Gesellschaft der Spätantike* (Stuttgart 1964).

The christian Church and cultural life.

C. Andresen (ed.), *Zum Augustin-Gespräch der Gegenwart* (Cologne 1962).
L. Bréhier, *Le monde byzantin*, 3 vols (Paris 1948–50).
H. von Campenhausen, *Griechische Kirchenväter* (2nd ed. Stuttgart 1956), E.T. *The Fathers of the Greek Church* by S. Godman (1963).
Ibid., *Lateinische Kirchenväter* (Stuttgart 1960), E.T. *The Fathers of the Latin Church* by M. Hoffmann, (1964).
F. Cavallera, *Saint Jérôme*, 2 vols (Louvain 1922).
P. Courcelle, *Les lettres grecques en occident* (2nd ed. Paris 1948).
E. R. Curtius, *Europäische Literatur und lateinisches Mittelalter* (Berne 1948), E.T. *European literature and the Latin Middle Ages* by W. R. Trask (1953).
H. J. Diesner, *Studien zur Gesellschaftslehre und sozialen Haltung Augustins* (Halle 1954).
S. Dill, *Roman Society in the last century of the Roman Empire* (2nd ed. New York 1958).
P. Fargues, *Claudien. Étude sur sa poésie et son temps* (Paris 1933).
E. Griffe, *La Gaule chrétienne a l'époque romaine*, 2 vols (Paris-Toulouse 1947).
F. G. Maier, *Augustin und das antike Rom* (Stuttgart 1955).
H. I. Marrou, *Saint Augustin et la fin de la culture antique* (4th ed. Paris 1958).
F. van der Meer, *Augustinus de zielzorger* (1947), E.T. *Augustine the bishop* by B. Battershaw and G. R. Lamb (1961).
P. Riche, *Éducation et culture dans l'occident barbare. VIe–VIII siècles* (in *Patristica Sorbonensia*, 4, 1962).
A. Schäfer, *Römer und Germanen bei Salvian* (Breslau 1930).
J. Steinbeiss, *Das Geschichtsbild Claudians* (Halle 1936).
J. Steinmann, *Saint Jérôme* (Paris 1958), E.T. *St. Jerome* by R. Matthews (1959).
J. Straub, *Augustins Sorge um die regeneratio imperii* (in *Historisches Jahrbuch* 73, 1954).
J. Sundwall, *Abhandlungen zur Geschichte des ausgehenden Altertums* (Helsingfors 1919).
R. Thouvenot, *Salvien et la ruine de l'empire romain* (in *Mél. Éc. fr. de Rome* 38, 1920).
A. Wachtel, *Beiträge zur Geschichtstheologie des Aurelius Augustinus* (Bonn, 1960).

The Völkerwanderung. *Germans and Celts.*

F. Altheim, *Geschichte der Hunnen*, 5 vols (Berlin 1959–62).
L. Bieler, *Ireland, harbinger of the Middle Ages* (1963).
E. Birley, *Roman Britain and the Roman army* (1953).
P. H. Blair, *Roman Britain and early England* (1963).
R. Buchner, *Die römischen und die germanischen Wesenszüge der neuen politischen Ordnung des Abendlandes* (Spoleto 1958).
J. B. Bury, *The life of St. Patrick and his place in history* (London 1905).
W. Capelle, *Die Germanen der Völkerwanderung. Auf Grund der zeitgenössischen Quellen dargestellt* (Stuttgart 1939).
P. Courcelle, *Histoire littéraire des grandes invasions germaniques* (2nd ed. Paris 1952).
C. Courtois, *Les Vandales et l'Afrique* (Paris 1955).
W. Ensslin, *Theoderich der Grosse* (2nd ed. Munich 1959).
J. Fischer, *Die Völkerwanderung im Urteil der zeitgenössischen christlichen Schriftsteller Galliens mit Einbeziehung des heiligen Augustinus* (Heidelberg 1948).
E. Gamillscheg, *Romania germanica*, 3 vols (Berlin and Leipzig 1934–6).
J. Godfrey, *The Church in Anglo-Saxon England* (Cambridge 1962).
H. von Halbank, *Das römische Recht in den germanischen Volksstaaten* 3 vols (Breslau 1899–1907).
H. Halbing, *Goten und Wandalen* (Zurich 1959).
F. Lot, *Les invasions germaniques. La pénétration mutuelle du monde barbare et du monde romain* (Paris 1935).
A. Loyen, *Sidoine Apollinaire et l'esprit précieux en Gaule aux derniers jours de l'Empire* (Paris 1943).
A. Momigliano, *Cassiodorus and the Italian culture of his time* (*Proc. Brit. Acad.* 41, 1955).
F. Petri, *Germanisches Volkserbe in Wallonien und Nordfrankreich* (Bonn 1937).
Ibid., *Zum Stand der Diskussion über die fränkische Landnahme und die Entstehung der germanisch-romanisch Sprachgrenze* (Darmstadt 1954).
E. Salin, *La civilisation mérovingienne*, 4 vols (Paris 1949–50).
Settimane di Studio del Centro Italiano di Studi sul Alto Medioevo. III: I Goti in occidente. IX: Il passaggio dall' antichità al Medioevo in occidente. (Spoleto 1956, 1962).
K. D. Schmidt, *Die Bekehrung der Germanen zum Christentum*, Vol. I (Göttingen 1939).
Ibid., and E. Wolf, *Die Kirche in ihrer Geschichte*, Vol. II (Göttingen 1961).
F. Steinbach, *Zur Grundlegung der europäischen Einheit durch die Franken* (Leipzig 1939).
W. von den Steinen, *Chlodwigs Übergang zum Christentum* (in *Mitteilungen Österreich. Instituts f. Geschichtsforschung*, Ergänzungsband 12, 1933).
E. A. Thompson, *A history of Attila and the Huns* (Oxford 1948).
J. Werner, *Beiträge zur Archäologie des Attila-Reiches* (in *Abhandlungen der Bayerischen Akademie*, N.F. 38, A.B. 1956).

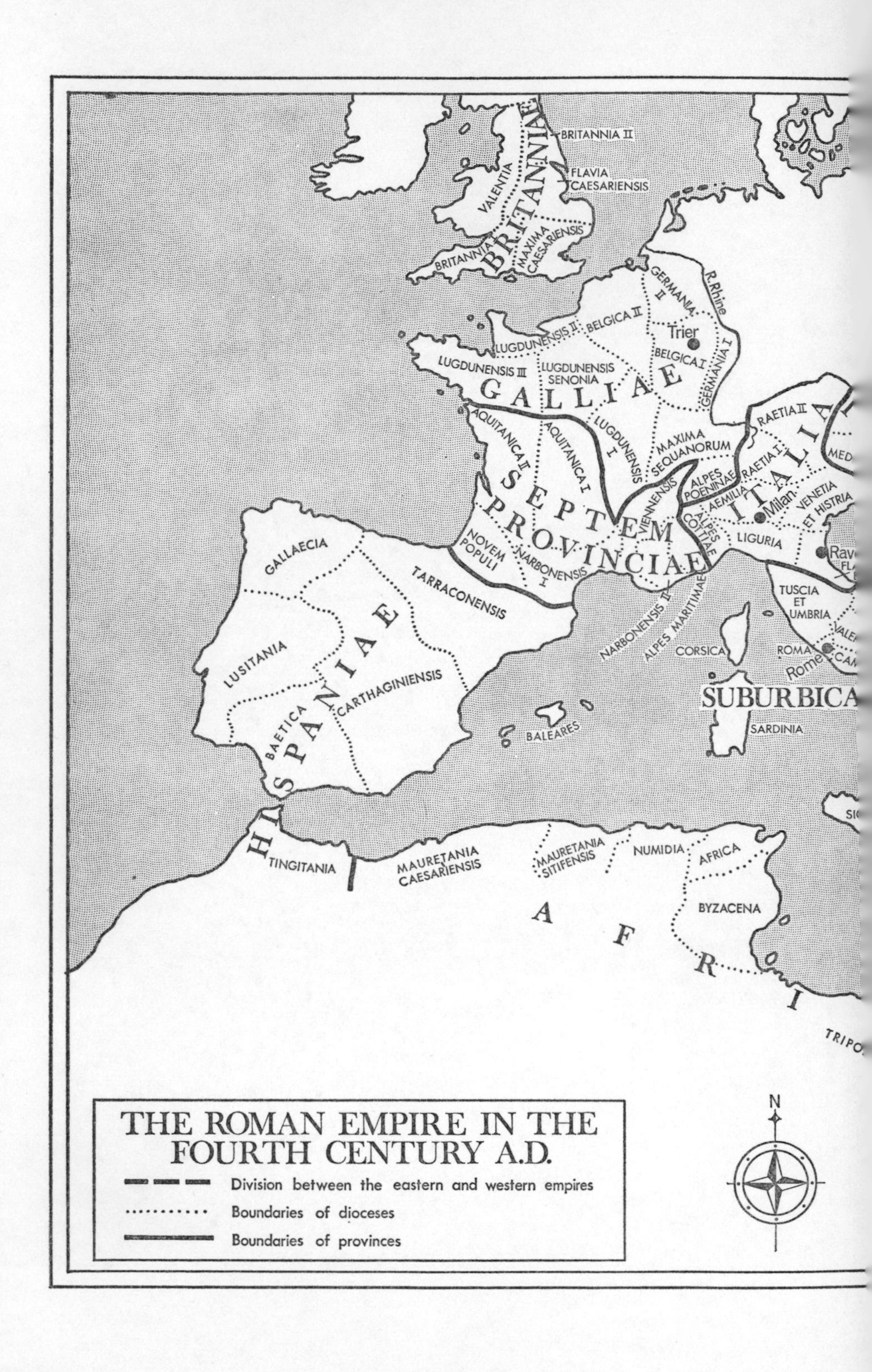
BRITANNIAE
BRITANNIA II
FLAVIA CAESARIENSIS
VALENTIA
MAXIMA CAESARIENSIS
BRITANNIA I
R. Rhine
GERMANIA II
BELGICA II
Trier
BELGICA I
GERMANIA I
LUGDUNENSIS II
LUGDUNENSIS III
LUGDUNENSIS SENONIA
GALLIAE
LUGDUNENSIS I
MAXIMA SEQUANORUM
AQUITANICA II
AQUITANICA I
SEPTEM PROVINCIAE
NOVEM POPULI
NARBONENSIS I
VIENNENSIS
ALPES POENINAE
ALPES COTTIAE
NARBONENSIS II
ALPES MARITIMAE
RAETIA II
RAETIA I
ITALIA
Milan
AEMILIA
VENETIA ET HISTRIA
LIGURIA
TUSCIA ET UMBRIA
ROMA
Rome
CORSICA
SUBURBICA
SARDINIA
GALLAECIA
TARRACONENSIS
HISPANIAE
LUSITANIA
CARTHAGINIENSIS
BAETICA
BALEARES
TINGITANIA
MAURETANIA CAESARIENSIS
MAURETANIA SITIFENSIS
NUMIDIA
AFRICA
BYZACENA
A F R I
THE ROMAN EMPIRE IN THE FOURTH CENTURY A.D.
Division between the eastern and western empires
Boundaries of dioceses
Boundaries of provinces
N

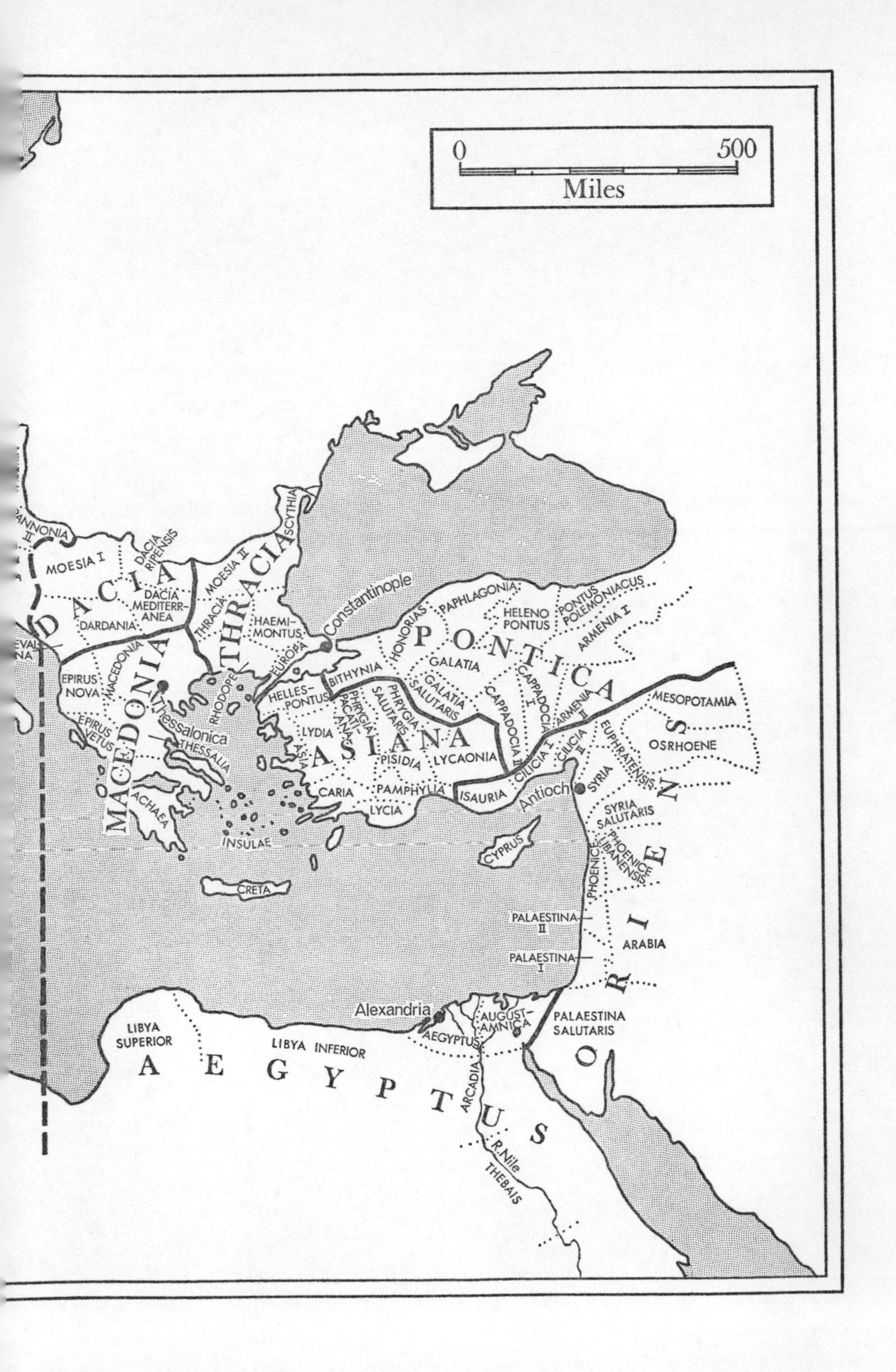
0
500
Miles
DACIA
MOESIA I
DACIA RIPENSIS
DACIA MEDITERRANEA
DARDANIA
THRACIA
MOESIA II
SCYTHIA
HAEMIMONTUS
EUROPA
RHODOPE
Constantinople
MACEDONIA
EPIRUS NOVA
EPIRUS VETUS
Thessalonica
THESSALIA
ACHAEA
INSULAE
CRETA
PONTICA
PAPHLAGONIA
HONORIAS
HELENO PONTUS
PONTUS POLEMONIACUS
ARMENIA I
ARMENIA II
GALATIA
GALATIA SALUTARIS
BITHYNIA
CAPPADOCIA I
CAPPADOCIA II
ASIANA
HELLESPONTUS
LYDIA
ASIA
PHRYGIA PACATIANA
PHRYGIA SALUTARIS
PISIDIA
LYCAONIA
CARIA
PAMPHYLIA
LYCIA
ISAURIA
CILICIA I
CILICIA II
ORIENS
MESOPOTAMIA
OSRHOENE
EUPHRATENSIS
SYRIA
Antioch
SYRIA SALUTARIS
PHOENICE
PHOENICE LIBANENSIS
CYPRUS
PALAESTINA II
PALAESTINA I
ARABIA
PALAESTINA SALUTARIS
AUGUSTAMNICA
Alexandria
AEGYPTUS
LIBYA SUPERIOR
LIBYA INFERIOR
ARCADIA
R.Nile
THEBAIS

INDEX